AN EMPIRE *of* PRINT

PREVIOUSLY PUBLISHED TITLES IN THE PENN STATE SERIES IN THE HISTORY OF THE BOOK

Peter Burke, *The Fortunes of the "Courtier": The European Reception of Castiglione's "Cortegiano"* (1996)

Roger Burlingame, *Of Making Many Books: A Hundred Years of Reading, Writing, and Publishing* (1996)

James M. Hutchisson, *The Rise of Sinclair Lewis, 1920–1930* (1996)

Julie Bates Dock, ed., *Charlotte Perkins Gilman's "The Yellow Wall-paper" and the History of Its Publication and Reception: A Critical Edition and Documentary Casebook* (1998)

John Williams, ed., *Imaging the Early Medieval Bible* (1998)

Ezra Greenspan, *George Palmer Putnam: Representative American Publisher* (2000)

James G. Nelson, *Publisher to the Decadents: Leonard Smithers in the Careers of Beardsley, Wilde, Dowson* (2000)

Pamela E. Selwyn, *Everyday Life in the German Book Trade: Friedrich Nicolai as Bookseller and Publisher in the Age of Enlightenment* (2000)

David R. Johnson, *Conrad Richter: A Writer's Life* (2001)

David Finkelstein, *The House of Blackwood: Author-Publisher Relations in the Victorian Era* (2002)

Rodger L. Tarr, ed., *As Ever Yours: The Letters of Max Perkins and Elizabeth Lemmon* (2003)

Randy Robertson, *Censorship and Conflict in Seventeenth-Century England: The Subtle Art of Division* (2009)

Catherine M. Parisian, ed., *The First White House Library: A History and Annotated Catalogue* (2010)

Jane McLeod, *Licensing Loyalty: Printers, Patrons, and the State in Early Modern France* (2011)

Charles Walton, ed., *Into Print: Limits and Legacies of the Enlightenment, Essays in Honor of Robert Darnton* (2011)

James L. W. West III, *Making the Archives Talk: New and Selected Essays in Bibliography, Editing, and Book History* (2012)

John Hruschka, *How Books Came to America: The Rise of the American Book Trade* (2012)

A. Franklin Parks, *William Parks: The Colonial Printer in the Transatlantic World of the Eighteenth Century* (2012)

Roger E. Stoddard, comp., and David R. Whitesell, ed., *A Bibliographic Description of Books and Pamphlets of American Verse Printed from 1610 Through 1820* (2012)

Nancy Cervetti, *S. Weir Mitchell: Philadelphia's Literary Physician* (2012)

Karen Nipps, *Lydia Bailey: A Checklist of Her Imprints* (2013)

Paul Eggert, *Biography of a Book: Henry Lawson's "While the Billy Boils"* (2013)

Allan Westphall, *Books and Religious Devotion: The Redemptive Reading of an Irishman in Nineteenth-Century New England* (2014)

Scott Donaldson, *The Impossible Craft: Literary Biography* (2015)

John Bidwell, *Graphic Passion: Matisse and the Book Arts* (2015)

Peter Shillingsburg, *Textuality and Knowledge: Essays* (2017)

AN EMPIRE
of PRINT

THE NEW YORK PUBLISHING TRADE

IN THE EARLY

AMERICAN REPUBLIC

· · · · · · · ·

STEVEN CARL SMITH

THE PENNSYLVANIA STATE UNIVERSITY PRESS

UNIVERSITY PARK, PENNSYLVANIA

Library of Congress Cataloging-in-Publication Data

Names: Smith, Steven Carl, 1981– , author.
Title: An empire of print : the New York publishing trade
in the early American republic / Steven Carl Smith.
Other titles: Penn State series in the history of the book.
Description: University Park, Pennsylvania : The Pennsylvania
State University Press, [2017] | Series: The Penn State series in the
history of the book | Includes bibliographical references and index.
Summary: "Traces the evolution of New York's publishing trade
from the end of the American Revolution to the Age of Jackson.
Explores the gradual development of local, regional, and national
distribution networks in the early republic"—Provided by publisher.
Identifiers: LCCN 2017006873 | ISBN 9780271078519
(cloth : alk. paper)
Subjects: LCSH: Publishers and publishing—New York (State)—
New York—History—18th century. | Publishers and publishing—
New York (State)—New York—History—19th century. |
Book industries and trade—New York (State)—New York—
History—18th century. | Book industries and trade—New York
(State)—New York—History—19th century.
Classification: LCC Z478.6.N5 S64 2017 |
DDC 070.509747/09033—dc23
LC record available at https://lccn.loc.gov/2017006873

It is the policy of The Pennsylvania State University Press to use
acid-free paper. Publications on uncoated stock satisfy the
minimum requirements of American National Standard for
Information Sciences—Permanence of Paper for Printed Library
Material, ANSI z39.48–1992.

Typeset by
COGHILL COMPOSITION COMPANY

Printed and bound by
SHERIDAN BOOKS

Composed in
SCALA PRO AND SCALA SANS PRO

Printed on
NATURES NATURAL

. . . .

For Mom and Dad

. . . .

CONTENTS

. . . .

TABLES

· · · · · · · · · · · · · · · · · · · ·

ACKNOWLEDGMENTS

I have accumulated a number of debts over the course of more than eight often difficult years writing this book. And while what I say here hardly comes close to expressing the depth of my gratitude, I hope at least to address the people and institutions that helped make this book possible. I am most indebted to Jeff Pasley. Jeff was able, time and again, to help me shape the unwieldy ideas I had about New York and print culture into a cohesive analysis. Jeff treated me like a colleague and, more important, like a friend. He has been a transparent, fair, supportive, and downright wonderful mentor. He has helped me along as a young scholar in immeasurable ways that I will never be able to fully reciprocate. I continue to follow his example as I move forward in my own career.

I also owe thanks to Michelle Morris, Catherine Rymph, Patricia Okker, Theodore Koditschek, John H. Wigger, John Bullion, and Russ Zguta for their patience, interest, and brilliance as mentors. Michelle always made herself available to read and talk about my work, and should be greatly credited for having a lasting influence on this project and on my thinking about early America. Hers is a mentorship and a friendship that will last well beyond this book. Catherine helped me develop a broad literacy on race, class, gender, and urban history that continues to inform my thinking. Ted helped guide my thinking on social, political, and economic life, while Pat offered an invaluable literary perspective. I would also like to thank Nancy Taube, Patty Eggleston, Jenny Morton, Sandy Kietzman, and Melinda Lockwood, who often went out of their way to lend a hand. No acknowledgment would be complete without a nod to T. J. Tomlin, Marly Ramsour, Will Mountz, Joe Beilein, Megan Boccardi, Marlin Barber, Kyle Miller, Kris Maulden, Jonathan Jones, Lucas Volkman, Daniel Connor, Andrea Weingartner, Leroy Rowe, Mike Snodgrass, Cassie Yacovazzi, Sarah Lirley McCune, Bill Lewis, Nina Verbanez, and Josh McMullen—don't give up the ship. Years ago, T. J. Tomlin took me under his wing, and he remains a model scholar, teacher, friend, and colleague. I also want to thank Marly Ramsour for all of her support during the many years I spent researching and writing this book.

The History Department at the University of Missouri funded some of my earliest research with several generous summer research grants, as did the Anna K. and Mary E. Cunningham Research Residency at the New York State Library. Without the 2010 short-term fellowship from the New York Public Library, *An Empire of Print* would not be what it is today. It was during the month I spent in the reading room at the NYPL that I found the basis for much of my project in Evert Duyckinck's financial records. A Reese Fellowship in the Print Culture of the Americas allowed me to spend June 2011 at the American Antiquarian Society, the nation's premiere research library for the early history of print in America. I was able to spend a month digging around in a variety of collections, including the Book Trades Collection, which contributed mightily to chapter 2. But it was in the summer of 2008 that I gained my first exposure to the AAS when I was invited to be part of the annual Summer Seminar in the History of the Book in America. It was during this week of extensive reading and discussion that I came up with the idea for my project. A fellowship from the Library Company of Philadelphia's Program in Early American Economy and Society allowed me to spend all of July and part of August 2011 in Philadelphia working at the LCP and the Historical Society of Pennsylvania, reading in particular the hundreds of letters to and from New York printers that I found in Mathew Carey's massive archive. A fellowship from the Gilder Lehrman Institute of American History allowed me to spend a month in New York in December 2011 and early January 2012 doing research at the New-York Historical Society, Columbia University, and the New York City Municipal Archives at 31 Chambers Street. It was during this trip to New York that I happened upon John Ward Fenno's estate inventory, a document at the heart of chapter 3. A 2014 Hackman Research Residency Fellowship from the New York State Archives and Archives Partnership Trust allowed me to spend another month in Albany doing research on probated wills. In 2015, I was fortunate to receive a Summer Institute Fellowship from the National Endowment for the Humanities, which allowed me to spend a month in New York City as part of the "City of Print: New York and the Periodical Press" NEH Summer Institute. The conversations with my colleagues at the institute helped to clarify some of my thinking and moved the project forward.

Finally, I was fortunate to receive a 2012–13 Andrew W. Mellon Early American Literature and Material Texts Fellowship from the University of Pennsylvania's McNeil Center for Early American Studies and the Library Company of Philadelphia. During that time, this project matured in ways I could not previously have imagined. The McNeil Center not only allowed me to focus exclusively on writing but allowed for an open, constructive, and at times intense interdisciplinary environment. It is doubtful that this book would be where it is today without my time there. I would like to thank Jim Green at the Library Company and Dan Richter at the McNeil Center for spearheading the Mellon Early American Literature and Material Texts Fellowship Initiative, and for inviting me to be part of its interdisciplinary community of scholars. My time at the center introduced me to some of the brightest young minds in early American studies, exposed me to cutting-edge research in the field, and allowed me unlimited access to one of the finest university libraries in the country.

Between 2011 and 2013, I presented three chapters of this book to the annual Early American Literature and Material Texts Initiative Workshop. I am so thankful for the sharp criticism and welcome feedback I received from my fellow EALMT colleagues, Sarah Scheutze, Mark Mattes, Seth Perry, Alea Henle, Kate Gaudet, Marcia Nichols, Danielle Skeehan, Joshua Ratner, John Garcia, Lindsay Van Tine, Kristina Garvin, Sonia Hazard, Daniel Couch, Andrew Inchiosa, Angel-Luke O'Donnell, Michael Winship, Jim Green, Dan Richter, Marcy Dinius, Eric Slauter, Christopher Looby, Meredith McGill, and Jessica Linker, and I am grateful for the great care and attention to detail they gave my work. *An Empire of Print* is the book it is today because of the EALMT Initiative. The friendships I made in Philadelphia at the McNeil Center and the Library Company will last well beyond the publication of this book.

I have also benefited immensely from the staff at the many libraries and research centers where I did research for this book. Paul Mercer made my time at the New York State Library all the more interesting with his constant curiosity and encouragement. At the New York Public Library, Thomas Lannon went out of his way to help me with my research. During my time there, we formed a lasting friendship, and he remains interested in whatever it is that I am doing. I am also indebted to him for arranging my fifteen minutes of fame, which took shape in a story about my work published in the *Huffington Post* (and thanks to Angela Montefinise of *Huff Post* for her candor and patience in interviewing me). The American Antiquarian Society staff have a well-earned reputation for collegiality, and I owe a special debt of gratitude to Elizabeth Pope, Tracey Kry, Laura Wasowicz, Tom Knoles, Dennis Laurie, Phil Lampi, and Andrew Bourque. Ashley Cataldo took a special interest in my project, and often brought me things she thought useful. I have known Paul Erickson, the former director of academic programs at the AAS, since 2008, and he constantly impresses me with his inquisitiveness, attention to detail, and good humor. At the Library Company, I am grateful to Cathy Matson and Jim Green, and am thankful for the sound guidance and helpful critiques they offered during the PEAES Colloquium. I am especially indebted to Jim, who took an early interest in my work. He helped guide me through the maze that is the Lea & Febiger Records, and was always ready for a conversation. I also owe a great deal of thanks to Connie King for her attentive and graceful stewardship of the LCP's reading room. I owe thanks to the Historical Society of Pennsylvania's helpful staff, including reference librarians Steve Smith, Sarah Heim, and Ron Medford. The Gilder Lehrman Institute's education coordinator, Kathleen Wesner, handled all of the arrangements and took the time to meet with me to discuss some of my research. Ted O'Reilly and Tammy Kiter, manuscript librarians at the New-York Historical Society, helped me during my two visits there. Kenneth Cobb at the Municipal Archives deserves a great deal of thanks for helping me during my time there and for subsequently sending me reels of microfilm. Finally, I would like to thank James Folts of the New York State Archives, whose endless knowledge of New York history helped me a great deal during my time in 2014 as a Hackman Research Resident in Albany.

While researching and writing a scholarly book can often be lonely, I have come to the conclusion that even this kind of work requires a devoted community willing to talk, listen, and lend a hand. I have made many lasting friendships working on *An Empire of Print*. Had it not been for this project, my life would not be as rich as it is today. The people I list here have read my work, offered helpful criticism, and provided much needed friendship and encouragement. Their sharp intellect, enthusiasm, solidarity, and good cheer helped lift me up even when things looked bleakest. I would therefore like to acknowledge and thank Craig Hollander, Tristan Tomlinson, Sam Seeley, Sarah Chesney, Sarah Rodríguez, Hannah Farber, Chris Parsons, Adam Lewis, Cameron Strang, Katie Howard, Emma Stapely, Ben Reed, Jess Hower, Andrew Fagal, Louis-Pascal Rousseau, Susan Brandt, Roderick McDonald, Michelle McDonald, Wayne Bodle, Andy Shankman, Bill Carter, Tom LeCarner, Lucia McMahon, Jim Gigantino, Anna Stewart, Erin Murphy, David Prior, Josh Brown, Anne Verplanck (who opened her beautiful Delaware home to me during a move to Philadelphia), Dominque Zino, Amber LaPiana, Kacy Tillman, Matt Sivils, Andy Burstein, Nancy Isenberg, Kristen Doyle Highland, Kristin Stone, Andrew W. Robertson, Joe Adelman, and the late Dallet Hemphill, whom we all miss. Josh Brown took an early and avid interest in my work and was always available to help me out whenever I needed him. Sarah Rodríguez generously read the manuscript from cover to cover, and it is doubtful that the book would be where it is today without her many helpful suggestions and support. Craig, Tristan, Chesney, and Fagal were especially encouraging as I was writing the afterword, and we often talked about ideas (big and small) while tossing the famed "Pigskin of Knowledge" around the McNeil Center. Craig went the extra mile to help me so many times, and he and Jeni Steinhardt Hollander opened their home to me whenever I needed a place to stay in New York. These wonderful friends and scholars have enriched my life and truly reshaped my understanding of the possibilities of interdisciplinary and collaborative scholarship.

I cannot express how fortunate I am to work at Providence College. I am so incredibly thankful to have such generous, brilliant colleagues and amazing students, who have made my time in Rhode Island fun, instructive, productive, and memorable. The dean of the School of Arts and Sciences, Sheila Adamus Liotta, and the provost, Hugh F. Lena, deserve special thanks for covering the cost of indexing the book. I have had the good fortune to work alongside friends and colleagues from across campus (and who, though they may not have realized it at the time, offered support and encouragement for this book): Anthony Rodriguez, Bob Reeder, Rob Stretter, Anthony Jensen, Tuire Valkeakari, Tom Strasser, Bill Hogan, Jon Scanlan, Pat Reid, Ian Levy, Arthur Urbano, Edmund Dain, and Vance Morgan. My research assistant, Patrick Atwood, helped compile essential data for chapter 2. The Department of History and Classics is, hands down, the best department at Providence College. I cannot imagine working with a better group of colleagues and friends, including Colin Jaundrill, Adrian Weimer, Margaret Manchester, Robin Greene, Ray Sickinger, Sharon Ann Murphy, Pat Breen, Connie Rousseau, Fr. Dave Orique, Jen Illuzzi, Vefa Erginbas, Paul O'Malley, Toby Harper, Fred Drogula, Matt Dowling, Richard Grace, Tom Grzebien, Karen Holland, John Lawless, Dara Mulderry, Mario DiNunzio, Paul Quinlan, and Fr. John Vidmar. Jeff Johnson and Ted Andrews deserve special mention for helping me in the early stages of the book by reading (many) drafts of my book proposal while also sharing with me their own work. Jeff went the extra mile by helping me with the response to my reader reports. Beyond that, Jeff has been a calming and encouraging voice and a steadfast friend—a true "Top Bro." Alex Orquiza was always available to discuss teaching, research, writing, baseball, and *Star Wars*. Alex and his wife, Erica Holland, also opened their home to me during several trips I made to Boston. And to the PC Bowling "Team" (you know who you are): the next round is on me!

Many previous versions of this book have been presented at conferences, invited workshops, and lectures. I am grateful for the comments and suggestions of the audience members, commenters, and fellow panelists at the annual Researching New York Conference; the Business History Conference; the annual Conference on New York State History, the American Antiquarian Society; the PEAES Colloquium at the Library Company; the North American Labor History Conference; the Urban History Association Conference; the New England Historical Association Conference; the Social Science History Association Conference; the Boston Immigration and Urban History Seminar at the Massachusetts Historical Society; the McNeil Center for Early American Studies Friday Seminar; the CUNY Graduate Center Early American Republic Seminar; the annual conference of the Society for the History of Authorship, Reading, and Publishing; and the May 2016 Early American Material Texts conference at the University of Pennsylvania's McNeil Center for Early American Studies. I was fortunate to be named the 2012 Malkin New Scholar by the Bibliographical Society of America, and, as part of my award, I was invited to present part of what became chapter 5 at its annual meeting in January 2012 at the Grolier Club in New York City.

Portions of this book have been published elsewhere, and I owe the editors thanks for granting me permission to use this material in *An Empire of Print*. I would like to thank the *Papers of the Bibliographical Society of America* and its editor, David Gants, for permission to incorporate portions of my December 2012 article, "'Elements of Useful Knowledge': New York and the National Book Trade in the Early Republic" into *An Empire of Print.* I also need to thank Wayne Franklin, editor of *Literature in the Early American Republic,* for granting permission to use some of my May 2014 essay "'A Rash, Thoughtless, and Imprudent Young Man': John Ward Fenno and the Federalist Literary Network" in the book.

I am grateful for the hard work, patience, and interest of Patrick Alexander at the Pennsylvania State University Press, and his dedicated staff, including Laura Reed-Morrisson, Jennifer Norton, Alex Vose, and Hannah Hebert. Patrick has been an ideal editor and has helped me develop this book in so many ways. I could not have asked for a better experience, as a first-time author, in working with a university press. I would also like to thank James L. W. West III, editor of the Penn State Series in the History of the Book, and the two anonymous readers, whose sharp criticisms helped make this a much stronger book. I would also like to thank Suzanne Wolk for her many heroics in copyediting the book.

But my greatest debts are to my parents, Rod and Pat Smith, to whom I dedicate this book. As the shy, bookish only child of an engineer and a nurse, how exactly I came to be a historian is a curious thing. I strongly doubt that whatever I say in this acknowledgment will do justice to the love and support they have given me. Regardless of my career choice, Mom and Dad were always there to support me in whatever way they could. It's been an up-and-down journey, but they stood by me and helped talk me through my lows and celebrate my highs. Both worried every time I made a research trip to some faraway place, and they always demanded a phone call in the evening to let them know I was okay. I fondly recall Dad taking test snapshots of old family letters with a digital camera and sending them to me in preparation for my first big research trip, to verify that, yes indeed, a digital camera would work just fine in the archive. They supported me at every step of the way, and this type of love and friendship is impossible to repay, and even more difficult to put into words. Sadly, my mom did not live to see this book in print. She passed away in February 2012 after a short, painful battle with cancer. While I was absolutely devastated, and had thoughts of giving up on the project, I knew deep down that she would have wanted me to finish. And so, with the love and support of my friends and family, I kept working. My dad has been extraordinarily supportive the past few years as I worked to finish the book. When times were tough and things looked bleak, he was always there for me. I will never be able to pay him back for what he has done for me, and so I hope this book will stand in as an expression of my thanks for all of his love and support. It has been a long, difficult, and often painful road to get to this point. But I did it.

I hope that I have made you proud, Mom and Dad. This is your book as much as it is mine.

Steven Carl Smith
Providence, Rhode Island

A NOTE ON CITING NEWSPAPERS

. . . .

Many of the newspapers cited in this book include the city as part of the title (e.g., the *New-York Packet*). In cases where the city is not part of the name on the paper's masthead, I have added it in roman type (the New York *American Citizen*). In cases involving common—or less well known—town names, I have included the state abbreviation (the Salem, Mass., *Impartial Register*). And while I have made every effort to record newspaper titles accurately, editors and printers all too often made subtle (and sometimes extensive) changes to newspaper names. Thus, for example, the four newspapers published in Carlisle, Pennsylvania—the *Carlisle Gazette*; the *Carlisle Gazette, and the Western Repository of Knowledge*; *Kline's Carlisle Weekly Gazette*; and the *Spirit of the Times & Carlisle Gazette*—are in fact the same paper, which went through various name changes over time. In the interest of thoroughness, and in the hope of being helpful to other scholars, I have used the name on the masthead when citing particular issues of these papers, preferring to err on the side of providing too much information rather than too little; and I have listed the many variations on these newspaper names in the bibliography. In the case of punctuation, I have made slight alterations for the sake of consistency, opting for the use of commas for subtitles (the *New-York Gazette, or The Weekly Post-Boy*).

INTRODUCTION

The Pertinent Details

In January 1852, Dr. John W. Francis gave a speech at a meeting of the Typographical Society in New York. A printer's apprentice before he entered medicine, Francis had developed relationships with many of the city's leading literary figures and the men who produced their work. The publishing trade, he remarked, brought "together the most productive elements of society" and "established a vital relation between intellect and mechanics, between labor and thought." Looking out into a large audience of the city's most prominent publishers, Francis declared, "I see before me in this assembly those who have achieved enduring literary fame, and those who are guides of public opinion." Although it had been a long time since Francis had traded in his leather apron for a doctor's satchel, he prepared some thoughts on his experiences as a "fellow laborer in your noble pursuits." Calling the industry the "representative of the intellectual man on earth," he argued that the press was "the expositor of his cognitive powers" and served as "the defence and maintenance" of "inherent rights." Francis added a few words about his respect for the trade. "Hence I have ever cherished the deep regard for those who have appropriated their time and talents to this vast engine of civilization," he concluded. "I have ever looked upon the vocation as holding the integrity of our highest privileges on earth."[1]

By the time Francis made these remarks, New York had become the center of publishing in the United States. But Francis did not celebrate the men historians so often credit with establishing that city as the nation's publishing capital in the mid-nineteenth century—men like the Harper brothers and George Palmer Putnam. Rather, he spoke of the printers and booksellers who produced and distributed thousands of books in the earliest years of the new Republic, using presses that had changed little since Gutenberg. "You have told me, gentlemen, that you would be gratified with some reminiscences touching New York—social, literary, personal—of men and books—all having a bearing, more or less immediate, either on the progress of human development, or the character of our metropolitan city."[2] The key figures in the transformation of the city's trade, for John Francis and his audience, were the men he knew at the turn of the nineteenth century who set the type, pulled the levers of the presses, bound the books, and sold them locally, regionally, and nationally.

While Francis acknowledged several newspapermen of the early Republic, including noteworthy Republican and Federalist editors, he dedicated most of his speech to celebrating the city's booksellers and publishers, "whose character and influence," he believed, "justly demand[ed] a detailed account." The first was Evert Duyckinck, who had been "quite extensively engaged as a publisher and seller" and whom Francis considered "rich in literary recollections." Isaac Collins was "most widely known" for his many editions of schoolbooks and his quarto Bible. Francis also remembered that, "some sixty years ago," Thomas and James Swords "began operations on Pearl-Street," when "New-York was little more than a village, and when literary projects were almost unknown." As printers and booksellers, the Swords brothers deserved "ample notice as most efficient pioneers" whose "integrity was never doubted" and whose "word was as good as their bond."[3]

Francis wrapped up his speech by wondering aloud whether a "comparative view of the past and present condition of the press" would yield an accurate assessment of the "existing condition of our city as a Literary Emporium." Over the course of his lifetime, Francis had witnessed the impressive growth of the trade in his native New York, due in no small measure to advancements in technology and the increased consolidation of labor and capital. Yet despite what he observed, and the experiences he drew from in his speech, he concluded that the early history of the city's publishing trade, upon which the successes of the press in the mid-nineteenth century had been built, was lost. "I have depended on a memory somewhat tenacious as my authority, in most instances, having no leisure at command for reference. A volume might be written of pertinent details."[4]

An Empire of Print traces the evolution of New York's publishing trade and its "pertinent details" from the end of the American Revolution to the age of Jackson. The book explores in five case studies the gradual development of local, regional, and national distribution networks in the early Republic, and in doing so reveals stories of the men who built the city's thriving trade just before New York became the nation's publishing capital, an unofficial designation it holds to this day. The book analyzes the economic relationships and shared social and cultural practices that connected printers, booksellers, and their customers. It focuses on the economic lives of the tradesmen who worked the printing presses and sold the books that formed the public sphere in the new nation. If the cultural matrix of printed texts served as the primary legitimating vehicle for political debate and literary expression—as scholars have suggested—then we need to understand the economic interests and political affiliations of the people who produced these texts. The printers, booksellers, and publishers at the heart of *An Empire of Print*, like their contemporaries in other major seaport cities, imagined for themselves a robust American book trade that could satisfy the new nation's desire for print, and many fulfilled their ambition by cultivating trade networks that crossed regional boundaries, delivering books to the masses.[5]

Scholars have shown that there was a reading revolution in the mid-eighteenth century, as middling-class libraries grew in both size and diversity. Consumers flocked to local bookshops to stock up on histories, geographies, biographies, encyclopedias, novels, dictionaries, spelling books, almanacs, and poetry collections. To meet this increasing demand, colonial bookshops often imported books from London. The War of Independence, however, put a halt to the flow of consumer goods from Europe, and while British booksellers raced to flood the American market in the immediate postwar period, American printers, booksellers, and publishers helped build up the trade by reprinting popular European titles for the domestic market. As scholars have pointed out, the book business boomed and as a result played an important role in the shaping of economic, political, and cultural life in the years after the Revolution. And because the book trade experienced such growth, there began to emerge a gradual differentiation between various elements in the trade. Printers began to ply their craft by financing the production of "American" books—deemed to be texts, whether reprints or original works, produced in America by American labor with American paper and American type for American audiences. Nascent capitalists that they were, these entrepreneurs coordinated the financing, production, and dissemination of print in the early Republic, evolving well beyond their traditional roles as "printers" and "booksellers" into "publishers" who focused on marketing and distribution while outsourcing the labor of producing a book to local job printers. Thus "printers," "booksellers," and, eventually, "publishers" worked together to make the popular books of the day readily and cheaply available for schools, churches, and homes. This appetite for print created a national market, and the New York publishing trade, with its advantageous port, began to thrive at the turn of the nineteenth century.[6]

For the past twenty years or so, scholars have examined how the production and distribution of books, pamphlets, newspapers, broadsides, and other ephemera shaped the development of the new nation. Some have focused on how communication networks helped spur political mobilization during the Revolution and early Republic. The growth of the domestic book trade also aided in the development of the professional class in antebellum America, as Michael Hoeflich has shown in his recent study of legal publishing. Others observe how the American people began to understand themselves as *Americans* in the years after the Revolution. But there is no such agreement that print culture had this kind of widespread political and cultural impact, as scholars have begun to question whether print actually influenced the evolution of the new nation. Trish Loughran argues forcefully that a national print culture did not exist in the early Republic, at least not prior to the widespread adoption in the 1830s and 1840s of steam presses and revolutionary forms of transportation such as canals and railroads. The "imagined community" held together by print was, in Loughran's estimation, just that: imagined. There could not have been a national print culture because the kind of distribution and communication infrastructure needed to achieve a national circulation of texts did not, Loughran argues, yet exist in the United States. And Robert Gross, in his wide-ranging introduction to *An Extensive Republic*, suggests that the early Republic's geography proved far too great a hurdle for the ordinary bookseller to overcome. Other than a few well-connected publishers, such as New York's Harper Brothers, who could claim a truly national market for their products in the 1830s and 1840s, most publishing in the early days of the new nation, Gross argues, remained a local affair.[7]

At the same time, however, scholars have broadened our understanding of the market economy and the role that the publishing trade played in shaping social, political, and cultural institutions in the early Republic. Many point to Philadelphia as an important center for the production and dissemination of print. This should not be surprising given the impressive productivity of the city's printers in the eighteenth and nineteenth centuries. But as recent studies of Baltimore and Charleston suggest, the trades in other American cities in the late eighteenth and early nineteenth centuries were just as dynamic. So, while renewed attention to the book trade has contributed to our understanding of print culture's role in shaping the course of the new nation—resoundingly affirmed with the publication of the second volume in the acclaimed History of the Book in America series—absent from the historiography is the story of New York's publishing trade in the early Republic. This is despite considerable work on the evolution of the city's antebellum book trade, ranging from case studies of leading midcentury publishers such as the Harper Brothers, George Putnam Palmer, the American Tract Society, and the American Bible Society, to the emergence of the so-called penny press, which changed the way Americans got their news. Additionally, extensive literature addresses New York City's evolving and increasingly important role in the market economy in the early Republic. *An Empire of Print* suggests that New York's early publishing trade should be considered alongside Philadelphia and Boston precisely because the men discussed in this book played an important role in distributing thousands of books to a nation hungry for print long before the Harper Brothers dominated the market.[8]

An Empire of Print, then, sheds light on how New York City's printers, booksellers, and publishers helped build up the new nation in print by developing sophisticated regional, and in some cases national, distribution networks for books hot off the city's presses. Each chapter examines an element of New

York's publishing trade in the early Republic—government printing, subscription publishing, the bookshop, the first national literary fair, and the wholesale book trade—and in so doing provides detailed snapshots of the critical years between the end of the Revolutionary War and the consolidation of the trade in the 1830s and 1840s. These five case studies belie the suggestion that printers and booksellers lacked access to a robust communication infrastructure that would have enabled them to form the kind of trade networks through which thousands of imprints could circulate nationally. Indeed, the financial records, business correspondence, and aspirational rhetoric that circulated in newspapers reveal how the city's printers, booksellers, and publishers engaged in extensive interurban and intrastate trade, their efforts coordinated with those of fellow tradesmen in port cities such as Philadelphia, Boston, Baltimore, Richmond, Charleston, and Savannah. And while readers may not have understood that they were participating in a shared cultural experience, made possible by the distribution networks of men like John Ward Fenno and Evert Duyckinck, the thousands of books shipped out of Manhattan to distant cities and towns in fact created possibilities for the simultaneous use of texts. The business archives of Samuel Loudon, Samuel Campbell, Fenno, Duyckinck, and Philadelphia's Mathew Carey illuminate not only their individual operations but the scope and impact of the larger trade in the early Republic.[9]

But the story of New York's publishing trade in the early Republic is not marked by innovation or high-minded idealism, things that John Francis knew all too well in 1852. Rather, the stories in *An Empire of Print* often speak to the same themes that marked the uneven development of the young Republic: uncertainty, struggle, unflappable ambition, pragmatism, and endurance in the face of difficult, sometimes seemingly insurmountable political and economic obstacles. Many of New York's printers, booksellers, and publishers lived through the imperial crisis and the War of Independence that followed. Suddenly on their own, in a city and a nation seeking political, cultural, and literary fulfillment in print, New York's printers, booksellers, and publishers looked to build a trade that could supply American-made books for a population that had an insatiable appetite for knowledge. This book shows that New York City may have been the capital of the nation's publishing trade in the early nineteenth century, much as it is today.

SAMUEL LOUDON AND THE BUILDING OF
THE EMPIRE STATE IN PRINT

In late January 1784, as New York was recovering from the British occupation, the printer Samuel Loudon sensed an opportunity. Loudon hoped to win the state's printing contract, so he drafted a petition to make his case for the job. The position was highly coveted among printers because it was partially subsidized by the state. Indeed, the legislature required any number of printed documents to function on a daily basis, ranging from the annual publication of state laws, to legislative proceedings, to the smaller stuff of governance, including individual legislative acts, city and state ordinances, and gubernatorial proclamations. Given the instability of the trade at the time, the annual stipend also gave printers some financial security, which in turn allowed them a little more freedom to pursue other projects, such as running a newspaper.[1]

There was a problem with Loudon's plan, however. When Loudon delivered his petition, fellow printer John Holt still had the job. Holt had become gravely ill, however, and as he lay dying, his wife, Elizabeth, had taken over the printing office and was doing her best to keep the business afloat. None of this seemed to matter to Samuel Loudon, who anticipated that the state would soon be searching for a new printer. Indeed, it was not the least bit uncommon for the state legislature to receive several petitions a year from printers seeking the position. It just so happened that Loudon was taking advantage of Holt's illness, while Elizabeth labored to keep up with the work orders rolling into their office.[2]

Given their professional history, not to mention the nature of the printing business in New York during the Revolution, Loudon's undercutting of Holt was not all that surprising. In fact, it was par for the course. In the previous decade, Loudon had competed off and on with Holt for job work from the New York Provincial Congress, and the two men seemed to have little admiration for each other. Personal rivalries aside, the printing business was profoundly unstable before, during, and after the war. In fact, Samuel Loudon's ability to keep his business afloat was nothing short of miraculous, considering that he had little experience. Unlike fellow members of the trade, Loudon did not apprentice in a printer's shop as a young boy. After a few short years running a small general store in New York City, he started selling books on the side, and eventually established a popular circulating library. After some success in the book business, Loudon branched out into the printing trade, launching the *New-York Packet* in January 1776, a paper that he continued to publish in exile during the war. Indeed, after the British forced the evacuation of New York, several printers fled the city along with Loudon. Hugh Gaine, who had been the king's printer in New York from 1769 to 1775, escaped to New Jersey, while Holt landed in Kingston. Loudon, meanwhile, wound up in Fishkill, a small village fifty miles north of Manhattan where the exiled Fourth Provincial Congress (which renamed itself the Convention of Representatives of the State of New York) had convened in a local church. Loudon had been the acting state printer since arriving in Fishkill, thanks to a sizeable £200 stipend given to him by the state's Committee of Safety. Loudon's good fortune would not last long, however, as the Committee of Safety gave the contract to John Holt, who held it for the remainder of the war. Loudon was suddenly left in the lurch despite his proximity to the legislature, and he could only watch with a mixture of nervousness and annoyance as Holt swooped in to take his job, and thus his means of survival. And while he and his family eked out a living in Fishkill as the war raged on, Loudon kept a close watch on the state legislature, hoping that the contract would soon become available again.[3]

Once back in New York City after the war, probably thinking that his days on the run were over, Loudon tried to get back the state printer's contract from John Holt. But before he could do that, he had to spruce up his shop. Loudon's loss of the contract to Holt can be partly blamed on his shoddy equipment. During his time in Fishkill, Loudon struggled to complete work because his type was so worn that even the simplest jobs became next to impossible. Loudon noted in his January 1784 petition that he had recently purchased new type. He wrote that he had "acquired a sufficient quantity of New Types fit to print the Laws & Journals of This State, & all other Printing business with which he may be favored." Once he allayed any concerns about the materials he would use, Loudon emphasized his past experience printing for the New York government during the war, a job that of course meant working with limited resources. Perhaps his greatest achievement while working for the state in Fishkill, however, was his printing of several thousand copies of New York's first state constitution in 1777. Loudon reminded lawmakers that he had also "Printed the Journal of the Legislature of both Houses, while at Fishkill," pointing out that he did so "at a time when no other Printer in the State could do them." This was reason enough, according to Loudon's logic, at least, to give him the contract. Yet another selling point for his renewed interest in the state printing contract was that he had a large, capable workforce. Loudon's petition also contained a personal appeal. The additional stipend earned as the state printer, he argued, would help support his growing family. He mentioned that his household was "numerous & expansive (being Twenty in number)," a situation that demanded "considerable employment in the Profession of a Printer to yield them a Moderate Support." Holt died three days after Loudon delivered his petition to the legislature. And while Elizabeth Holt carried on John's work for a short time, Loudon's case was apparently persuasive enough, for he was appointed state printer shortly thereafter.[4]

But whatever hopes he had of living a settled, stationary life in Manhattan were dashed almost as soon as he reopened his printing office. The state legislature, after initially meeting in New York City, relocated several times in the 1780s. There for each move was the printer Samuel Loudon. Remaining true to his promise, Loudon trudged up and down the state, his printing equipment in tow, so that he could remain near the proceedings of the legislature. Most of Loudon's career as an itinerant government printer, then, was marked as much by personal struggle as it was by economic instability. This chapter tells the story of Loudon's life on the run.

Once described by a nineteenth-century essayist as a "sober-sided old Scotchman" and a "stanch Wig," Samuel Loudon was dogged by complications on his journey to the state printer's office.[5] Hardly a "meer mechanic" who set aside ideology in favor of fiscal expediency, Loudon was a shrewd, opportunistic businessman who always seemed to be in the right place at the right time. He deftly maneuvered through New York's networks of influence beginning in the late 1760s, while he still traded in dry goods, putting himself in advantageous positions to receive political patronage during the Revolutionary War and in the early years of the new nation. He was also a survivor. His career as a printer was limited by material shortages and fiscal challenges. Unlike many fellow printers, who were forced to shut down their presses because of financial difficulties, Loudon managed to remain afloat. Despite his meager circumstances—which included periodic supply shortages, especially of paper—he managed to be a productive printer while in Fishkill. And while things did not always work out in his favor before, during, or after the war, the "stanch Wig" positioned himself to be an important participant in New York state politics. By taking over the state printing contract and printing the laws and proceedings of the New York legislature in the early years of the Republic, Loudon and his well-traveled press helped to rebuild commercial and political distribution networks that had been all but severed during the British occupation of the city. So, while Loudon's life on the run in revolutionary New York may seem to us both tedious and disheveled, the years he spent following the legislature as the state's official printer had political significance, as the work he did played an important role in creating the Empire State.[6]

"They Intend to Incourage a Number of Their Friends to Come Over from Scotland"

Though he was most probably born in Scotland in 1727, little is known about the first twenty-six years of Samuel Loudon's life. While we do not know the precise year of his arrival in New York, we do know that Loudon opened a general store near the Old Slip, a boat slip in lower Manhattan, in 1753.[7] The sheer variety of goods lining Loudon's shelves reflected the evolving tastes of a colonial consumer steeped in a simple, rustic past while also adapting to sophisticated material and cultural trends. Loudon, for example, accommodated local farmers and laborers by stocking "red clover seed," as well as "brimstone, Durham Mustard, dishes, saws, files, axes, shovels, speaking trumpets, lanthorns, pots and kettles, paper and twine, nails, hinges, locks, hats, powder and shot." This kind of stock would have met the needs of the city's growing population, especially in the rural environs north of Manhattan. His Old Slip shop was not limited to stocking items useful to working men and their families, however. Loudon advertised a selection of "ready made coats and breeches, in the newest fashions" in order to appeal to merchants and gentlemen looking to keep up with the latest London styles.[8] As the increasingly affluent colonial consumer began desiring the finest English-made goods in the mid-eighteenth century, merchants like Samuel Loudon tried their best to meet those needs.[9]

Loudon's general store did not last long. In September 1757, Loudon closed the store and opened in its place a discount ship chandlery. He had on offer in his new a shop a variety of cheap, essential maritime goods, ranging from cables, cartridge paper, and "half worn sails"—all at "the Lowest Prices."[10] Loudon's transition to a specialized, if cheap, ship chandlery suggests that he understood well the nuances of the city's evolving market economy. Recognizing that he was unlikely to make it selling a diverse lot of items, Loudon pivoted and began catering to the constant need to outfit maritime vessels in one of the busiest ports in colonial North America.

In February 1766, Loudon got involved with the powerful Livingston and Schuyler families in a land speculation scheme. Having taken out a loan from his creditor, Thomas Livingston, Loudon purchased two tracts of land worth nearly £550. Evidently finding little success in selling his acquisition for a profit, Loudon grouped his holdings together with several fellow speculators in January 1768 and transferred the holdings to Philip Schuyler. The idea behind the merger was that Schuyler could secure a better price for land given his political influence as a member of the New York Assembly. Schuyler, Loudon reasoned in releasing the land holdings, could "sell the same for the benefit of the creditors."[11] On behalf of his fellow speculators, Loudon implored Schuyler to get the best possible deal. After corresponding with "the People concerned with Mr. Thos. Livingston's Lands," Loudon gently reminded Schuyler that he had been tasked with making an "advantageous sale" and that the "Lands" should not "go off for a Trifle."[12]

The scheme dragged on for several years. With each passing season, Loudon and his partners grew increasingly uneasy. Writing on behalf of the creditors, Loudon indicated to Schuyler in April 1773 that all involved were "anxious to have the sale closed."[13] In order to expedite the process, Loudon proposed an ambitious marketing plan, suggesting to Schuyler that they "get an advertisement put in the News Papers" in addition to printing a "parcel of hand bills, to put up at Country taverns and other Publick places in the Country."[14] The advertisement Loudon had published in the *New-York Gazette* described five tracts of "happily situated" land totaling more than twenty-one hundred acres, all "well watered and timbered, in the neighborhood of grist and saw-mills." Potential investors, Loudon pointed out, would find that the tracts could be acquired on the most generous of terms.[15]

As the weeks passed by with no sale in sight, Loudon grew impatient with Schuyler's inability to close a deal of any kind. No longer able to conceal his frustration, he revealed to Schuyler in June 1773 that he had already lost quite a bit of money in the venture. In an act of true desperation, Loudon begged Schuyler to return his shares, at a loss. His plan was to sell "some of the Saratoga Lands" to the Scottish and Irish immigrants pouring into the province. "There are numbers from both places expected soon," he wrote, as they had "yet a little cash."[16] New York, as Loudon clearly recognized, was a demographic marvel in the late eighteenth century. In ten short years, from 1760 to 1770, the city's population increased by 20 percent to more than twenty thousand, surpassed only by Philadelphia in sheer size. In the fifteen years or so before the Battles of Lexington and Concord, nearly 140,000 Europeans descended upon the North American colonies, including about 125,000 Britons. The surge was largely the result of a massive influx of Irish and Scottish migrants—55,000 Irish and an additional 40,000 thousand from Scotland. Approximately 25,000 ended up in New York province. Many of the new arrivals fled Great Britain's beleaguered textile industry, which had witnessed a sudden and dramatic wave of joblessness in the mid-eighteenth century. Most of the Irish and English migrants came as indentured servants. Relatively few Scottish immigrants, by contrast—about one in five—tethered their passage across the Atlantic to a fixed labor term. Scholars have speculated that many of the Scottish immigrants avoided indentured servitude because they were probably older and somewhat more affluent, and had transferable skills as artisans; they also tended to travel with their families. The biggest draw to colonial North America for them was cheap and readily available land.[17] Recognizing this potential market, Loudon sent two Scottish gentlemen—Captain William Loudon and Peter M'Robert—to Albany to consult with Schuyler. Loudon emphasized to Schuyler that the meeting with Captain Loudon and M'Robert seemed the key to a profitable return. "They intend to incourage a number of their friends to come over from Scotland next year," Loudon wrote, and it was "probable that they may bring over some wealthy people with them as the spirit of emigration seems to operate strongly in Britain & Ireland."[18]

"Authors of the Most Established Reputation"

With the upstate lands possibly sold to Scottish immigrants, Loudon remade his business for a third time. In December 1771, he announced in Hugh Gaine's *New-York Mercury* that he had opened a bookstore. While his shop remained a ship chandlery, "as usual," Loudon at the same time touted the "great variety" of books he had in stock as well as a standard assortment of stationery.[19] Loudon did not think twice about badgering friends and acquaintances to buy his books. Writing to his brother-in-law, Elijah Backus of Norwich, Connecticut, in September 1773, Loudon slipped a copy of his inventory into the package. But it was not enough merely to include the book catalogue in the correspondence; Loudon insisted that his brother-in-law place an order. He encouraged Backus to "purchase a few useful Books" for his daughter, Lucy, "& your other children." At the same time, however, Loudon was contrite, acknowledging to Backus that his correspondence was indeed motivated in part by his desire to spread the word about his new bookshop. "Self interest is partly included in my advice," he confessed.[20] Loudon seemed unfazed by entering into an increasingly competitive trade without the least bit of formal training, relying instead on instinct and, to a certain degree, luck.

After several abandoned business ventures, Loudon landed on his feet at the bookstore. Even with early success in the trade, he continued exploring new ways to make money. As a member of and shareholder in the New York Society Library, Loudon probably recognized that he could profit by lending books in addition to selling them. Founded in 1754, the New York Society Library was a private corporation in which potential members could buy the "rights," or shares, to the library at a cost of five pounds. Members also paid an annual subscription of five shillings just for borrowing privileges, a princely sum that made membership far too expensive for many city residents. Early on, the library attracted more than one hundred subscribers, and could count among its number the wealthiest and

most prominent families of the city, including the Livingstons, the Van Cort-
landts, and the Stuyvesants. The library did not fare well during the American
Revolution. The building was ransacked during the British occupation of Manhattan in September 1776, and members faced the difficult choice between
remaining loyal to the British Crown or siding with the upstart Americans.
Because of the inner turmoil that rocked the library, it did not reopen until late
1788. By the following year, it could count nearly 240 members who borrowed
from shelves lined with more than three thousand books.[21]

The opening of the New York Society Library was part of a larger trend that
witnessed the formation of hundreds of similar social, or membership, libraries
in early America. Many took the shape of local voluntary associations, formed
by citizens eager to work together in order to get their hands on all the latest
reading material. And while many of these libraries resembled the New York
Society Library in that most of the patronage came from a small, often elite
group of founding members, they were designed to function as public libraries
and not as private reading rooms.[22]

Loudon established the city's second circulating library in late December
1773. He advertised its opening in James Rivington's newspaper. At first glance,
Loudon's choice of venue for this advertisement seems odd given Rivington's
Tory politics. But a closer look reveals that it was a pragmatic move. By advertising in Rivington's paper, Loudon could reach the largest possible audience. In
October 1774, only a few months after Loudon's advertisement appeared in
Rivington's New-York Gazetteer, Rivington claimed that he had more than thirty-
six hundred subscribers—by far the largest newspaper subscription roll in the
North American colonies.[23] Heeding the call of "several very respectable inhab-
itants," Loudon promised to stock books in the library that would be "both
instructive and entertaining," written by "authors of the most established reputation."[24] Three weeks later, Loudon announced in Hugh Gaine's *New-York
Gazette* that the circulating library's catalogue was available and "ready to be
delivered to the subscribers, *gratis*." Loudon boasted that he had on hand "a neat
collection of books" and that he would work diligently to find titles to suit the
evolving tastes of his patrons.[25] The circulating library grew so rapidly and
developed such a devoted following in its first year that Loudon published a
second catalogue that reflected the expansion of his stock. "The Library will be
much enlarged," he wrote in a late November edition of the *New-York Gazette*,
promising the public that "no endeavours will be wanting to render it a real
public benefit." Loudon insisted that his library would help contribute to the
public's civic engagement. "Books are standing counsellors, always at hand,
and always disinterested," he wrote. Because books had "this advantage over
all other instructions," he reasoned, "they are ready to repeat their lessons as
often as we please."[26]

Loudon counted among his most loyal customers women with broad literary and political interests. We know this because he was compelled to make a
public statement on the number of women who borrowed books from his
library. In response to a derogatory remark in a London magazine about the
intellectual capacity of the city's women, Loudon objected to the charge that New
York women did not read as widely as their London counterparts. "If ever there
was in former times any reason for such an invidious observation," he wrote, "it
is hoped it exists no more, but rather that there may be just occasion, on this
subject or a remark of an opposite kind." In fact, he insisted that the opposite
was true. "The proprietor of the CIRCULATING LIBRARY informs all such connois-
seurs, that the ladies are his best customers, and shew a becoming delicacy of
taste in their choice of books."[27] Loudon's statement in the *New-York Gazette*
proved to be an astute observation. Elsewhere in eighteenth-century North
America, women borrowed and read library books at impressive rates. In Philadelphia, for example, Thomas Bradford opened a circulating library in 1769.
His surviving charging ledgers, which recorded the library's book circulation
between early December 1771 and mid-December 1772, reveal that Philadelphia
women borrowed books from the library nearly as often as men did.[28]

Like the Bradford and Loudon circulating libraries, the New York Society
Library counted among its members several women with a wide range of literary interests. By the time she joined the library in 1789, Henrietta Maria Colden
was part of an elite social circle that included the Hamilton and Burr families.
She was also reported to have had a brief flirtation with James Madison in 1791,
when the Virginian was in New York serving his term in Congress.[29] Colden
was an active book borrower. She checked out forty titles between August 1789
and the end of April 1792, including David Ramsay's *History of the Revolution in
South Carolina* and *History of the American Revolution;* Edward Gibbon's *Decline
and Fall of the Roman Empire;* the *Posthumous Works of Frederick the Second, King
of Prussia, Arundel,* by a Mr. Cumberland; *Fortunate Country Maid; Gamesters;*
the collected works of Jean-Jacques Rousseau, Georgiana Cavendish's novel *The
Sylph; The Englishman's Fortnight in Paris,* by Jean Jacques Rutledge, and Charlotte Smith's *Romance of Real Life,* among many others.[30] Catharine Bradford,
like Colden, was also an active New York Society Library patron. Her second
husband, Cornelius Bradford, bought the Merchants' Coffee House in 1776,
which he later renamed the Old Coffee-House.[31] The couple fled the city to
Rhinebeck, New York, during the British occupation.[32] They returned after the
evacuation in 1783, picking up where they left off.[33] Despite the loss of her
husband three years after their return to the city, Catharine continued to operate
the coffeehouse for many years, and it functioned as a meeting place during the
recovery of the city's economy.[34] During her time as the proprietor of the coffee-
house, Catharine checked out seventy-two titles from the New York Society

Library, among them novels such as *The Sylph;* Robert Bage's 1787 *Fair Syrian;*
The Woman of Fashion, by Phoebe Gibbes; a pseudonymously authored novel
titled *Arpasia, or The Wanderer;* and *Caroline of Litchfield* by the Swiss translator
and novelist Isabelle de Montolieu.[35]

"A Compleat and Accurate News-Paper"

His bookstore thriving and the circulating library growing, Samuel Loudon
added a printing press to the business in 1775. He purchased the equipment
from his former partner, Frederick Shober. Shober & Loudon was a short-lived
partnership. As tension between Great Britain and the American colonies wors-
ened, Shober wanted out of the partnership. According to Isaiah Thomas's
version of the story, "the commencement of hostilities [between Great Britain
and the colonies] alarmed Shober," and, in the late winter of 1775, he sold his
shares of the business—which included the press and all of the printing equipment—to Loudon and retired to the country, where he spent the remainder of
his days as a farmer.[36] In only a few short months, Samuel Loudon fell into
ownership, quite by accident, of a fully stocked printing shop. The press Loudon
inherited from Shober was well traveled, to say the least. Probably purchased by
Hodge and Shober in Philadelphia, the partners took it with them to Baltimore.
And when the venture in the Chesapeake proved to be a failure after only a few
short months, Hodge and Shober relocated yet again, to New York, where Samuel Loudon was eventually brought on board.

Because Loudon lacked a formal printer's apprenticeship, his partnership
with Shober was also something of a crash course in how to operate a printing
press. A printer was a working mechanic with an "inclination for books," as
Benjamin Franklin observed in his autobiography. The printer's world was hardly
one of scholarly pursuit, however. Rather, as Loudon no doubt discovered, it was
a grimy, physically demanding profession, and years of training were required
to effectively operate the complicated machinery and finish a printed object. The
production of print, whether for a book, a newspaper, or a bill of lading, was the
end result of many hours of often tedious labor. Apprentices and journeymen
first dampened the paper. Next, a typesetter carefully placed the text in a composing stick, gathered from the nearby letter case, onto the press. The type was then
vigorously beaten with heavy leather balls soaked in ink, often made in-house by
the apprentices. The last step involved the impression of the heavy wooden press
onto the wet paper. The actual presswork was the most taxing aspect of the trade.
Pressmen working in a preindustrial print shop often overdeveloped the muscles
in the arm they used to pull the press, a deformity that drew attention and ridicule
from fellow artisans on the streets and in the pub.[37]

After acquiring Shober's well-traveled press, Loudon immediately made the best of his former partner's bad luck. In early January 1776, Loudon established a newspaper called the *New-York Packet, and the American Advertiser*. And, much like his foray into the book business, Loudon did so without the least bit of formal training. Loudon's aim in printing the *Packet* was to provide Manhattan with a reliable and informative newspaper. "In the course of this publication," he wrote in the paper's prospectus, "the editor engages to do everything in his power to render it a compleat and accurate NEWS-PAPER, that the Public may thereby receive the earliest intelligence of the state of our public affairs." After assuring potential subscribers that he had cobbled together a "neat and sizeable set of TYPES for the above-mentioned purpose," Loudon predicted that his newspaper would serve as a living record of the extraordinary events then unfolding in New York and elsewhere in the British North American colonies. "The Publisher flatters himself that the NEW-YORK PACKET, will be conducted on such principles," he reasoned, "as will influence every discerner of real merit, who may encourage the work, to preserve it in volumes, as a faithful Chronicle of its own time."[38] Rather than make his politics known, Loudon envisioned a newspaper that would serve as a witness to and guardian of a revolutionary moment.

By adding a printing press to his bookshop and circulating library, Loudon was taking a financial risk. Newspapers had become visible, and important, parts of everyday life in the mainland colonies—especially the major port cities. By the time the Stamp Act threatened to shutter printing shops from Charleston to Boston, there were twenty-three newspapers in circulation, and by 1775, when fighting began in western Massachusetts, thirty-seven. Yet printing was far from a lucrative business in the late eighteenth century, especially shops that published newspapers. Some papers folded almost overnight, while most printers scraped by on the slimmest of margins, begging subscribers to forward payment. Printers also accepted just about anything as currency, including foodstuffs and firewood. Most printers kept shops open by printing and selling almanacs, blank account books, and legal forms, in addition to taking on random job-printing contracts.[39]

Having sidestepped politics in the December 1775 prospectus, Loudon addressed the issues dividing the British Empire in the *Packet*. In the first issue, published in early January 1776, he embedded his fervent patriotism in cautious, conciliatory language. The first order of business was to seek the approval of New York's residents by making the paper relevant to the public. "The difficulty of the times requires much prudence in conducting a Work of this nature," he wrote, a subtle reminder of the dire state of politics in New York and elsewhere. Loudon was not looking to placate either Tory or Whig readers, however. Rather, he hedged a risky bet by announcing his intention to support "any considerations that may illustrate and animate the glorious cause of Constitutional

Liberty," while at the same time applying rhetorical salve to "the bleeding wounds of the extended empire." Loudon did not stop there. He suggested that his newspaper, however small it may have been on the imperial stage, would nonetheless aim to bridge the ever-widening gap between Great Britain and its colonies. "For this purpose," Loudon invited "the Friends of America and the British Constitution" to join him in thinking through the issues at hand, and he hoped that by doing so, "the year 1776 may be the happy Era, in which Peace and union, on a Constitutional Basis, shall be concluded between Great-Britain and her Colonies."[40] Invoking the British constitution in the first issue of the newspaper was a subtle yet compelling announcement of what he intended to address in the *Packet*. Colonists had been complaining for years about the violations of their rights and liberties as fellow Englishmen. So, while Loudon was careful in how he worded the first issue, those reading between the lines would have detected the political subtext. At the same time, Loudon's tone suggested that hope for reconciliation with the mother country still existed, at least for some, in January 1776.

Like many newspapermen of the time, Loudon intended his paper to circulate beyond New York City. Even with limited experience in the business, he used his contacts as a bookseller to connect with fellow printers and postmen in other cities. Readers could get a subscription to Loudon's *New-York Packet*, for example, in Philadelphia, in Albany, Fishkill, and Schenectady in upstate New York, in thirteen Connecticut towns, and in nine more towns in nearby New Jersey. And while Loudon's distribution network was limited to towns, large and small, in the mid-Atlantic region and nearby Connecticut, the *New-York Packet* was part of a growing network of newspapers that circulated stories about protests throughout British North America. As scholars have pointed out, disseminating localized moments of hardship, protest, or outright resistance to British policy helped to shape and define a sense of shared purpose and sacrifice.[41]

Unlike his other business ventures, Samuel Loudon's *New-York Packet* seemed less about turning a profit than about serving a higher political purpose. However much he may have styled the *Packet* as a nonpartisan newspaper, Loudon's decision to enter the newspaper business was a political move. Otherwise, founding a newspaper with limited knowledge of the economics of the business, at the height of the imperial conflict, was a questionable decision at best. Loudon's logic in establishing a paper was all the more perplexing given the fragmented relationship between the press and the public in New York. Indeed, publishing a newspaper in late eighteenth-century New York had become a risky business, marked by drama, skullduggery, and shifting partisan loyalties. The newspaper trade was filled with dubious characters—the men Loudon called his peers—who undercut one another just to get ahead and stay afloat. What is remarkable about Samuel Loudon's career as a newspaperman in revolutionary New York, then, was how deftly he negotiated this increasingly perilous political landscape.[42]

Before Loudon fashioned the *Packet* into a newspaper that catered to Whig politics, John Holt was the only patriot newspaper printer in New York City. Holt was an outspoken critic of the Stamp Act and conducted himself so well during the ensuing crisis that he became a favored printer of the Sons of Liberty. In fact, Holt was able to use his newfound political leverage to get the Sons of Liberty to help pay down his debts, which totaled nearly £450. And when it seemed that Holt would be forced to close his doors after returning both his printing press and the rights to the *New-York Gazette, or The Weekly Post-Boy* to his business partner, James Parker (Holt had been renting the equipment and editing the paper owned by Parker)—the Sons of Liberty swooped in and bought Holt his own printing equipment, which he then used to found his own newspaper, the *New-York Journal*. Holt repaid his debt to the city's patriot leaders by making the *New-York Journal* into one of the leading Whig papers in the British North American colonies. The *Journal* was so well known in patriot circles that when the Massachusetts delegation to the First Continental Congress—which included both John Adams and Samuel Adams—stopped in New York for a night of rest on their way to Philadelphia, they made sure to set aside time to meet with "Friend Holt, the liberty printer."[43]

But John Holt concealed a shady past filled with deception, dishonesty, and dubious circumstances. Unlike most men in the colonial printing trade, Holt did not start out as a printer's apprentice. Rather, he was a self-styled Virginia gentleman and social climber who made his mark financially in the high-risk, high-reward profession of selling tobacco. In 1752, Holt somehow (inexplicably) got himself elected mayor of Williamsburg, despite being a relative unknown in Virginia politics. He could be vindictive, and he used his position to exact revenge on rivals. When a local shopkeeper's house mysteriously caught fire, Holt, as mayor, prohibited any resident from providing aid to the family—all because of a petty disagreement the two had had over the sale of alcohol to slaves. Not long after becoming mayor, things began to fall apart for Holt. In 1754, he was faced with foreclosure after going bankrupt. Rather than stay and settle his debts, Holt fled to New Haven, Connecticut, where he tried to reinvent himself as a newspaperman working under Benjamin Franklin's protégé James Parker.[44]

However hard he may have tried to get his life in order, trouble seemed to follow John Holt wherever he went. Much of his misfortune was of his own making, caused largely by his own dishonesty. While Holt was overseeing Parker's New Haven businesses, an unknown burglar broke into the local post office in June 1757 and stole a considerable number of lottery tickets and a lot of Connecticut currency. Holt aggressively went after the culprit in strongly worded notices in his newspaper. A little more than a year after the theft, Holt blamed the robbery on Charles Roberts, his mulatto servant, and his alleged accomplice, a slave named George owned by the president of Yale College. Roberts and George stood trial for the theft, but Holt was later accused of making up the whole thing. Amazingly enough, Holt's deception did not end with the fabricated charges against his servant.[45]

Looking to leave his troubles behind, Holt moved yet again. This time, he traveled south to Manhattan, where he took over Parker's *New-York Gazette, or The Weekly Post-Boy* in July 1760. Unlike the move to New Haven, where he was largely able to escape his reputation as a debtor, New Yorkers knew that John Holt was a lying drunk who constantly borrowed money he could not repay. In fact, he was known to have embezzled money from both the New Haven post office and Parker's printing shop to build a house worthy of a learned gentleman. Of course, he never repaid the stolen funds. Relations between Holt and Parker soured so thoroughly that the latter tried repeatedly to end their business partnership. And while Holt gained the favor of the city's Sons of Liberty during the imperial crisis, he was still known in whispers around town as a "Smooth tongued" con man and a "deceitful knave and Villain."[46]

When Loudon established the *Packet,* Tory politics had for some time dominated the city's newspapers. Indeed, patriots described James Rivington's and Hugh Gaine's papers as "Lord North's Press."[47] Born in London in August 1724, Rivington was brought up in the printing business. Owing largely to his early exposure, Rivington honed an understanding of the trade that few in the British Atlantic could match. "No man in the trade was better acquainted with it than he," Isaiah Thomas tells us. Rivington "possessed good talents [and] polite manners" and was "well informed, and acquired so much property as to be able to keep a carriage."[48] Despite being part of a successful London partnership, Rivington ran the business into the ground, largely because he was a gambler with expensive tastes. Having filed for bankruptcy in 1760, Rivington fled London for New York in the hope of striking it rich in the colonial American book trade. Once in the British colonies, Rivington moved around quite a bit, stopping in Philadelphia, New York, Boston, and eventually Annapolis, achieving some measure of success as a bookseller. He settled down in New York in 1769 with a wealthy widow named Elizabeth Van Horne, starting his newspaper—*Rivington's New-York Gazetteer, or The Connecticut, Hudson's River, New-Jersey, and Quebec Weekly Advertiser*—four years later. Almost overnight, Rivington's paper was credited as the city's best. Isaiah Thomas praised Rivington for his editorial skills and for supplying the most up-to-date and complete coverage of foreign news, British parliamentary debates in particular. "Few men, perhaps, were better qualified," Thomas wrote, "to publish a newspaper"—high praise indeed coming from the early publishing trade's curator of institutional memory.[49]

Within two short years of establishing the *New-York Gazetteer*, Rivington could boast of having nearly four thousand subscribers.[50]

Like most printers in colonial America, Rivington pledged, initially at least, to make the pages of his newspaper available to all viewpoints, regardless of political affiliation. In April 1773, when he began publishing *Rivington's New-York Gazetteer*, Rivington assured his readers that he would sidestep "acrimonious Censures on any Society or Class of Men." He was steadfast in his commitment to political neutrality. "The printer of a newspaper," he argued more than a year later, "ought to be neutral in all cases where his own press is employed."[51] He designed the *Gazetteer* to be "as generally useful and amusing as possible." Rivington understood that making such a statement was risky, given the increasingly high stakes of imperial politics. "When so many Persons of a vast Variety of Views and inclinations are to be satisfied," he admitted, "it must often happen, that what is highly agreeable to some, will be equally disagreeable to others."[52] In fact, for the first year and a half of the *Gazetteer's* existence, Rivington made the extraordinary promise under the masthead of each issue that the paper was "EVER OPEN and uninfluenced." By November 1774, however, as Isaiah Thomas discovered when writing the second volume of his history of the early press, Rivington had added the king's arms to the paper; and by August 1775, the phrase "EVER OPEN and uninfluenced" no longer graced the front page of the paper.[53] The imperial crisis now mattered more than press neutrality, and printers like Rivington, for better or worse, had to choose sides.

As time wore on, and as reconciliation with Great Britain became increasingly less likely, Rivington's Loyalist politics began to show in his newspaper. Rivington saturated New York with all manner of Loyalist political statements, including handbills, pamphlets, broadsides, and essays in the *Gazetteer*.[54] Rivington's aggressive Loyalism, Isaiah Thomas tells us, "soon became obnoxious to the whigs."[55] The situation became so heated that in mid-April 1775, an effigy of Rivington was hanged in nearby New Brunswick, New Jersey.[56] In November 1775, Rivington published Joseph Galloway's pamphlet *A Candid Examination of the Mutual Claims of Great-Britain, and the Colonies.* A Pennsylvania assemblyman, Galloway had publicly expressed skepticism about whether independence from Great Britain was feasible, let alone advisable. In his pamphlet, Galloway condemned those he called "American demagogues," whose only goal, he argued, was to achieve an "ill-shapen, diminutive brat, INDEPENDENCY." In Galloway's world, the only plausible outcome of the imperial conflict was a stronger "union between two great countries whose interest and welfare are inseparable."[57]

Rivington's publication of Galloway's pamphlet was controversial and generated a great deal of resentment in the city. Much of the anger directed at Rivington can be traced to the activism of "King" Isaac Sears. That Sears, a militant privateer of working-class origins, moved a group of workingmen to action was not the least bit surprising. Not only was Sears renowned for his ability to rile up a crowd at a moment's notice he was also known throughout the city as one of the founders of New York's Sons of Liberty and had been a leading voice in the protests against the Stamp Act and the Townshend Acts. After marching into the city from Connecticut, Sears and his men surrounded Rivington's shop, weapons drawn, and forced their way inside. Sears then demanded that Rivington and his pressmen hand over the type, and once it had been stuffed into sacks, they "destroyed the whole apparatus of the press," as Isaiah Thomas reported in the *Massachusetts Spy*. The destruction of Rivington's press created quite a stir. A crowd of more than fifteen hundred people gathered around Rivington's shop and shouted "their approbation by three huzzas."[58] Thomas recounts that Sears's men paraded out of Rivington's office with all of his type, later melting it down into bullets. As Sears and his men galloped out of town on their way back to Connecticut, legend has it that they belted out the lyrics of "Yankee Doodle," a not so subtle dig at Rivington's foppish reputation. Not long after the attack on his shop, Rivington and his family returned to England.[59]

Loudon recognized that starting the *Packet* was a calculated risk, perhaps even a dangerous move. In a March 1776 letter to his cousin Dudley Wood-bridge—who was then the postmaster at Norwich, Connecticut—Loudon touched on the addition of the printing press and newspaper to his already busy bookshop, decisions that he made against the backdrop of an intense imperial conflict. Loudon acknowledged that the stress of shifting the focus of the business had a negative impact on his family. "I have this opportunity by Mr. Jno Griffiths," he wrote, to "inform you that our Family enjoy health, but we cannot say, but that, at Times our minds are uneasy on account of the exposed state of this City." His decision to go into the newspaper business, at least as he expressed it to Woodbridge, seemed more about expediency than about a commitment to the public good. "I lately engaged in the Printing Business," he wrote, "as there was nothing to be done in the Merchantile." Yet at the same time, Loudon promised to keep the paper up and running, at the behest of several influential supporters, no matter the toll. "I have had good encouragement to prosecute it," he told his cousin, insisting that "it will not do to leave the City till I'm obliged." Loudon realized that an escape from New York loomed on the horizon. He assured Woodbridge that in relocating his family, his business, and his newspaper, he would be sure to find a spot convenient for receiving and distributing the news. "I intend to keep my Office by head Quarters where the Posts meet, which will be in or near this city, and if there is any apparent danger, to move my Family a little way in the Country."[60] Loudon's commitment to remaining in New York until the bitter end was a perilous gambit. He certainly understood that with each passing week at the helm of the *Packet* he was putting his family in increasing danger. He also probably recognized his limitations as a printer, given his lack of professional training. And given the timing of the *Packet*'s establishment, Loudon, whether or not he realized it at the time, was making his professional life difficult and complicated.

"Our City Is Now Fortifying"

Just as Samuel Loudon was starting out in the newspaper business, he watched with a mixture of wonder and horror as New York prepared for what the city's leaders expected to be a full-scale British invasion. The city and the province had been in near-constant chaos since February 1775. The colony's government all but collapsed when the assembly refused to send delegates to the Second Continental Congress. Not long afterward, in late April 1775, New Yorkers first heard the news that the Massachusetts militia had defeated British regulars at Lexington and Concord. The municipal government, meanwhile, had been effectively taken over by the so-called Committee of One Hundred, which drew up Articles of Association in which signers pledged their loyalty to the Continental Congress, not to Parliament. New Yorkers had drawn a line in the sand. By October 1775, William Tryon, New York's royal governor, sensed that whatever goodwill remained toward the royal government had all but dissipated. He had only to look outside his mansion to see a ragtag militia drilling in the open fields on the edge of town, while unskilled laborers erected defenses around the city. Realizing that he was greatly outnumbered, Tryon fled the city under cover of darkness to a fortified merchant ship.[61]

Tryon's assessment of the situation was astute. Not long after his escape to New York Harbor, residents learned that Parliament had rejected the Olive Branch Petition and that King George III had declared the British North American colonies to be in open rebellion. With reconciliation seemingly no longer on the table, the public was galvanized in January 1776 by the publication of Thomas Paine's *Common Sense*. As the winter of 1776 gave way to spring, General Charles Lee rode into the city with two hardened New England militia regiments. Samuel Loudon noticed the newcomers, writing to Dudley Woodbridge, "Some of the Troops from Boston are arrived here, and many more expected." The Continental Congress recognized, as did Lee, that New York was a likely target for Sir William Howe, the newly appointed commander of the British army in North America. New York had, after all, been a hub of activity for the British army until General Gage departed for Boston in 1768, and the city's large, navigable harbor would surely be hotly contested. Lee knew that the city needed to be fortified. Loudon witnessed much of the feverish building of defenses in and around the city. Lee, for example, ordered a series of forts to be constructed on both Manhattan and Long Island to guard against a naval assault, while also erecting barricades around the city's busiest streets. Several forts and batteries popped up along the road that led north from lower Manhattan to the King's Bridge. Loudon commented on the changing character of the city in the letter to Woodbridge. "Our City is now Fortifying," he told his cousin. "Every street is strongly Barricaded & entrenched, & Battery's in every part 'round the City; and they are making a strong fortification on a Hill behind the City; and opposite on Long-Island." Lee fortified Brooklyn and its advantageous high ground with forts, redoubts, and trenches. Loudon reflected on the sheer number of people working on the city's defenses. "Some thousands of Citizens & Army are employed every day at the Works," he wrote, "which make them go on very rapid." Having witnessed all of this near-constant building and the arrival in the city of thousands of troops from Boston, Loudon could not help but look to the heavens for protection. "And may the God of Armies grant success," he wrote.[62]

As the city prepared for a possible British invasion, Loudon took on a job that changed his life dramatically. In the spring of 1776, a "gentleman of the city"—later discovered to be the Episcopalian bishop Charles Inglis—approached Loudon about printing a rebuttal to the "celebrated pamphlet entitled *Common Sense*."[63] Loudon agreed to the print the pamphlet, titled *The Deceiver Unmasked, or Loyalty and Interest United,* not only because was it a paying job but also because he sincerely believed that all sides in a debate, however, rancorous, should be heard. At the same time, however, Loudon was no buffoon. Knowing full well that taking on a job like this carried certain risks, he insisted that Inglis take great care in finishing his work. Loudon demanded, for instance, that the pamphlet be "written with decency," and that it "not express or even imply any disapprobation of the proceedings of the Honourable Continental Congress or the glorious Cause."[64] Satisfied that Inglis had met his expectations, Loudon took the job.

As he finished the presswork, Loudon made a critical error: he advertised the pamphlet in Hugh Gaine's *New-York Gazette* before it was finished. Once word hit the streets, opposition to the pamphlet quickly mobilized. Loudon was invited—compelled, really—to attend a meeting of the Committee of Mechanics. At the meeting, a sailmaker named Christopher Duyckinck, the committee's chair, interrogated Loudon. Duyckinck wanted to know, first and foremost, who had written the pamphlet. In his myopic cross-examination, Duyckinck threatened to smear Loudon's reputation and publicly burn all copies of the text if he did not reveal the author's identity. Loudon refused to comply with Duyckinck's demand.

Duyckinck refused to take no for an answer. He continued to press Loudon for the author's name, and when Loudon refused, Duyckinck set into motion a series of events that turned Loudon's life upside down. That night, six uniden-tified men broke into Loudon's home and stole dried sheets of the pamphlet. Obviously shaken, Loudon still refused to give up Inglis as the author of *The Deceiver Unmasked,* and the next day he filed a complaint with the General Committee of Inspection. His grievance did not have the desired effect, however. Rather than reprimand Duyckinck and his henchmen, the committee recom-mended that Loudon cut his losses and discontinue publication—a clear impli-cation that Loudon's life was in danger. Loudon grudgingly complied, vowing not to distribute the remaining copies he had on hand. This, seemingly, should have brought an end to the ordeal.

Christopher Duyckinck, however, was not convinced of Loudon's contrition. Worried that Loudon would at some point resume work on the noxious pam-phlet, Duyckinck decided to take matters into his own hands. That very night, he and forty fellow mechanics marched to Loudon's home. The chain of events that followed eerily resembled the attack on James Rivington's printing shop less than one year earlier. According to Loudon, Duyckinck and his men rushed into his house. "Some of them ran up stairs to the Printing Office," he said, "while others guarded the door." The invaders made off with "the whole impres-sion of said Pamphlets" and, once out of the house, carried the nearly fifteen hundred copies of the text "to the Commons and there burnt them as I have been informed." Only two copies of Loudon's edition survived the attack.

Obviously convinced that their actions against Loudon were just and had sent the right message, Duyckinck and his men capitalized on the destruction of the pamphlet by circulating an ominous communiqué to the city's printers. "Sir, if you print, or suffer to be printed in your press anything against the rights and liberties of America, or in favor of our inveterate foes," the message read, "death and destruction, ruin and perdition, shall be your portion." The message, most probably nailed to the doors of print shops, was signed "by order of the committee of tarring and feathering" by a man calling himself "Legion."[65]

Duyckinck and his mob did not touch Loudon's printing press. In Novem-ber 1775, as noted above, James Rivington's press had been smashed by "King" Isaac Sears and his band of Connecticut men for roughly the same crime: printing a text the city's Whig leaders did not like. Loudon had taken on the project not because he championed Inglis's message, which he knew would be deeply unpopular among a large segment of New York's population. Rather, he recognized that *Deceiver Unmasked* would be a best seller because, not in spite, of its content. By this point, few could seriously question Samuel Loudon's politics. Unlike Rivington, who masked his Loyalism under the guise of press neutrality, Loudon made little effort to hide his support of the patriotic cause in either his newspaper or the other jobs he did as a printer. Indeed, Loudon printed two pamphlets in 1776 favored by American Whigs, Richard Price's

Observations on the Nature of Civil Liberty and Samuel Sherwood's *The Church's Flight into the Wilderness*. The case of Charles Inglis's pamphlet, then, reveals the cost of doing business for a printer in revolutionary New York.

"I Don't Know That a Supply Can Be Had"

The city's worst fear was realized in September 1776. "The City of New York is now invaded by a powerful Fleet and Army," Hugh Gaine wrote in the *New-York Gazette*. Manhattan's residents, he reported, had to "seek a Retreat in the Country."[66] Loudon and his family fled the city in September, according to an announcement he made in an early September issue of the *Packet*. Like thousands of fellow New Yorkers, they had little choice in the matter. While revolutionaries had succeeded in overthrowing royal governance in the North American colonies—accomplished in New York with the destruction of the gilded statue of King George III on Manhattan's Bowling Green in July 1776—royal forces overran the city not long after, in the fall of 1776. George Washington, the Continental army, and thousands of residents were thus forced out of the city into the countryside as the British army moved in and occupied New York and Long Island. More than half the city's population deserted their homes, businesses, and places of worship, which the British army then converted into barracks, warehouses for munitions, and prisons.[67]

Once out of the city, Loudon and his family escaped to Norwich, Connecticut. Loudon wasted little time getting his business up and running. He set up a small bookshop in the corner of "Col. Jedediah Huntington's Store," announcing a "Neat Assortment of BOOKS, to be Sold cheap."[68] Loudon did not stay in Norwich for very long, however. The family packed up yet again and moved to Fishkill, New York, approximately fifty miles north of Manhattan. Loudon was not the only printer forced to relocate during the war. Many printers had to pack up shop and move in order to stay out of the way of the British army. Isaiah Thomas famously escaped Boston in the spring of 1775, while Daniel Fowle moved out of Portsmouth, New Hampshire, not long afterward, in November. Solomon Southwick *buried* his printing equipment in Newport a year later, and John Holt, like Loudon, moved out of Manhattan just before the British occupied the city.[69]

It was no accident that Loudon and his large brood landed in Fishkill. Loudon knew that by relocating to this small village on the banks of the Hudson River, he would be able to deliver the most up-to-date news coming out of the Provincial Congress, which decided to meet in Fishkill. Loudon was unable to get the *Packet* up and running immediately, however, largely because of the difficulties of packing up and moving a large assortment of books, paper, type, printing equipment, and his already well-traveled press. But he was also forced to adjust to the limited availability of supplies, especially paper. Loudon seemed to recognize that shortages would be likely, and he all but predicted hardships before he even left Manhattan. With the prospect of settling down in Fishkill on the horizon, Loudon wrote that he was "under the necessity of informing his Customers" that the *Packet*'s relaunch would be delayed "for several weeks, occasioned by the trouble in moving as well as the Great scarcity of Printing Paper." He would not resume publication of the newspaper in Fishkill until January 1777.[70]

In late September, Hugh Gaine packed up his shop and trudged across the Hudson River to Newark, New Jersey, where he continued publishing the *New-York Gazette: and the Weekly Mercury*, a paper he had established in 1752. Gaine arrived in New York in 1745 via Ireland, a precocious eighteen-year-old, after apprenticing in a Belfast printing shop for five years. He bounced around the city before landing in James Parker's shop as a journeyman. Gaine scrimped and saved for six long years while working for Parker. He eventually opened his own business at Hanover Square, which he named the Bible & Crown. Gaine quickly gained a reputation as an honest businessman who did good work. His years of toil paid off in 1768, when the Provincial Assembly appointed him the royal printer in charge of producing all of the colony's official government documents; the city of New York followed suit a year later.[71] But Gaine would not limit his enterprise to publishing a newspaper and printing the colony's laws. Much as Loudon had done, Gaine began speculating in land north of Manhattan, investing in approximately six thousand acres on the outskirts of Albany. On top of his land speculation and publishing business, Gaine partnered with a newly established Long Island paper mill in 1774 as a way to generate a reliable supply of paper for himself and his fellow printers.[72]

Not long after he moved to Newark, Gaine returned to Manhattan, a decision as practical as it was political. Gaine was probably surprised when he discovered that in mid-September 1776—after he had fled Manhattan—a newspaper with his name on it had appeared in New York espousing pro-British views. Unbeknownst to him, the Crown had instructed Sir Ambrose Serle to publish a British paper in New York; instead of starting a new one, Serle moved into the Bible & Crown and picked up where Gaine had left off, using the *Weekly Mercury*'s title and masthead. When Gaine discovered that someone was printing his paper without his consent, he made what must have been an agonizing decision: he accepted William Howe's offer of amnesty and returned to the city so that he could publish his newspaper. In early November 1776, Gaine, along with nearly five thousand fellow colonists, returned to Manhattan. He resumed publication of the *Mercury* on the agreement that the paper meet the standards dictated by Serle, who maintained ultimate editorial control. Gaine remained in British-controlled New York for the next six years, publishing his now pro-British paper until the end of the war. And while he played the part of the turncoat by returning to British-occupied New York and was persona non grata among the Whigs, the British did not trust him, either. Gaine felt the sting of this distrust when the British appointed James Rivington the colony's royal printer in 1777, stripping Gaine of the post he had worked so hard to attain.[73]

Samuel Loudon and his family struggled to make ends meet during the war. Loudon intermittently published the *New-York Packet* despite a scarcity of supplies. Suddenly cut off from commodity chains, Loudon had to scramble for enough paper. Writing to merchants as near as New Haven and as far away as Boston, Loudon reflected a stark reality on the revolutionary frontier: commercial and political networks had been either severely curtailed or disrupted entirely. Indeed, he feared that the *Packet* would be permanently shuttered if he could not locate enough paper. Writing to New Haven's Isaac Beers, Loudon expressed his anxiety. "I have wrote to Milton near Boston, but have got no Answer; if I can't get supplyed from boston [*sic*] or from you, I must stop—for I don't know that a supply can be had nearer."[74]

The War of Independence was a trying time for American printers. Readership for some newspapers rose because of a genuine and justifiable interest in the military conflict. But for most printers, including Loudon, getting materials, let alone information to print, proved frustratingly difficult. Once independence had been declared and the war picked up steam, printers no longer had ready "access to imported supplies of presses, types, ink, and paper from Great Britain," as historian Carol Sue Humphrey observes. Many newspapers folded because of the scarcity of these necessities. Isaiah Thomas, like so many of his fellow printers, complained bitterly in 1778 that "printing utensils are no where to be procured in this country at present, types in particular, are not made in America."[75]

Paper became especially hard to come by in the late eighteenth century. Importation slowed considerably after passage of the Stamp Act in 1765 and all but ended in 1775. The crippling lack of imported paper forced printers to either scour the countryside looking for crudely made domestic paper or shut down operations entirely, which is exactly what Ebenezer Watson of the *Connecticut Courant* did in December 1775. A number of printers, such as Worcester's Thomas, implored the local population, especially women, to save rags that could be used to make paper. "Earnest requested that the fair Daughters of Liberty in this extensive country," he wrote in an advertisement that he printed several times, "would not neglect to serve their country, by saving for the Paper-Mill at Sutton, all Linen and Cotton-and-Linen Rags."[76] Samuel Loudon published a similar advertisement in August 1776 that offered "Four pence per Pound" for "the best sort of CLEAN, WHITE LINEN RAGS."[77]

The struggle to locate paper remained a constant concern for Loudon. In March 1776, he begged women in upstate New York to bring him "all kinds of cotton and linnen rags." "If the LADIES neglect these hints," he wrote ominously, "the consequences will be awful," not least of which would be the end of the *Packet*. Like many clever politicians, before and since, Loudon made the issue about education. "Our children are destroyed for the lack of knowledge," he wrote. Loudon endured several lean months between October 1778 and April 1779, when he published only half a dozen issues of the newspaper for want of paper. Makeshift mills in Boston and Connecticut were able to provide him with only "a few scanty supplies," and a desperate trip to Philadelphia yielded little return. Facing further shortages, Loudon and blacksmith Robert Boyd drafted a petition requesting that the New York State Legislature build a paper mill funded by lottery ticket sales. There are no surviving records to indicate whether the state ever seriously considered Loudon's plan.[78]

Printers also faced a labor shortage during the war, as young men joined either the local militia or the Continental army. Samuel Hall, printer of the *New England Chronicle*, was in constant need of help. In April 1776, he printed an advertisement that promised "constant Employ, good Wages, and punctual Payment" to any journeyman printer who showed up at his shop.[79] Loudon faced a similar situation a few months later. In August 1776 he lamented that "some of our hands being called out to duty obliges us to publish a half sheet this week," a sobering apology that was placed just above a desperate advertisement seeking "a good Pressman."[80]

Despite his difficulties, Loudon stuck out the war in Fishkill. Even though he had lost the state printer's contract to John Holt, he kept his press busy. A few small, crudely printed issues aside, the *Packet* remained in print throughout much of the war. Loudon scrimped and saved where he could to keep the paper afloat, deciding to shut it down only occasionally. In fact, Loudon was remarkably productive during the war, despite the material limitations he endured. A significant hindrance was the size of his workspace. The temporary shop he set up on Theodorus Van Wyck's farm on the outskirts of Fishkill was, to his mind at least, unfit for a printing business. Indeed, Loudon's shop "on the King's Highway near the Fishkill Village" was "by far the smallest" in "N. York."[81] In addition to keeping the *Packet* in circulation, Loudon printed two thousand copies of the state's first constitution in May 1777, along with various odd jobs given to him by the legislature. He also published Tom Paine's *American Crisis* essays as a series of small pamphlets.[82] And while Loudon was able to sustain his business during the war, his return to New York City did not bring the peace he had hoped to find.

"A General Peace Between All the Powers at War"

News of peace between Great Britain and the newly created United States sent shockwaves through New York. In February 1783, King George III issued a royal proclamation finally ending the war. By late March, the good news had reached Fishkill. "A GENERAL PEACE between ALL the POWERS at WAR was *Signed the Twentieth* January last," Loudon wrote in the *New-York Packet,* concluding breathlessly "LAUS DEO!"[83] Two weeks later, he announced with excitement that he was preparing to return to Manhattan. This, of course, meant that his deadbeat subscribers in Fishkill needed to settle up to help pay for the relocation. "As the Printer expects in a few weeks to remove his office to New-York, he requests all those in arrearage to be speedy in settling their accounts."[84] But Loudon remained in Fishkill for several months, unable, for whatever reason, to make the return trip home.

Residents of British-occupied New York City had a dramatically different reaction to the sudden end of war. Many American Loyalists and British regulars gathered at City Hall on a cool morning in April 1783 for a public reading of the king's statement on the "cessation of arms, as well by sea as land."[85] And while they vehemently opposed what had happened and publicly cursed the king, many began to prepare for an immediate evacuation of the city, packing their personal valuables and selling their homes and businesses. But the British army occupying New York, led at that time by Sir Guy Carleton, was in no rush to leave. Carleton wanted to give every person who desired to leave under the British flag the opportunity to do so; therefore, he waited several months in order to allow Loyalists and their families plenty of time to flee the city.

Loudon, like many thousands of New Yorkers in exile, waited patiently for the British to evacuate the city. He continued publishing the *Packet* in Fishkill until the end of August 1783. In the final issue of the paper printed in Fishkill, Loudon announced that he intended to resume publication of the *Packet* once settled in Manhattan. Evidently satisfied that subscribers had come forward with payment—something few printers in early America could boast of—Loudon thanked his loyal supporters, who "by the punctuality of their payment" helped sustain the paper "under many difficulties" and "at a great expense" to both his bottom line and his personal life.[86] Not long after stopping production of the *Packet,* Loudon and his family began the arduous task of packing up the shop. Much of their furniture and finer things, in fact, remained in Norwich with Dudley Woodbridge. Just before setting off on the fifty-mile journey to Manhattan, Loudon wrote to his cousin with detailed instructions on how to ship the family's beloved "Looking Glasses" and "Mahogany Furniture" safely and cheaply. "Get the freight as moderate as you can," he wrote; "your shippers are exceeding extravagant in their charge."[87] Thus, after eight years on the run, living first in Norwich and then in Fishkill, Samuel Loudon was on the road for what he hoped would be the last time.

The New York that Loudon discovered on his return did not resemble what he had left behind eight years earlier. In many places, the city had been reduced to rubble as a result of two disastrous fires, which nearly gutted the city, and the British army's hard use of buildings during the occupation. East of Broadway, as William Alexander Duer tells us, vacant buildings dotted the streets. "No visible attempts had been made since the fire to remove the ruins," Duer said in a speech to the St. Nicholas Society, "and as the edifices destroyed were chiefly of brick, the skeletons of the remaining walls cast their grim shadows upon the pavement, imparting an unearthly aspect to the street."[88] A number of residents returned to the city only to discover that their former homes had fallen into disrepair. Having returned with high hopes on Evacuation Day, James Duane observed grimly that his homes looked "as if they had been inhabited by Savages or wild beasts."[89] Not only had private residences been neglected and abused by the British. The occupiers also took over government buildings, public squares, and churches for use as stables, hospitals, and living quarters for their troops. After nearly eight years of hard use and little or no upkeep, many buildings were in terrible condition. The army also chopped down the trees that had once lined residential streets, replacing them with all manner of fortifications. The city streets had become a festering sewage pit strewn with garbage, while the city's wharves were all but ruined.[90]

By the time Loudon returned to Manhattan, the British army continued to linger in the city. For this reason, Loudon did not immediately resume publication of the *Packet* but busied himself with job printing. "I've now got pretty well fixt in my House," he explained in a letter to the mechanic-turned-revolutionary Alexander McDougall, who was by that time in charge of overseeing the return of patriot citizens to the city. He revealed that he was hard at work on a variety of projects. "And intend to employ my People in printing an Almanac for the next year," he wrote, "the Constitution of the United States, hand bill Advertisements, etc, but don't mean to bring a newspaper till the Government of this place is changed." Had Loudon resumed publishing the *Packet* on arrival, he knew that he might well have been "obliged to compromise" the political integrity of the paper.[91]

At the same time, however, Loudon observed that the remaining Loyalists in New York walked about the city in fear, second-class citizens at constant risk of "personal abuse and seizure of property."[92] And while Loyalists lived in constant fear of mob attacks, patriots streaming in from upstate and elsewhere also had to watch their backs. Several fires threatened to burn down the city not long after the war ended. Loudon's home itself was nearly destroyed by two mysterious fires after his return from Fishkill.[93]

Loudon and the scores of New York patriots returning to the city put great strain on a permanently fractured relationship with the British army. Many New Yorkers were counting the days until the British finally decided to leave. "When the B. will evacuate is unclear," Loudon wrote. "Reports say that they will be nearly out by the end of October." A month after Loudon's prediction, in late November 1783, Carleton and his troops began the arduous task of leaving behind the city they had held since 1776. On 25 November 1783—a day remembered for many years as Evacuation Day—thousands of New Yorkers made a triumphant return to New York as the last remnants of the British army trudged toward the East River waterfront to board ships departing the city.[94]

"A Variety of Other Articles"

As the city rebuilt after the British evacuation, the publishing trade started taking shape in Hanover Square, near the municipal markets and coffeehouses. The Fly Market, the oldest municipal market in the city, was located in the First Ward, at the southeastern tip of Maiden Lane at the intersection with Front Street. It consisted of several open-air structures where butchers, fishmongers, and grocers sold meat, fish, and produce. The Fly Market must have been an arresting sensory experience for the New Yorkers who worked, shopped, and milled about near the open stalls. In addition to the sights and smells—slaughtered livestock and produce in various states of decomposition mixed with the scent of saltwater wafting in from the wharves—the Fly Market was also home to hucksters and small children peddling cheap foodstuffs, their cries sure to annoy nearby printers and booksellers tending to their accounts. "Do you want any radishes?" asked little girls patrolling Maiden Lane and Front Street, baskets resting on their heads and draped over their arms. There was also the arabber who barked at passersby to buy his "fine ripe Water-Milyons," a fruit described by the printer Samuel Wood as "very palatable, cooling, and refreshing." Marketgoers might also have walked past a horse-drawn cart filled with onions driven by a rumpled old man bellowing, "Here's your beauties of Onions: here's your nice large onions!" Perhaps most annoying for neighboring businesses was the man who trudged "round in the afternoon, with a long and loud cry of 'Hot Muf-Fins,'" which he tried to sell as the appropriate complement for a midafternoon tea. And early in the evenings, marketgoers could count on hearing the man who roamed the streets crying, "Oysters, Oysters, here's your beauties of Oysters, here's your fine, fat, salt Oysters!"[95]

According to the city's trade directories, first published in 1786, printers, booksellers, and bookbinders tended to open shops on Pearl and Water Streets near the Fly Market, Hanover Square, and the Tontine Coffee House. Winding through what is now lower Manhattan, Pearl and Water ran (and still run) parallel to each other, intersecting with Wall Street, Maiden Lane, and the Old Slip. These streets cut through the First, Second, and Fourth Wards, with Pearl Street ending at Chatham Street (now Park Row), which connects Broadway to the Bowery, while Water Street ends at St. James Place. Both streets were crowded thoroughfares in the early Republic, crawling with the city's leading merchants and master artisans. Bankers, brokers, insurance men, accountants, and lawyers rubbed elbows as they walked among the many print shops, binderies, and bookstores, venturing between various offices amid the noise of wagons, carts, and carriages. Merchants on Pearl and Water Streets tended to be specialized wholesalers who catered to the needs of local, regional, national, and international markets. The nexus of the city's social, political, and economic activity in the early Republic was at the corner of Wall and Water Streets, the location of the Tontine Coffee House, which became home to the city's first stock exchange. The construction of this coffeehouse in 1793 was undertaken by a group of merchants and politicians who owned among themselves more than two hundred shares in the building. The Tontine became an important gathering place for the city's leading merchants, politicians, and aspiring men of letters, who congregated there to discuss the latest national and international news.[96]

Samuel Loudon's rise to the state printer's position in 1785 boosted business. While Loudon devoted much of his energy to fulfilling orders for the state legislature, which had relocated to Manhattan after the British evacuation, he also continued publishing the *New-York Packet*. Even with the kickback he received as the state's printer, publishing a newspaper in the early Republic was an expensive business. In the two short years since Evacuation Day, the city's print market had been revitalized. By 1785, the year Loudon and his brother took over the state printer's job, eleven fellow printers lived and worked in Manhattan, including several who published newspapers. In November 1783, four days after Loudon resumed publishing the *Packet*, Charles Webster and John M'Lean founded the *Independent Journal*. That same year, William Morton and Samuel Horner rebranded the *New-York Evening Post*—a triweekly they had started in September 1782—the *Morning Post*, a paper they rolled back to a twice-weekly printing.[97] A week after her husband's death in late January 1784, Elizabeth Holt continued his paper, the *Independent Gazette*, which she renamed the *New-York Journal and State Gazette* in mid-March 1784. Elizabeth was involved with the paper, on and off, until she sold it to Thomas Greenleaf in January 1787.[98] In March 1785, Francis Childs founded the *Daily Advertiser*, a paper that remained in print until August 1806.[99] In short, only a few years after the Revolutionary War, several robust newspapers were available to the New York reading public.

Given the number of newspapers in postwar New York, Loudon recognized that he was in competition for not only subscribers but also, more important, advertisers. Advertisements were as ubiquitous as they were essential to the layout and financial well-being of early republican newspapers. If a printer like Loudon expected to profit from a newspaper, his hopes would have rested with the number and cost of advertisements, not with the number of subscribers. Indeed, any newspaper that turned a profit probably filled three of its four pages with advertisements, including several that the printer ran for weeks, if not months, at a time in the same space on the page. In many ways, the early republican printer was one of the most important people in the local, regional, and national economy, because what was printed in the local paper drove every-day commerce.[100]

Surely aware that his margin of error was razor thin in an increasingly competitive market, Loudon started tracking every facet of his newly expanded printing office. His first order of business was to make note of the money paid for advertisements printed in the *Packet*. For roughly nine months in 1785, Loudon recorded in his account book a brief description of the ads he ran, the name of the person who paid for the space, and, quite often, his fee. During this time, Loudon ran a large assortment of advertisements (table 1.1). Not surprisingly, property transactions—ranging from farmland to boardinghouses—made up a large percentage of the advertisements that appeared in the *Packet*. Indeed, nearly 40 percent of the advertisements he recorded in his account book dealt in some way with property transactions.[101]

The advertisements in *New-York Packet* were not limited to property, how-ever. Loudon recorded transactions with nearly thirty trades and professions. For example, two young, brash attorneys—Alexander Hamilton and Aaron

TABLE 1.1 Types of Advertisements Appearing in the *New-York Packet*, January–September 1785

	Advertisements (N)	Advertisements (%)		Advertisements (N)	Advertisements (%)
Business/Labor	29	7.8	Livestock	5	1.3
Almshouse	2	0.5	Maritime	22	5.9
Auction	26	7.0	Notice	30	8.1
Brewery	1	0.2	Politics	2	0.5
Items for Sale	39	10.5	Real Estate	145	39.1
Indentured Servant/Slave	11	2.9	School	11	2.9
Lectures	8	2.1	Sheriff	3	0.8
Legal Notice	33	8.9	Society Meeting	3	0.8
			TOTALS	370	99.3

SOURCE: Samuel Loudon Account Book, 1785–1789, Samuel Loudon Papers, AAS. This table was created by transcribing all of the advertisements listed in Samuel Loudon's Account Book from 22 January to 5 September 1785 (newspapers numbered 457 to 521) into a database and assigning each of them to one of the sixteen categories listed above.

Burr—took out advertisements in Loudon's paper. Burr was the acting attorney for the estate of a man named Peter Grim, and he requested that "ALL persons indebted" to Grim "make payment to Aaron Burr, at his office, No. 10 corner of Nassau and Little Queen streets."[102] Several auctioneers—Viner Van Zandt, Anthony Bleecker, Frederick Jay, and Isaac Moses—placed nearly thirty advertisements for a range of sales taking place in the city and surrounding countryside. Hugh Gaine, who shuttered his newspaper and opened a bookstore after the British evacuation, placed an advertisement in Loudon's *Packet* touting his large assortment of Bibles, dictionaries, history books, and "a great variety of School Books for children."[103] An earthenware dealer, Eugene M'Farlane, paid for two advertisements to promote his "GOLDEN TINCTURE," which he described as a sort of cure-all for maladies of the mouth. It was, he said, the "PERFECT remedy for the cure of the Tooth-Ache" and was also good for common ailments such as "the scurvy, and all scorbutic humours in the mouth," not to mention "all disagreeable smells from the breath."[104] The Hanover Square merchant Joseph Blackwell announced in late February 1785 the arrival of a variety of imported goods, including broadcloth, corduroy, calico, Irish linen, hats, penknives, pocketbooks, desk furniture, "a few Chests of most excellent BOHEA TEA," which had just arrived from Amsterdam aboard the ship *Grace,* and the "best Philadelphia manufactured SNUFF."[105] The Queen Street merchants Buchanan & Thompson—around the corner from Blackwell's—touted their goods, imported on "the last vessels from Glasgow, Liverpool, Bristol, and London," which included tartans, ivory and horn combs, razors, buttons, ribbons, "black and white gause," sewing silk, "and a variety of other articles."[106] The variety of advertisements in Loudon's newspapers suggests that New York's economy was on the rise.

Like many early American newspapers, the advertisements in Loudon's *Packet* had a dark side. Loudon did job work for residents seeking the return of runaway indentured servants and slaves. In early March 1785, for example, he printed one hundred handbills that detailed the likeness of several servants who had run away from the ironmonger Samuel Kempton. William Pemberton paid eight shillings for a late February 1785 advertisement seeking the return of "A NEGRO MAN named BOB NESBIT." The twenty-six-year-old Nesbit, according to Pemberton, was "well known in the city," a tad overweight, and wore a decorative piece in his right ear.[107]

The ads Loudon recorded in his account book also reveal the costs of doing business in New York. Nearly half of the paid advertisements in Loudon's *Packet* cost between six and ten shillings, and most of them appeared only once or twice (table 1.2). These data suggest that the average cost of an advertisement fell somewhere in this price range. As expected, the price of running an ad in several issues of the newspaper would have been higher. For advertisements printed in

TABLE 1.2 Advertising Rates in the *New-York Packet,* January–September 1785

Printings	£0 1s–5s (N)	(%)	£0 6s–10s (N)	(%)	£0 11s–15s (N)	(%)	£0 16s–18s (N)	(%)	£1–2 (N)	(%)
1–2	7	4.9	55	38.7	8	5.6	7	4.9	1	0.7
3–4	—	—	9	6.3	26	18.3	—	—	3	2.1
5–6	—	—	—	—	2	1.4	2	1.4	1	0.7
7–8	—	—	—	—	1	0.7	—	—	3	2.1
more than 8	—	—	—	—	—	—	—	—	18	12.4
TOTALS	7	4.9	64	45	37	26	9	6.3	26	18

SOURCE: Samuel Loudon Account Book, 1785–1789, Samuel Loudon Papers, AAS. This table shows the cost of advertising in the *New-York Packet* for merchants, artisans, and auctioneers.

three to four issues of the *Packet,* the price was somewhere between eleven and fifteen shillings. Advertisements printed eight or more times cost between £1 and £2. And while there is some variation in the price Loudon charged for ads, he sold more than twenty ads at a fixed rate of eight shillings. Loudon's fee structure was universal, and he did not charge more for certain kinds of advertisements. Indeed, New Yorkers could expect to be quoted the same price whether they were wealthy merchants or farmers. Loudon's records suggest that while the average cost of an individual advertisement was approximately eight shillings, he offered a small percentage discount for multiple printings.[108]

Loudon abandoned his project to annotate and record the price of the advertisements that appeared in his newspaper in September 1785, but the records illuminate an important aspect of a printer's daily life in the early American Republic: the negotiation of advertising space in a newspaper. Advertising was a necessary revenue generator for businesses that were often plagued by a serious lack of capital. Although printers like Loudon relied on subscribers to a certain degree, bringing in advertising was the surest way to keep a newspaper in print. And while Loudon probably gave up this useful practice when the demands of the state printer's position became too much to handle, the accounts he left behind reveal an otherwise elusive element of the printing business.[109]

"He's Both a Devil and a Saint"

The legislature remained in New York City for the first three years of Samuel Loudon's term as state printer. With the start of the eleventh session, however, a series of expensive moves complicated Loudon's life. In January 1788, the legislature relocated to Poughkeepsie. The following December, lawmakers met in Albany for the twelfth session, and the thirteenth, which met from July 1789 to April 1790, was held in New York City. As the state's printer, Loudon had to remain near the legislature so that he could publish the laws and proceedings at a moment's notice, not only for lawmakers and public officials but for any citizen with an interest in how the government functioned on a daily basis. He was responsible for printing and distributing the output of the legislature, which included the journals of the proceedings and the laws passed by the assembly during each session. This was an enormous task that required not only deft operation of the press but coordination to get the necessary documents out to subscribers in a timely manner. Despite the toll it took on his family, the journeymen in his shop, and the equipment he was forced to drag across the state, Loudon uprooted his life each time so that he could remain at the state's disposal.[110]

Loudon's life on the road is materially preserved in a messy account book he kept during his tenure as the state's printer. Much of the account book chronicles his fleeting attempts to print the state laws and journals of the tenth, eleventh, and twelfth meetings of the legislature. The account book reveals the stress and uncertainty of a printer struggling to gain a footing in the unstable postwar New York market as he moved from place to place, just trying to keep up with the pace of work. Broken into roughly nine sections, Loudon's accounts provide the rough sketch of a businessman overwhelmed by the duties required of the state printer. Indeed, the slapdash system he used—which does not seem to be rooted in any kind of formal bookkeeping method—and the frenzied notations he made represent not only the great demands placed upon him by his employer but also uncertainty about whether he and his family would remain in the same place for more than a few months at a time. We can see him flailing wildly, often out of control, in an attempt to provide some semblance of order to his already chaotic life at a time of profound political and economic instability. Despite the hard life he continued to lead in postwar New York, Samuel Loudon helped build the Empire State in print.

While the account book appears to be unorganized and sloppily kept, a closer look does suggest a structural logic, a kind of controlled chaos barely contained by the large folio pages. Loudon divided his state printing accounts into two large, easily discernable sections: subscriptions he took and items he shipped, broken up by legislative session and subdivided by county. While these two categories may seem one and the same, in Loudon's printing office they took place at two very different points in time. Loudon, for whatever reason, recorded subscriptions at the end of the account book. When it came time to deliver the sets of laws and proceedings, Loudon picked up the same account book and opened it to the front section, where he recorded the distribution lists for the ninth, tenth, eleventh, and twelfth state assemblies. In between these two large, densely annotated sections of the account book were more than 160 blank leaves.

Each year began the same way for Samuel Loudon, regardless of where the legislature met. As politicians arrived to take their seats in the assembly, one of their first stops was the state printer's office. Several of New York's most influential men appear in Loudon's accounts. In 1786, for example, Alexander Hamilton stopped by Loudon's office. So did Aaron Burr. Henry Brockholst Livingston, Morgan Lewis, and Philip Livingston all walked into Loudon's shop to buy their subscription for the forthcoming legislative session. Next to each subscriber's name, Loudon recorded the date and what each individual was scheduled to receive. By keeping his subscription list separate, writing it down at the start of the legislative session in the back of his account book, Loudon knew precisely how many copies he would need to print.

All the more remarkable was Loudon's practice of shipping the subscriptions *as they came off the press* rather than waiting to complete the edition. He returned to the subscription list time and again throughout the legislative session to hastily record the date that an individual section of a particular volume was printed *and* sent to subscribers. Loudon kept track and made sense of this unorthodox system of production and distribution by writing down the segments printed and delivered using the text's binding signatures. These fleeting moments of input and output, in which Loudon marked each individual subscriber's account repeatedly, probably occurred over the course of several weeks, perhaps even months. For example, a man named "John L., Esq."—probably John Livingston—stopped by Loudon's shop on 24 January 1786. John L. paid in advance for his subscription of "the laws only." Just below his new subscriber's name, Loudon made a small note to himself that John L.'s subscription would be delivered "as they come out." Louden then went about his business of taking additional subscriptions. Later on during the legislative session, Loudon returned to John L.'s account to record that he had delivered segments of "the laws only" with the binding signatures "B, D, E, G, L, O." Loudon eventually closed this account, scribbling on an undetermined date that John L.'s "whole set" had been delivered. While this kind of bookkeeping did not follow the traditional double-entry method so often employed by merchants and artisans in the early Republic, Loudon developed a system that worked for him, especially given the material constraints he faced so soon after the British evacuation.

In addition to traipsing around New York, dragging his press and family with him to wherever the state legislature decided to meet, Loudon took on other jobs in order to get by. In 1786, for example, he accepted a job to print the state's currency. Loudon had competition for the appointment, however. The printer Shepard Kollock had also expressed interest and submitted a proposal to do the work. For whatever reason, Kollock shared his bid with Loudon. Loudon turned around and underbid Kollock, a devious move that won him the contract. Incensed, Kollock lashed out at Loudon in the *New-York Gazette* for doing such a dishonest thing to a fellow printer. "To good and evil equal bent," Kollock wrote of Loudon, "He's both a Devil and a Saint."[111] Even though the war was over, Loudon continued doing whatever he had to do in order to get business, even with the additional income he received as state's printer, meager though it may have been. In an eerie parallel to the dubious business practices of his former nemesis, John Holt, Loudon valued work far more than he did friendship and loyalty.

Loudon's busy period fell between the end of April and the middle of June. Typically, sessions of the New York State Assembly lasted from January until the spring, with some ending as early as March while others ran until May. As soon as the legislature concluded its business, Loudon went to work, composing a polished printed edition of the proceedings of the assembly and a collection of the laws it had passed. It usually took him and his journeymen about a month to complete at least part of that year's job. Once they had enough material ready for shipment, Loudon started filling orders. In the spring of 1787, very few of his orders were ready—he shipped only nine in April and May. But by the start of summer, activity in Loudon's shop usually reached a fever pitch. Loudon shipped a significant majority of the items documenting the tenth meeting of the legislature, in June 1787—119 orders, to be precise. Loudon shipped most of the orders during the first two weeks of June, with nearly half going out in the second week alone. This suggests that Loudon's press had reached maximum productivity. Loudon distributed state publications on a county-by-county basis. Predictably, New York, Albany, and Westchester counties typically received most of the annual publications (table 1.3). Most of the subscriptions shipped in June 1787, for instance, went out in bulk orders. For example, 90 percent of Loudon's Albany subscribers received their texts in the second week of June. Loudon still had a few orders unfilled by the first of July, but by the start of August much of his work was complete. The following spring, Loudon's work cycle remained largely the same. While the people's business was conducted in the cold, dark winter months, making a record of that business in print was an ongoing process, one that came to fruition in the summer months, when subscribers up and down the state could examine for themselves the inner workings of a newly formed representative democracy.[112]

Once his work on the annual laws and proceedings was complete, Loudon shipped the state's documents to people affiliated with local and state government. County, township, and municipal clerks made up nearly half of the recipients of the laws and proceedings for the tenth and eleventh legislative sessions, while thirteen local treasurers subscribed. More than 40 percent of the documents ended up going to members of the New York Assembly and the

TABLE 1.3 Samuel Loudon's Distribution Network by County, June 1787

	Shipments (N)	(%)	Texts (N)	(%)	Week 1 (N)	(%)	Week 2 (N)	(%)	Week 3 (N)	(%)	Week 4 (N)	(%)
Albany	20	16.8	62	37.5	2	10.0	18	90.0	0	0	0	0
Columbia	4	3.3	4	2.4	0	0	1	25.0	3	75.0	0	0
Dutchess	10	8.4	10	6.0	4	40.0	3	30.0	1	10.0	2	20.0
Kings	3	2.5	3	1.8	3	100	0	0	0	0	0	0
Montgomery	14	11.7	14	8.4	1	7.1	0	0	0	0	13	92.8
New York	18	15.1	18	10.9	6	33.3	10	55.5	0	0	2	11.1
Orange	3	2.5	1	0.6	2	66.6	1	33.3	0	0	0	0
Queens	6	5.0	6	3.6	3	50.0	3	50.0	0	0	0	0
Richmond	6	5.0	12	7.2	3	50.0	3	50.0	0	0	0	0
Suffolk	8	6.7	8	4.8	5	62.5	1	12.5	1	12.5	1	12.5
Ulster	15	12.6	15	9.0	2	13.3	13	86.6	0	0	0	0
Washington	2	1.6	2	1.2	0	0	0	0	0	0	2	100
Westchester	10	8.4	10	6.0	5	50.0	2	20.0	2	20.0	1	10.0
TOTALS	119	99.6	165	99.4	36		55		7		21	

SOURCE: Samuel Loudon Account Book, 1785–1789, Samuel Loudon Papers, AAS. This table (like the tables that follow) is based on sections 3 and 4 of Loudon's account book, which consist of distribution lists by legislative session, broken down by individual county. In order to determine patterns, and in an attempt to make sense of these sections of the account book, which are difficult to read in their current state, I transcribed each individual transaction—340 in all—using categories such as location, occupation, texts received, and date shipped.

state senate, while the governor's office received one set. Five members of the judiciary received copies in 1787 and 1788 (table 1.4). Two auditors and the state's surveyor general appeared on Loudon's distribution list, along with Andrew Onderdonk, owner of a Long Island paper mill. By distributing the state's laws and proceedings each summer, Loudon connected members of the state government at a crucial point in the rebuilding process. The June and July arrival of the printed record of the state's business was an annual material reminder of just how far the state had come in only a few short years. Indeed, Loudon's role, simple and small though it may have been, nevertheless helped rebuild the state's political communication network.[113]

Loudon's decision to distribute the laws and journals during production turned out to be a disastrous mistake that forced him to constantly scramble to fulfill orders, as evidenced by the haphazard records he kept. Despite his best efforts to serve the needs of the state legislature, he created a situation that probably caused him more work and even greater anxiety than he could possibly have anticipated. Loudon's accounts reflect the situation of a printer who was unable to meet the heightened demands of working for the state while also

TABLE 1.4 Recipients of State Publications, 1787–1788

	Shipments	
	(N)	(%)
Assembly Member	89	32.2
Auditor	2	0.7
Clerk (county, township, municipality)	133	48.1
Executive	1	0.3
Judiciary	5	1.8
Manufacturing	1	0.3
Member of the Senate	31	11.2
Surveyor General	1	0.3
Treasurer (county, township, municipality)	13	4.7
TOTALS	276	99.6

SOURCE: Samuel Loudon Account Book, 1785–1789, Samuel Loudon Papers, AAS.

continuing to publish a newspaper. Given his often frosty relationship with the state legislature, which had not hesitated in the past to hand over his job to a competing printer, his frantic bookkeeping tells the story of a man just trying to stay one step ahead of the work orders coming into his office.

"Such Removals Have Cost Your Memorialist"

Samuel Loudon did not last long as the state's printer. He gave up the job—or rather was replaced—in 1790, when the assembly appointed John Swaine and Francis Childs to share the considerable duties required of the position. After five years of working with the state legislature, Loudon had grown weary from relocating every winter, moves that he paid for out of his own pocket. He was also frustrated by the lack of financial support from the legislature. Despite the troubles he experienced, he sought reappointment in 1790. But Loudon was also clearly frustrated. He made his annoyance known in a series of petitions to the state legislature. Every argument he made in favor of staying in the state printer's office was accompanied by a complaint regarding the unanticipated costs of doing the job.

The first petition, which Loudon filed with the legislature in mid-January 1790, outlined several unanticipated expenses. First, Loudon claimed he was grossly underpaid, a far cry from his pleading with state lawmakers for his old job in January 1785. "When your Memorialist agreed with your Commissioners in January 1785," he reasoned, "his proposal for Printing was then the lowest offer," which suggests that he had perhaps underbid Elizabeth Holt for the job. Loudon also complained that he was in charge of gathering supplies on his own and had not received any kind of payment. When Loudon "undertook the business," he "was unprovided with Paper, which had to procure at a dear rate." Loudon's main point of contention, however, was that the state had required him to reprint a revised set of laws, labor that not only went unpaid but that "greatly augmented the printing work." His financial troubles were exacerbated, moreover, by the constant relocation of the legislature. Loudon pointed out that he had not been told when he took the job that "the Legislature would be removed out of this City to Albany, Poughkeepsie or to any other place." The "expence of such removals," he wrote, "have cost your Memorialist considerable sums." Despite listing his many grievances, though, he still wanted the job—provided he was paid more money. "Make him some adequate allowance for printing the revised laws," he requested, while also paying him the "balance due on his last Year's salary."[114] His case for reappointment was evidently not good enough, and the state chose Swaine and Childs for the job.

Still feeling the sting of being passed over, Loudon went on the offensive. He had little else to lose, so he drafted two additional petitions that he hoped would convince the legislature to pay him what they owed. By this time, Loudon argued that his five years of faithful service to the state was reason enough for not only the full payment of his salary but also the additional expenses he incurred in the course of doing his job. "That your Memorialist having served you faithfully as printer for the State, from January 1785 to January 1790, five years, is, he presumed, intitled to his salary without any deduction." To avoid any confusion, Loudon included in the second petition what can only be described as an expense report. Loudon estimated that the State of New York owed him nearly £350. He argued that the state owed him £30 for additional "expenses in carrying Paper Printing materials to Poughkeepsie" in 1788 and for hiring additional "hands there for the Work." The state's tab, he pointed out, increased in 1789 on top of his £330 annual salary—which he had never been paid in the first place. He billed the state an additional £50 in 1789 for "expenses removing my Printing Apparatus to Albany," and also for the costs of hiring journeymen, buying paper, and renting a house. If this was not enough, the state legislature was also a deadbeat newspaper subscriber. The assembly owed Loudon nearly £2 for six subscriptions to the *Packet*.[115] Loudon's memorial to the state was not limited to a list of expenses; he also made an emotionally charged appeal.

> Your Memorialist appeals to the surviving members of the committee who agreed with him to print for the state, whether they know any thing at that time of the revision of the laws, which for the four last sessions has greatly

augmented the printing work; or, whether they ever mentioned to your memorialist, that he was under obligation to remove his Printing office out of this City without an additional consideration. Even now, tho he supposes the printing work will be far less than he had to perform, he asserts, and is ready to prove, that no printer can do your work for 100 pounds, nor for 200 pounds per annum, find paper, and subject himself to remove his office out of the City for the purpose. . . . During the sitting of the past sessions of the Legislature, Your Memorialist complained repeatedly to several of the Members, that their work was greater than he agreed for on account of the Revision of the Laws they acknowledged it, and said He ought to be allowed for it, and that he should Memorial [i.e., petition] your honorable body for the purpose which, with due deference, he has now done.[116]

The next day, Loudon delivered a *third* petition to the legislature. The impetus was Loudon's discovery that the state had actually *reduced* his pay. He made sure to point out that he had included a detailed list of expenses, yet, much to his dismay, he was informed that the committee "chosen to report on the same" had actually "deducted *thirty pounds* from the salary" for reasons he was "unable to determine." Loudon reminded the legislature that he had "completed five Years and did all the Work of the several Sessions within that Time." Loudon was obviously furious at what he described as an "overlooked" account. He repeated his demand that the state settle the debts that had resulted from his being required to move "his printing Office Paper &c to Albany & Poughkeepsie." In his concluding remarks, Loudon suggested that he was far from profiting from the work he had done and that he was only looking for just payment for duties performed. "Your Memorialist assures you that he has scarcely saved himself by the public Works, and he wants nothing more than is contained in the spirit of his Contract."[117]

If his own calculations are taken at face value, Samuel Loudon had a legitimate gripe. Monetary considerations, while certainly pertinent, do not tell the entire story of Loudon's troubled relationship with the State of New York. The physical logistics of uprooting and relocating a massively sedentary business for three consecutive years placed a considerable burden on Loudon, his large family, and the journeymen and apprentices in his employ. While moving the printing press alone—a large, cumbersome wood and iron device weighing several hundred pounds—would have been a logistical nightmare, the several thousand pounds of type that went everywhere with him must have made the annual moves enormously taxing. Printing shops in this era typically had between one and three presses, depending, of course, on anticipated production and the printer's finances. Since Loudon was simultaneously printing for the state and publishing his newspaper, he probably had at least two presses in his shop. In that case, he would have had four pairs of ball stocks, ten chases, seventeen galleys, eight frames (stands that held type cases), eight composing sticks, two imposing stones, twelve type cases, and eleven letter boards. Further, a two-press shop would probably have possessed more than twenty-two hundred pounds of type. In other words, it would have taken Loudon and his crew days to pack and load the equipment, not to mention the gruesomely slow pace of overland transport to their new shop. Yet, presented with Loudon's repeated pleas for help and the supporting evidence he submitted, the cash-strapped New York State Legislature did not take pity on the embattled printer. In an undated and unsigned note that presumably ended up on Loudon's desk, the state denied his request for retroactive payment. "The Committee to whom was referred the Petition of Samuel Loudon report that the former report of your committee was the full Ballance due to Samuel Loudon or State Printer agreeably to the contract made with him—and that no further allowance ought to be made."[118]

Near the end of his tumultuous career as the state's printer, Samuel Loudon began putting more time into publishing his long-standing newspaper, the *New-York Packet*. He had kept up the paper for many years, despite the hardships he faced during the Revolutionary War. As his tenure as the state's printer ended, Loudon expanded the scope and reach of the *Packet*. In early May 1789, for example, he started issuing the *Packet* three times per week. He was able to keep pace with this increased workload until February 1791, when he made the *Packet* a weekly paper. About a year later, in late January 1792, Loudon stopped printing the *Packet*, this time for good. It did not take him long to pick up where he had left off, for he established a daily newspaper—the *Diary, or Loudon's Register*—in mid-February 1792. Not long after taking on the considerable task of publishing a daily paper, Loudon brought his son Samuel Loudon Jr. into the business. Three years later, in February 1795, Loudon allowed Samuel Jr. to take over the publication. Loudon's secondary role in the *Diary* did not last long, however, as the younger Loudon died suddenly in September 1795.[119]

The death of Loudon's son proved to be the penultimate chapter in a career marked by pain and hardship. By 1800, still reeling from young Samuel's sudden demise, the elder Loudon retired to Middletown Point, New Jersey, a small town about fifty miles south of New York City that hugged the Jersey shore. But Loudon was a restless retiree. In 1805, he was approached by the young and ambitious Thomas Ronalds, and the two went into the book business together. It was likely that Loudon was more of a silent partner, while Ronalds took care of the day-to-day operations in New York. Had he known the misfortune he was to face as Ronalds's partner, Loudon might have invested more than just money in the shop, or declined the partnership altogether.

Loudon's enterprise with Ronalds was doomed from the start. While Loudon was enjoying the peace and quiet of the Jersey shore, away from the bustle of lower Manhattan, Ronalds faced a crisis. Like many New Yorkers in the late summer of 1805, he suspended the business when an outbreak of Yellow Fever consumed the city. "We have been under the disagreeable necessity with our fellow citizens to shut our store on acct. of the Fever having appeared among us," Ronalds and Loudon wrote to Philadelphia's Mathew Carey; "consequently Business must be suspended for a time."[120]

Ronalds and Loudon, however, faced problems that went beyond shuttering their business to avoid Yellow Fever. By December 1805, the partners had encountered difficulties with their creditors—to the tune of an $800 debt to the Manhattan Bank and Loudon's old colleague Hugh Gaine.[121] By 1806, Ronalds and Loudon had dissolved their partnership, and Ronalds entered into business with his brother James.[122] Thomas Ronalds's run of bad luck did not end with the dissolution of his partnership with Loudon, however. The Ronalds brothers closed their doors almost as soon as they opened, as they ran into financial difficulties with their creditors before they could really make a fresh start. Loudon, meanwhile, slipped back into retirement until his death in 1813.[123]

As a shrewd, opportunistic businessman, Samuel Loudon spent much of his life as a printer on the move, his printing press and large brood in tow. His constant moves, made out of necessity—first to avoid capture by British troops, then to follow the state legislature as it searched for a home after the American Revolution—were reflected in the way he kept track of his accounts. Loudon spent much of his career as a printer sparring with the New York legislature. Although he often received the short end of the stick, he helped rebuild the Empire State from the ground up by printing and distributing its earliest laws and proceedings. In this particular case, Loudon was in constant contact with local merchants in order to develop consumer space in the pages of the *New-York Packet*. Additionally, he served as a political intermediary, connecting well-known politicians, local officials, and ordinary New Yorkers with the goings-on in the state legislature. His account book suggests that Loudon was a man crumbling under the stress of a job that required him to play an important role in rebuilding the state's fractured political communication network. Despite the hardships he faced, Loudon adapted to change. If the production of his newspaper and the distribution of the legislative proceedings are any indication, Samuel Loudon was, at the very least, a survivor.

2

WILLIAM GORDON, PRINT CULTURE, AND
THE POLITICS OF HISTORY

On an early June morning less than a year after the Treaty of Paris was signed, William Gordon arrived at Mount Vernon just in time to enjoy breakfast with George Washington. Washington typically sat down for his breakfast at seven in the morning. By that time, the general had usually been up for several hours, catching up with his correspondence or enjoying a good book. Gordon, like many guests at Mount Vernon, would have been summoned by what another visitor described as "the great bell," which called everyone to meals. Before being shepherded into the dining room, though, visitors typically gathered in a sitting room, where they had access to a number of newspapers. The actual meal, of course, depended on the season, but guests could reasonably expect a spread of tea and coffee, cold, cured, and broiled meats, fish, and fowl, all finished with a dash of parsley and whatever was fresh from the garden that morning. After breakfast, during which Gordon no doubt peppered the general with questions about the recent war, Washington introduced Gordon to what he had come all the way from Massachusetts to see: a stack of his private papers compiled during the War of Independence. A minister from Roxbury, on the outskirts of Boston, Gordon had for many years been diligently collecting material for a history of the American Revolution. Washington provided Gordon with all of his correspondence, apparently concealing nothing, and then left the ambitious minister and fledgling historian alone in the study while he made his daily ride about the plantation.[1]

Gordon did not waste the opportunity. He was so committed to his research that he stopped only for meals, never once visiting with his host after that initial breakfast. "I sat into work and followed it closely," Gordon recalled of his time at Mount Vernon, "rising by day light and being at his [Washington's] books as soon as I could read, and continued it till evening, breaking off only for meals, and never went once to visit tho' invited." Gordon remained at Mount Vernon, his nose buried in Washington's writings, for more than two weeks. During that time, he "searched and extracted thirty and three folio volumes of copied letters," military orders, and "bundles upon bundles of letters" addressed to Washington. In reflecting on his experience, Gordon asked his friend Horatio Gates, "don't you think I labored hard?"[2]

Gordon's arrival at Mount Vernon in early June 1784 marked the pinnacle of his career in America. But his research trip to Mount Vernon was an unusual event, one that historians, then and now, rarely have the opportunity to experience: Gordon was digging around in the private correspondence and personal records of a living symbol of American independence. Just a few months earlier, the nation's obsession with Washington as an object of affection began with his willing resignation of his military command, a selfless act that Gordon commended. "It afforded me peculiar pleasure to learn, how your Excellency had secured your public character by your manner of retiring to the private walk of domestic happiness," he wrote in a letter to Washington, "after having been, in the hands of the Supreme Governor, a glorious instrument in establishing the rights of the American states."[3] A eulogy given years later in Charlestown, Massachusetts, reminded parishioners of the unifying effect of Washington's resignation. "Former heroes were stimulated to deeds of civil enterprise or exploits of martial achievements by ambitious designs of personal aggrandizement or the lawless lust of power," said Thaddeus Harris. "But he accepted command with reluctance; exercised it with moderation; voluntarily resigned it. . . . How matchless this conduct! How unrivaled does WASHINGTON appear."[4] Gordon's initial meal at Mount Vernon, and the work he had taken on there, held as much contemporary significance as it seemingly did for posterity.

Born in Hitchin, England, in March 1729, William Gordon trained for a godly life in Plaisterers' Hall, London, a dissenting academy founded to provide ministers for congregations not affiliated with the Anglican Church. After serving for many years as a pastor, first in Ipswich and then in Southwark, Gordon set sail for Philadelphia with his wife, Elizabeth, in 1770.[5] Gordon had long sympathized with the American colonists in their dispute with the mother country, and he wasted little time in seeking out patronage and making important political connections that would serve him well in the long run. Almost immediately after arriving, he and Elizabeth stayed for a time with the Philadelphia patriot and noted physician Benjamin Rush. Gordon eventually befriended Ezra Stiles, preaching from his Rhode Island pulpit in June 1771 on a tour north from Philadelphia to Boston.[6] Shortly thereafter, William and Elizabeth settled in Roxbury, where he served as the town's minister from June 1772 to March 1786. While Gordon made no attempt to hide his contempt for the ways in which the British Parliament had dealt with its brethren in the American colonies, he was also willing to invite controversy in his adopted country by openly questioning the sincerity of the Declaration of Independence in light of the continued existence of slavery.[7]

William Gordon's *History of the Rise, Progress, and Establishment, of the Independence of the United States* was one of several "histories" published in the early years of the Republic that chronicled the American War of Independence. Publishers of these so-called histories hoped to capitalize on the emotional and political need of the American people to understand, come to terms with, and celebrate their recent past. Gordon's *History* was published by subscription. Subscription books in early America were often published for local and elite audiences. But the New York edition of Gordon's *History* cut across regional, class, and indeed gender boundaries. Despite being a controversial text, Gordon's *History* connected readers, British and American, in a transatlantic reading public. The text itself was composed and written in America during and immediately after the War of Independence, yet it was first published in London. Not long after the original London edition arrived in the United States, word spread that a pirated American edition was in the works. A partnership of three New York printers, led by the Scottish émigré Samuel Campbell, engineered a multicity advertising campaign to secure subscriptions and at the same time fulfill their own national ambitions. In reprinting Gordon's history of the war in the United States for an American market, Campbell, Robert Hodge, and Thomas Allen helped shape the new nation's understanding of its history and its possibilities for the future by creating a national reading public attentive to its recent past.[8]

Gordon's history of the American Revolution had a complicated publication history wrapped up in the material and economic intersection of books and newspapers. The national subscription campaigns, first by Gordon and later by the New York printers, took place across dozens of newspapers. Booksellers and printers relied heavily on newspapers, advertisements in particular, to spread the word about their publishing ventures. The large and diverse list of subscribers they printed in their pirated edition of Gordon's *History* was almost entirely the result of publicity drummed up by local editors, who reprinted advertisements for the book in their newspapers. But the democratization of the new nation's history was more far-reaching than either Gordon or Campbell and his partners could have imagined. However many people the book reached, its distribution paled in comparison to the number of people exposed to the newspaper advertisements touting the book's merits. And while the pirated edition did reach every corner of the new nation, the New York printers William Morton and Francis Childs undermined Campbell's campaign to pirate the text by serializing the *History*, effectively creating crude, informal "story papers" that appeared in their newspapers. This kind of literary subterfuge exposed far more readers to the history of the war than the physical books, printed by subscription, did. What this particular case reveals is that while book publishers and newspaper printers often had codependent relationships and frequently worked closely with one another, newspapers, as material texts, remained far more accessible to ordinary Americans than did even the cheapest books produced for a national market.[9]

Scholars have shown that the revolutionary "histories" written in the late eighteenth and early nineteenth centuries marked a departure from the colonial past. The works of Jeremy Belknap, Mercy Otis Warren, David Ramsay, and William Gordon (among many others) helped shape the course of American history in the early Republic. All the more intriguing was these self-proclaimed historians' awareness that the very act of writing their histories—which often required months, if not years, of research—represented a form of revolution, both intellectual and political. As civic-minded participants in the public sphere, the early historians of the Revolution felt a sense of patriotic duty to chronicle the story of American independence for the people of the new nation and for posterity. But history, for these early historians, was as much a political tool as it was an important story to tell, and evident in their works is an emphasis on presenting American independence as a natural, and national, progression. Their histories often represented the political and ethical mores of American society on the brink, and eventually in the midst, of a prolonged struggle with an imperial master. The justification for revolution, so their stories go, resided not with divine providence but rather with the actions and thoughts of the people. And while they did not either participate in or directly influence the protests that led to rebellion, the long war that won independence, or the policy making that shaped America's political present and future, they did play a role in how future generations would view this formative period in the nation's history. In the course of writing their histories so soon after the events they described, Marshall, Warren, Ramsay, Belknap, Gordon and others depicted the deeds of great American men in what amounted to a historical romance, creating in the process a heroic, shared, and uniquely American past.[10]

In his *History*, William Gordon presented an elite narrative of the Revolution. Gordon aggressively sought the patronage and friendship of John Adams, George Washington, and other founders—a public spat with John Hancock not withstanding—and advertised his *History* as a story based in large part on the lives and actions of the Revolution's leading men. And while a large number of ordinary people throughout the new nation eventually subscribed to the New York edition of the *History*, many no doubt did so knowing that the story Gordon told was not actually *their* story. At the same time, however, the very act of seeking subscriptions subverted the way in which Gordon wrote the text and the likely audience he sought. The subscription list drawn up by the three New York publishers effectively *democratized* Gordon's contemporary version of "founders chic."[11] By placing their names in the text next to the great heroes Gordon celebrated, the subscribers could thus imagine themselves as part of the story, making history alongside Washington and Adams. Gordon's *History*, then, as fraught and contested as it was with an equally complicated publishing history, was nonetheless an attempt to chronicle a heroic American past. The necessity of an American edition of Gordon's book, produced in New York City on American paper with American ink by American labor, was realized all too well by the hundreds of subscribers who proudly offered their names.

"Readers Are Increasing in These States"

Despite the political and intellectual aspirations of the early historians, writing the history of the American Revolution was by no means big business. While representing an interesting confluence of commercial and political nationalism, the early histories were often commercial failures for authors and publishers alike. David Ramsay wrote two histories of the war, financing the production and distribution of both.[12] And while he had high hopes for financial success and a national audience for his work, he ultimately failed at the endeavor, bemoaning the expenses involved in writing and publishing in the new nation. "Readers are increasing in these states, and I trust the day is not far distant when the sale of two thousand copies of an original work might be counted upon," he later wrote, concluding that "this would make it worth while to write books. All that I have ever done in that way, has not cleared actual expenses."[13] Ramsay laid much of the blame on Robert Aitken's slipshod presswork. His choice of Aitken to print his *History of the American Revolution* was curious, especially after Aitken botched the binding work on Ramsay's first history. Aitken deflected the criticism, blaming the poor work on his woeful finances. He considered his pecuniary state to be "so low on Account of My Losses in trade that I find Cr[editors] ready for it before I am possess'd of my income." Ramsay's flawed logic in reasoning that "because he was a Scotchman" Aitken "must be a linguist and grammarian" ultimately led him to a second disappointment. Writing to his friend Ashbel Green, Ramsay complained bitterly that "the printing the spelling the ink the forms of the lines are in many cases execrable."[14] For Ramsay, the line between commercial failure and a compelling national narrative grew all the more murky with each pull of Aitken's press.

Even with the loss, Ramsay's *History of the American Revolution* did have an extensive readership. Buried at the end of his "waste book," Aitken recorded the distribution list of Ramsay's text, after leaving dozens of blank pages between the day-to-day operations of his shop and his subscription lists. By separating his waste book and the Ramsay distribution list, Aitken created a critical distance between two facets of his business: the ordinary, daily pace of life in his Philadelphia shop, where books moved in and out of the store, in the hands of customers and exchange partners alike, and this unique printing job. While the space between the chronological list of transactions and the distribution list accomplishes this separation, the fact that both are in the same account book also signifies just how intertwined these various facets of the publishing trade were in the late 1780s. Given that Ramsay engaged in a subscription campaign in order to drum up interest in the text, it is not surprising that he and Aitken gained a few potential readers, in addition to shipping a case of the books to London. On 23 October 1789, for example, Aitken noted that he "sent 300 vols" of "Ramsay's Revolution in a case directed [to] S. Vaughn & Son, Lond." Aitken listed the occupations of some of the subscribers and the location of others. For example, two days before Christmas in 1789 he sent Robert Smith, a merchant, "1 sett" of Ramsay's text, while a "Mr. Bloomfield" of New Jersey likewise received one set of the history; on the same day, Aitken shipped a set of the text to a grocer by the name of Captain Cochran Jr. The distribution of Ramsay's history was a fluid process. In April, Aitken fulfilled an order for "A Doctor in Virginia," and in mid-June he shipped one set of the text to an Alexander William Thompson in Maryland.[15]

Although Ramsay considered his *History of the American Revolution* a commercial flop, Aitken continued receiving queries about the text long after the initial publication. In May 1790, more than a year after printing enough copies for the original subscribers, Aitken received a substantial request for sixty-two sets of the history from a man the printer described in the waste book as "the Scot." The order was clearly unexpected, as Aitken recorded it on a small slip of paper that he later inserted between the pages of his waste book. The tone of the note also suggests Aitken's surprise, perhaps even his frustration. He wrote, in part, "& now May 10th rec'd in quires being in full on acct of David Ramsay Esq., Sixty-two Setts—of his hist. of Revolution."[16] Why "the Scot" wanted sixty-two sets of Ramsay's history remains unclear. But, from a practical perspective, this kind of sizeable order would have been a boon to Aitken's shop at a time when he was still smarting from his venture in Bible publishing, which nearly put him out of business. Still, Aitken's two jobs for Ramsay were not enough to rescue him from years of bad financial decisions, and he died miserable and broke in July 1802, leaving his daughter to clean up the mess.[17]

"You Have Obliged Me Greatly"

Early in the military conflict with Great Britain, William Gordon felt compelled to tell the story of what he rightly perceived as an important moment in the history of the Western world. A self-aware witness to history, Gordon began collecting materials not long after the first shots had been fired at Lexington and

Concord. At that point, Gordon began a search for documents that would last thirteen years and would bring him into contact with many luminaries of the revolutionary generation. He left few stones unturned, casting about for any kind of source, ranging from newspapers, to state and federal documents, to the personal correspondence of George Washington, Horatio Gates, and Nathanael Greene, among others, which he often traveled to look at in person. In an effort to play the part of the impartial, objective compiler, Gordon used the remnants of Thomas Hutchinson's private papers, many of which had been destroyed during the Stamp Act crisis in 1765.[18]

The papers that Washington accumulated during the war had been the object of Gordon's desires for some time. Indeed, Gordon had been badgering Washington for a look into his private records since the early days of the conflict. In December 1776, for example, Gordon wrote to "acquaint" himself with Washington, and to pass along notice that he was "preparing for that history in which you are so deeply concerned and make so eminent a figure." In the course of briefly describing the work, Gordon expressed his hope that Washington would be "so obliging as to assure me that you would assist by furnishing materials."[19] Washington was apparently easy to convince, because Gordon boasted a year later to John Adams that "His Excellency Gen. Washington has promised me his assistance" and that others "had done the same."[20] Once Washington gave him permission to look through his private records, Gordon tried to schedule a time to meet. In July 1778, he asked that "when your Excellency can retire to y[our ha]bitation, and have your papers about you, [I] must then apply for the honor of being admitted [there] for a few weeks," so that he could "collect the proper materials" for his "intended history."[21] Washington, though, asked Gordon to first petition Congress for permission to look at his private papers, which Gordon gladly did prior to setting off for Mount Vernon.[22]

Gordon sought the widest possible source base for his *History*. In the early spring of 1777, he petitioned the Massachusetts legislature for access to records kept by the Committee of Safety. He hinted at this ambition in a letter to Adams. Gordon was thankful to Adams "and the other gentlemen of the Congress" for helping him gain access to "certain intelligence that may not be easily gained in any other way."[23] In June, Gordon excitedly fired off a letter to his friend Horatio Gates, telling Gates that he was needed in Boston "on special business" and was making his way "in great haste."[24] The legislature, as it turned out, approved his request one month later, as the secretary of the commonwealth was "directed to deliver to the Revd. Doctor William Gordon, all the late Com[mit]tee of Safety's Papers, now in the Secretaries Office."[25] This resolution continued to allow Gordon access to state-level information. Since 1775 at least, Gordon had had access to documents that few outside the legislature had seen. Indeed, according to a May 1775 resolve of the Provincial Congress, Gordon was to have "free access" to "all persons who have the care of any Prisoners detained at *Concord, Lexington,* or elsewhere . . . whenever he shall desire it," and "all civil Magistrates" should provide him aid and assistance "in examining and taking Depositions of them and others, without exception."[26]

Now that his access to important state documents was all but guaranteed, Gordon continued his feverish campaign to supplement the *History* with private correspondence from important men involved in the war. Gordon had hoped to secure manuscripts from Adams, for instance, but was ultimately disappointed. "I am happy in finding that I had planned beginning the history as early as you proposed," he wrote to Adams in June 1777, but he was disheartened because Adams was not forthcoming "as to any considerable assistance."[27] In September, in a letter to General Gates in which he gave his "heartiest wishes for success," Gordon asked that either Gates or his amanuensis procure for him "the best materials for my history," and that if a certain "Col. Meigs is with you, pray my compliments, and renew my request that he would favour me with his journal thro' the woods under Arnold to Quebec"; Gordon insisted that Gates send this material "under cover to me when you write to the Council of this State."[28] After Gates had fulfilled his favor, Gordon was profuse in his thanks.

> You have obliged me greatly by promising your papers, and raising my expectations of some excellent and curious garnish. I am likely to possess the best materials, tho' I shall not have the best pen; but in history truth is the diamond; fine composition is but the polish—labored elegance and extravagant colouring only brings her into suspicion, hides her beauty, and makes the cautious reader afraid lest he is in company with a painted harlot. Tho' ever so naked, yet if as well proportioned and as truly wrought as the Venus de Medicis she will enrapture in the private retirements of the study: but being designed to appear in public she must be decently and neatly appareled so as not to offend the eye. I will seek to dress her in a colour that shall suit her complexion—in a taste that shall please the present and future generations—and in a dress that shall improve instead of concealing her beauties.[29]

After receiving permission from a number of men to scour their private archives, most notably George Washington's papers, Gordon assured his subjects that he was interested in pursuing the impartial truth in writing his history. Writing to Washington in August 1781, Gordon thanked the general for his "assistance in my designed history of the present glorious contest for liberty." The heart of this particular letter, though, was Gordon's surprisingly modern justification for access to Washington's private papers: he wanted to produce an accurate, objective history of the war. "Truth and impartiality are what I aim at," he wrote, "and therefore am for getting the best information possible, which must be by having a recourse to original papers in the possession of those who have borne a distinguished and active part in the transactions of the day." In a letter to Gates, Gordon indicated that he would seek "not only the *truth* but the truth *truly* represented." But Gordon's pursuit of the truth had its limits. He was willing to withhold certain information that might have painted an unflattering portrait of the men at the heart of the *History,* or that would have jeopardized peace. He promised Washington that he would "conscientiously conceal whatever . . . may be imprudent and unsafe to divulge" so as to "promote peace and prevent or destroy dissentions."[30]

A little more than a year later, Gordon was clearly trying to repair his fractured relationship with John Adams. Over the course of several meetings, Adams seemed to have developed a less than favorable opinion of Gordon, and was not keen about Gordon's flattering letters. According to Adams, Gordon was "an eternal talker, and somewhat vain, and not accurate nor judicious," and while he praised Gordon's commitment to "the Cause," he cast him as "incautious, and not sufficiently tender of the Character of our Province." Adams also called Gordon out on his ambition. He was, Adams wrote, "Fond of being a Man of Influence, at Head Quarters and with our Council and House, and with the general Officers of the Army, and also with Gentlemen in this City, and other Colonies."[31] Gordon promised Adams that his only aim was to report the truth. "I have not seen Braintree a long while," he wrote, "but went the last October across the country to Traveller's rest in Virginia, the seat of our common friend Genl. Gates, with whom I spent a fortnight in searching after historical knowledge and truth."[32] John Adams's caution in dealing with Gordon should not be taken lightly. Gordon's research can be viewed as an aspirational pursuit. As both a compiler and an author, Gordon wanted to be considered part of the same intellectual and social circle as the subjects in his history. Because he could not hope to accomplish much in the way of actual influence on matters of policy or diplomacy, he opportunistically banked on wielding influence with his pen. In this way, Gordon went to great lengths to present himself to the leading men of the Revolution as a reliable, objective historian and thus as a person to be taken seriously.

Despite Adams's rebuff, Gordon pressed on. Writing again to Washington in June 1783, Gordon announced that he intended to "prosecute the history of the late Revolution with the utmost diligence." He thanked Washington yet again for his promise of access and assistance, and offered to visit Mount Vernon at Washington's earliest convenience. "With the greatest pleasure I recollect your approbation of my original design, and your repeated kind assurances of affording me your assistance, which is of capital concern in it," he wrote, "for I am in search of genuine truth and not a fairy tale."[33] And while he promised an impartial story of the American War of Independence, Gordon was later accused, by his London printer at least, of producing a one-sided story.

Gordon's research, in particular his pleading with the U.S. Congress for access to material, became an object of public fascination. Gordon mentioned his petition to Congress in letters to Horatio Gates and George Washington. In January 1783, for example, he told Gates of his intention to travel to Philadelphia to "present a petition to Congress for liberty of inspecting their papers with a view to my history."[34] To Washington he revealed his impatience at having to wait on word from Congress. "Should my memorial be complied with, shall repair to Philadelphia with all possible expedition," he wrote, hinting that a trip to Mount Vernon would not be far behind. "Shall hope for the pleasure of inspecting your papers after having examined the Secretary's office," he exclaimed confidently to Washington.[35] Once word got out that not only had the petition been approved but that Gordon had been busily inspecting official and private papers, several newspapers reported on Gordon's research and the importance of his project. In August 1784, for example, Samuel Hall, the printer of the *Salem Gazette*, reported to his readers that "the Rev. Dr. Gordon has lately petitioned Congress" with "the desire of cherishing the love of liberty." Hall enthusiastically reported that Congress had made available "any papers or files . . . which may be desired," except for "instructions to the Ministers of the United States in foreign countries, letters to or from those ministers, or other foreign ministers, or any acts or records which hitherto have been considered as confidential or secret." Hall also indicated that Congress had given Gordon its blessing to travel to Mount Vernon to examine Washington's records. "The Congress, having the fullest confidence in the prudence of the later Commander in Chief," Hall wrote, "have no objection to his laying before Dr. Gordon any of his papers, which he shall think at this period may be submitted to the public eye."[36] News of Gordon's successful petition, taken from Hall's original notice, appeared two days later in Boston, in both the *Independent Chronicle* and the *Continental Journal and Weekly Advertiser*, in Worcester's *Thomas's Massachusetts Spy* on the same day, and later in the *Essex Journal and the Massachusetts and New-Hampshire General Advertiser* and the *Boston Gazette*. The details of his research moved beyond the Boston area as well, appearing in Hartford's *American Mercury*, New London's *Connecticut Gazette*, Philadelphia's *Pennsylvania Packet*, and Trenton's *New-Jersey Gazette*.[37] In September 1784, Samuel Loudon notified his New York readers that Gordon had been doing the "necessary but arduous work" of "collecting materials for an History of the late Revolution," after receiving the permission of the Congress to look through its files.[38] Later that month, John Carter, the publisher of the *Providence Gazette*, received a letter from a traveler regarding Gordon's *History*:

On a late journey to the southward, I found that numbers had entertained an opinion, that Dr. Gordon of Roxbury, was concerned in the History of the War, published at Boston; and having reason to believe that the story was artfully propagated, by interested persons, to promote the sale of that performance, please to inform the public, through the channel of your Gazette, that Dr. Gordon has been favoured with the inspection of the papers belonging to the late Generals Washington, Gates, Lincoln, and Greene; but that, as he has not been in the *least* concerned in any historical publication which has *yet* appeared, neither will he engage in *any*, till he has announced the same to the United States by his own signature.[39]

In September 1785, Gordon wrote to Nathanael Greene to inform him that he had shipped "part of a map of New York and its environs, containing the portion of Long Island." Gordon asked that Greene mark out on the map, "with a pencil or ink, the lines and fortifications and every thing else that may prove explanatory to the transactions that passed upon it." For purposes of comparison, Gordon also sent Greene "a Map of the Carolinas executed for Dr. Ramsay's History," and he asked Greene to make any additional markings on Ramsay's map that would "make every thing as plain to the reader as possible." Gordon was after as much detail as he could find; he was interested in "marches and countermarches, the same of Cornwallis's," rivers crossed, "where battles were fought, and important matters transacted," and "whatever else may tend to the illustration of the history of the war." Greene evidently complied, at least in part, for Gordon wrote him two weeks later to thank him for his "obliging letter, with the map part of Long Island improved."[40]

"Have Now Sent You One of My Proposals"

William Gordon's *History*, both the London edition he financed and the pirated edition that appeared in New York a year later, was published by subscription. The subscription book trade functioned organically within the early modern bookshop, yet at the same time it was governed, informally, by a different set of social, cultural, and economic rules. A key difference that set the subscription trade apart from other publishing ventures was its *publicness*, in contrast to the private, individualized shopping experience of walking into a store and browsing the shelves, an experience that often ended with the purchase of a book. The subscription trade hinged on an agreement, at first private and then public, between a publisher and the person who decided, in advance, to buy that book. Publishers reached their potential market not through face-to-face interactions within the controlled space of the bookshop, but rather through regional and national networks of printers, booksellers, and literary agents. And the local term of purchase, an individual's act of agreeing to buy a book in advance of publication, suggests the creation of a national reading public. In a way, then, subscribing to William Gordon's *History* created a national *imaginary* that gradually became a material *actuality*, as each copy of the text was either bundled or bound and then shipped to the man or woman who bought it.[41]

Subscription was common in early America. People helped support a wide variety of projects in the late eighteenth and early nineteenth centuries, ranging from road surveys, privateering ventures, postal delivery, fire insurance, coffeehouses, expeditions, debt relief, civil societies, discussion clubs, and circulating libraries, to name a few. Subscribing to books was just one of many ways in which Americans expressed themselves publicly and politically by lending their names, and thus their reputations, to whatever cause they believed in at the time.[42]

Publishers often asked subscribers to lend their names to a list to be published as part of the text. Although subscription publications were common, actual subscription lists did not appear in every published subscription book. In many cases, publishers failed to follow through on their promise to include a subscription list, for whatever reason. Some pointed to a lack of space—likely due to a shortage of either paper or ink—or placed blame squarely on subscription agents who did not return subscription lists in time for inclusion. Yet another reason why publishers neglected to include a subscription list was that they often lacked enough names to warrant one. Subscribing to a book, which often meant handing over a deposit without first seeing the material object itself, was a risky purchase for many consumers. Attentive to the difficulties they faced in procuring subscribers, publishers often cast their call for subscribers in cautious terms. "A list of Subscribers will be prefixed," so read a proposal in a June 1788 edition of the *Connecticut Journal*, "if received in season."[43] Given the challenges publishers faced in getting enough subscribers on board to justify the inclusion of a list—let alone to publish the book at all—it is remarkable that both the London and New York editions of Gordon's *History* were published with what seem to be complete lists. In fact, when Samuel Campbell, Robert Hodge, and Thomas Allen had their contacts scouring the nation seeking subscribers, around one hundred additional subscription projects were ongoing, and only about one-quarter included a list of some kind when published.[44]

Publishers announced potential subscription books in a number of ways, ranging from broadsides printed and distributed locally to advertisements that circulated in the nation's growing network of newspapers. News of a subscription campaign also traveled by word of mouth and in notes shared in particular social networks. William Gordon, and later the New York publishers who pirated his work, took advantage of these methods in order to generate national interest in his *History*. A proposal seeking subscriptions for Gordon's book circulated in several newspapers after first appearing in Samuel Loudon's *New-York Packet*. "The writer, in the beginning of 1776, made known his intention to his Excellency, the late Commander in Chief of the American army, and, meeting with the desired encouragement, applied himself to collecting materials for the history," read the initial advertisement. The proposal also indicated that Gordon had been "an acquaintance and correspondent with a number of gentlemen of the first consequence, in both the civil and military line," including, in addition to Washington, "GATES, GREENE, LINCOLN, AND OTHO WILLIAMS." This kind of social network gave Gordon, in his own estimation at least, "the most authentic and interesting information" through a "liberal examination of their papers, both of a public and more private nature." Gordon imagined his *History* as helping to foster a civic consciousness, especially at such a formative moment in the young nation's history. The first volume of his book would list "the names of subscribers" in an effort to buttress the text with the public support of the American people. But the invention of American history by subscription came at a price. "It is proposed to embellish the work with a good collection of maps, plans and cuts, should the subscription be so far countenanced by the public as to answer the expence," the proposal indicated. Because of the potential importance of the text, Gordon expected subscribers to have "no objection against advancing one half of the subscription money at the time of subscribing." No mention was made of Gordon's publication plans.[45]

Wherever Gordon's proposal was reprinted in a local newspaper, it was identical to Loudon's initial advertisement, the only differences being typographical and aesthetic. Over the course of nine months, Gordon's request for subscribers was published in eight newspapers in eight cities, stretching from New England to Charleston, South Carolina. After Loudon's initial publication in mid-January, the advertisement appeared again a week later in the *New-York Packet* and continued on a weekly basis until the second week of February. The ad appeared next in Thomas Bradford's *Pennsylvania Journal*, where it was published thirty-three times between the end of January and the second week of September 1786. From that point on, Gordon's project was publicized by several papers, including John Carter's *Providence Gazette*; Isaac Collins's *New-Jersey Gazette* in Trenton; the *New-Hampshire Gazette*, published in Portsmouth by John Melcher; George Goodwin's *Connecticut Courant*; the *Carlisle Gazette* in rural Pennsylvania, published by partners George Kline and George Reynolds; and the Charleston *Columbian Herald*, published by a partnership of Thomas Bowen, James Vandle, and S. Andrews.[46]

What emerge from Gordon's correspondence and the advertisements are the contours of a national network of booksellers, printers, and merchants willing to take subscriptions for him. Given that he had cultivated epistolary relationships with many important military and political figures, Gordon did not hesitate to call upon his contacts in seeking subscribers. Gordon told Nathanael Greene in November 1785, "Have now sent you one of my proposals," and politely asked Greene's assistance in "promoting and hastening subscriptions." Whatever names Greene could secure, Gordon continued, should be sent to "Messurs. May & Hills, Merchants in Savannah," who were receiving "subscriptions on my behalf." Four days later, Gordon told George Washington that he expected the proposal to be "circulated through the United States by the first week in January." Gordon implied to Washington, much more delicately and deferentially than he had with Greene, that he expected the general to distribute proposals to his friends and acquaintances near Mount Vernon in addition to subscribing himself. "I gave direction that a few should be forwarded to your Excellency from New York as soon as printed," he wrote, flattering Washington that he was "greatly honoured and served by your countenance." Gordon told Washington, much as he had Greene, that he had an agent nearby ready to take names. "I have requested of my friend Mr. Roberdeau to receive subscriptions for me at Alexandria," he wrote, "and promise myself from his former acts of kindness, that he will oblige me in it."[47] Remarkably, Washington noted in his diary that he had done as Gordon requested. "Thursday, 16th [February 1786] Put one of Doct. Gordon's Subscription Papers (yesterday) in the hands of Doct. Craik to offer to his acquaintances."[48] Gordon's years of insistent correspondence, it seems, were finally paying off.

In addition to the printers and merchants mentioned in the letters to Greene and Washington, the newspaper advertisements listed the agents responsible for receiving subscriptions in each city. Overall, the ads named thirty men. In New York, for instance, Gordon listed three printing shops that potential subscribers could visit: the printers of the *New-York Packet,* Samuel Loudon and his son John, Hugh Gaine at 36 Hanover Square, and John Berry and John Rogers's bookshop across the street. The ads directed Connecticut subscribers to several places, including the post office in Hartford, Elias Beers in New Haven, and George Goodwin, publisher of the *Connecticut Courant.* The *New-Hampshire Gazette* listed William Woodbridge of Exeter, the postmaster of Portsmouth, Jeremiah Libbey, and the printer John Melcher as possible contacts. In Philadelphia, newspapers listed Robert Aitken as Gordon's primary contact, and also the printer of the *Pennsylvania Journal,* Thomas Bradford, while Isaac Collins, publisher of the *New-Jersey Gazette,* asked Trenton subscribers to forward their requests to his shop. A number of names appeared in the *Carlisle Gazette* in Pennsylvania, including George Kline and George Reynolds, printers of the *Gazette*; Ephraim Steel; James Ross, a "Professor of Languages"; Shippensburgh's William Rippey; and Chambersburg's James Riddle, a local attorney. And in Rhode Island, the *Providence Gazette* posted the information that Newport's Daniel Mason, merchants Brown & Benson of Providence, and the printer John Carter would be available to take subscriptions. The Charleston *Columbian Herald* listed the merchant Nathaniel Russell, in addition to printers Thomas Bowen, James Vandle, and S. Andrews as contacts alongside the Savannah mercantile firm of May & Hills, two men whom Gordon mentioned in his letter to Greene.[49]

A number of newspapers carried the advertisement for several weeks, which was a typical practice. Printers regularly took payment for several runs of the same advertisement and, once placed, the listing remained in the same fixed location on the page for weeks, even months, alongside other long-running ads. Gordon paid for multiple advertisements in five newspapers. His efforts did not go unnoticed by observers in nearby Boston. Writing to Jeremy Belknap, John Eliot sneered, "Gordon is in the zenith of subscription glory. He offers his proposals and then a printed receipt."[50] The ad ran weekly between mid-January and mid-February in Loudon's *New-York Packet,* while Isaac Collins published it twice—on 6 February and again on 13 March—in his *New-Jersey Gazette.* Likewise, the ad appeared twice in Kline and Reynolds's *Carlisle Gazette* and was published six times between 20 February and 10 April in Charleston's *Columbian Herald.* By far the largest paid advertising run, however, was in Bradford's *Pennsylvania Journal,* published on Wednesdays and Saturdays in Philadelphia. Between the end of January and mid-September, Gordon's proposal appeared a remarkable thirty-three times, a run that allowed Philadelphia readers ample time and opportunity to learn about the forthcoming *History.* Gordon's persistence in saturating the Philadelphia market eventually paid dividends.[51]

In encouraging his correspondents to subscribe to his *History,* Gordon also sought the patronage of influential military and political leaders. Writing to Samuel Osgood in January 1786, shortly after the publication of the subscription proposal, Gordon hoped for the "honour of your name among the subscribers to my History," insisting that such practice was necessary to publicize the production. "The printing of the work cannot be undertaken" without "*advancing* money," Gordon informed Osgood, tipping his hand that his own material circumstances were not "equal" to the task of financing the book without subscriptions. In asking—pleading, really—for a subscription from Osgood, Gordon requested that he stand up for the project. "Stand by me as a *patron,*" he implored Osgood, "and argue for me against all reasonings that may be made to the mode of subscribing." Despite this plea, Osgood declined to lend his name to Gordon's *History.* In his attempt to use Nathanael Greene as part of his network of subscription agents, Gordon leaned on Greene's sense of friendly obligation. "After such experience of your friendship," he wrote, "I cannot doubt of your countenance, in promoting and hastening subscriptions."[52] Like Osgood, however, Greene did not add his name to Gordon's subscription list.

"An Historian May Use the Impartial Pen There"

On 21 April 1786, the *Connecticut Gazette* reported that Gordon had boarded a ship, the *Neptune,* en route to London. Gordon's sudden departure from Boston was a newsworthy event given his sudden celebrity as the "historiographer" of the Revolution. News of Gordon's departure was also announced in Samuel Loudon's *New-York Packet* on 29 April.[53] Gordon's return to London was necessitated not by any kind of animosity between himself and his Roxbury congregation but by Gordon's belief that "an Historian may use the impartial pen there with less danger than here," as he wrote to Horatio Gates. Gordon eventually came to see the American Revolution, which he had championed for so many years, as having gone too far in its embrace of democracy. "The spirit of the Americans in continuing to abuse Britain, *etc.,* tho' peace has been established," he wrote to his friend John Temple in March 1786, "has reconciled me greatly to the thought of leaving the continent where I should have had no quiet in case of a future rupture, unless I would have gone with them in all their extravagances." He wished, he told Temple, to return as "a Briton" to his "native country" to finish out "his days there as a *peaceable subject.*" He persuaded Temple to ship all of his possessions, which consisted of "eight to ten boxes and cases" of furniture (including a number of pieces long held by his family), books, artworks, linens, and clothing, and "two or three small boxes with papers, sermons, etc.," which included all of his research and an early draft of the *History,* which he would publish two years later in London. Though this was already a lot to ask of Temple, Gordon requested in addition that his friend ship the goods without their "being subject to duties, as they were formerly British, and are not meant for sale, but my own private use."[54]

There was a loud public backlash against Gordon's decision to return to London. Many people saw Gordon's decision to publish a history of the American Revolution in London, after years of research and writing in the United States, as an insult to their growing sense of national pride. In February 1786, John Trumbull lashed out at Gordon in his Norwich *Packet.* "It is currently reported," he wrote, "that the History of the late War, by the Rev. Dr. Gordon, for which he has issued Proposals is to be printed in London—We hope the Doctor will give us an Opportunity to contradict this Report, as such a Proceeding must be a Disgrace to this County, or to the Rev. Author." John West Folsom of the *Independent Ledger* had a similar reaction, writing that "the eastern prints abound with squibs against Dr. Gordon, the historiographer of the Revolution of America, for taking his work to London, which they term an enemy's country, to be printed, when it might be done equally well here." Publishing the book in London, according to Folsom, slighted not only the newly formed American Republic but its emerging publishing trade as well. "Indeed it appears to be so generally resented in the eastern states," he wrote, "that the people shew no disposition of encouraging it."[55] Gordon's return to London, and the negative reaction to it, fed spiteful gossip. Writing to Jeremy Belknap in March 1786, John Eliot asked what Belknap thought of "poor Gordon's basting," concluding that the would-be historian "will not obtain subscribers." Eliot laid much of the blame for Gordon's abrupt departure on the Boston publishing trade and publishers' apparent demand for more money than Gordon could afford. "Yet how strange that *printers* should have so much influence in society," he wrote.[56]

Gordon's return to London, with an important yet potentially divisive text in his possession, worried Americans a great deal. Philadelphia's John Dunlap and David C. Claypoole, printers of the *Pennsylvania Packet*, published a letter from Halifax that expressed concern for Gordon's safety. While he thought that the publication of Gordon's *History* in London would be "sufficient ground for a vexatious prosecution," the author of the letter wondered how the book would be received in England at a time when publishing works critical of the British government was a dangerous risk for London's printers. The author of the letter speculated on rumors later confirmed by John Adams: that Gordon had tinkered with the text to make it acceptable to the English print market but also to avoid a possible sedition trial in politically charged London. "He must certainly either consider himself as being able to withstand such prosecution," the author wrote, "or, to avoid it, he must, as has been suspected, render it palatable to English-mens stomachs."[57] As fate would have it, Gordon would do just that.

Gordon arrived in London expecting to find a ready market for the *History*. What he discovered instead was a publishing trade reluctant to take on his book. Indeed, Gordon's landing in Great Britain caused as much a stir as his departure from Boston had. Even before the *History* went to press, it was reshaped by a London printer because it was a problematic project, for two important and interrelated reasons. First, in the printer's estimation, it was entirely too sympathetic to Americans. Second, the printer feared that some within both Parliament and the military might take offense at Gordon's characterization of them. Gordon's initial draft of the *History*, then, was as unprintable as it was unsellable. Gordon's printer had to worry about not only the financial risk but a political backlash. In an apparent panic, Gordon revised the entire work, changing both "the form and the stress" of his magnum opus.[58] He removed citations and, in many instances, conveyed the thoughts of his subjects as though they were his own words. He confessed as much to George Washington. "I apprehend it to be often necessary to introduce sentiments and information, while I suppressed the names of the writers from those letters they were taken, and at times inserted them as though they were originally my own," he wrote to Washington from Newington just outside London.[59] Gordon told James Bowdoin that he had made the changes because he feared being sued for libel: "I shall not be able to publish as soon as I intended; but shall make as much haste as good speed. Several on this side of the water have protection of the law against libels; and as they will be likely to suffer by the truth, I must give it in that artful guarded way that even the fangs of law cannot fasten upon me, or they may hoist me into the pillory which is a post I am not fond of occupying, besides plundering me of all the profits I wish to gain from the History."[60]

At the urging of his nervous London publisher, Gordon reshaped the manuscript. The answer to why he did so lies, in part, in the often unstable place of the publishing trade in early modern English society. By the time Gordon arrived in London, there was a long-standing and tenuous relationship between the press and the British government. Far from acting as a fourth estate, the press in Britain—despite the lapse of the Licensing Act in 1695, which led to the proliferation of newspapers—often operated in a burdensome regulatory climate and was subject to widespread political censorship of what was printed, and when.[61] London newspapers could print certain aspects of official parliamentary business, such as the king's speeches and legislation adopted at the conclusion of a session, without fear of reprisal. Scholars have shown that in order to criticize, or even remark upon, the actions of Parliament, printers in Walpole's Britain resorted to criticizing policy indirectly, through such cryptic tactics as short verses and epigrams.[62] To do otherwise risked prosecution for seditious libel. Printers and publishers in London operated cautiously, seemingly averse to risky projects, for fear that they could endanger not only their careers but the livelihood of their families. Britain's seditious libel law was extremely far reaching, both in how it defined sedition and in who could be brought to trial. If men in power deemed printed material—whether a newspaper, pamphlet, or book—either dangerous or slanderous, everyone involved in the production of that text could face prosecution, from the author, to the printer, to the network of shopkeepers that stocked and sold the item.[63]

A number of high-profile cases, ranging from Richard Francklin's 1731 trial to the 1752 prosecution of William Owen, would have been known to British citizens in colonial America, but none more so than that of John Wilkes. North American colonists had embraced the radicalism of Wilkes, whose forty-fifth issue of the *North Briton* incurred the wrath of Lord Halifax in 1763; Halifax had everyone involved in the publication of the paper arrested on the charge of seditious libel.[64] As historians have shown, "Wilkes and Liberty" became something of a cause célèbre and a rallying cry in revolutionary America.[65] Indeed, shortly after Gordon's return to England, the publisher John Stockdale was brought before the House of Commons on a seditious libel charge after he printed a book critical of Parliament's impeachment of Warren Hastings.[66] Commentators observing Gordon's return to London speculated openly about whether the former Roxbury minister, along with any printer who took on the project, would face political reprisals. Gordon, it seems, had made a gross mis-calculation in thinking that London presented the best opportunity to publish his book.

Gordon's revisions to the *History* did not go unnoticed. While serving as the American minister to Great Britain, John Adams was able to get his hands on Gordon's original manuscript. After receiving his personal copy—he had been a subscriber to the London edition—Adams tore into the revised and toned-down version of the *History*. In his marginalia, Adams sympathized with the author's plight and acknowledged, privately, at least, that the published edition differed greatly from what he had seen earlier.

> The Historian had a brother in Law, Field the Printer in London, who was to print the Work. . . . I know that the Brother Field would not print the original Manuscript until it was inspected and corrected by some Gentle-men of Letters in London. . . . These Judges were of opinion the Book would not succeed, i.e., would not sell, if the Style was not softened, and if the Praises of Americans were not moderated. All this was done. And if Gor-don's original Manuscript should be preserved, all this in substance will appear. For I had it in substance from Dr. Gordon's own Mouth. I had indeed opportunity of comparing the original Manuscript in several Sheets with the Print and I know the variation to be very great. The form of Letters too was the effect of the Booksellers advice.[67]

Adams remained perplexed by Gordon's excessive editing long after the book's publication. In an 1813 letter to Elbridge Gerry, he pointed out that Gordon had been told by his friends and advisors that the *History* was too "bold" and that Gordon's over-the-top style "would damn the work" in London's elite reading circles. Adams also blithely reminisced that the *History*, at least as Gordon ini-tially intended it, was "so favorable to America" and "so disgraceful to Britons that neither would be borne." Adams assumed that Gordon had revised the book in "style and spirit" so as to accommodate "British taste and feelings."[68] One of Gordon's Boston friends confirmed John Adams's hunch; the original "was not suited to" English readers "and consequently would *never sell*." Apparently, the *History* was taken out of Gordon's hands and given to a hack writer in London, who "*modelled* and made [it] agreeable to English readers."[69]

American readers became increasingly fascinated by the drama surround-ing Gordon's editing of the *History*. Indeed, the printer of the *Massachusetts Centinel*, Benjamin Russell, published the rumors that Gordon had heavily revised the book. "It is a fact, that Dr. Gordon has met with so many crosses in England, on account of his 'History,' as to determine him to give over all endeav-ors to accomplish the object of his voyage," he wrote. Russell reported that a high-ranking British official had "rebuffed him license for his publication, on account of its partiality to the Americans."[70] This assertion was reprinted two weeks later in Philadelphia; after three weeks, news of Gordon's troubles had arrived in South Carolina; the gossip probably gave many Philadelphia and Charleston subscribers pause.[71] In contrast to the original report, however, "a correspondent" from London wrote to the *Massachusetts Centinel,* asserting that it was "*not* a fact that 'Dr. Gordon has met with so many crosses.'" The correspondent maintained that letters from Gordon himself, just received in Boston, "speak very differently," and that "subscription papers are yet open" in London, and "those persons who wish to add their names to the list of subscribers, may be satisfied that they will receive their books as soon as they can reasonably expect, considering the length of the work."[72] This corrective to the reports of Gordon's censorship, however, failed to extend beyond the Boston papers.

Despite the national circulation of his subscription proposals, Gordon's decision to return to London significantly reduced the number of American subscribers. In fact, to examine the London subscription list is to see a missed opportunity (table 2.1). An overwhelming majority of the subscribers—nearly 80 percent—were in fact Britons. Additionally, a handful of subscribers resided in France, Canada, the Caribbean, and the Netherlands. American subscribers made up less than 20 percent of the overall number, despite the book's being a text about the American War of Independence.

The London subscription list lacked any kind of regional diversity. Given that Gordon spent most of his career as a minister in Roxbury, Massachusetts, it is little surprise that most of the American subscribers to the London edition called New England home (table 2.2). The eighty-nine New England subscribers hailed from fourteen towns and villages, ranging from Andover, Salem, Boston,

TABLE 2.1 Distribution of William Gordon's *History* (London Edition), 1788

Region	Subscribers (N)	Subscribers (%)
Great Britain	506	78.2
United States	125	19.3
Scotland	12	1.8
France	1	0.1
Canada	1	0.1
Jamaica	1	0.1
Netherlands	1	0.1
TOTALS	647	99.7

SOURCE: Gordon, *History of the Rise, Progress, and Establishment, of the Independence of the United States* (1788), vol. 1.

TABLE 2.2 Distribution of William Gordon's *History* (London Edition), 1788, by American Region

Region	Subscribers (N)	Subscribers (%)
New England	89	71.2
Mid-Atlantic	4	2.2
South	32	25.6
TOTAL	125	99

SOURCE: Gordon, *History of the Rise, Progress, and Establishment, of the Independence of the United States* (1788), vol. 1.

Marblehead, and Middleburgh in Massachusetts to Providence and Warwick, just south in Rhode Island. A handful of his Roxbury residents had their names listed in the London edition, including three attorneys—Benjamin Clarke, Increase Sumner, and D. S. Greenbough—and a fellow minister, Eliphalet Porter. Thirteen subscribers hailed from Boston, among them a number of attorneys and two U.S. congressmen—Jonathan Jackson and former delegate to the Continental Congress James Lovell. In Providence, John Jenckes and Jabez Bowen each purchased a set of the *History*, while Warwick's Caleb Greene also appeared on the list.

Very few subscribers to the London edition listed their occupation in the text. The professions given in the London edition, though, paint a singular social and gendered portrait of the reader of Gordon's *History*—an elite, wealthy, professional man. In both the United States and the British Empire, attorneys, politicians, and ministers dominated the London subscription rolls. In Great Britain, for example, ninety-one lawyers, eighty-two ministers, and eight doctors subscribed, as did three members of Parliament (Watkins Lewes, William Middleton, and Clement Taylor), the recorder of London, Sergeant Adair, and the rector of Langar, Edward Gregory. During their time in London as American diplomats, John Adams and Thomas Jefferson subscribed to the text. A similar readership existed in the United States (table 2.3). Elbridge Gerry of Marblehead, Massachusetts, and John Bayard of Philadelphia—both members of Congress—could be counted as subscribers alongside Benjamin Lincoln, the lieutenant governor of Massachusetts, and George Washington.

Gordon and his *History* had staunch defenders. Isaiah Thomas and Francis Childs, printers of the *Massachusetts Spy* and the New York *Daily Advertiser*, respectively, encouraged readers to take a sympathetic, even pragmatic, view of Gordon's decision to return to London to publish the book. Thomas published a critical defense, a piece Childs reprinted, word for word, in the *Daily Advertiser* nine days later. Thomas derided those who had "squibbed, roasted, and basted

TABLE 2.3 Occupations of Subscribers to William Gordon's *History* (London Edition), 1788

Occupation	Subscribers (N)	Subscribers (%)	British Empire[a] (N)	British Empire[a] (%)	United States (N)	United States (%)
Army officer	4	1.6	1	0.4	3	1.2
Attorney[b]	119	48.5	91	37.1	28	11.4
Doctor	9	3.6	8	3.2	1	0.4
Member of Congress	6	2.4	0	0	6	2.4
Member of Parliament	3	1.2	3	1.2	0	0
Minister	97	39.5	82	33.4	15	6.1
Occupations with one subscriber[c]	7	2.8	5	2.0	2	0.8
TOTALS	245	99.6	190	77.3	55	22.3
		N=245				
Occupation Missing		N=402				

SOURCE: Gordon, *History of the Rise, Progress, and Establishment, of the Independence of the United States* (1788), vol. 1.
[a] British Empire here includes Scotland, Canada, and Jamaica.
[b] Includes one subscriber who resided in Halifax, Canada, and another in Jamaica. This category also includes seven subscribers from Glasgow, Scotland.
[c] Occupations with one listing: ambassador, British consul, diplomat, dowager, the lieutenant governor of Massachusetts, the recorder of London, and the rector of Langar in Nottinghamshire, Great Britain.

[Gordon] on all sides"; much of the abuse, in his opinion, was "propagated without any foundation in truth." He did concede that the proposal, which had been circulating in the nation's newspapers since early January 1786, contained "a deception by no means to be justified," namely, that Gordon had been less than forthright about his publishing plans when asking for subscription money. In Thomas's estimation, Gordon should have "informed the public, in his proposals for printing his work, that he intended to have it printed in England or Scotland," thus allowing his potential subscribers a choice. Yet despite this critique, Thomas could not fault Gordon for trying to make money. "In short, it is supposed the doctor intends, if possible, to make a fortune by this publication," he wrote, "and who can blame him for his intention?" Thomas defended this position by reiterating that Gordon's book defended the American War of Independence. "It is well known that in many instances he has shewn himself to be a most furious and flaming whig, and very inveterate against his countrymen the Britons," he wrote. In Thomas's view, it was "best to let the doctor revisit his native country in peace," and those who "chose to send their money with him" by subscribing to the *History* "certainly have a right so to do; the risk is theirs."[73]

Despite comparatively few American subscribers, New York's elite did eventually read Gordon's *History*. Patrons of the New York Society Library actively checked out the book in the years following its initial publication in London, and it proved to be one of the most popular titles in the library's stacks in the late 1780s and early 1790s.[74] Between late July 1789 and early May 1792, Gordon's *History* was checked out nearly 150 times. Only twenty-three titles of the more than three thousand listed in the 1789 catalogue had a greater circulation in the library's earliest surviving charging ledgers. In fact, members checked out Gordon's history of the American Revolution more than David Ramsay's two histories *combined*.[75] Given the library's status as an elite cultural institution, borrowers of Gordon's *History* tended to be men and women of some means (table 2.4). Most of those who read Gordon's *History* were either merchants or professionals, including ten doctors, nine lawyers, six auctioneers, four dentists, and one auditor. Two artisans checked out the text, including a Federalist mason named James Robinson who, incidentally, did the masonry on New York's Federal Hall.[76]

Although the readership of Gordon's *History* consisted predominantly of men of standing, women patrons did borrow the text. In 1791, as March drew to a close, Henrietta Maria Colden checked out the first volume. Curiously, she returned it the next day, either having finished reading it or, possibly, out of dissatisfaction with its tone and content. She did not check out any of the remaining volumes.[77] Catharine Bradford borrowed three of the four volumes and, unlike Colden, spent considerable time reading each one. She held on to the first volume for nine days in December 1791, and when she returned it on 14 December she checked out the second volume, reading it intermittently for the next two weeks.[78]

TABLE 2.4 Occupations of Patrons Checking out William Gordon's *History* from the New York Society Library, 1789–1792

Occupational Category	Patrons (N)	Patrons (%)
Merchant	25	42.3
Professional	17	28.8
Politics	4	6.7
Artisan	2	3.3
Military	1	1.7
Occupation Unknown	10	16.9
TOTAL	59	99.7

SOURCES: First Charging Ledger, 1789–1792, Special Collections, NYSL; M'Comb and Tiebout, *New York Directory* (1789); Hodge, Allen, and Campbell, *New-York Directory* (1790); Duncan, *New-York Directory* (1791, 1792).

"Most of the Book-Sellers and Printers on the Continent"

Early in 1789, three New York printers—Robert Hodge, Thomas Allen, and Samuel Campbell, in partnership—announced their intention to publish, by subscription, an American edition of William Gordon's *History*, complete with a "list of the names of the subscribers." In their proposal, which first appeared in New York in February 1789, the partners placed their pirated edition of the book alongside the supposedly superior London publication, touting the abilities of New York's printers to publish a text equal to any that could be produced in Europe, and at a fraction of the cost. Hodge, Allen, and Campbell solicited "PROPOSALS, for printing by subscription, in three large octavo volumes," they wrote in the advertisement, "neatly printed on new types and fine paper, handsomely bound and lettered," and priced at "only *thirty shillings*." They also claimed that their edition was "less than one half of the price" of the London edition. In outlining the terms of the subscription, in which they pointed out that presswork on the text had already begun, the partners further touted the abilities of the city's printers and bookbinders. "Each volume will contain about 500 pages," they wrote, "and shall, in point of execution, be little inferior to the British edition." Hodge, Allen, and Campbell also reminded potential subscribers of Gordon's sympathy to the American cause and his many years of travel and research as reason enough to subscribe to their edition. His residence in the United States during the war, along with his "access to the papers of Congress" and his extensive correspondence with Washington "and most of the principal officers in the American and British Armies," proved "the authenticity and impartiality of his information."[79]

As with Gordon's advertising campaign of the previous year, the ligaments of a national network of subscription agents emerged more clearly the further Hodge, Allen, and Campbell's proposal traveled. In one of their initial advertisements, published in the *Federal Gazette and Philadelphia Evening Post,* Hodge, Allen, and Campbell pointed out that subscriptions would be taken not only in their individual New York print shops but also "by the other booksellers in the state of New-York," by "J. Cruckshank, T. Dobson, W. Young, and W. Spotswood" in Philadelphia and, perhaps most significantly, by "the other book-sellers and printers on the continent."[80] This phrase—"the other book-sellers and printers on the continent"—circulated in the nation's newspapers for five months, between February and June, and evoked not only the vastness of the American landscape but also the interconnectedness of the publishing trade. Indeed, the use of this phrase can be interpreted as an echo of the similarly nationalistic language in the proposal itself. In Elizabethtown, New Jersey, where the advertisement ran from early March to May 1789, Shepard Kollock made known his intentions to take any and all subscribers to the New York edition. Interested readers could pay for the text by visiting Benjamin Larkin's bookshop at "Shakespear's Head, no. 46, Cornhill" in Boston, while Nathaniel Patten, Barzillai Hudson, and George Goodwin took subscriptions in Hartford, Connecticut. In Savannah, Georgia, subscriptions were "taken at the Printing Office" of James Johnston, who published the *Georgia Gazette*. In Norfolk, Virginia, the proposal could "be seen at the Printing Office (of J. & A. M'Lean, near the Town-Hall)," and in Poughkeepsie, the printer of the *Country Journal* advertised in mid-June—five months after the initial appearance of the proposal—that he would be taking subscriptions for the New York edition of the *History*.[81]

Hodge, Allen, and Campbell had national ambitions in addition to publishing Gordon's *History*. In a signed broadside dated 10 January 1789, the partners, along with fellow New York printers Hugh Gaine and William Ross, called upon the "*Booksellers* and *Printers* of the *United States of* AMERICA" to unite in a common cause to print, publish, and disseminate "a correct Edition of the common *School Bible*." This ambitious proposal was born, they wrote, out of several meetings of allied tradesmen where "the Importance of promoting the Extension of Literature, and particularly those Books which are the real Use to Society at large," was discussed at length. The group decided to act because of the trade's continued reliance on London publishers for books commonly used in everyday life; in their estimation, this undermined the growth of the American publishing trade. "It must be a Matter of sincere Regret to every Well-wisher to *American* Manufactures, that now being an independent Nation, we must have Recourse to another Country for that very Book (viz. the HOLY BIBLE) the printing and publishing of which," they wrote, "dignifies every Christian Country where it is manufactured." The solution was to petition Congress for financial support to produce a common text of the Bible that could be shared among printers and booksellers. And while this proposal eventually backfired—a host of publishers, among them Philadelphia's Mathew Carey, Worcester's Isaiah Thomas, and even Gaine, printed and sold their own Bibles for local and regional markets— the national print market imagined by Hodge, Allen, and Campbell in the January 1789 Bible proposal suggested that while printing was very much local in practice, its practitioners had begun to think nationally.[82]

New York printers had worked to build a national readership for subscription books prior to the ambitious plans of Hodge, Allen, and Campbell. In 1774, for instance, James Rivington aggressively sought subscribers to his edition of John Hawkesworth's *New Voyage, Round the World*. His promotion of the text was manifested in a subscription list that included more than six hundred names. And while a great many called New York, New Jersey, and Philadelphia home—228, to be precise—about half of the people on the list resided in locations farther afield. For example, a number of Rivington's subscribers resided in the Caribbean. Rivington secured 168 from Kingston and Savanna-La-Mar, Jamaica, thirty-three from Antigua, eighteen from Dominica, and five from Pensacola, Florida. In addition, fifty-seven subscriptions from New Bern, North Carolina, arrived in Rivington's New York office. Rivington also received subscriptions from Massachusetts, Connecticut, and Quebec.[83]

The remaking of the London edition, in which Hodge, Allen, and Campbell reduced the text from four volumes to three, effectively Americanized Gordon's *History*.[84] As noted earlier, the *History* had been entirely researched and largely composed in the United States during and immediately after the War of Independence. The text was then essentially rewritten, according to observers who saw the earliest manuscript, to suit the British print market, disregarding any good will Gordon had established with American readers and further damaging his reputation with the nation's publishers. Probably recognizing the potential for an American edition, Hodge, Allen, and Campbell seized the opportunity to reshape the *History* yet again, ignoring entirely the animosity toward Gordon as turncoat. In this instance, rather than alter the text in any significant way, they redesigned its *material* form, and in the process created an edition distinct from that produced in London a year earlier.

In mid-May 1789, the New York printer Francis Childs announced in his *Daily Advertiser* that the first volume of Gordon's *History* had been published by Hodge, Allen, and Campbell. In addition to publicizing the availability of the first volume, the advertisement in Childs's paper served as a final stage of the national project imagined by the New York partnership. The advertisement requested that agents "who have been entrusted with proposals will please to be expeditious in sending on their lists of subscribers," so that the names "may be inserted in the last volume."[85] By the end of August, the project was complete, and Hodge, Allen, and Campbell used the back page of the *Daily Advertiser* to announce that all three volumes would be shipped to subscribers. Interestingly, like the dozens of advertisements that circulated throughout the countryside in 1789, the trio's ad announced that the text would be available "at their respective Book-Stores in New-York" as well as at the shops of "most of the Book-sellers and Printers on the continent."[86]

After announcing plans for their edition of the *History*, Hodge, Allen, and Campbell engaged in a heartfelt defense of Gordon's text. "Various have been the opinions respecting this history of the late Warfare," they wrote, acknowledging the many criticisms of the *History*. The publishers condemned the disparaging remarks by "self-interested" men and those who disliked Gordon's "plain and unornamented style." In fact, the simplicity and straightforwardness of Gordon's *History* was, they argued, a reason to celebrate the text. "The circumstances and events are faithfully, plainly, and impartially related," they wrote, and "Dr. Gordon's simplicity in diction, his easy narration of facts, and the agreeable manner by which he places his auditor as a spectator" made the *History* "the most authentic and genuine History of the Revolution that has yet been published either in Europe or America."[87] By materially remaking the book, the partners could now place the New York edition alongside the London edition and declare unequivocally that their edition—which retained the heavily edited London text, by the way—was superior. In order to better state their case, Hodge, Allen, and Campbell quoted at length from a positive review published in a London journal.

> The accounts here given of American affairs, are so different in several respects from what have been the conception of many on each side of the Atlantic, that it was necessary to insert a variety of letters, papers, and anecdotes, to authenticate the narrative. The publication of these, it is presumed, will obtain credit for such parts as could not with propriety be supported by the introduction of similar proofs. The excellencies and the defects of this work are of a sort directly opposite to those which distinguish the historical productions of the present times. In these volumes, the reader will find none of the ornaments of style, or artifices of composition; no elaborate delineations of character, and no parade of moral or political philosophy. But instead of these ambitious and unnecessary decorations, he will meet with an impartiality truly praise worthy, and an extent as well as accuracy of information highly entertaining and instructive. The events are so circumstantially and plainly related, without any reflections upon them, either common-place, or far fetched; and the reader is left (as he ought to be left) to form his own judgment of the different men and measures, unassisted, or rather undeluded, by the opinions and prejudices of the writer. In the composition of this work, he seems to have imitated rather the simplicity and winning plainness of the Greeks, than the embellished magnificence of the Romans; or the sententious brilliancy of the modern historians. Whether he has acted wisely, in thus departing from the fashions of his co-temporaries, is not for us to determine, but he has at least the authority of Hobbes, and the practice of Thucydides, to justify him.[88]

The advertising campaign for the New York edition was successful in attracting a large, diverse list of subscribers. Overall, Hodge, Allen, and Campbell secured better than one thousand subscribers in 173 cities, towns, villages, and townships in fifteen states and the western territories, a very respectable, even outstanding, effort for the period (table 2.5). Comparatively speaking, the pirated New York edition of Gordon's *History* was an overwhelming success. The number of book subscribers varied widely after the American Revolution, with some books having as few as ninety-two subscribers. Scholars have esti-

TABLE 2.5 Distribution of William Gordon's *History* (New York Edition), 1789

Region	Subscribers (N)	Subscribers (%)
Mid-Atlantic	612	54.4
South	403	35.8
New England	101	8.9
Western Territories	2	0.1
Caribbean	1	0
Canada	1	0
Great Britain	1	0
Not listed	3	0.2
TOTAL	1,124	99.4

SOURCE: Gordon, *History of the Rise, Progress, and Establishment, of the Independence of the United States* (1789), list of subscribers, 3:3–28.

mated that, on average, printers could count on approximately 370 subscribers, depending on the project. Printers often failed to secure subscribers for even the best-known authors. For example, a 1797 edition of Rousseau's *Social Contract* had only two hundred subscribers, while Montesquieu's *Spirit of the Laws* never went to press because it did not generate enough interest to cover the cost of production. Novels published by subscription met with similar lack of interest. A 1795 edition of Susanna Rowson's *Trials of the Human Heart* had fewer than 150 subscribers, while Samuel Relf's *Infidelity, or The Victims of Sentiment,* published in the same year, was also a flop, with 146 named subscribers. There were some successful subscription books, as evidenced by the 1813 edition of Daniel Bryan's *The Mountain Muse: Comprising the Adventures of Daniel Boone,* which was published with a list of 1,350 subscribers drawn from ten states.[89]

The subscription list published in the pirated New York edition of Gordon's *History* had a remarkable geographical range. A handful of subscriptions arrived from the Caribbean, Canada, and Great Britain. More than half of the subscribers resided in the mid-Atlantic region, no doubt owing to the aggressive marketing campaign by Philadelphia and New York printers. A smaller yet still significant number called New England home. Southern subscriptions accounted for more than a third of the overall number. Once completed, the New York edition was distributed to forty-one locations in Georgia, Maryland, North and South Carolina, and Virginia. A little fewer than half of these subscribers called Charleston, South Carolina, home, where three years before, the printers of the *Columbian Herald* campaigned aggressively for what became the London edition. It is possible that once word reached South Carolinians that a domestic edition of the text was in the works, subscribers walked into the *Herald*'s shop seeking to add their name to the list. The New York edition even reached subscribers in the sparsely settled western territories, in this case William Carey of Marietta in the Ohio territory and John Holden in Kentucky. In a way, then, the New York edition of Gordon's *History*—an earnest attempt to help define the nation's identity by using the recent past—was also a nod to future settlement and the move to expand west.

Hodge, Allen, and Campbell published Gordon's *History* for a national market that extended beyond the early Republic's largest cities (table 2.6). A handful of subscribers resided in towns with populations between twenty-five hundred and five thousand, including Albany and Hudson, New York, Hartford and New Haven, Connecticut, Alexandria and Richmond, Virginia, and Richmond, North Carolina. What is remarkable about the dissemination of the New York edition is that it can be traced to small villages and counties across the early national landscape. And while a great many subscribers did indeed reside in the two largest cities, with populations that exceeded twenty-five thousand—New York and Philadelphia—a significant percentage resided in more than 160 small towns, villages, and counties with populations below twenty-five hundred. The largest concentration of areas under twenty-five hundred fell in the mid-Atlantic region. In New York, for example, Gordon's *History* reached Palatine Township, Orange County, Shelter Island, Dutchess County, Germantown, Schenectady, Troy, Mount Pleasant, Hempstead Harbor, Lansingburgh, Goshen, and Poughkeepsie, to name only a few. In New Jersey, copies ended up in Trenton, Elizabethtown, Newark, Hackensack, South Amboy, Morristown, Cumberland, Essex, and Somerset counties, Hope, Millstone, and Acquackanonk. Pennsylvania subscribers hailed from Northumberland County, Montgomery, Haddonfield, Springfield, Nazareth, and Lancaster. Only two subscribers lived in

TABLE 2.6 Distribution of William Gordon's *History* (New York Edition), 1789, by American Region and Population

Population Range	Subscribers (N)	Subscribers (%)	Towns/ Cities (N)	Towns/ Cities (%)	New England (N)	New England (%)	Mid-Atlantic (N)	Mid-Atlantic (%)	South (N)	South (%)	West (N)	West (%)
25,000–35,000	345	33	2	1.1	0	0	2	1.1	0	0	0	0
10,000–24,999	207	19.8	2	1.1	1	0.5	0	0	1	0.5	0	0
5,000–9,999	1	0	1	0.5	1	0.5	0	0	0	0	0	0
2,500–4,999	75	7.1	6	2.4	2	1.1	2	1.1	2	1.1	0	0
Below 2,500	417	39.9	162	93.6	49	28.3	74	42.7	38	21.9	1	1.1
TOTALS	1,045	99.8	173	98.7	53	30.4	78	44.9	41	23.5	1	1.1

SOURCES: Gordon, *History of the Rise, Progress, and Establishment, of the Independence of the United States* (1789), list of subscribers, 3:3–28; U.S. Bureau of the Census, "Population of Urban Places" (1790), https://www.census.gov/population/www/documentation/twps0027/tab02.txt.

Delaware—Joshua Fisher, an attorney from Dover, and Thomas Ricket, a Kent County artisan. Gordon's *History* also reached thirty-eight small towns in the South, including Chestertown and Somerset County in Maryland; Caroline and Lunenbergh counties in Virginia; Georgetown, Dorchester, and Santee in South Carolina; and Savannah, Georgia. In North Carolina, subscriptions reached twenty-eight small towns, including Edenton, Chowan, Franklin, Bertie, Williamsborough, Newbern, Currituck, Granville, Anson, Lumberton, Wilkes, Chatham, and Lincoln.[90]

As with similar projects, merchants and professionals dominated the subscription rolls (table 2.7). Of the professionals, attorneys accounted for 153 sets of the text, along with forty-three military officers, nineteen ministers, seventeen doctors, seven officers of the peace, and four teachers. Several politicians subscribed, including George Clinton, the governor of New York; Georgia senator Joseph Clay; Simeon DeWitt, the surveyor general; the treasury commissioner, John Edwards; John Hobart, a justice of the New York Supreme Court; U.S. Postmaster General Ebenezer Hazard; Richard Henry Lee, a Virginia senator; Thomas Mifflin, the president of the Commonwealth of Pennsylvania; the chief justice of the Pennsylvania Supreme Court, Thomas McKean; the congressional sergeant at arms, Joseph Wheaton; and the French consul, J. Hector St. John de Crèvecœur. In addition to politicians, military officers, ministers, peace officers, attorneys, and teachers, there was a remarkable mix of professions on the subscription list. Among these, for example, was the Charleston auctioneer Joseph Gaultier; Joseph Jadwin, a New York beef and pork inspector; two city treasurers; the president of the College of Rhode Island (renamed Brown University in 1804); a New York customs officer; three southern judges (Samuel Ashe of North

TABLE 2.7 Occupations of Subscribers to William Gordon's *History* (New York Edition), 1789

Occupation	Subscribers (N)	(%)	Towns (N)	New England (N)	(%)	Mid-Atlantic (N)	(%)	South (N)	(%)	Other (N)	(%)
Artisan	127	19.5	14	0	0	87	13.3	40	6.1	0	0
Merchant	133	20.4	22	10	1.5	69	10.5	53	8.1	1	0.1
Unskilled	2	0.3	2	0	0	1	0.1	1	0.1	0	0
Planter	18	2.7	1	0	0	0	0	18	2.7	0	0
Professional	322	49.4	91	33	5.0	156	23.9	132	20.2	1	0.1
Shopkeeper	49	7.5	10	5	0.7	32	4.9	12	1.8	0	0
TOTAL	651	99.8	—	48	7.2	345	52.7	256	39	2	0.2
Occupation Missing	470										

SOURCE: Gordon, *History of the Rise, Progress, and Establishment, of the Independence of the United States* (1789), list of subscribers, 3:3–28.

Carolina, William Gibson of Savannah, and John Faucheraud Grimké of South Carolina); the civil engineer Pierre L'Enfant; a major in the Army Corps of Engineers; a notary public; and a South Carolinian surveyor named Joseph Parsell.[91]

Readership of the New York edition was not limited to the wealthy and the elite. While merchants and professionals made up a large segment of the subscription list, a significant percentage of the subscribers were either artisans, unskilled workers, or shopkeepers. Nearly 30 percent of subscribers worked in some way with their hands or ran a small shop. Five of the shopkeepers, all booksellers, lived in New England—Isaac Beers and Abel Morse in New Haven, Nathaniel Patten in Hartford, Isaiah Thomas in Worcester, and Benjamin Larkin in Boston—while forty-four resided in either the mid-Atlantic or the South. Not surprisingly, most of the mid-Atlantic shopkeepers, among them grocers, tobacconists, booksellers, innkeepers, and an apothecary, lived in either New York or Philadelphia. All twelve southern shopkeepers lived in Charleston, including the booksellers and stationers John Campbell and James Muirhead, the tavern keeper Edward McCredy, and nine grocers.[92]

Artisans made up 20 percent of the overall subscription list. Men from some fifty different trades appeared on the subscription list, from fourteen cities, towns, and counties in seven states across the mid-Atlantic and the South (table 2.8). Of the trades on the list, tanners and printers were most heavily represented, with eleven and ten, respectively. Interestingly, nine of the eleven tanners resided in Manhattan—the other two resided in Orange County, New York, and South Carolina. It is perhaps not surprising that several printers subscribed to the New York edition of Gordon's *History*. Six mid-Atlantic printers appeared on the list: Philadelphians Andrew Brown, Francis Bailey, and Alexander Bilsland; the Albany printer Charles R. Webster; Goshen, New York's David Mandeville; and Shepard Kollock from Elizabethtown, New Jersey. Additionally, four southern printers added their names to the list: T. B. Bowen and Patrick Burton from Charleston, and two North Carolina printers by the names of Hodge and Wills. Tanners and printers were not the only occupations with more than one subscriber, however. Seven carpenters and seven painters subscribed to the *History*, along with six tailors, six cabinetmakers, five shipwrights, and four each of bakers, blacksmiths, coopers, and upholsterers. The subscription list included a Charleston, South Carolina, gardener and a Goshen, New York, farmer.

Perhaps overwhelmed by the number of subscriptions, Hodge, Allen, and Campbell took a number of shortcuts in producing their edition. A copy owned by a subscriber named Luke Bernus, from Watertown, Massachusetts, tells the story of an inconsistent publishing venture. The advertisement indicated that the partners planned to distribute the *History* serially, promising to ship the first ninety-six pages of the first volume to the subscribers. Given that more than a

TABLE 2.8 Occupations of Artisan Subscribers to William Gordon's *History* (New York Edition), 1789

Occupation	Subscribers (N)	Towns (N)	Mid-Atlantic (N)	South (N)
Baker	4	2	1	3
Blacksmith	4	3	3	1
Bookbinder	2	2	2	0
Brewer	2	1	2	0
Bricklayer	2	2	1	1
Brush maker	2	1	2	0
Cabinetmaker	6	5	5	1
Carpenter	7	5	5	2
Cooper	4	1	0	4
Currier	2	1	2	0
Engraver	3	2	2	1
Hatter	2	2	1	1
Joiner	2	2	2	0
Leather dresser	2	2	2	0
Limner	2	2	2	0
Mason	2	2	2	0
Painter	7	3	3	4
Printer	10	5	6	4
Saddler	3	3	2	1
Shipwright	5	3	4	1
Shoemaker	3	3	2	1
Smith	2	2	1	1
Stone cutter	2	2	2	0
Tailor	6	2	1	5
Tanner	11	3	10	1
Upholsterer	4	4	3	1
Wheelwright	3	2	3	0
Occupations with one subscriber[a]	23	5	16	7
TOTALS	127	—	87	40

SOURCE: Gordon, *History of the Rise, Progress, and Establishment, of the Independence of the United States* (1789), list of subscribers, 3:3–28.

[a] Occupations with only one subscription: bootmaker, coach maker, coach painter, distiller, engine maker, goldsmith, gun maker, hairdresser, house carpenter, jeweler, mariner, miller, paper maker, parchment manufacturer, pump maker, rope maker, ship chandler, silversmith, stoneware manufacturer, tin plate worker, turner, watchmaker, whitesmith.

thousand people from all corners of the nation wanted to own Gordon's *History*, this serialization plan proved unworkable. The Bernus copy, for example, does not appear to have been issued serially; the markings made by a binder that would have indicated a serial production are absent from the spine of the book, an indication that Hodge, Allen, and Campbell fell short of fulfilling the promises made in their sweeping advertising campaign. The materiality of the New York edition, when compared against the distribution data, suggests that the partners became victims of their own success. It is likely, then, that Bernus—and doubtless many subscribers like him—received either one volume at a time or all three volumes at once. Hodge, Allen, and Campbell probably used this tactic as a way to drum up greater national interest.[93]

An expensive purchase like this was no trifling matter, and so it is reasonable to suggest that those who subscribed to Gordon's *History* intended that it would be read by everyone in the household. That said, a handful of women did subscribe to the *History* under their own names. Hannah Laboyteaux of New York, Mary Stockton of Elizabethtown, New Jersey, and Judith Barnes of Bristol, Connecticut, all purchased a subscription. Elizabeth Geyer of Charleston, South Carolina, was the only woman in the South to subscribe.[94] Laboyteaux was a widow and by no means from a prominent family. She had lived in New York with her husband, John, a tailor, until the British took over the city during the War of Independence, at which time they apparently fled to Philadelphia. In 1764, John Laboyteaux announced that he had relocated his tailoring shop to a location "between the Fly-Market and the New Dutch-Church, next door to Mr. *William Keen,* confectionary." This new location evidently allowed John and Hannah to expand their shop to offer a "small but neat Assortment of Clothes," including "Flannels, Buckrams, glaz'd Linens, black Serge Denim, 4 Thread Black Breeches Patterns, and a large Assortment of Mohair Edgings," in addition to space enough for "Private Lodging."[95] Hannah and John's new shop became something of a mixed economic space, as their spare room was occupied by Robert Woffendale, a "Surgeon Dentist, lately arrived from London."[96] In November 1767, John and Hannah relocated again, this time to Beekman's Slip, where they continued to offer tailoring services, clothing for sale, and what they described as "Genteel Lodgings," with a "large commodious Cellar," both available to rent.[97] John and Hannah remained in New York for at least a decade; a 1779 advertisement in the *Pennsylvania Packet* for an assortment of calicoes and clothes places them in Philadelphia, where they remained until John's death in 1780.[98] After John passed away, Hannah returned to New York, where in early 1784 she began the arduous task of tracking down her husband's debtors. "All persons indebted to the estate of JOHN LABOYTEAUX, late of this city, deceased, are, for the LAST TIME, requested to make payment before the first day of March next, to the subscriber," said a terse advertisement Hannah placed in the *Independent Gazette.*[99]

While it is impossible to pinpoint the exact motivation that led someone like Hannah Laboyteaux not only buy to Gordon's *History* but to lend her name to the subscription list, it is nevertheless compelling to imagine her wanting to own the text as a way to revisit and add a narrative to memories of days long since passed. The New York edition of Gordon's *History* and its large subscription list, then, acted as a public monument to the nation's collective memory of the War of Independence, still very fresh in the mind of someone like Hannah, who endured great hardship during and after the war. The subscribers, so prominently advertised and displayed as part of the Americanized version of the text, stood in as curators of the past.

"This Subject Will Engage a Considerable Part of Our Paper"

In addition to the London and New York editions, Gordon's *History* was remade a third time by New York printers. Gordon's decision to return to London to publish the *History* resulted in a dramatic transformation of the written text. A pirated American edition, published only a year after the London edition had arrived in American ports, further altered the material form of the text. Not only did the New York collaborative of Hodge, Allen, and Campbell publish a truncated "Americanized" version, but the pirated edition was yet again transformed by newspaper editors who serialized it in their daily papers not long after it rolled off the press.

The serialization of Gordon's *History* was presented by New York newspaper editors as an alternative to book ownership. The newspaper's form radically transformed the materiality of Gordon's *History* from a staid, traditional narrative into a daily cliffhanger, as readers of and listeners to the paper had to wait until the following afternoon to pick up where the story left off. And despite the disposability of the daily newspaper, readers and subscribers were afforded the opportunity to essentially re-create Gordon's *History* on their own terms. The collectability of the serialized *History* was promoted by the printers who excerpted it, a shrewd move that made the text available to an even wider audience than Hodge, Allen, and Campbell could possibly have imagined.

William Morton, the printer of the *New-York Morning Post,* published excerpts of Gordon's *History* in his daily paper for ten months. In this way, Morton surreptitiously circumvented Hodge, Allen, and Campbell's attempt to capitalize on the nation's need for a heroic past. Subscribers to the *Morning Post,* and readers who may have either borrowed the papers or read or listened to them at the local tavern or coffeehouse, experienced Gordon's work without parting with the thirty shillings needed to buy their own bound copies. Morton justified the excerpting by pointing to the influence of his readers, who seemed to be pestering him to publish the *History*. "The Printer, at the solicitation of a number of his Customers proposes publishing GORDON'S HISTORY OF THE AMER-ICAN WAR in this paper," he wrote. Morton indicated that he would devote "a large portion" of the *Morning Post* to the endeavor in each issue until he published "the whole four volumes (consisting of more than 2,000 pages)," which he believed would take a few months. Once finished, he argued, "the public" in New York and beyond would be "furnished with a valuable historical treasure at a very inconsiderable price." This statement, in which Morton deferred to the alleged desires of his readers, was printed at the top of each excerpt of Gordon's book.[100] Interestingly, Morton also appealed to readers who may have wanted to own Gordon's *History* in its entirety, but in serial form. In so doing, he hoped to bring in additional subscribers to the *Morning Post*. In a miniscule advertisement, tucked away in the bottom third of the left column on the third page of the paper a week after he began serializing the *History*, Morton indicated that "Gentlemen *wishing to have the* History of the late War (by the Rev. Dr. Gordon) *complete, through the Channel of* The Morning Post, and Daily Advertiser," should stop by the printing shop at 231 Queen Street, where they could "*have the Papers from its Commencement, and so continued till the whole is finished, which will be in the course of a few Months.*" Morton could not help but add, just below this notice, that "SUBSCRIPTION *of the* Morning Post, &c." could be had "at the LOW RATE *of THIRTY-TWO SHILLINGS per ANNUM.*" Ironically, Morton's notice for his serialized edition of Gordon's *History* was placed next to an advertisement for Samuel Campbell's book shop.[101] Morton's serialization of Gordon's *History* in its entirety for nearly a year was remarkable. Although the subscription list for the pirated New York edition suggests a diverse national readership, Gordon's *History* was further democratized by Morton's suggestion that consumers could amass the text on their own, using the *Morning Post*, for a fraction of the price. By giving in to the pressures of his readers, Morton returned the history of the War of Independence to the ordinary citizens of New York and the nation.

William Morton was not the only New York printer who devoted space in his newspaper to reprinting Gordon's *History*. Francis Childs, publisher of the *Daily Advertiser*, announced to his readers that "when GORDON'S History of the American Revolution" first appeared in New York, he "early obtained a copy thereof, with intent to re-publish the same, for the amusement and gratification" of his readers. Childs considered the *History* an important and timely work, one worthy of continued public debate. He argued that because Gordon had done a great deal of research and had used "a variety of papers, and anecdotes, to authenticate the narrative," the *History* was "interesting, and worthy of our attention." Childs acknowledged that reprinting Gordon's *History* was a considerable task, in terms of both time and space. "Tho' this subject will engage a considerable part of our paper," he wrote, "we do not intend to neglect those who may wish for other matter."[102] Shortly after announcing that he would reprint excerpts of Gordon's *History*, in March 1789, Childs commenced with the serialization in medias res. In early March, Childs told his readers that he thought it "most prudent to commence the publication of the 5th letter, in which *Hutchinson's* dispute with the general court of *Massachusetts*—the burning of the *Gaspee* schooner—committees of correspondence—and the *supremacy* of Parliament, are brought into view." The very next day, Childs published the first part of Gordon's fifth letter.[103] Childs, of course, had been involved in the subscription campaign by Hodge, Allen, and Campbell. Only two days before announcing his intention to reprint the *History*, Childs ran the subscription proposal advertisement, probably handed to him personally by one of the three partners.[104]

Childs had been involved in a similar campaign two years earlier. The end result of that effort took the opposite route, as the serialized newspaper essays published in his paper resulted in the printing of a book. Beginning in October 1787, Alexander Hamilton arranged for several New York City printers to publish the so-called Publius essays, written primarily by Hamilton, James Madison, and John Jay—all posing as the eponymous Publius—to promote the ratification of the recently drafted U.S. Constitution. Appearing first in John M'Lean's *Independent Journal* in late October 1787, the Publius essays would be reprinted, at regular intervals, in Samuel Loudon's *New-York Packet*, Childs's *Daily Advertiser*, and Thomas Greenleaf's *New-York Journal and Daily Patriotic Register*. Five months later, in late March 1788, M'Lean and his brother Archibald published the first bound edition of what became known as *The Federalist Papers*. In May, the M'Lean brothers published a second volume that included the remaining forty-eight essays, and the *Independent Journal*, after a brief hiatus in the spring and early summer of 1788, finished printing the series in mid-August 1788. As Elaine Crane and Trish Loughran have shown, the "Publius" essays had a limited reach beyond Manhattan, appearing in fewer than twenty newspapers in Massachusetts, New York, Virginia, Pennsylvania, New Hampshire, and Rhode Island, in addition to Mathew Carey's Philadelphia magazine, the *American Museum*, and Noah Webster's ambitious new literary project, the *American Magazine*, published in New York.[105]

While the circumstances surrounding the serialization of Gordon's *History* were certainly unusual, excerpting long texts in newspapers and magazines was common practice in the early Republic. After taking a considerable financial hit publishing *The Power of Sympathy*—the text that literary scholars have identified as the first American novel—Isaiah Thomas hedged his bets in order to increase sales. Surely recognizing that he had erred in taking the kind of risk involved in publishing *The Power of Sympathy*, Thomas reprinted around a dozen excerpts of the novel in his fledgling literary magazine, the *Massachusetts Magazine, or Monthly Museum*. In what can only be described as a desperate move, Thomas posed as a reader named Calista in order to "share" the published novel with the subscribers to his own magazine. Thomas's pseudonymous tactic did little to increase either the visibility or the sales of *The Power of Sympathy*, and the novel languished in obscurity for nearly a century.[106]

The serialization of Gordon's text by Morton and Childs created an entirely different reading public for the *History*. The act of taking an already published book and excerpting it in the daily papers effectively created a third edition. In the process, Morton and Childs formed an expansive new discursive space that allowed for greater access to and interaction with the very recent history of the Revolution in public and private spaces that the bound editions of Gordon's *History* may not have reached.

Despite embracing economic and political nationalism in their proposal and the resulting reading public created by their subscription list, Hodge, Allen, and Campbell's edition of Gordon's *History* remained largely unpopular with most Americans. In fact, the book received an intellectual dressing down one hundred years after its initial publication by one of the nation's first professional historians.[107] Critics at the time of the New York edition's publication could not get past Gordon's writing style and his heavily edited book to see any kind of symbolic importance in its publication by American printers for an American market. Describing the work as "the rise and progress of inconsistencies and palpable falsehoods," Boston's *Herald of Freedom* pointed to the "various errors and omissions" as reason enough not to trust the narrative, despite Gordon's years of travel and research. Shortsightedness when it came to facts and evidence notwithstanding, the major flaw of the *History*, argued the reviewer (writing under the pseudonym Punctilio), was the author's perspective: Punctilio accused Gordon of celebrating the virtue of the losing Brits. "The conduct of the infamous Arnold is palliated," wrote Punctilio, "and held up as brave and heroic," while Gordon failed to fully acknowledge the systemic consequences of Benedict Arnold's decision to switch sides. Punctilio also condemned Gordon for his dull writing style, perhaps his greatest offense. "But his affected language plainly indicates his inability to do justice to the subject," wrote the critic, and he "suffered his partial views to reduce his judgment."[108] Francis Childs published Punctilio's sentiments six days later.[109]

As we have seen, however, Gordon's *History* was not without its defenders. An anonymous reader, identified only as "A Subscriber to Gordon's History," took to the pages of the *Daily Advertiser* to defend not only the text but the reputation of the men and women who subscribed to the New York edition. The subscriber made the case that a group of Boston booksellers, still smarting from Gordon's refusal to work with them to publish the *History*, had engaged in the smear campaign purely out of spite. "I have been informed that when Dr. Gordon was writing this history," wrote the subscriber, "those Booksellers had seen the manuscript and were lavish in its praises." The situation apparently turned sour when the Boston booksellers made an excessive "demand for printing it," offering Gordon "such humiliating terms that he would not have received a sum sufficient to defray his bare expenses." When Gordon turned down the offer, "he was forced to the alternative of printing it in London," after which, the subscriber alleged, "they began to change their panegyrics into the most illiberal and even personal abuse." The subscriber's suspicion that Gordon had a nasty disagreement with Boston booksellers emerges from Gordon's correspondence. Writing to Horatio Gates in February 1786, after he had decided to return to England, Gordon hinted that he published the *History* in London to spite Boston publishers. "I shall take ample revenge on the printers," he wrote, "by letting them see that they cannot come near me in printing binding and cheapness, all things considered." In an April 1786 letter to George Washington, Gordon complained about the negative press he and his project had received. "The abuse with which I have been loaded by the public prints, shall only make me the more cautious in answering the character of the faithful Historian," he wrote. Ultimately, according to the subscriber, the judgment of Gordon's *History* should be left to "critical reviewers" and not to a "PARTY of Printers in Boston."[110]

In this attempt to build support for the New York edition of Gordon's *History* and to counter criticism of the book and its author, the subscriber suggested that supporters and critics alike should look no further than to the subscribers themselves. Judgment of Gordon's work, he wrote (and we can be fairly certain it was a "he," perhaps even Gordon himself), should consider the men and women who not only paid in advance for a copy of the text but lent their names to the third volume. "The concurring approbation of many hundreds of subscribers," wrote the subscriber, "whose names are signed to a proposal for printing an American edition, induced me to add *my* own to the list." He had done so, he claimed, not because of peer pressure or desire for a heightened public profile, but rather for the experience of reading the book itself. "I had read and judged for myself, and I will venture to assert that 500 OTHER subscribers, of very superior abilities and learning to what I can pretend, had likewise read the English edition." Mocking the temerity of the Boston booksellers, the subscriber questioned whether the booksellers were better equipped to judge Gordon's *History* than the men and women who paid for the publication of the New York edition. "But a club of Bostonian booksellers," he sneered, "have more knowledge than 500 gentlemen of liberal education." Gordon, in the estimation of this anonymous writer, had gone about his research in the right way by corresponding and visiting with many prominent American statesmen, who had all provided encouragement. The same could not be said of the Boston publishers, who evidently felt slighted when they could not print the *History* on their terms. "Not so with a pack of sneaking haberdashers in literature, a club of Bostonian Printers, whose assertions are unsupported," the author wrote, "but whose mercenary hearts seem to be eager in their pursuit of revenge, without possessing sufficient judgment to know, that they never have been injured in the object of their resentments."[111]

The list of subscribers from every region of the new nation, given prominent place in the first volume of Gordon's magnum opus, must have filled readers with a sense of pride. Although some faulted Gordon for moving to England to publish his edition, the return of the book to American soil, produced using American funds by American printers, was as significant for the city's publishing trade as it was for the shaping of the new nation's understanding of its recent past.

3

JOHN WARD FENNO'S BOOKSHOP POLITICS

In December 1798, on yet another cold night in Philadelphia, John Ward Fenno was startled by rustling at the porch step of his Chestnut Street home. "There came last night to my House two ruffians," he wrote the next day in his paper, the *Gazette of the United States*, "one of whom lurked about the porch, while the other, as I stood at my own door, struck me on the head with a bludgeon." After absorbing the initial attack, from a man he later identified as a "United Irishmen," Fenno retreated into the *Gazette*'s office, along the way grabbing a piece of printing equipment to fend off further violence. He later reflected that this "fortunate" decision to duck behind the press may have saved his life. To retaliate would have had dire consequences. "I should have been murdered," he concluded.[1]

This was not John Ward Fenno's only brush with violence. Much of Fenno's career in Philadelphia was colored by a heated rivalry with fellow printer Benjamin Franklin Bache. The grandson of Benjamin Franklin and the editor of the *Aurora,* Bache was the foremost voice in a vibrant and growing Republican newspaper network. The bad blood began when Fenno's father—also named John Fenno—traded rhetorical jabs with Bache's *Aurora* in the pages of his *Gazette of the United States*. As caustic as the language between Fenno's *Gazette* and Bache's *Aurora* was, the animosity between the two men reached a boiling point in early August 1798.[2]

In a series of scathing editorials, Bache accused the Fennos of playing a role in fellow Federalist Joseph Thomas's alleged theft of nearly $20,000. "We understand that the recent discovered scheme of swindling and forgery, has but barely budded," Bache wrote, and that the "branches of this grand affair promise to appear in several quarters of the Union in a short time."[3] Referring to Fenno's father as a "*mercenary scoundrel,*" Bache insinuated that he was somehow involved in Thomas's grand scheme. Infuriated, John Ward Fenno stormed into the *Aurora*'s Market Street office and demanded that Bache retract the accusation that his father had covered for Thomas.

Fenno's young sprig plucked up courage enough to go as far as the office of the *Aurora* yesterday evening, in order to deny that his *pappy* was the friend of *Jozey Thomas*—the lad was accompanied by a gentleman, who acknowledged he had reason to be ashamed of the youth's behaviour. *Fenno's* young lady in breeches came to require the name of the writer that called his papa a *mercenary scoundrel,* and to demand *satisfaction* for his being billed Jozey Thomas's friend—but when the person he was offended with rose from his seat, behold the "poor little foolish, fluttering thing"—literally ran away with its mouth full of froth, and its knees trembling![4]

Naturally, the Fennos had a remarkably different interpretation of the shakedown. Young Fenno maintained that he had visited the *Aurora* to confront Bache and the "villainous terms" used against his father. The young man portrayed himself as having an imposing countenance, so much so that Bache—a "mean and contemptible coward"—began trembling upon his entrance. In a striking contrast to Bache's story, Fenno insisted that he stood his ground, telling Bache that if "he neglected to recant the obnoxious terms, that I should treat him as a scoundrel, and that he was a lying, cowardly rascal." Taking exception to Fenno's thinly veiled threat, the other men in the office "bristled up," while Bache "doubled his fist, and made some shew of striking a blow at me."[5] It was at this time that Fenno's unnamed companion insisted they withdraw.

The quarrel in Bache's office, and the competing narratives that appeared in the *Aurora* and the *Gazette,* would only be resolved by a brawl. On the same day that the *Gazette* and the *Aurora* published their stories, the two men happened upon each other at Fourth and Market Streets. Enraged not only by Bache's language about his father but also by the way in which he was characterized as a drooling, inarticulate ne'er-do-well, Fenno—at least in Bache's recounting of the incident—"muttered up courage enough last evening" and lunged at Bache "with *tooth* and *nail.*" A violent scrum ensued during which Fenno apparently bit and scratched his antagonist. Bache gave himself the last word, pointing out that Fenno "got in return a sound rap or two across the head and face." Fenno gave a startlingly different account. Casting Bache as a "villain whose detestable propensities present to an Indignant world, a combination of vice and depravity, which both in degree and variety, challenge the whole annals of mankind," Fenno reminded *Gazette* readers that Bache had derided his father as a "MERCENARY SCOUNDREL," and explained that this "crying affront, which struck with the force of thunder to the heart," sent him into a rage. Fenno, convinced that he must "resort to prompt revenge," ran into Bache while on a leisurely stroll with his younger brother; Bache happened to be walking down Fourth Street "with his bludgeon, accompanied by John Beckley."[6]

Upon which I immediately proceeded towards him; and after advancing full in his view, for about one third of the square, came up with him. He drew back, and brandished his club—I advanced and seizing him by the collar, struck him at the same instant in the face, and repeated my blows as fast as possible. He repeatedly attempted to push his stick in my face; but having closed in with him, his arms were so cramped, that his attempts proved very feeble. The scuffle issued in my driving him against the wall, when I should have soon wrested the club from his hand—had not his companion, very improperly seized my left hand, and disengaging it from round his body, held it fast. Bache instantly drew off. My attempts to get at him again were rendered ineffectual by those around, one of whom seized me round the body, and held me fast, while Bache sneaked home, his nose barked, and his sconce covered with blood, conspicuous marks of Jacobin valour. I had no weapon, but my fist and received no hurt in the transaction. It is not without reluctance that I further intruded upon the public. The active misrepresentations of Bache and his partisans, seemed to call for a true statement of the affair.[7]

The assault at his home, and the long-standing quarrel with Bache, typified John Ward Fenno's career as a partisan newspaperman. Born in Boston in March 1778, the oldest of fourteen children, Jack, as he was affectionately called by his family, was trained as a printer by his father, the founder of the influential Federalist newspaper the *Gazette of the United States*. In addition to this formal training, young Fenno received a classic liberal education, first at Mr. Payne's Academy in New York and later at the University of Pennsylvania. Jack's ultimate ambition was to read for the bar, but his father's sudden death during the Yellow Fever epidemic of September 1798 forced him to take over the *Gazette*. Jack Fenno kept the paper afloat, at least early on. To make up for the exodus of journeymen and apprentices due to the outbreak, not to mention a dramatic decrease in circulation, Fenno's brothers Charles and George provided much needed help with the production of the *Gazette*. No longer able to publish the *Gazette*, he sold the paper and left for New York in 1800, opening a small book-shop soon thereafter.[8]

Characterized by the Philadelphia publisher Mathew Carey as a "rash, thoughtless, and imprudent young man" and by a fellow newspaper editor as an "unfortunate lunatic," Fenno tried to pick up the pieces of his failed career in New York.[9] Opening a bookstore would seem, at least at first glance, to have been an apolitical move for a man like John Ward Fenno. As one of dozens of booksellers in early nineteenth-century Manhattan, though, Fenno engaged in bookshop politics during his brief but colorful career in the trade. Competing with the likes of Hocquet Caritat, who had for many years operated a prominent

Broadway bookstore and circulating library that catered to a largely Jeffersonian clientele, Fenno set himself apart in New York's crowded print market by running a shop that became a gathering place for the city's Federalists. Viewing his own store as a counterpoint to Caritat's, which was only a few feet away from his own, Fenno followed business practices that reveal for us how literary politics influenced the development of the new nation's publishing trade. And while he certainly catered to local consumers, Fenno had much larger ambitions. Like the publishers involved in creating a national reading public for William Gordon's history of the American Revolution, Fenno aspired to create a Federalist reading public. Building on the work of his predecessor in the New York book trade—the English rogue and political provocateur William Cobbett—Fenno built a national network of retail agents who agreed to hawk his hawkish books and periodicals, including many British works critical of the radicalism of the French Revolution. Fenno's distribution network connected American readers to a larger transatlantic, particularly British, and especially conservative, literary culture.[10]

Fenno imported most of his books and periodicals from London. Despite the efforts of activists in Philadelphia and New York to reduce the trade's reliance on imported European books—the subject of chapter 4—many early Republic printers and booksellers continued doing business with British publishers. In addition to selling books he considered superior material objects, Fenno also maintained a cultural and political connection to Great Britain. He was not alone in his commitment to preserving an Anglophile culture in the new nation. Scholars have shown how a cultural break from Great Britain was far more complicated than severing political ties and creating a new nation. Building on Paul Giles's work, which traces the "twisting and intertwining" of British and American literature between the American Revolution and the Civil War, Leonard Tennenhouse suggests that American writers in the early Republic appropriated existing British literary tropes for their own projects. In Tennenhouse's telling, literary culture in the new nation was part of a "literature of diaspora." Thus the process of "unbecoming British"—to borrow Kariann Yokota's provocative phrase—was marked by fits, starts, and years of cultural and material self-reflection on just what it meant to be an "American," and how it was different from being "British." The reality, Yokota tells us, was both simple and stark: despite winning the war against Great Britain and thus political independence, Americans could not fully shake their "Britishness"—at least not initially. Indeed, Americans depended on British merchants to keep up social and cultural appearances, continuing to import manufactured goods in part out of a need to project the image of refinement necessary to combat the European perception that the new Republic was little more than a savage, parochial backwater.[11]

But for John Ward Fenno, the commitment to selling British books and periodicals was as much a bold political statement as it was a reflection of the uneasiness many Americans felt at figuring out who they were as a people. Fenno helped articulate a Federalist desire to re-create close cultural, economic, and political ties with Great Britain by advertising and selling the latest editions from London and acerbic British magazines critical of the French Revolution. Far from imagining the future course of the new nation, independent of its former colonial master, Fenno maintained an Atlantic gaze, looking to England for inspiration and purpose, a business strategy that no doubt contributed to the cultural anxieties many New Yorkers and Americans felt as subjects who were becoming citizens.

"Fenno Has Sold Out His Establishment in Philadelphia"

John Ward Fenno left Philadelphia in a hurry. In the frenzy of packing for his move to New York, he apparently forgot some of his clothing. In two letters, Fenno asked his friend and protégé Asbury Dickins to ship what he had left behind to Manhattan. In July 1800, Fenno implored Dickins to "send me my boots &c." Two weeks later, Fenno again brought up his missing threads. "Has there been no opportunity by sea or land, for the Costumes . . . Boots &c?"[12] Dickins evidently did not care to respond. Fenno had good reason to flee Philadelphia in such haste. In addition to his bitter rivalry with the editors at the *Aurora,* he faced mounting financial difficulties. Not long after taking over the *Gazette of the United States,* Fenno was slapped with a libel suit in September 1798 by the secretary of Pennsylvania, Alexander Dallas. Libel suits remained constant threats to newspaper editors, as they could bankrupt a printer's shop seemingly overnight.[13] Fenno did not contest the case and apparently "did not appear" before the court, "nor was any counsel engaged in his defense." Not surprisingly, Fenno lost, and the Pennsylvania Supreme Court forced him to pay Dallas $2,000. News of the judgment circulated widely in the nation's newspapers, from Portland, Maine, to Augusta, Georgia.[14] The negative publicity of the case, not to mention his mounting money troubles, handicapped Fenno's ability to oversee the publication of the nation's most important Federalist newspapers.

Fenno became editor of the *Gazette of the United States* at a time when newspapers played an increasingly important role in partisan politics. As scholars have shown, opposition to George Washington and his acolytes—specifically Treasury Secretary Alexander Hamilton—grew first from within his presidency and then, especially, during John Adams's administration. Newspapers were at the heart of this simmering conflict. Used at first by Thomas Jefferson and

James Madison to distribute their fundamentally different visions for the future of the young Republic, newspapers and the ambitious men helming them quickly became, as historian Jeffrey L. Pasley argues, "the political system's central institution, not simply a forum or atmosphere in which politics took place." Central to this development, Pasley tells us, were the printer-editors who made themselves into "purposeful actors in the political process, linking parties, voters, and the government together," all in order to pursue "specific political goals." The invention of politically minded editors like Fenno and the newspapers that advocated for specific politicians and parties was directly tied, Pasley suggests, to the evolving federal government. The spirit of disinterested public service, without the stain of faction or party, quickly evaporated as a deep ideological and partisan divide overtook the First Congress. Helping to articulate the division, and, consequently, to hasten the development of a national two-party system, was the partisan newspaper editor.[15]

John Ward Fenno, like his father, was typical of the new partisan editor who emerged in the 1790s. No longer simply "meer mechanics" who either printed all sides of political arguments or sidestepped politics altogether, these young, ambitious, and politically minded printer-editors made themselves into professional political operatives, choosing to embrace the messiness of politics. These "new kinds of men" were, as Pasley points out, "political communicators by trade, working in a new sector of the publishing industry devoted to and subsisting on partisan politics."[16] Fenno witnessed the development of newspaper politics firsthand, so that by the time he took over his father's influential Federalist paper, he was familiar with the political economy of partisan newspapers in the new nation.

Fenno's brief career as the editor of the *Gazette of the United States* was haunted by the boom-and-bust economics of the printing trade in the early Republic. Printing was a notoriously expensive trade given the high costs of procuring a press, type, ink, and paper. Even successful shops could fold at a moment's notice. Newspapers were particularly risky ventures, given the time, labor, and expense involved in producing a single issue. Indeed, it often took the printer, his journeymen, and the apprentices up to *sixteen* hours to produce a standard four-page paper. And while many young men, like Fenno, entered the business looking to make their reputations as well as their fortunes, most printer-editors either lost money or at best broke even. Newspaper editors relied heavily on advertising and subscription revenue to make ends meet, and the larger partisan papers, such as Fenno's *Gazette,* the Philadelphia *Aurora,* and the New York *American Citizen* (to name only a few), were forced to count on political patronage—local, state, and federal printing contracts and advertisements by and for the party—for additional income. The father-and-son team that published the *Gazette of the United States* was not immune to these invisible market and political forces.[17]

Fenno's father took an unusual path to his career as a newspaper editor. Born in August 1751 to a Boston leather dresser, the elder Fenno spent much of his adult life trying to distance himself from his humble beginnings. Educated at the Old South Writing School near the Boston Common, Fenno took a job as an assistant teacher at the school after his graduation in 1768—a post he held for six years. While we know little about his activities, political or otherwise, for much of his adult life beginning in 1774, we do know that he worked for a time at the *Massachusetts Centinel* for the printer Benjamin Russell, a job that gained him the admiration of the city's leading politicians. After failing as a Boston dry goods merchant, Fenno relocated with his family to New York City in January 1789, looking to establish himself as a printer. Fenno's move to New York, at the time the capital of the new nation, was financed by several leading Boston Federalists. Indeed, Fenno arrived in the city with a letter of introduction addressed to the prominent New York Federalist Rufus King, a letter that no doubt supplied him with the kind of necessary connections and possibilities for political patronage he would need in order to establish a successful newspaper. Once settled in the city, Fenno began publishing the *Gazette of the United States* in mid-April 1789. Fenno and the *Gazette* remained in New York until mid-October 1790, when he relocated to Philadelphia along with the U.S. government. After a brief delay, Fenno rebooted the *Gazette* in early November 1790 from his new office on Market Street.[18]

Fenno had ambitions plans for his newspaper. He imagined the semiweekly *Gazette* as "A NATIONAL PAPER" that he would publish "at the Seat of the Federal Legislature, wherever situated." He would devote much of the *Gazette*'s focus, he argued in his January 1789 prospectus, to the "support of the Constitution, & the Administration formed upon its national principles." Fenno's initial purpose was political unity, not division. In order to achieve this lofty aim, Fenno sought subscriptions in every state capital and refused to print advertisements. He also had an idealized vision of himself as an editor. Removing himself entirely from the material production of the *Gazette*, choosing to instead hire out labor to print the newspaper, Fenno shaped the public persona of a gentleman editor, a respected man of letters who did not, unlike his fellow newspapermen, work with his hands.[19]

Fenno's early work as editor of the *Gazette* reflected his intention to offer a national platform for the newly formed federal government. And while he did not envision the *Gazette* as a political paper—boasting that it would extol "NATIONAL, INDEPENDENT, and IMPARTIAL PRINCIPLES"—bolstering the Washington administration's policies was a deeply partisan act.[20] The *Gazette* helped disseminate Federalist policies to political leaders and fellow newspapermen alike. Because of his national ambitions, Fenno's subscription rolls grew. Yet despite an impressive number of readers, the *Gazette* was hemorrhaging money, owing in no small part to Fenno's inability to collect money efficiently from subscribers. Recognizing his struggles to keep the paper afloat, leading Federalists came to Fenno's rescue and helped to ensure, in whatever way they could, the *Gazette*'s survival. As the administration's policies, especially Alexander Hamilton's ambitious financial plan, became more controversial, additional revenue trickled into Fenno's office in the form of government printing contracts, specifically all business related to the U.S. Senate and Hamilton's own Treasury Department. Hamilton even went so far as to give Fenno a staggering amount of money, without any expectation that Fenno would repay the loan. Hamilton also led a campaign in Philadelphia and New York, aided by Rufus King, to raise funds to help sustain the paper. The survival of the *Gazette*, not to mention the tireless work by Fenno and his political patrons to keep it afloat, was in serious doubt after Fenno died in the late summer of 1798 during the Yellow Fever outbreak that devastated Philadelphia. Not long afterward, John Ward Fenno stepped up and took over his father's paper, even as the *Gazette* faced continued financial difficulties.[21]

By the time he assumed control of the *Gazette*, John Ward Fenno had grown disillusioned with the state of American politics. As the 1800 election season drew near and Republican newspapers stoked the fires of opposition, Fenno bristled at the prospect of a Jeffersonian administration. "Reflection and Experience have convinced me that it will be in vain to look for a moral principle or fidelity to engagements," he wrote to his friend Joseph Ward, "in the conduct of any Republican govt. whatsoever."[22] Making matters worse, subscriptions to the *Gazette* had "fallen off much" since Fenno took over the paper.[23] Clearly in over his head, Fenno made overtures to Joseph Dennie in February 1799 to become a full-time salaried editor of the *Gazette*. Dennie was the obvious choice to take over and revive the paper. Between 1796 and 1799, Dennie had transformed the *New Hampshire Journal, or Farmer's Weekly Museum* from a local newspaper into arguably the nation's most important literary publication. Possessed of what Fenno described as a "liberality of sentiment," Dennie had earned a reputation as a man of impeccable taste.[24] Dennie was also resoundingly Federalist in his politics. He was intensely hostile to Republicans, Thomas Jefferson in particular, for fear that a Republican administration would usher in a new age of revolution inspired by the events in France. Given Dennie's politics and literary acumen, it should come as little surprise that Fenno begged him to take over the editorship of the *Gazette*. Dennie ultimately declined Fenno's offer, though he did write for the *Gazette* on occasion under the pseudonym "Oliver Oldschool, Esq." after moving to Philadelphia in 1799.[25] Unable to secure the replacement of his choice, and evidently fed up with the daily grind of editing the paper, Fenno put the *Gazette* up for sale on "the most liberal terms" in the spring of 1800.[26] Not long after Fenno posted the ad, Caleb Parry Wayne announced that he had taken over the paper.[27] Seemingly retired from Philadelphia politics, Fenno packed his bags and moved to New York City.

The New York that greeted Fenno, much like the city he had left behind, was in the midst of dramatic social, political, and economic changes. Foremost was the emergence of the Tammany Society and its commitment to establishing a strong Republican base in the city. By the mid-1790s, hundreds of Manhattan residents—including many artisans and mechanics—had become involved in the society and, in turn, in local politics. Inspired in large part by the French Revolution, the city's mechanics became increasingly disaffected with Federalist moneyed men such as Alexander Hamilton. New York's artisans and laborers began supporting local Republican candidates—led by and identified with the powerful Clinton family headed by longtime governor George Clinton and his up-and-coming nephew, Dewitt. At the heart of the political shift was the perception that republicanism, at home and abroad, was under attack. Concern grew that President Washington's administration did not have the interests of urban workers in mind, and discontent among mechanics and small merchants in Manhattan and elsewhere led to the rise of so-called Democratic-Republican societies. The city's Democratic-Republican societies were unequivocally pro-French in their politics and openly campaigned for the United States to go to war with Great Britain. Distrust of Federalists deepened as a result of the unpopular 1795 Jay Treaty, which granted Great Britain most-favored-nation status in international trade, effectively isolating the new French Republic. In the tense aftermath, the city's Republicans held massive town meetings to protest the treaty.[28]

Despite Republican gains in the 1796 city and state elections, the Federalists quickly regained the upper hand. Federalist saber rattling in response to the 1798 Quasi-War with France and its new conservative government, the Directory, all but neutralized the Republican ascendency. Recognizing an opportunity to permanently immobilize opposition newspapers, Federalists pushed what came to be known as the Alien and Sedition Acts through the U.S. Congress. Justified as a wartime measure, the Alien and Sedition Acts, which Federalists hoped would stifle criticism of the administration and the Congress, had the opposite effect. Rather than silence the Republican opposition, the reactionary and controversial laws galvanized Republican printer-editors. A suddenly emergent network of Jeffersonian-leaning newspapers played a decisive role in electing Republican candidates to local, state, and federal positions. In the spring of 1800, around the time that Fenno sold the *Gazette of the United States* to Caleb Parry Wayne, the Republicans swept New York City's elections. Manhattan's congressional seat went to a Republican, as did all of the city's state assembly seats. The Republican insurgency effectively guaranteed that New York's electoral votes would go to Thomas Jefferson in the presidential election later that fall, the final chapter in the so-called Revolution of 1800 that pushed many

Federalists out of power, though they maintained pockets of influence, especially in New England.[29]

Fenno's move to New York, then, made for compelling political theater. Shortly after learning that Fenno had sold the *Gazette*, David Denniston announced in the *American Citizen*—Manhattan's leading Republican newspaper—that "Fenno, as we predicted a few days ago, has indeed *sold out* and is succeeded by a young man of the name of Caleb P. Wayne—of whom as yet we know nothing." In the same issue of the *Citizen*, Denniston made it known that Fenno had also bought out William Cobbett's New York bookstore and looked to open his own shop in the city. "Fenno has sold out his establishment in Philadelphia," he wrote, and "purchased Porcupine's load of filth and iniquity."[30] The deck, it seems, was stacked against Fenno's bookshop long before his arrival in Manhattan.

Fenno's decision to sell the *Gazette* and leave Philadelphia hinged on his taking over Cobbett's Manhattan bookstore. Formerly an enlisted man in the British army, Cobbett ended up in Philadelphia after running afoul of corrupt officers when he loudly protested the abuse of enlisted men. In Philadelphia, Cobbett took a different tack, assuming an ardently pro-British identity with the pen name Peter Porcupine. Cobbett, as Porcupine, was the author and editor of several satirical pamphlets and a newspaper, *Porcupine's Gazette*, that skewered Republicans, propped up Federalists, and tacitly endorsed the policies of Great Britain while simultaneously criticizing the excesses of the French Revolution. Given their shared politics, Cobbett became a close friend of the Fenno family while living in Philadelphia.[31]

Cobbett's career took a dramatic turn in 1799, however, when he became embroiled in a bitter libel case brought against him by Benjamin Rush, the noted Philadelphia physician, reformer, and Republican politician. In the Pennsylvania Supreme Court judgment, Cobbett was expected to pay Rush $5,000—a princely sum that all but ended Cobbett's career as a Philadelphia publisher.[32] Cobbett tried to pick up the pieces of his career by fleeing Philadelphia in 1800 and settling in New York as a bookseller, but he ultimately determined that a return to England was in his best interest, both politically and personally. In a farewell address he published in June 1800 that would later achieve wide circulation in the nation's newspapers, Cobbett announced his intention to transfer the business to his friend and protégé, John Ward Fenno. "THIS is to inform all those of you, whom it may concern, that, being upon the point of returning to that *'insular bastille,'* Great Britain," he wrote, "I have fully and legally authorized Mr. John Ward Fenno (late of Philadelphia) who is my successor in business, to make final adjustment of all my unsettled accounts." By the time Cobbett published his address in the *Daily Advertiser* and the *New-York Gazette*, he was well on his way to England. It is probably for this reason that the erstwhile Porcupine could not resist the opportunity to take one last jab at his enemies. "When people care not two straws for each other, ceremony at parting is mere grimace," he wrote, "and, as I have, for some time past, felt the most perfect indifference, with regard to a vast majority of those whom I now address, I shall spare myself the trouble of a ceremonious farewell." Cobbett saved his best insult for Benjamin Rush: "With this I depart for that HOME, where neither the moth of Democracy, nor the rust of federalism doth corrupt, and where thieves do not, with impunity, break through and steal five thousand dollars at a time."[33] Cobbett's acrimonious farewell address became a national news story. Word spread quickly from Manhattan, first to Philadelphia and then to Massachusetts, Virginia, Connecticut, South Carolina, Rhode Island, and finally Vermont.[34]

Fenno had a complicated financial relationship with Cobbett. After he moved to New York, he got himself into financial trouble helping Cobbett flee the country. Short on funds, Cobbett called on his old friend, who in turn hit up the Philadelphia bookseller Asbury Dickins for cash to help cover Cobbett's legal fees and relocation costs. When Dickins was not forthcoming with money, Fenno panicked and obtained a loan from the Manhattan Company. Ever paranoid, Fenno worried that his debt was now tied to the political machinations of the likes of Aaron Burr, the bank's founder. "At present I cannot stir," he told Dickins, "for my note is in the Manhattan Bank—they are all Jacobins, & I can have no reliance for a renewal—1381 dolls. in amount."[35]

After arriving in New York, with or without his shoes, Fenno opened his bookshop at Hanover Square in Manhattan's First Ward. In 1800, the year Fenno settled down in Manhattan, forty-seven printers, twenty-three booksellers, and fourteen bookbinders lived and worked in New York City. Several booksellers and a number of printers and bookbinders lived and worked on either Pearl or Water Street near Fenno's new Hanover Square shop. Along Pearl Street, Fenno could walk out his front door to find the printers Thomas & James Swords (99 Pearl Street), John Lang (116 Pearl Street), Ebenezer Belden (131 Pearl Street), George F. Hopkins (136 Pearl Street), Philip Ten Eyck (148 Pearl Street), Hugh Gaine (44 Hanover Square), George Forman (64 Water Street), and James Oram (102 Water Street), in addition to fellow booksellers Evert Duyckinck (110 Pearl Street), Samuel Campbell (124 Pearl Street), Thomas Arden (186 Pearl Street), Isaac Collins (189 Pearl Street), William Falconer (94 Water Street), John Reid (106 Water Street), and Brown & Stansbury (114 Water Street). Fenno's new store was thus at the center of the city's emerging publishing trade.[36]

Fenno inherited a robust business from Cobbett. His first move was to retain Cobbett's customer base. "Having succeeded to his business here," Fenno wrote, "I shall, at all times be happy in executing the orders of his friends and customers."[37] According to Cobbett's accounts, a number of important, well-connected men patronized his Philadelphia and New York shops. Foremost among Cobbett's customers were Robert Liston, the British minister to the United States, several additional British commissioners, and the Swedish consul. Several American politicians—all Federalists—frequented Cobbett's shop, including Connecticut senator Uriah Tracy, Pennsylvania congressman Samuel Sitgreaves, and two U.S. representatives from South Carolina, Robert Goodloe Harper and William Loughton Smith. Thus Fenno could almost certainly count on a prestigious and like-minded group of customers waiting to patronize his new store.[38]

Because Fenno took over Cobbett's business, many of the books in his new shop had at one time lined the shelves of the Porcupine's bookstore (table 3.1). When Fenno opened his store at Hanover Square, he bought out a large selection of Cobbett's books, including nearly seventeen hundred copies of 318 titles valued at more than $4,000. Unlike other booksellers just starting out, Fenno had something of a competitive advantage because he knew the reading preferences of his patrons. Fenno's new inventory was not limited to one genre or category of books, however, as the store came with a variety of educational, professional, and reference texts in addition to a large assortment of Bibles and religious works. Belles lettres texts, broadly defined, made up a large percentage of the stock that Fenno inherited from Cobbett, among them twenty Greek and Roman classics, including twenty-two copies of the Roman satirist Persius, seven copies of Aesop's *Fables*, four copies of Virgil's *Aeneid*, and the writings of Cicero, Tacitus, and Ovid. Cobbett also left two copies of the Homeric epics on the shelf, but Fenno's accounts do not distinguish between *The Iliad* and *The Odyssey*. Fenno's new store came with quite a bit of Shakespeare—nearly 160 copies—and twenty-nine history titles, including William Belsham's *History of Great Britain* and William Playfair's *History of Jacobinism*. Cobbett also left Fenno nineteen travel books by Jonathan Carver and John Hawkesworth, among others. Cobbett had also stocked nine political philosophy titles, ranging from thirty copies of Edmund Burke's essays, three copies of John Locke, and one copy of Adam Smith's *Wealth of Nations*. Shoppers could also find Milton's *Paradise Lost* and the works of Oliver Goldsmith and Geoffrey Chaucer, along with the anthology *Poetical Beauties of Modern Writers*. Fenno's new shop had sixty titles in economics, law, mathematics, medicine, and science, totaling 150 copies. Thus, despite the forces acting against him in the Republican press, specifically David Denniston's *American Citizen*, Fenno's store was already something of a known commodity in New York's print market.[39]

With such a large and diverse inventory already on hand, Fenno promoted his new store with a series of newspaper advertisements. Over the course of several issues of the *New-York Gazette* and the *Daily Advertiser*, Fenno touted "*new and interesting Novels*," history books and travel literature, legal books, works of poetry, books on architecture and carpentry, and gardening books; most

TABLE 3.1 Total Book Stock Left Over from William Cobbett, 1802

	Itemization of Stock				Valuation of Stock
	Copies		Titles		
	(N)	(%)	(N)	(%)	($)
Belles Lettres					
Advice	8	0.4	2	0.6	4.50
Biography	39	2.3	14	4.4	367.15
Classics	75	4.4	20	6.2	255.55
Essays	112	6.7	30	9.4	296.47
Fiction	114	6.6	24	7.5	162.00
Geography	11	0.6	5	1.5	103.50
History	98	5.8	29	9.1	386.50
Music	28	1.6	2	0.6	56.61
Periodicals	221	13.1	18	5.6	280.74
Philosophy	40	2.3	9	2.8	75.49
Plays	188	11.2	4	1.2	88.90
Poetry	91	5.4	9	2.8	179.62
Travel	35	2.0	19	5.9	186.12
Misc. Texts	167	9.9	14	4.4	225.99
TOTAL	1,227	72.3	199	62	2,669.14
Education					
Foreign Language	53	3.1	4	1.2	21.97
Juvenile	17	1.0	10	3.1	37.24
Language	4	0.2	3	0.9	2.62
Text	24	1.4	7	2.2	30.50
TOTAL	98	5.7	24	7.4	92.33
Professional					
Economics	12	0.7	2	0.6	16.00
Law	45	2.6	18	5.6	200.00
Math	26	1.5	2	0.6	16.77
Medical	40	2.3	18	5.6	114.00
Science	27	1.6	20	6.2	166.72
Technical	38	2.2	7	2.2	128.20
TOTAL	188	10.9	67	20.8	641.69
Reference					
Dictionaries	13	0.7	7	2.2	51.00
Misc.	1	0	1	0.3	1.25
TOTAL	14	0.7	8	2.5	52.25
Religious					
Bibles	—		—		—
Misc.	151	8.9	20	6.2	780.73
TOTAL	151	8.9	20	6.2	780.73
Book Stock TOTALS	1,678	97.8	318	98.9	4,236.14

SOURCE: Estate Inventory of John Ward Fenno, John Ward Fenno Papers, NYHS.

of these books, Fenno pointed out, were the *"best London editions."*[40] Like Cobbett before him, Fenno preferred books imported from London to those produced in the United States. He balked at selling American-made books that were, in his estimation, "so damnably high charged as to frighten the poor American bookmonger." Fenno did recognize that the New York printers in his neighborhood would eventually supply his shop, however. He expected that trade with London would become difficult because of the continued political strife that made international commerce uncertain. "The trade of importing must be suspended till the War is Over," he confided to Asbury Dickins, referring to the French revolutionary wars then ravaging Europe. He lamented that a mid-June 1801 shipment from London would be "the last that will come, I suspect, to so large an amount."[41]

Fenno's reliance on the London book trade was not all that unusual. Despite the determined effort by American printers to produce more books for the domestic market, a topic I explore in the next chapter, booksellers continued importing books from Europe. Between 1785 and 1805, the London publisher Joseph Johnson sold books to a number of New York booksellers. Writing to John Fellows in 1795, Johnson insisted that the shipment "are all books of character, I have sent you no trash."[42] Johnson also corresponded with the printers Thomas and James Swords. "I have sent you seven trunks of books," Johnson wrote the brothers in October 1800, "for schools, general reading, arts & sciences." Johnson followed up in March 1801 by sending "300 prints of Washington," which he considered "the best likeness yet published of that immortal character."[43] In November, the brothers received yet another "case of books" from London, but their records do not indicate whether Johnson shipped this particular order.[44] Johnson's tidy business with New York ended abruptly in January 1806, when much of his stock was destroyed by a fire that enveloped his warehouse. After the fire, the Swords brothers received only two letters from Johnson to settle outstanding debts, communication made all the more complicated by the passage of the Embargo Act of 1807, which halted American trade with Great Britain and France.[45]

Bookshop Politics

Fenno did not open his bookshop without making a political splash. In early October 1800, Fenno fanned the flames of the long-standing, bitter dispute between Anglophile Federalists and pro-French Republicans. He indicated in the *New-York Gazette* that he stocked in his Hanover Square store a number of "engravings, elegantly printed in colours . . . just received from London." In this advertisement, Fenno tipped his avidly pro-British hat, celebrating a number of prints that commemorated British victories in the Napoleonic and Anglo-Spanish Wars. Fenno in particular celebrated Horatio Nelson's victory at the Battle of the Nile, noting that he had for sale four plates, including images of the "blowing up of l'Orient by the fire of the Bellerophon and vanguard" and "Zealous Capt. Hood's" pursuit of "le Genereux, le Guilliaume Tell, la Justice and la Diane." Fenno claimed that this collection of prints would eventually form a "compendious Naval History of the War."[46] The following January, Fenno appealed yet again to Manhattan's Anglophiles by advertising a number of engravings, "among which are Portraits of the most distinguished worthies of Great Britain"—Samuel Johnson, Lord Mansfield, Lord Kenyon, Lord Camden, and Lord Loughborough, among others.[47]

At the end of October 1800, Fenno took additional shots at the city's Republicans and the French Revolution in his promotion of several newly imported "political works." Fenno celebrated the work of Sir Francis d'Ivernois, a Genevan exile who resided in London during the French revolutionary and Napoleonic wars. D'Ivernois was a friend and correspondent of fellow English intellectuals Joseph Priestley, Richard Price, and Jeremy Bentham, and an avowed opponent and outspoken critic of the French Revolution; he had worked directly with the British prime minister William Pitt as a diplomat in support of Great Britain's war against the French Republic. Fenno imported several copies of d'Ivernois's 1799 *Historical and Political Survey of the Losses Sustained by the French Nation*, a stinging critique of the excesses of the new French Republic. Of this text, Fenno was effusive in his praise and admitted that he sold "this work at an uncommonly low price, because I am anxious to impart the important & extensive information which it conveys on French affairs." In his estimation, there was no book of greater importance to global politics. "No work of equal size, contains more valuable and useful information," he wrote, arguing that it would be "interesting to every class of readers."[48]

In the same advertisement, Fenno lauded the writing of John Gifford, a British Tory and historian. After achieving some notoriety in London for publishing his *History of England* in 1790, his four-volume *History of France* between 1791 and 1793, and finally a history of the French Revolution titled *The Reign of Louis XVI: A Complete History of the French Revolution*, Gifford took up his pen to translate several pamphlets critical of the French Revolution written by French nobles in exile. Gifford would go on to found the *Anti-Jacobin Review* in 1798, a Francophobic periodical that remained in publication until 1821. Fenno praised Gifford's *Letter to the Earl of Lauderdale*, a pamphlet that explored, he wrote, "the sophistries of the Republican peer, with fallacies of the Republican commoner, and the falsehood of all, with a keen spirit and steady mind." Fenno did not stop there, however, suggesting that Gifford presented "the map of patriot putridity" which was, he argued, "rank to the nose, offensive to the eye, and disgustful to the stomach."[49]

Fenno's criticism of the French Revolution even bled into his otherwise mundane business correspondence. In a letter to Asbury Dickins, Fenno listed a shipment of books he had recently forwarded to Philadelphia. And while this letter is fairly typical in most respects, Fenno made it deeply personal with a misogynistic comment about Stéphanie Félicité du Crest de Saint-Aubin, comtesse de Genlis, the author of a popular collection of children's comedies. The letter took a vicious turn when Fenno mentioned that he had sent Dickins several copies of "~~Theatre of Education~~ Little Bruyère by that bitch of a whore the *Comptesse de Genlis.*"[50] Fenno's remark reveals deeply rooted political and gender animosities. Madame de Genlis had been born into old nobility but grew up in poverty because her father lost the family's fortune when she was young. Her marriage to the comte de Genlis gained Madame de Genlis entry to the royal court as *dame d'honneur.* In 1772, her political and social fortunes shifted considerably as a result of a brief, opportunistic affair with the duc de Chartres, Philippe Egalité, who appointed her *gouverneur* (head tutor) of his sons, including Louis-Philippe, making her the first woman to be charged with educating a royal prince. Initially supportive of the French Revolution, Madame de Genlis fled France after the fall of the Girondins in 1793. She eventually landed in London without her husband, himself a Girondist and a casualty of the Reign of Terror. While in London, she supported herself by writing a number of popular novels and educational tracts, including *The Theatre of Education* and *Le petit La Bruyère*, the texts that Fenno apparently received in a shipment from London and clearly despised, though it is not immediately clear why. His slight of Madame de Genlis in the letter to Dickins probably had a moral dimension, as Fenno seemed critical of her very public affair with Philippe Egalité, which of course catapulted her to literary renown, at least for a time.[51]

Fenno saved his most colorful critiques for his book catalogue. Like his fellow booksellers in early America, Fenno used the catalogue to entice customers into stopping by his store. Booksellers' catalogues became increasingly ubiquitous in North America around the middle of the eighteenth century. Evolving from single-sheet broadsides that could be distributed, read, and displayed in any number of private and public spaces into small, stitched texts that resembled pamphlets, these highly portable catalogues were published by booksellers as an inexpensive way to promote their wares. Booksellers often pointed out in newspaper advertisements that if customers wanted to know more about their store, they could stop in and flip through the catalogue. Over time, the structural logic of book catalogues became increasingly complex. By the turn of the nineteenth century, booksellers like Fenno were designing their catalogues to appeal to a particular segment of the population, eschewing broad popular appeal in favor of a targeted consumer base.[52]

Fenno designed his *Supplementary Catalogue,* which he published in October 1800, to draw the city's Federalists to his Hanover Square shop. Building on the series of advertisements that appeared in the *Daily Advertiser* and the *New-York Gazette,* he emphasized that he stocked a wide variety of books and pamphlets critical of the French Revolution, while also calling attention to texts that celebrated the new nation's British colonial past. The *Supplementary Catalogue,* then, was a material reflection of Fenno's bookshop politics. The message was clear: Republicans, or at least patrons sympathetic to the French Revolution, were not welcome. And while Fenno was no longer in the business of making flamboyant pronouncements in his own daily paper, the advertisements he placed in New York's newspapers, along with his *Supplementary Catalogue,* allowed him to use a subtler, more nuanced political voice.

Fenno annotated twenty-eight titles listed in the *Supplementary Catalogue.* In many cases, he inserted his often sarcastic editorial voice to promote books that opposed the French Revolution and to mock French authors. By constructing the *Supplementary Catalogue* in this way, Fenno began a conversation with his customers, who probably expected to discuss Federalist politics while browsing the stacks. For example, Fenno described Napoleon Bonaparte's *Egyptian Correspondence* as a "very curious and interesting display of Gallic Perfidy," while M. Mercier's *New Picture of Paris* offered the finest description of "the present deplorable state of that metropolis." Fenno did occasionally find a silver lining in books with which he disagreed. Despite insulting the duc de La Rochefoucauld-Liancourt's social standing and politics, Fenno seemed to find value—at least grudgingly—in the duke's *Travels Through the United States,* Liancourt's careful meditation on his tour of North America in the late 1790s, after his forced exile from Paris. "The amusing delusions of this Sansculotte, double-faced *Duke,*" Fenno wrote, "being blended with much curious research, and some ingenious speculation, will be found to possess a degree of interest sufficiently ample to reward perusal."[53]

Fenno's biting remarks in the *Supplementary Catalogue* did not go unnoticed by his political enemies. In early December 1800, David Denniston took umbrage at Fenno's criticism of Benjamin Franklin. The offending remark, Denniston pointed out in the *American Citizen,* appeared in Fenno's lengthy celebration of Jonathan Boucher's series of pro-British sermons, delivered in the 1760s and 1770s and published in 1797 under the title *A View of the Causes and Consequences of the American Revolution.* An Anglican minister and avowed Loyalist, Boucher had preached to his parishioners in St. Anne's County, Maryland, that obedience to the English Parliament was the spiritual duty of all Americans. Aware that his message was unpopular in his parish and elsewhere in the North American colonies, Boucher fled Maryland and sailed for London in September 1775. In the *Causes and Consequences of the American Revolution,*

Boucher used Robert Filmer's *Patriarcha* to justify English rule in the colonies.[54] Denniston took exception to how Fenno praised Boucher's insult of Benjamin Franklin. "In an appendix to one of his Sermons," Fenno wrote in his catalogue, "he unfolds many private facts and anecdotes, tending to place the character of the arch hypocrite and impostor, Franklin, in a more detestable point of light, if possible, than that in which it stood before."[55] Fenno was probably referring to Boucher's suggestion that Franklin had "stolen from an Irish gentleman, of the name of *Kinnersly,* many of his useful discoveries respecting electricity."[56] It was this slur against Franklin that incensed Denniston, and in early December he lashed out at Fenno in an essay that would later appear in Norwich, Connecticut, and the District of Columbia.

> Thus it is that a shameless young man can dare to insult a whole country, by attempting to rob the honoured dead of his fair fame. Where is the spirit which ought to protect the sacred memory of America's brightest orna- ment? Shall an hireling of a foreign country! Shall an avowed foe to the interests of his own, be permitted to vilify a face, whose patriotism and eminent virtues will be held in the highest veneration, whilst honour and gratitude exists among Americans? None, but those who are callous to every generous feeling, can view without the utmost indignation, the calumniat- ing of departed worth, by sacrilegious wretches, whose infamy is as notori- ous as the name and character of Franklin are inestimable. Too long did that British emissary Porcupine, libel the same great and good man; being an Englishman, and the tool of his government, he was more excusable than an American, who has no pretext to apologize for such scandalous depravity. Mr. Adams has had the merit of patronizing this snake, who emits his poison with so much virulence upon whatever is praise-worthy, or has been respectable in the country.[57]

Denniston was of course referring to William Cobbett's habitual Franklin bashing in the pages of his newspaper, the *Porcupine's Gazette.* Cobbett had made quite a name for himself in Philadelphia going after Benjamin Franklin Bache, the printer-editor of the *Aurora* and the grandson of the late Benjamin Franklin. Cobbett was merciless in his attacks, suggesting that the steadfastly Jeffersonian Bache was the "prostitute son of oil and lamp-black" and "notori- ously in the pay of France." In November 1797, Cobbett let loose on Bache—and his cousin Temple Franklin—while also, as Denniston would later point out, undermining Franklin's good name. "This atrocious wretch (worthy descendant of *old Ben*) knows that all men of understanding set him down as an abandoned liar, as a tool, and a hireling."[58] Inspired by his mentor, Fenno—even in the fairly innocuous business of bookselling—continued this line of attack against Franklin, much to the chagrin of Jeffersonian editors like Denniston.

"Gentlemen Who Subscribed Through Him for the British Periodicals"

What could Fenno's customers expect to find upon entering his shop? By 1802, Fenno had accumulated more than thirty-five thousand items, ranging from individual copies of books and pamphlets to various types of paper and writing instruments. Much of his capital was tied up in books, pamphlets, and periodicals—almost ten thousand printed items lined the shelves of his shop. Fenno stocked more than six hundred titles, which amounted to nearly seven thousand individual copies. A majority of his book inventory was valued at nearly $6,000, while a smaller portion was valued in British pounds, probably because this was the portion of his stock imported from London. Fenno also stocked seven pamphlet titles valued at £39 and 168 pocket books worth more than $600. The shop also carried twenty-one hundred items categorized as "monthly publications" and valued at better than $100. And while he had comparatively little capital tied up in stationery—about £250—he did have approximately a thousand individual paper items. Fenno, like many booksellers in the early Republic, carried a wide variety of stationery, ranging from reams of demy paper, to thick folio, to superfine medium paper, to foolscap, as well as black and red ink powder, playing cards, writing instruments, and sealing wax. Stationery, while not the most exciting of products, was essential to a successful bookselling enterprise. Whatever form it took, paper was prohibitively expensive and time-consuming to make and was thus in high demand. Fenno probably displayed paper goods designed for the marketplace—bills of lading and exchange, both foreign and domestic, and copy slips—alongside other useful commercial items such as large folio volumes that merchants and artisans used as daybooks, letter books, and ledgers.[59]

While Fenno stocked a wide variety of books in his shop, ranging from eponymous chapbooks, to reference books, to schoolbooks, customers could also expect to find literary texts (table 3.2). Indeed, books catalogued, broadly, as belles lettres—advice, architecture, Greek and Roman classics, contemporary fiction, history, geography, political philosophy, and poetry, among many others—made up more than 60 percent of Fenno's overall inventory. Fenno specialized in several categories, including history, political philosophy, fiction, and travel literature (table 3.3). He carried, for example, nearly four hundred copies of sixty-six history titles—including many that chronicled the history of Great Britain and its empire—ranging from John Pinkerton's *Enquiry into the History*

TABLE 3.2 Total Book Stock in John Ward Fenno's Bookstore, 1802

	Itemization of Stock				Valuation of Stock	
	Copies		Titles			
	(N)	(%)	(N)	(%)	(£)	($)
Belles Lettres	4,727	69.5	368	63.4	655 04s 05d	3,540.00
Chapbooks	760	11.1	—	—	62 0s 05d	—
Education	149	2.1	39	6.7	22 05s 06d	95.83
Professional	294	4.3	112	19.3	128 04s 10d	616.94
Reference	126	1.8	27	4.6	128 01s 07d	59.50
Religious	572	8.4	34	5.8	63 15s 06d	1,072.36
Pocket Books	168	2.4	—	—	—	618.12
Book Stock TOTALS	6,796	99.6	580	99.8	1,059 12s 3d	6,002.75

SOURCE: Estate Inventory of John Ward Fenno, John Ward Fenno Papers, NYHS.

of Scotland, Bryan Edwards's *History of the British Colonies in the West Indies,* and John Payne's *Epitome of History.* Fenno's New York customers could browse a large selection of contemporary fiction, as he stocked more than 140 copies of thirty-one imprints. Readers could immerse themselves in a number of picaresque novels, including Alain-René Lesage's *Adventures of Gil Blas,* four copies of Henry Fielding's comic *History of Tom Jones, a Foundling,* and three copies of Tobias Smollett's *Adventures of Roderick Random,* among many others.

Like many of his fellow booksellers, Fenno stored books in various stages of production. In addition to fully bound books, he had on hand a variety of titles in boards without any decorative binding and in sheets. By 1802, he had more than three thousand copies of eight titles stored in sheets and 174 copies of fifty-four titles in boards. A store stocked with books in sheets was a common sight in bookstores of the era. Because of interior space constraints, booksellers often stored books either in rolls or stacked flat, "in sheets," after the printer delivered them. As the nineteenth century progressed, publishers began warehousing excess stock of rolls and sheets at neighboring binderies so as to avoid wasting precious shelf space on books for which there was little demand. John Adams's *Defence of the Constitutions of Government of the United States of America* was no longer in demand in 1802, so it is not surprising that Fenno kept nearly two hundred copies, valued at $470, in storage. Fenno also inherited quite a few copies of William Cobbett's collected works. Once Cobbett fled New York for London, customers probably lost interest—hence the fifteen hundred copies, in sheets, of *Porcupine's Works* that Fenno stored either in his shop or at a bindery not named in his accounts.[60]

TABLE 3.3 Total Belles Lettres Stock in John Ward Fenno's Bookstore, 1802

	Itemization of Stock				Valuation of Stock	
	Copies		Titles			
	(N)	(%)	(N)	(%)	(£)	($)
Advice	19	0.4	5	1.3	3 18s	18.50
Architecture	50	1.0	12	3.2	30 12s 2d	—
Biography	81	1.7	30	8.1	29 08s 08d	137.25
Classics	107	2.1	29	7.8	17 8s 6d	291.67
Cooking	230	4.8	1	0.2	7 13s 04d	—
Essays	190	4.0	58	15.7	126 9	281.22
Fiction	143	3.0	31	8.4	26 06s 11d	163.00
Gardening	3	0	2	0.5	2 11s 6d	—
Geography	22	0.4	7	1.9	1 07s	123.50
History	390	8.2	66	17.9	141 15s 08d	581.50
Music	47	0.9	4	1.0	4 18s	56.61
Philosophy	1,748	36.9	19	5.1	6 11s 02d	611.74
Plays	218	4.6	9	2.4	42 15s	92.90
Poetry	272	5.7	33	8.9	94 01s 01d	195.37
Travel	120	2.5	42	11.4	85 15s 01d	285.75
Misc.	1,087	22.9	20	5.4	9 14s 01d	700.99
TOTAL	4,727	98.3	368	99	631 05s 02d	$3,540.00

SOURCE: Estate Inventory of John Ward Fenno, John Ward Fenno Papers, NYHS.

Fenno, like Cobbett before him, imported several British periodicals. When he announced his takeover of Cobbett's business, Fenno reassured New York readers that subscriptions to their favorite magazines would continue unimpeded. "Having succeeded to his business here," Fenno wrote, "subscriptions for the four Periodical British works advertised by Mr. Cobbett, will be received by me and forwarded as heretofore." Once in business in New York, he avidly promoted the London weekly *Anti-Jacobin, or Weekly Examiner* in his book catalogue. The *Anti-Jacobin,* he wrote, brought together "the finest wits and geniuses of England," suggesting that it was "of course, one of the most ingenious productions of the present day."[61] Although he was probably preaching to the choir, Fenno's endorsement was nonetheless a stirring appeal that surely brought in a few new readers, given his celebrity as the former editor of the *Gazette of the United States.*

By 1802, Fenno carried a large selection of periodicals, including several British publications critical of Jacobinism in France and beyond that formed the heart of his collection. He had two copies of a two-volume, thirty-six-issue set of the *Anti-Jacobin, or Weekly Examiner.* Groundbreaking and widely read during its brief run, the *Anti-Jacobin* effectively combined literature and politics and was designed by its publishers to curtail British sympathy for the French Revolution.[62] Fenno also stocked four copies of *Beauties of the Anti-Jacobin,* a compendium of essays by George Canning, John Hookham Frere, George Ellis, and William Gifford that had originally appeared in the *Anti-Jacobin.* Patrons would also have found seven sets of the *Anti-Jacobin Review and Magazine* next to the *Anti-Jacobin, or Weekly Examiner* on the shelves of Fenno's shop. Like the *Anti-Jacobin, or Weekly Examiner,* the *Anti-Jacobin Review* was an attempt to subvert French radicals and their supporters. The editors even went so far as to call for the persecution of political dissidents in Great Britain. In their prospectus, the editors of the *Anti-Jacobin Review* advocated the use of the press to control the "vehicles of JACOBINISM" that had been allowed to spread from revolutionary France to Great Britain. "The press has been too long an engine of destruction," they wrote, and should "be rendered a means of preservation, and an instrument of protection" of the state.[63] As estimable as they made their aims seem, the editors of the *Anti-Jacobin Review* advocated the silencing of radical voices, including the prosecution of Thomas Paine in an actual criminal trial as a symbolic muting of Jacobin voices. Likewise, Fenno stocked the *British Critic,* yet another reactionary British journal—in this case a High Church publication—critical of the French Revolution.[64] In addition to periodicals damning the French Revolution, Fenno imported titles that celebrated British culture, including fifteen volumes of the *Annual Register,* a London periodical that brought together in one issue the previous year's major developments in politics, economics, and literature.[65]

Fenno was an important distributor of these conservative British periodicals. In October 1800, for example, he sent a case of magazines to Asbury Dickins in Philadelphia "by the Sloop *Patience,*" including twelve copies of the *British Critic,* six of the *Anti-Jacobin,* six of *Gentleman's Magazine,* and six volumes each of the first through fifth run of the *Anti-Jacobin Review.* Fenno asked his protégé to take subscriptions for the magazines on his behalf. "I send you a number of the above works for persons who subscribed to me in Philadelphia," he wrote, adding that he would make "no apology for putting you to the trouble of delivering these, as I know you will do it with cheerfulness, and I hope besides, that it may be of advantage to you, by bringing customers for other articles in your shop." Fenno also asked Dickins to place an advertisement for the British periodicals in the *Gazette of the United States.* "Please have this note published in Wayne's paper," he told Dickins: "J. W. Fenno acquaints those Gentlemen who subscribed through him for the British Periodicals works; and those who sent out orders for miscellaneous books, either thro' him or Wm. Cobbett, that Mr. Dickins will deliver their Books, at his store in Second Street, opposite Christ Church."[66] Dickins apparently went straightaway to the office of the *Gazette* to place the ad, which appeared on 25 October 1800.[67]

In two short years, Fenno had built up his stock to nearly ten thousand copies of more than six hundred individual titles, not to mention a variety of stationery and related items he offered to the merchant community and individual customer alike. And while he stocked a large assortment of books, Fenno specialized, as we have seen, in belles lettres: history, novels, travel stories, classics, and so on. But perhaps Fenno's most significant contribution to the early national print market was his continued importation of well-known British periodicals like the *Anti-Jacobin Review*, which he not only stocked locally but shipped to cities beyond New York. If the advertisements in New York's newspapers and the *Supplementary Catalogue* were not enough, his avid promotion of reactionary British publications left no doubt about Fenno's political sympathies.

"The Feast of Reason and the Flow of the Soul"

In early May 1801, Fenno moved his bookshop from the crowded quarters at Hanover Square to 141 Broadway, a few doors down from the elegant City Hotel. Once settled in his new space, Fenno excitedly announced the arrival of "a variety of the latest publications" from London, including the most recent issue of the *Anti-Jacobin Review*.[68] Fenno's move to Broadway, so soon after his arrival from Philadelphia, reflected the harsh reality that many New York merchants and artisans faced each spring. Moving was an annual tradition. In an unregulated housing market, unscrupulous landlords did not think twice about evicting tenants when a competing merchant or artisan offered more money for the space. Moreover, in a Dutch tradition passed down through the ages, leases across the city expired at the same time, on the same day. As a result, the first of May—which became known around town as "moving day"—witnessed the pandemonium of thousands of merchants, artisans, bankers, stockbrokers, jobbers, importers and exporters, and auctioneers spilling out into the street, the tools of their trade in tow and merchandise strewn about, to journey to their new place of business. Relocation for men in the book trade was an especially onerous task: packing up the shop's stock made for a long and challenging day of heavy work for white-frocked city cart men who transported the inventory from the old location to the new. The chaos of moving day, felt by thousands of New Yorkers each spring, was aptly described in the *Monthly Magazine, and American Review* by a woman named Amy Armstrong.

Now I scarcely know any grievance greater than that of being compelled to move once a year from one house to another. The people of this city are seized, on the first of May, by a sort of madness, that will not let them rest till they have changed their dwelling. No matter how conveniently and *cleverly* they may be situated. No sooner does spring appear, than preparations are made to move on the first of May. A new house must be looked for, and nothing must be thought or talked of, for the next three months, but what house we shall take.[69]

Fenno's Broadway storefront presents an interesting case study of competing literary politics. A few doors down from his new shop was Hoquet Caritat's bookstore and circulating library. A French national championed by Paine, promoter of French Enlightenment philosophy, steadfast defender of the French Revolution, and proponent of republicanism, Caritat would have made Jack Fenno's skin crawl. Born in 1752 in Vitry-le-François, just east of Paris, Caritat immigrated to the United States in 1792 after having tried, unsuccessfully, to establish a business in Paris at the height of the Revolution. In 1793, not long after the Citizen Genêt Affair, Caritat opened a circulating library in New York along with the publisher of Paine's controversial *Age of Reason*. By 1802, the circulating library, now located at the City Hotel, had grown to include a bookstore that boasted more than thirty-thousand titles—by far the biggest in the city. Caritat's catalogue, *The Feast of Reason and the Flow of the Soul*, provided customers with a detailed, partially annotated list of the books to be found in his City Hotel shop; only occasionally did Caritat allow his voice to interject into this carefully constructed text. Building on the success of his shop and circulating library, in 1801 Caritat founded what he called a "Literary Assembly"—consisting of the city's most influential politicians, attorneys, writers, scientists, clergymen, and physicians—that met regularly to discuss literary, philosophical, political, and scientific texts. Hoping to draw more members of substance, Caritat began encouraging women to attend the gatherings in 1803. Caritat's business, then, became a gathering place for New York's intellectual and literary elite, including recently arrived radical émigrés. Caritat was known to stock Voltaire, Rousseau, Diderot, Buffon, Holbach, Volney, and Condorcet, among others, old and new volumes of the *Encylopédie*, books documenting the French Revolution, and works by British Jacobin authors. He also regularly had on hand the same anti-Jacobin literature from Great Britain that Jack Fenno sold down the street; unlike his neighbor Fenno, Caritat was on good terms with both Federalists and Jeffersonians. Indeed, few men in the new nation could legitimately claim to count as friends both Thomas Paine and Alexander Hamilton.[70]

Caritat's large bookstore and circulating library was housed in the City Hotel on Broadway, a tony Federal-style brick building built in 1794. The City Hotel was Manhattan's first "modern" hotel and was built to accommodate overnight guests visiting the city in its nearly 140 neatly appointed rooms. But the hotel was not limited to providing lodging to business travelers and pleasure seekers. As the largest and most majestic building in Manhattan, the City Hotel became a hub of social, economic, and political activity as soon as it opened. The New York Customs House, for example, relocated to the City Hotel in 1795, and the building became an important meeting place for Manhattan's leading politicians. The hotel was also known for its elegant dining hall, and its labyrinthine wine cellars became the talk of the town in elite social circles. The exterior of the building was just as important to the city's economy as the spacious and sophisticated interior. On the ground level, a busy coffeehouse and several shops fronted Broadway. Once built, these shops became the most sought-after business addresses in the city. But the draw of the City Hotel was not limited to the building itself. The adjacent buildings became just as desirable, as merchants looked to capitalize on the elite clientele that frequented the hotel and its many shops. Fenno, like other ambitious merchants, recognized the potential of relocating to the area near the City Hotel, which included businesses such as ice-cream shops and pleasure gardens. Fenno was also surely aware that moving to 141 Broadway would put him in a position to compete with Caritat.[71]

Fenno's decision to relocate to 141 Broadway, then, was a shrewd political and business move. Fenno's bookshop politics, so carefully crafted in the *Supplementary Catalogue* and advertisements in the city's newspapers, can be read as an imitation and satirical inversion of Caritat's store. Whereas Caritat's bookstore would have been patronized by the city's radical Republicans, poring over French Enlightenment philosophy while humming *"liberté, égalité, fraternité!"* between the stacks, local Federalists just a few doors down could flip through copies of the *Anti-Jacobin Review* and discuss rascally Jeffersonians with the former editor of the *Gazette of the United States*. Fenno's relocation to Broadway was a deliberate effort to create a political counterpoint to Caritat's carefully curated bookstore and circulating library. The competing literary politics that overtook Broadway in the early nineteenth century also reflected in microcosm the city's—and indeed the nation's—struggles with the emergence of a two-party political system. Given that Caritat had been in business for several years prior to Fenno's arrival in the city, it was only fitting that Fenno become an insurgent of sorts and confront Caritat's store with his own brand of bookshop politics.

The Federalist Literary Market

After establishing himself in New York, Fenno used his political connections to develop a national distribution network of retail booksellers to distribute his brand of literary politics. The estate inventory prepared shortly after his death in 1802 outlines the distribution network he built during his brief career as a New York bookseller. The men charged with assessing Fenno's accounts probably used his ledgers to record all of his unsettled local, regional, and national accounts in their inventory. The assessors did not include the total number of transactions between Fenno and his retail agents, nor did they indicate the number of titles or copies Fenno sent to each bookseller. Rather, they copied the summaries of transaction histories from Fenno's ledgers, noting only the dollar amount for the outstanding balance due from booksellers.

The contours of a national distribution network of printers and booksellers emerge from the pages of Fenno's estate inventory. The assessors recorded sixty-five accounts that fell into the categories "Books on Commission," "Unsettled," "In Dispute," and "Failed."[72] Fenno's estate inventory provides only a partial summary, however, because it lists contacts who still owed Fenno money on the commission accounts. The reach of his business was probably far greater than the inventory suggests. I have identified with certainty thirty-five men in Fenno's network of booksellers working on commission. Commission accounts, like the names listed in the Fenno estate inventory, allowed booksellers and publishers to unload portions of their stock to smaller shops while also providing the agent a vast assortment of risk-free titles. Booksellers retained the rights to the books distributed to commission agents, and if they did not sell in their new markets, the commission agent could return them without penalty. Commission accounts, then, created sophisticated local, regional, and national networks of credit. Aside from the twelve New York booksellers and the six in Philadelphia on account with Fenno, more than half of Fenno's commission accounts were in locations beyond the mid-Atlantic.

It is possible that Fenno inherited many of the commission agents from his predecessor, William Cobbett. When Fenno assumed control of Cobbett's New York bookstore in June 1800, he probably also gained control of Porcupine's distribution network, which was quite extensive. Indeed, when Cobbett handed over the keys to the shop, Fenno would have inherited a network of seventy-five booksellers. In announcing the opening of his shop, Fenno made it known that he hoped to retain Cobbett's customer base, and this hope almost certainly included keeping in contact with the booksellers in Cobbett's commission network. Cobbett and his successor developed several connections in New England. Cobbett had three contacts in Boston—David West, Joseph Nancrede, and James White—in addition to Isaac and John Beers in New Haven, Connecticut, Edmund Blunt in Newburyport, Thomas Cushing in Salem, and W. Van Schaak in Pittsfield in the Berkshires. Only one New England bookseller—John Neilson of Providence, Rhode Island—appeared in Fenno's estate inventory. Cobbett and Fenno also had several international contacts in their distribution networks.

Cobbett worked with an Edward Edwards in Montreal, a London bookseller named John Wright, the Glasgow firm of James & Andrew Duncan, and the Jamaican bookstore Aikman, Smith & Stevenson. Fenno inherited the account of Anthony Henry, a Halifax bookseller, and an "unsettled" affair with a "Capt. Williamson" of Geneva, Switzerland.[73]

Fenno, like Cobbett before him, also did extensive business with southern booksellers. According to his estate inventory, he had at least thirteen southern booksellers on commission in five towns and cities (table 3.4). Fenno had ten accounts with booksellers in the Chesapeake region, three in Alexandria, Virginia, two in Norfolk, and five in Baltimore, Maryland. Fenno developed a relationship with the Alexandria partnerships of Cotton & Stewart and Bennett & Watts and with the Reverend Needler Robinson and B. Pollard & Co. in Norfolk. Fenno's five Baltimore booksellers were Campbell, Conrad, & Company; Ryan St. John; Robert Walsh; William Taylor; and Samuel Cole. Cobbett likewise

TABLE 3.4 Fenno's Unsettled Accounts by Region, 1802

Region, City, State	Accounts		Stock Received	
	(N)	(%)	($)	(%)
Mid-Atlantic				
New York, NY	12	34.2	307.08	10.6
Philadelphia, PA	6	17.2	1,817.00	63.2
TOTAL	18	51.4	2,124.08	73.8
New England				
Providence, RI	1	2.8	17.25	0.6
TOTAL	1	2.8	17.25	0.6
South				
Alexandria, VA	3	8.5	38.50	1.3
Norfolk, VA	2	5.7	60.75	2.1
Baltimore, MD	5	14.2	139.25	4.8
Charleston, SC	2	5.7	87.50	3.0
Washington, DC	1	2.8	9.32	0.3
TOTAL	13	36.9	335.32	11.5
International				
London, England	1	2.8	316.21	11.0
Halifax, Nova Scotia, Canada	1	2.8	79.25	2.7
Geneva, Switzerland	1	2.8	2.00	0
TOTAL	3	8.4	397.46	13.7
OVERALL TOTALS	35	99.5	2,874.11	99.6

SOURCE: Estate Inventory of John Ward Fenno, John Ward Fenno Papers, NYHS.

had a number of Chesapeake connections in towns ranging from Easton, Fredericktown, Georgetown Crossroads, and Williamsport in Maryland, and Chambersburg, Petersburg, and Richmond in Virginia. Cobbett and Fenno maintained several accounts in towns farther south, including Thomas Miller in Savannah and the Charleston, South Carolina, bookseller William Young, who was listed in both Cobbett's account book and Fenno's estate inventory.

Much of Fenno's distribution network was tied up with mid-Atlantic booksellers, Philadelphia in particular. Cobbett, likewise, traded frequently with several Philadelphia booksellers, reflected in the fifteen men listed in his account book.[74] Of the six booksellers listed in Fenno's estate inventory, quite a bit of the money still owed to him was held by two men: Asbury Dickins and John Conrad. Conrad was the patriarch of an interstate publishing family with outposts in Baltimore and in Petersburg and Norfolk, Virginia. The Conrad family built a sizeable publishing business in the early years of the nineteenth century, becoming a leading distributor of schoolbooks and literature. The Conrads' success was not immune to the ebbs and flows of the market, however, as they succumbed to what one historian describes as a "spectacular bankruptcy" in 1813.[75]

Asbury Dickins traveled, or at least hoped to, in the same intellectual circles as aspiring men of letters. By the time Dickins was twenty-one, his Second Street bookshop had become, according to the English traveler John Davis, a "rendezvous" point for a great many of Philadelphia's "sons of literature."[76] The oldest son of the Methodist clergyman John Dickins, Asbury—named after the itinerant Methodist preacher Francis Asbury—chose a life among men "of Affluence, Men of Liberality, and Men of Letters," a path that surely did not sit well with his stern father, who wanted him to enter the ministry.[77] Characterized by one historian as little more than a "snob, a social climber, and a Federalist toady," Dickins was nonetheless important to John Ward Fenno's literary and political ambitions.[78]

Fenno and especially Dickins hitched their wagons to the literary and editorial career of Joseph Dennie. As an essayist and the editor of the Walpole, New Hampshire, *Farmer's Weekly Museum,* Dennie had developed a reputation among Federalists as an outspoken critic of Republicans and champions of democracy such as Thomas Paine. With the *Farmer's Weekly Museum* facing financial troubles, Dennie relocated to Philadelphia in 1799—after a failed bid to become Walpole's congressional representative in 1798—where he worked for a time as Secretary of State Timothy Pickering's personal secretary. In January 1801, with Dickins as his printer, Dennie published the first issue of the *Port Folio,* without doubt the leading political and literary magazine in early nineteenth-century America. Writing as "Oliver Oldschool, Esq.," Dennie was ruthless in his criticism of ordinary people and their champion, President Thomas Jefferson. Over the course of eleven years, Dennie and the writers who gravitated to him fashioned in the pages of the *Port Folio* what historian Catherine O'Donnell Kaplan has called a "profoundly oppositional community" in an increasingly Jeffersonian nation.[79]

From the vantage point of his New York bookshop, Fenno looked to involve himself, as best he could, in Dennie's new Philadelphia project. Fenno wrote Dickins that "whenever Mr. D. sees fit to come forward in seriousness & commence with his publications," he would make "exertions to promote the success of his book." Dennie's skills as a polemicist excited Fenno a great deal, and he promised to help out in the publication and distribution of the magazine. On this note, Fenno suggested that his endorsement of the *Port Folio* carried great weight. "I do not choose to commit myself upon the abortive projects of other men," he told Dickins, apparently with no sense of irony. Yet Fenno had grown weary with Dennie's apparent lack of initiative in moving forward with the magazine, and he complained to Dickins that Dennie "ought, by this time, to be half through the Press," yet given the uninspiring pace, it was doubtful "whether he has a page ready."[80] Dennie's slow pace notwithstanding, Fenno was confident that the *Port Folio* would help invigorate Federalists nationwide.

Despite the early production hiccups, prospects for Dennie's project seemed high in January 1801. Responding to Dickins's request for advice about how best to construct a feasible distribution system for the *Port Folio*, Fenno suggested that Dickins contact a number of reliable booksellers in his own circle to help take subscriptions and disseminate the magazine. The names Fenno gave to Dickins reveal the national aspirations that he and his protégé shared for the *Port Folio*. In the process, Fenno reflected on his experiences in publishing and distributing the *Gazette of the United States*. "The subject which you suggest to my consideration will prove one of the most delicate points in the construct of your establishment," Fenno wrote to Dickins in February 1801.

I tell you from experience that you cannot be too cautious in appointing your agents. I would recommend to you Geo. Hill at Baltimore, and Augustine Davis of Richmond, to whom you are welcome to use my name. I think 2.5 per cent an adequate compensation for collecting $5 each from 20 people—tho I think it likely that you may have to give 5. When I printed the Gaz. I made particular agreements on the best terms I could, without any particular standard. I would have you to look well to a man's ability as well as honesty, and select men either rich or in good business: I lost more by the poverty of agents than by dishonesty. Indeed, I do not see what need you have of a great number of agents. The two whom I have mentioned, White at Boston, appear to me adequate to every purpose. If you extend your views to the Southern air, W. P. Young at Charleston is a proper man.[81]

Dickins evidently took Fenno's guidance to heart, at least initially. He reached out to George Hill—a Baltimore bookseller to whom Fenno had once referred as "that hog of a fellow"—to propose establishing a commission account to distribute the *Port Folio* throughout the Chesapeake region.[82] Despite his initial enthusiasm for Fenno's suggestions, two surviving letters indicate that Dickins's attempt to extend the *Port Folio*'s distribution network into the Chesapeake Bay area was half-hearted at best. Writing to Dickins in June 1801, Hill asked to have $200 assigned to his credit. Perhaps wanting to stroke Dickins's ego, Hill praised the books Dickins had sent him. "When I get a little more leisure I will tell you the success of your Goods sent me on commission and perhaps slip you a few more dollars."[83] Less than a month later, Hill chastised Dickins for his failure to respond. "I wrote yours of the 18th inst . . . begging you to acknowledge receipt of the money," Hill fumed. "Why this is not done in course I know not," he said, adding, "when I send you cash again I will take care to guard against such disappointment."[84] Dickins's lack of response to Hill's angry letters foreshadowed troubles lurking just over the horizon.

Publication of the *Port Folio* was troubled from the start. Fenno seemed particularly vexed by Dickins's inability to get the *Port Folio* out to subscribers—himself and his New York customers included—on time. While he did acknowledge that "a very handsome subscription will be had" in New York, Fenno was not impressed with Dickins's skill as a magazine publisher. "Care must be taken, however, to forward the numbers with more punctuality," he wrote. "Tho published Saturday, they never reach us until Thursday. You should see to this." Distribution of the *Port Folio* remained a concern for Fenno in his correspondence with Dickins for the next eight months. "For God's sake send on your papers earlier," Fenno begged in February; "instead of coming on Monday, they never reach us 'till Wednesday, & others not till Thursday." Fenno insisted that the slow pace of production should have been corrected by then, as he considered it a short-term problem. And of course Fenno filled his letters with passive-aggressive comments and what he considered helpful advice. "While your establishment was new[,] men overlooked inequalities," he pointed out, "but believe me, the continuance of those inequalities . . . will materially affect the interests of the concern." Fenno was annoyed that he still had not received his copies of the *Port Folio* more than a week later. "The papers still come on very irregularly," he noted. "We are now at Thursday, without the paper on Saturday last, tho' I suspect the mail of this day to bring it." A full five months later, in July, Fenno's irritation with Dickins persisted. He told Dickins about an Albany subscriber who had paid him five dollars for the *Port Folio* but had never received it. And yet, despite this frustration, the Albany subscriber remained committed to the *Port Folio*, for he paid Fenno again, this time requesting a full run of the magazine "from 1st no." The problems continued into August, as New York subscribers began complaining not only to Fenno but to men at the post office. "No Port Folio this week," he wrote Dickins with palpable irritation. "The fellows in the Post Office here (not the best natured scoundrels in the world) swear & fret not a little at being men as they are by enquiries, from the subscribers."[85] These early production and distribution issues, however, were temporary. The *Port Folio*'s surviving account books reveal that not only did subscriptions span the entire early American landscape, from New England, to the South, and west into Kentucky, but the magazine remained a successful venture for many years on Dennie's watch.[86]

The *Port Folio*'s success was not the result of Dickins's correcting these early problems. Even with Fenno's continued support, which bordered on obsession, Dickins began to wilt from the stress caused by the mountain of debt he had incurred. After Dickins read a hastily composed note from Fenno in July 1801, begging him to forward two volumes of the index to the *Annual Register* "as soon as this gets to hand," he seems to have considered following in William Cobbett's footsteps, or at least to have daydreamed about it. On the reverse of the note, in two sloppy columns, one on either side of his Second Street address, Dickins scribbled the word "London" ten times, one half-hearted "Lond" falling below his panicked scrawl on the right-hand side.[87] It was not long before Dickins's tortured fantasy would become reality. In late October 1801, he received a letter from one C. W. Hare that began, "It is with pain that I find myself in some measure compelled to send you the enclosed Notice." "You will please take notice," the letter continued, "that unless you enter special bail in the above case in the sum of fifteen thousand dollars on or before Wednesday next at twelve o'clock at noon at the office of Edward Burd, Esq in Fourth Street near Walnut capias ad respondendum will be issued against you at the suit of the above mentioned Samuel Blodget."[88] Dickins did not stick around for the legal proceedings. The day after receiving the summons, he granted power of attorney to Thomas W. Armat; amazingly enough, Joseph Dennie signed as a witness to the transfer.[89] Hours later, Dickins crossed the Delaware River to New Castle, a small town just south of Wilmington, where he hopped a ship to Liverpool.[90] The move was so sudden that, as with Fenno's abrupt departure from Philadelphia two years earlier, Dickins's attorney was put in the awkward position of shipping clothes and providing his client with cash. According to Armat's records, he sent along "To Cloaths at Newcastle—50," in addition to "Pocket 20 Guineas—$93.33."[91]

And just like that, Asbury Dickins was gone, leaving his friends to clean up the mess he had left behind. Obviously furious, Fenno began the difficult task of reclaiming the books, stationery, and periodicals he had sent to Dickins while simultaneously trying to recoup cash owed him on the commission account. Both Fenno and John Rodman drew up detailed debt sheets that ended up in

Armat's hands. "You have on the other side a general statement of my a/c against A. Dickins," he wrote to Rodman in January 1802, though he admitted that "without documents that could be furnished only by Dickins himself," he was unable to "come at any thing like the true Balance."[92] The total debt that Dickins owed Fenno came to $1,303.32. After Fenno's death, Rodman drew up yet another assessment, a document that paints an unflattering portrait of Asbury Dickins as an untrustworthy merchant. The debt sheet indicates that Fenno provided Dickins with at least $3,075.21 worth of books and prints—the latter, apparently, at cost—during the course of their business arrangement. And while Dickins seems to have returned a portion of the unsold stock, to the tune of $1,341.90 worth of "sundry books," Fenno received only $160.20 from Dickins for books actually sold on commission, hardly a profitable return given the size of the overall investment. All told, even after Fenno's death, Dickins was still in considerable debt to his friend and patron.[93]

Dickins's sudden flight to Liverpool was a fitting end to a year in which Fenno pestered him to do a better job at keeping up with his accounts. "Business is deplorably dull, with everybody," Fenno complained to Dickins in March 1801. Despite his boredom that day, Fenno was clearly annoyed with Dickins's inability to keep accurate books. "I wish you would make out a statement of your sales on the Comm. a/c as I want to close several affairs, particularly with Mr. Boucher, for the sale of his books."[94] Dickins, though, eventually disputed Fenno's numbers. Writing from his self-imposed exile in London, Dickins pleaded his innocence. "I owe Pratt 1500 dollars, which I am to repay whenever it be convenient," he wrote to his attorney. "Fenno," on the other hand, "must be mistaken; it is impossible he should be accurate in his statement."[95] Armat, however, told Dickins that his fortunes in Philadelphia were indeed bleak, partly owing to Dickins's slapdash account books. Amazingly enough, in Armat's expert legal opinion, Dickins's flight to London was a legitimate response to the situation. "Have only one moment to say that your note to John Vaughn is this day protested for non payment & that he has intimated a determination to send it to London to collect of you there," Armat wrote to Dickins. Claims against Dickins and his estate amounted to "ten thousand Dollars" in Armat's estimation. Not only that, but his friendship with Fenno seems to have completely disintegrated. "Fenno has taken away the books he sent you on Commission & says there is still 1700 Dollars due," a debt made worse by Dickins' inability to keep accurate records. "Your Books throw no light on it." In the end, Armat recommended that Dickins remain abroad, and thus out of the reach of his creditors. "In the Interim," he warned ominously, "I know not what you have left for it but flight."[96]

Armat did not exaggerate in his stark assessment of Asbury's situation. Dickins left behind considerable debt—nearly $6,500—and a large book inventory: three thousand copies of nearly 350 titles that he had neglected. If this was not enough to make Dickins and his attorney sweat, the Philadelphia shop also had a large assortment of stationery and blank books gathering dust on the shelves.[97]

The failed partnership with Dickins was the final chapter in Jack Fenno's brief, tumultuous career in public life. Fenno's attempt to create a national distribution network of Federalist booksellers was, ultimately, a failure. His literary ambitions were cut short by his untimely death, in 1802, after a bout with Yellow Fever, and also by the incompetence of Asbury Dickins, who stiffed not only Fenno but numerous other business partners and spent the remainder of his days in debtors' prison.[98] Fenno left dozens of commission accounts in limbo, the fragmentary remains of what he surely envisioned as a counterpoint to the network of Republican newspapers that catapulted Jefferson to the presidency in 1800.[99] There was an urgency in Fenno's endeavor to publicize and distribute texts that supported his conservative ideas and the Federalist cause, but in the end it came to nothing.

Still, Fenno's bookshop politics lived on in New York after his death. Ezra Sargeant—the man responsible for drawing up Fenno's estate inventory—announced in 1802 that he had opened his own shop on Water Street using Fenno's stock. Sargeant made sure to point out that he had "purchased the valuable stock on hand of Mr. John W. Fenno, deceased," and that Fenno's customers could find the latest copies of the *Anti-Jacobin Review* and *British Critic* at Sargeant's new shop. In addition to the British magazines on hand, Sargeant, like Cobbett and Fenno before him, advertised "an extensive and valuable collection of the latest and best London editions, many of which are executed in a style superior to the generality of Books usually imported into America." Although Fenno was no longer around to build a Federalist reading public connected to a transatlantic conservative British literary culture, Sargeant carried on his work using "connections in England" that enabled him to "receive by the earliest opportunities, the principal new works that merit attention."[100]

4

LITERARY FAIRS AND NATIONAL AMBITIONS

In mid-June 1804, the American Company of Booksellers gathered in New York's Lovett Hotel for its semiannual national literary fair. Important rituals of the nineteenth-century American publishing industry, trade sales and literary fairs were restricted to members of the book trade, and organizers solicited participation from both local and out-of-town sellers. Books went up for sale in lots, and prices, based on the suggestions of the seller, were determined by bids. Trade sales allowed large publishers to distribute their stock while simultaneously giving small booksellers the opportunity to diversify.[1]

After selecting Philadelphia's Mathew Carey to serve as the fair's president, and New York's Isaac Collins and Thomas S. Arden as vice president and secretary, respectively, the booksellers celebrated the skilled workmanship of American printers by awarding medals. Typically, the presentation of a medal was a symbolic gesture meant to commemorate politicians and military heroism. In this instance, however, the medals commemorating American presswork on European texts represented a form of economic patriotism. After giving the first-place medal to Philadelphia's Robert Carr, the booksellers celebrated the work of New York printers George F. Hopkins and Jonathan Seymour with a second-place medal for their edition of *History of the Reign of the Emperor Charles V*. The inscription on their medal read, in part, "Presented by the American Association of Book Sellers to Hopkins and Seymour for the Second Best Specimen of Printing" in the United States in 1804.[2]

Both Hopkins and Seymour enjoyed long and varied careers, though their paths intersected only briefly. Born in 1769 in Amenia, New York, Hopkins arrived in Manhattan in 1796 after bouncing around New Jersey for a few years, striking up a partnership with Joseph D. Webb and Noah Webster. His relationship with Webb, however, quickly soured. In May 1797, Hopkins and Webster dropped Webb from the firm because the three apparently could not work together. "Differences have arisen between Noah Webster, George F.

Hopkins, & Joseph Dudley Webb," they wrote, which made it "impossible to adjust with said Webb in an amiable manner."[3]

Webster kept Hopkins busy. Hopkins was in charge of maintaining Webster's newspaper, the *Commercial Advertiser*, and its twice-weekly "country" edition, the *Spectator*, and "such other articles of printing as shall be judged to be advantageous." Webster withdrew "himself from the ordinary business of the office" and instead spent his time "preparing original matter for the press." Hopkins, meanwhile, oversaw the daily operation of the shop. In particular, he was responsible for the content in Webster's *Commercial Advertiser*. According to his contract with Webster, Hopkins was in charge of handpicking "matter for the newspaper" in addition to rejecting the "personalities, calumny, and whatever may tend to injure their credit and circulation."[4] This sort of arrangement, while not explicit in the contract, suggests that Hopkins spent much of his day poring over the "exchange papers" that arrived in the office each week from American printers near and far, in addition to news received from Europe. In this type of situation, Hopkins probably scoured newspapers as they arrived and published the material fit to print in the *Advertiser*.[5] And while Hopkins was tasked with keeping his eyes on national and international news, Webster gave himself far-ranging editorial powers. "The said Noah Webster shall supply original matter, political, literary, and miscellaneous in such a manner as to promote the essential interests of the business."[6] The partnership did not last long, however. In early April 1799—less than two years after the original contract was signed—Hopkins and Webster dissolved their partnership, though it seems to have been an amicable separation. Webster was granted ownership of the shop's equipment and the *Commercial Advertiser* and *Spectator*, while Hopkins received a cash buyout.[7]

By 1803, George Hopkins was back in business, this time with Jonathan Seymour. The partnership was immediately recognized as one of the best in the city and in the new Republic, evidenced by the recognition the two men received at the 1804 literary fair. Despite their reputation as meticulous and talented pressmen, their partnership lasted only a few years. Whatever their differences may have been, Seymour was well regarded by the city's journeymen printers. Reflecting on his time working in Seymour's shop, Thurlow Weed later wrote that his "situation at the office of Mr. Seymour was a very pleasant one," pointing out in his memoir that "Mr. Seymour himself was a kind-hearted man, who had an encouraging word for all" and ran a "well-regulated shop."[8]

The medal presented to George Hopkins and Jonathan Seymour was an important symbolic and material representation of the American book trade's growth and economic independence. The story of how the book trade arrived at this point is the subject of this chapter. New York tradesmen organized in two separate moments in 1802 to promote their economic interests: a crisis in early February involving an increased duty on printing type, and the meeting of the first American literary fair in July. While these events, half a year apart, seemed like entirely different reasons for organizing, the two meetings struck a familiar chord: the protection and expansion of the American book trade. Both meetings encouraged independence from European publishers and conveyed a tone of mutual, nationwide economic improvement. The 1802 meetings reveal how a nationally conscious political constituency took shape as printers and booksellers mobilized to improve their trade. By the time the trade met again in 1804, organizers financed the production of commemorative medals celebrating the best printing done in America. And while medals given out during the fair embodied the trade's ambitions (and also its anxieties), the message was loud and clear: books produced in America with American labor for an American readership could compete with the best that London had to offer.

These meetings were part of a broader political movement to protect American economic independence. No longer bound by the restrictions of British mercantilism, American mechanics began manufacturing their own consumer goods, and merchants began participating in local, regional, national, and international commerce on their own terms. Nevertheless, British merchants saturated the former colonies with cheap manufactured goods, making it difficult for American industry to keep pace. Taking exception to the increased level of competition from Europe, mechanics and merchants promoted economic independence and manufacturing self-sufficiency as a way to fulfill the promise of independence, a form of political economy that the historian Lawrence Peskin has called "popular neomercantilism." Pro-manufacturing protectionists in major seaport cities pushed for state and federal intervention to protect American industry, which was still growing. Many groups lobbied for higher tariffs, legislation that they hoped would slow the flood of British goods to the United States in the years after the War of Independence.[9]

But promoters of American economic independence had to fight an uphill battle. Inflation was high in the late 1780s and early 1790s, and so there was little reason for Americans to turn away from Great Britain and cheap, plentiful manufactured goods. Yet it was precisely at this moment that "patriotic pride in independence, a less economically rational concern, captivated a broad portion of the public," a movement, Peskin suggests, that "spread enthusiasm about the potential for the new economy." Proponents of popular neomercantilism pushed for an expansion of domestic manufacturing that would lead to less reliance on foreign trade. In the process, these economic protectionists convinced "a substantial segment of the population, especially in the cities, that manufacturing was in the best interest of the new nation and that it could provide important economic gains."[10] Printers and booksellers publicly defended their economic

interests by encouraging domestic manufacturing and discouraging the importation of European books. They had much to lose and even more to gain in
trying to protect the new nation's book trade. Had they not joined together in a
common national cause against the real threat of foreign competition, their
growing empires of print would have dwindled almost as fast as they had grown.

The actions of the city's printers and booksellers, then, were part of a
long-standing tradition of trade activism. New York had for some time been
home to advocates of American manufacturing. The Society for the Encouragement of American Manufactures, formed in January 1789 at a Water Street
tavern by several prominent merchants, hoped to establish Manhattan as the
nation's preeminent manufacturing center. The society had high hopes after
building a lavish textile factory on Crown Street at a cost of nearly $60,000,
aspirations that were ultimately left unfulfilled when the factory's doors closed
after only two years. Despite such early hiccups, advocates continued to stress
the importance of establishing American domestic manufacturing. In 1791,
Robert R. Livingston helped found the New York Society for the Promotion of
Agriculture, Arts, and Manufacturers, which for many years lobbied the federal
government to help support the development of American industry. Likewise,
smaller groups of merchants and mechanics—including the city's printers and
booksellers—demanded that the U.S. Congress intervene in foreign trade to
help protect domestic manufacturing from competition from abroad, especially
Great Britain.[11]

In striking contrast to John Ward Fenno's business model, the printers
and booksellers who gathered in New York imagined a trade free from the
influence of the powerful London publishing guild, which they had relied on
for many years to line the shelves of their shops. The two meetings in New
York, which began with interstate trade in mind, became formative political
events. The publishing trade's own brand of popular neomercantilism resonates in stories about these meetings that circulated in newspapers. Communication between tradesmen in distant cities occurred in many ways, including
the exchange of newspapers in which accounts of meetings were published
and then disseminated by the postal routes. This system of publication and
distribution of local papers for a national reading audience was a useful, not
to mention cost-effective, way for mechanics and merchants to communicate
with far-flung communities. While the meetings may have been of little interest to the general reading public in 1802, printers in eastern port cities made
the challenges confronting the trade national issues by reprinting stories in
their local papers. When Americans read their newspaper at home or listened
to a public reading of the paper at the local tavern, they learned about a publishing trade at a crossroads. But they also read about a group of men equally
willing to meet head-on the challenges that confronted the nation's growing

trade, using language all too familiar to a nation born out of political conflict with a distant imperial master.[12]

"Materially and Injuriously Affect the Whole Business of Printing and Bookselling"

In February 1802, New York's booksellers became political actors when they sensed a threat to their economic interests. After reading William Coleman's request in the *New-York Evening Post* that the city's printers and booksellers meet to discuss "the proposed additional duty on Printing types," fifty-four men of the trade met at the Merchant Coffee-House on Wall Street.[13] What initially seemed an innocuous issue concerning tradesmen in New York and Philadelphia quickly spread beyond the Northeast. For several weeks, the talk in the city's printing offices and bookshops had been the news that Congress had not only eliminated a duty on antimony—the lustrous gray metalloid used in the production of printing type—but had also proposed an additional duty on foreign-made type. Such legislation would have made European-produced type prohibitively expensive for many of America's printers, especially those just starting out. According to a report by the House Committee on Commerce and Manufactures, the decision to raise the price on imported type was made to protect American domestic manufacturing. "Such manufactures as are obviously capable of affording to the United States an adequate supply of their several and respective objects," the report read, "ought to be promoted by the aid of Government. Two modes of administering this aid have presented themselves to your committee: The one, to permit, free of duty, the importation of such gross articles as are essential to those manufactures. The other, to impose higher duties on such articles (on importation) as can be supplied by our own citizens to advantage."[14]

The controversy began when the Philadelphia type founders Archibald Binny and James Ronaldson petitioned Congress. At the time, Binny and Ronaldson were the only type founders in the United States. Even so, they struggled because they often had trouble getting their hands on the material needed to produce moveable type. Indeed, Binny and Ronaldson told the House Committee that they had tried, repeatedly and in vain, to procure antimony domestically. They were forced to "send to Europe for it, and with much difficulty and after long delay" they procured a large supply from London, at an astronomical cost. As a result, Binny and Ronaldson sought the help of Congress, pleading to the committee for a reduction in the duties on imported antimony. "Your Petitioners have established the Manufacture of Printing Types in Philadelphia, in the prosecution of which they have had many obstacles to encounter," they argued, noting "that the high price of the Metals of which their Types are composed, together with the difficulty of procuring some of them, particularly Regulus of Antimony, is a considerable bar to the success of their establishment."[15] The House committee read and debated the petition, and while its members decided to revise the protective tariff by lifting the duty on antimony, they did not stop there: in addition to eliminating the tax on the metal, they also *increased* the tax on imported type by 7.5 percent. By eliminating the duties on antimony while also raising taxes on imported type, the Congress unwittingly gave Binny and Ronaldson a virtual monopoly, as they were the only type foundry in the United States at the time. And by giving almost complete control of the domestic market in printing type to a foundry ill equipped to meet the demands of the nation's growing publishing trade, the Congress provoked an unintended backlash.

Once sheltered in the warmth of the coffeehouse, the fifty-four printers and booksellers in attendance organized themselves. Samuel Campbell was nominated to chair the meeting, and George Hopkins was appointed secretary. James Swords read a circular letter sent by Philadelphia printers and booksellers that requested cooperation in petitioning "the general government against the proposed duty." The men agreed unanimously with "their brethren in Philadelphia, and the union, on this subject" and accordingly drafted a petition articulating the "impolicy of the proposed additional duty on the importation of Printing Types." The petition was signed that day and mailed to the House of Representatives.[16]

The New York petitioners argued that the proposed duty on type, which protected Binny and Ronaldson but little else, posed a risk to the book trade's growth. To allow the duty to go into effect would "do extensive injury to all persons concerned in printing," they claimed, "and indirectly to tax every reader in the United States for the involvement of the few persons who are concerned in the business of Type-founding." In drafting the petition, the New York printers and booksellers also acknowledged the role of newspapers in helping to spread news about the proposed duty on imported type. "Thro the medium of the public papers and private correspondence, your memorial is to have been informed that a proposition is now before your Honorable House for imposing a duty of Twenty per cent on imported printing types," a measure, they argued, that was "highly impolitic in itself." They claimed that Binny and Ronaldson's firm was not up to the task of supplying the type needed by printers and booksellers to fulfill the needs of a growing print market, and observed "that at present there exists but one Type Foundry in the United States," and that it was "wholly out of the power of this concern to supply a twentieth part of the demand from printers in America." The petitioners also made the case that Binny and Ronaldson did not cast "many species of letters" they considered necessary in order to properly conduct the printing business. To this end, they asked the committee to repeal the duty on type: "On these grounds your memorialists respectfully trust that your Honourable House, taking the premises into consideration, will not impose a further duty on Printing Types, which would almost amount to a prohibition; a result which your memorialists, from their professional knowledge and pursuits, are persuaded would operate as a public evil, and would materially and injuriously affect the whole business of Printing and Bookselling throughout the United States."[17]

One week later, a second New York petition drafted by the city's journeymen printers was presented to the House of Representatives. Drawn up at a meeting of the Franklin Typographical Society, this document, while echoing the petition drafted by their employers, illuminated the concerns of journeymen printers, bookbinders, and papermakers. The journeymen's petition reasoned that the proposed duty would force booksellers to import more books assembled in Europe, which would dramatically reduce the number of titles printed and bound domestically. This alarming possibility, they argued, spelled doom for the American book trade, in particular for increasingly vulnerable journeymen and apprentices who relied on job printing. If allowed to remain on the books, the duty would eventually "deprive two thirds of the Journeymen Printers in the United States, of their means of subsistence."[18] In making their case to Congress, New York journeymen insisted that the continued importation of foreign type was vital to the survival and growth of the American economy.

The city's journeymen printers characterized the duty on foreign-made type as a hindrance to upward social and economic mobility. The business of printing, they argued, was an expensive craft to begin anew, let alone to maintain. "Very few of those, who are obliged to resort to journey-work when they become free," they wrote, "ever have it in their power to realize a capital sufficient to commence business on their own accounts." To make the procurement of raw materials increasingly difficult diminished "their number, to the very great injury of the whole."[19] The journeymen insisted that the new tax posed a serious risk to the future growth of the domestic publishing trade. They did not stop there, however. They made a compelling case that these additional burdens—which made the purchase of much needed imported type prohibitively expensive—would create a glut of insolvent permanent journeymen wandering the countryside in search of job work, unable to advance in their chosen craft.

This localized anxiety evolved into a national concern. Following the drafting of petitions in Philadelphia and New York, printers and booksellers in Boston, Baltimore, and Charleston delivered their own petitions to Congress. The increased pressure on Congress to repeal the duty reveals that the controversy was a national issue and that members of the trade, regardless of place, had an obligation to protect their brethren in cities near and far. Indeed, to remain inactive, the petitions suggested, would have spelled almost certain doom for the American book trade in the long run.

The Baltimore petition conveyed the same palpable sense of urgency found in the New York and Philadelphia documents. Leonard Yundt and Matthew Brown, publishers of the Baltimore *Federal Gazette,* described the severity of the situation: "As no time ought to be lost in arresting the progress of a bill which aims so deadly a blow at one of the most flourishing mechanic arts in the country, those interested in this city should be early in co-operating with their brethren of Philadelphia. A meeting therefore of the printers, booksellers, paper-makers, bookbinders and stationers, of this city, is requested at James Bryden's Fountain Inn, on Friday evening next at 6 o'clock—All of whom will, more immediately or remotely, be affected by the operation of the contemplated duty."[20] Echoing concerns expressed by the Franklin Typographical Society, the Baltimore meeting called attention to the potential economic ramifications of the type duty. Indeed, Baltimore's printers and booksellers argued that the increased duty on type would actually "materially injure other and essential branches" of the publishing trade, namely, papermaking and bookbinding.[21] Systemic economic collapse, in their view, would be the long-term result of the duty on foreign type.

In the days that followed, the mobilization of the publishing trade continued to move south. Seven days after the petitions from New York, Philadelphia, and Baltimore arrived in Congress, graced with more than 170 signatures, twelve men met in Charleston's Carolina Coffee House to draft a petition of their own. The Charleston printers and booksellers agreed with their northern comrades that the "intended additional duty" on type would "distress your memorialists, and all others concerned in the business of Printing, Bookselling, &c., and not add to the general good of the Country." Like the Baltimore trade and the Franklin Typographical Society before them, the South Carolinians conveyed a feeling of impending doom, arguing that the duty would make it increasingly difficult for journeymen and apprentices to get ahead: "Your memorialists beg leave also to observe to your honourable body, that while duties on almost every species of merchandise will fall but lightly on individuals, being borne by the great mass of consumers, duties on Mechanical Implements, coming out of the pocket of the laborious artisan alone, must tend to check the progress of trade, and damp the incentives to industry."[22]

These printers and booksellers followed in the footsteps of American mechanics who had for many years advocated economic protection. In the immediate aftermath of the War of Independence, mechanics in Philadelphia and New York took strong anti-British and, especially, anti-Loyalist positions, going so far as to demand that Tories be prohibited from engaging in trade unless they demonstrated "their uniform attachment to the cause of independence of America." In both cities, mechanics sent petitions to the state legislatures pleading for increased duties on imported manufactured goods. Soon thereafter, as Peskin points out, the young nation saw the "first coordinated, national effort by the mechanic protectionists" to petition for protective tariffs. Originating in Boston in April 1785, an organization calling itself the Committee of Tradesmen and Manufacturers won a dramatic victory when the Massachusetts House of Representatives passed a strong protective tariff in July. Not wanting to rest on their laurels, the Boston mechanics looked to spread the gospel of economic protectionism. In August, "they drafted a circular letter to mechanics throughout the nation," a document that, Peskin argues, rallied "other mechanics to the protectionist cause."[23] And, like the circulation of news on the type controversy nearly twenty years later, the circular letter was shared by mechanics in port cities and small towns alike.

The campaign by the nation's printers and booksellers actually worked. In 1804, after debating the numerous petitions, Congress repealed the duty on imported type.[24] Printers and booksellers in New York shared economic interests and held the same sense of mutual obligation for the trade as did printers and booksellers in Philadelphia, Baltimore, Boston, and Charleston. Regardless of location, printers and booksellers worked together to protect the growing American publishing trade. At the same time, the petitions reveal that they were willing to sacrifice one facet of the trade—the domestic manufacture of moveable type—in order to protect their immediate economic interests. In their petitions to Congress, printers and booksellers argued that protecting the trade as a whole was more important to the domestic economy than buttressing the infant American manufacture of type, an industry that they probably assumed would grow over time. The successful interstate and interurban organization in response to the tariff, then, provided a useful template for men in the trade who sought to protect and promote their local, regional, and national economic interests.

"A More General Extension and Sale of Useful and Valuable Books"

Leading New York booksellers, including several involved in the type controversy, played an active role in organizing literary fairs. These meetings brought together printers and booksellers from dozens of cities to celebrate the ingenuity and growth of the new nation's publishing trade. The literary fairs also allowed booksellers and printers to form new regional and national distribution networks. These trade organizations and the public meetings they organized shared a common goal: to promote the manufacture of American books for the domestic market that would compete with European imports.

In 1801, the newly formed American Company of Booksellers appointed New York printers Thomas Swords, James Swords, and Hugh Gaine to organize and host the nation's first literary fair.[25] Organizers mobilized booksellers by publicizing the plans for the June 1802 meeting in newspapers. The idea for the fair, however, originated with Philadelphia's Mathew Carey. According to the notice that ran in Noah Webster's *Commercial Advertiser* in December 1801, "Mr. Matthew [*sic*] Carey has just published an address to the Printers and Booksellers of the United States, recommending a LITERARY FAIR, on the plan of those held at Frankfort and Leipsic [*sic*], in Germany." Webster and his printer, Ebenezer Belden, insisted that the literary fair was a practical necessity not only for the book trade but for the nation as a whole. Their encouragement of the meeting can also read as a reflection on the status of American political independence: "The plan is good and deserves encouragement. When we consider that in consequence of the union between Ireland and England, *cheap* books from the former place can no longer be imported into the United States—that *authorship* in England is high, and the duties on paper enormous, it will occur to every one who thinks that in a short time, we shall be able to print all books of merit at a much cheaper rate than we can possibly import them."[26]

The Philadelphia printer Mathew Carey played an important role in proposing, planning, and running the nation's first literary fair. The son of a Dublin baker, Carey apprenticed as a printer until he fled his native Ireland after publicly criticizing the British government. And while he did return to Dublin for a brief period, during which he provoked the ire of the Irish government for his anti-British publications, Carey fled yet again, this time landing in Philadelphia. Not long after his arrival, he opened a printing shop and began publishing the *Pennsylvania Herald*. It was in this newspaper that Carey advocated the development of American industry, in part out of his loathing for Great Britain.[27] Carey's crusade to educate Americans on the importance of American manufacturing found its largest audience in his ill-fated *American Museum*, a magazine that Carey hoped would have a national circulation. And while Carey was able to keep the magazine afloat for five years, from 1787 to 1792, it proved challenging from the start. Despite the financial straits Carey was put in by the *American Museum*, he filled the magazine with essays promoting a "nationalistic political economy."[28]

The first literary fair was several months in the making, but members of the trade recognized its value in enabling booksellers to make trade connections. The fair, they argued, would be especially helpful for small-town shopkeepers who lacked access to major markets like New York, Boston, or Philadelphia. Eight days after the *Commercial Advertiser* announced the event to New York readers, Thomas Cushing of the *Salem Gazette* in Massachusetts published a brief note about the literary fair, but in slightly altered terms. While acknowl-edging its usefulness as an opportunity for booksellers in Philadelphia and New York to swap their texts, Cushing articulated the greater purpose of the meeting. Praising Carey as an "enlightened and liberal bookseller," the *Gazette* considered the fair a "measure which would greatly benefit the trade in general, but more especially those who are situated in interior places."[29]

Promotional material circulated widely in newspapers. In many cases, newspaper editors copied word for word the advertisements published in either the *Commercial Advertiser* or the *Salem Gazette*. The notice initially published by the *Commercial Advertiser,* for example, found its way to Boston, Salem, and Providence by the end of December, appearing in the *Commercial Gazette* and the *Providence Journal, and Town and Country Advertiser.* After the turn of the year, the notice wound up in New Bedford's *Columbian Orator,* and eleven days later it was published in the *Herald* in Rutland, Vermont. Two days later, two Connecticut papers, the New London *Bee* and the Norwich *Courier,* carried the advertisement. A week later, the *Salem Gazette* published a plea for the literary fair and a similar notice appeared in the *New-Hampshire Gazette.* The following day, the *Salem Gazette's* notice was published in *Thomas's Massachusetts Spy, or The Worcester Gazette,* and ten days later the notice appeared in yet another Portsmouth paper, the *United States Oracle, and Portsmouth Advertiser.* In March, the *Gazette* notice appeared in two Massachusetts papers, Leominster's *Telescope, or American Herald* and Dedham's *Columbian Minerva.* This was not the last appearance of the *Gazette's* reprint, however. One month later, the notice appeared in the New York *Mercantile Advertiser,* and shortly thereafter in the New Bedford, Massachusetts, *Columbian Courier.* Overall, the versions published in the *Commercial Advertiser* and *Salem Gazette* appeared in nineteen newspapers in fifteen towns and municipalities in eight states.[30]

As news spread, Philadelphia and New York booksellers moved quickly to plan the fair. In mid-April 1802, Federalist newspaper editors Noah Webster and William Coleman announced the plans for the fair, as did James Cheetham, the new editor of the Jeffersonian *American Citizen.* The next day, the same announcement appeared in six additional New York newspapers. New York's printers and booksellers expected that the literary fair would draw participants from across the country. "Twenty four of the booksellers of the City of New-York have agreed to attend the *Literary* or *Book fair,* to be held in the City on the first of June next," the notice ran, adding that the group had reserved "Mr. Barden's Long Room at the Old Coffee House" in order to accommodate the anticipated crowd. Organizers especially encouraged "those remotely situated" booksellers to visit the city and to bring with them "all the articles they mean to dispose of" at the fair. The men also pleaded with the nation's newspaper printers to publi-cize the event. In making this request, the organizers revealed not only their national ambitions for the gathering but also their anxiety about protecting their economic interests against foreign competition. "The Newspaper Printers in the several States, who are desirous of encouraging Book Printing in this Country," they wrote, "are respectfully requested to insert this notice two or three times in their several papers."[31] Recognizing the urgency in this language, the *Commercial Advertiser's* Ebenezer Belden immediately sent an issue of his newspaper to Philadelphia. Upon arrival, the literary fair was announced in the *Gazette of the United States* and the *Philadelphia Gazette and Daily Advertiser,* and in *Poulson's American Daily Advertiser* two days later. Several days later, printers in the Chesapeake region published the announcement. Shortly thereafter, word of the fair traveled from New York to Providence, Rhode Island, and on to Boston, Salem, and Dedham in Massachusetts and Norwich and New London, Connecticut. By the second week of May, news of the literary fair had reached Brattleboro, Vermont.[32]

Answering Carey's call to action, dozens of booksellers arrived in Manhattan in June 1802 for the first American literary fair. Printers captured much of the action that took place in the Old Coffee House in their newspapers and in doing so highlighted the regional diversity, and the national ambitions, of the attendees. The *Commercial Advertiser,* for example, published an early report of the proceedings. "In pursuance of arrangements previously made," its notice read, "there was this day a general audience of booksellers at the Old Coffee-House, from various parts of the Union." The *Commercial Advertiser* touched on the politics of the fair, announcing that Hugh Gaine—by then a well-respected elder statesman of the printing trade who had put his political indecision during the War of Independence behind him—would chair the fair and that Mathew Carey would serve as secretary. The paper also highlighted the resoundingly nationalist tone of the discussions, conversations that returned time and again to the interconnectedness of the publishing trade. The attendees insisted that "correct and decent printing, with the various branches of domestic manufactures connected therewith," would lead to "a more general extension and sale of useful and valuable books" throughout the young nation.[33] On 2 June, Philadelphia's *Gazette of the United States* reported that "several booksellers have arrived in New-York, from Philadelphia, and the eastward," bringing with them a "large assortment of books . . . to be exhibited to the trade."[34]

The next day, a story appeared in the *Commercial Advertiser* that further articulated the organizers' goal of establishing a national literary culture that would equal or even surpass what then existed in Europe. "THE LITERARY FAIR that has just commenced in this city promises considerable advantage to American Literature," it read, in that "A new Republic—The Republic of Letters, is about to be formed—one that will vie in usefulness with those lately formed" in Europe. In imagining the economic impact of the literary fair, the *Commercial*

Advertiser appropriated the symbolic significance not only of the 1787 Constitutional Convention but of the Committees of Correspondence that connected the nation during the imperial crisis: "The meeting of the book-sellers who are now assembled in this place from different parts of the U. States reminds us of the first committees and conventions that associated with the view of organizing a federal republic." Webster had high hopes that the "labors" of the meeting would "be equally propitious" and that the meeting would result in a "new *imperium in imperio*, destined to enlighten and to increase the happiness of the U. States." Aside from the strong political metaphors, the *Commercial Advertiser* adopted language of unity and cooperation. "By a judicious direction of capital—by a proper harmony of design and execution—by a perfect and mutual understanding with each other," Webster argued, "there is no doubt but the members of the Republic, while they promote their own interest will save vast sums of money to their country." This improvement in publishing standards would "extend learning, and essentially contribute to the dissemination of both virtue and knowledge."[35] Webster's message was loud and clear: the economic independence of the new Republic hung in the balance. But more was at stake than economic patriotism. The continued development of the publishing trade, he believed, would help educate the new nation's growing and ambitious population. Webster's promotion of the literary fair was reprinted in several newspapers. It appeared first in Philadelphia three days after the initial publication, and two days later was published in the Baltimore *Republican*. From then on, Webster's piece began a circuitous journey through New England and the mid-Atlantic region, appearing a week later in three Connecticut papers. By mid-June, it had arrived in Rhode Island and the Finger Lakes region in upstate New York. Seven days after a reprinting in Cooperstown, New York, the report was published in Carlisle, Pennsylvania. By the end of the month, it had appeared in Vermont and New Hampshire, first in Burlington's *Vermont Centinel* and five days later in Walpole's *Farmer's Weekly Museum, or Literary Gazette*.[36]

Booksellers hailing from Boston, Hartford, Stonington, New Haven, Albany, New York City, Philadelphia, Baltimore, and Richmond attended the fair. The initial tally, first published in Jonathan Seymour's New York *Daily Advertiser*, counted forty booksellers, though the notice in the paper indicated that "considerable numbers of other Booksellers from different parts of the Union are expected to arrive in town in the course of this week."[37] A follow-up list, however, never appeared. New York booksellers arrived with hundreds of books pulled from their shelves. The city's booksellers, along with those arriving from out of town by either stage or ship, probably hired local cart men—municipally regulated employees who monopolized transportation in early American port towns—to transport their crates of books to the coffeehouse.[38]

"A More Extensive and Certain Trade"

News of the inaugural literary fair spread far and wide in pamphlets, broadsides, and newspapers. In addition to toasts delivered at New York's Lovett Hotel, printers published orations and reports that served as political manifestos. These bold public proclamations articulated the national ambitions of the fair wrapped up in the promotion of domestic production of books.

At the conclusion of the first day's business, the booksellers retired to the Lovett Hotel for supper. After the meal, which no doubt included many rounds of ale, the booksellers rose for sixteen carefully crafted toasts, which functioned as acts of symbolic loyalty for groups of people with shared political or fraternal interests. Written with a broader readership in mind, these convivial political statements often appeared in local newspapers and were thus transformed into public declarations. In many cases, toasts circulated between cities and appeared in newspapers far afield, as printers swapped their dailies and weeklies, for free, via the postal routes. The publication and circulation of toasts in the early Republic's newspapers, scholars have pointed out, record public dialogue that might otherwise be lost.[39]

The organizers prepared toasts that touched on themes of literary nationalism, economic independence, and the history of the trade. The second toast, for example, commemorated the "memory of Faust and Gutenberg," while the third celebrated the "memory of Franklin." Franklin was an especially common celebratory trope at large gatherings of the New York publishing trade. The inclusion of Faust seems a peculiar choice. The historical intertwining of the Faustian legend and the invention of the printing press was, however, not all that far-fetched. The connections between Faustus the scholar, Faustus the dastardly necromancer, and Gutenberg reflected an unease about the potential power—for both good and evil—of the printing press. This toast can thus be read as a metaphor for the rapid expansion of the American publishing trade insofar as Faust, who made his fateful bargain in order to have unlimited knowledge, was linked with Gutenberg, whose invention made possible the democratization and wide availability of such knowledge. Perhaps the booksellers conflated Faust and Gutenberg as a way to reflect on the growth of the nation's book trade and its contribution to the emergence of an American republic of letters, which had been the first toast of the evening.[40]

The organizers also rallied the attendees in support of the domestic production of books. Three toasts promoted American book publishing and its allied trades. After hoisting their pints to celebrate the "elegant art of engraving," the booksellers feted the "sister arts of Letter founding and papermaking, printing and bookbinding." The inclusion of type founding was an interesting choice, considering that only four months earlier printers and booksellers in New York, Philadelphia, Baltimore, and Charleston had tried aggressively to repeal a protective duty meant to boost domestic manufacturing. The booksellers attending the fair probably recognized the irony of toasting American type foundries, most notably Philadelphia's Binny and Ronaldson. Immediately following this toast, which no doubt made some in the audience uneasy, the booksellers celebrated paper manufacturing with a clever rhetorical turn. "May America increase in rag manufactures," they proclaimed, hoping to encourage the production of linen paper for their newspapers, books, pamphlets, and broadsides, "but never see her manufactures in rags." This final, ominous line revealed an understated anxiety. Clever though it may have been, the very next toast in the progression indicated that future prosperity hinged on the success of their endeavors at the fair. "The *American Literary Fair*," it stated, "may the benefits resulting from it be as extensive as the views of its supporters are liberal." If not, then manufacturing might well end up in rags. After a rousing series of toasts, the booksellers passed a number of additional resolutions, including the planning of future meetings. "It was proposed, and agreed to at the meeting, that a LITERARY FAIR be held twice a year in one of the largest cities in the United States."[41] Emboldened by the success of the first fair, the booksellers agreed that their next meeting would be held the following October in Philadelphia. Reprints of the toasts circulated between ten newspapers in nine towns. Initially published in the New York *Mercantile Advertiser,* the toasts moved immediately south, first to Philadelphia, and then to Alexandria, Virginia, and Baltimore, Maryland, followed by Salem, Massachusetts, Providence, Rhode Island, and finally Portsmouth and Keene, New Hampshire, and Brattleboro, Vermont.[42]

In a rousing, inspirational speech delivered to the literary fair on the Fourth of July, the New York printer Hugh Gaine emphasized the importance of the trade's independence from European competition. That the nation's booksellers and printers gathered at all, Gaine pointed out, was something of an accomplishment. "Assembled, as you are, from different parts of the United States, for the promotion of our common interest," Gaine reminded attendees, the "pursuit of one object, the literary welfare of our country," was made all the easier by uniting "in one body" for "the benefits of all its parts." The language of cooperation, friendship, and mutual obligation to the trade resonates throughout Gaine's address. By adopting this rhetoric, Gaine hoped to overcome regional prejudices. "Yes, we are brethren," he said, "and I feel a pride in the idea, that the mean and narrow jealousies, which have too long prevailed, are now to vanish, and give place to the generous emotions of mutual good will." Of paramount importance to Gaine was the protection of domestic manufacturing: "In contemplating the future greatness of this establishment, which, though now in its very birth, adds a dignity to our avocation before

unknown; the mind is led, by a natural transition, to the first rise of our manufacture in this country: a period, interesting from a thousand causes, to every
American, and rendered peculiarly to us, by the happy contrast of our present
situation."[43]

Gaine reminded the audience that the necessity of printing, publishing, and
binding American books was made all the more paramount by their former
reliance on Great Britain. "It is not long, since Great-Britain," he said, "was
resorted to for the supply of almost every want." London publishers cashed in
on their efforts to bring literature to the new nation. "Her manufactures enabled
her, without the expense of government or protection, to reap all of the benefit
of our labours," he said bluntly. The message was loud and clear: the nation's
leading booksellers had a responsibility to protect and increase their trade for
the betterment of the nation as a whole. "As a Citizen of New-York, I feel gratified
by your attendance," Gaine said, "as an American, I feel proud." But he maintained that private interest did not drive up attendance at the literary fair; rather,
the "nobler aim" as "booksellers, and guardians of the press" was to join together,
"as one man to raise the name of American literature." In the end, he concluded
that the resolutions the men adopted, as a national body, made up a "constitution
of our literary republic." Their meeting, then, promised to greatly benefit not
only their trade but the very soul of the nation.[44]

A broadside printed in New York during the fair reiterated many of Gaine's
points. Probably written by Mathew Carey, the broadside was signed by Philadelphia's John Conrad, Boston's John West and Ebenezer Andrews, and New
York's Isaac Collins and James Swords, signatures that authenticated and thus
lent the authority of the fair's organizers to Carey's argument. The fair, according to Carey, had been "constantly and actively attended every day," in spite of
logistical challenges. Complications ranged from the fair's initial "novelty," the
"want of previously fixed regulations," the "remoteness of the persons concerned," and travel expenses. Despite these obstacles, which probably caused
organizers a great deal of anxiety, Carey boasted that the fair was a smashing
success. In his estimation, it exceeded "the most sanguine expectations," much
to the advantage of the "art of printing, and the interests of literature in our
fortunate country." The organizers estimated that the number of books
exchanged between printers, booksellers, and publishers large and small numbered more than half a million. "By the simple operation of exchange," according
to Carey, "perhaps not less than half a million volumes are put into circulation,
which might have lain on the shelves for years, under the limited operations of
trade hitherto existing." Small booksellers benefited from these exchanges, and
the deals made in the coffeehouse created new interstate trade networks. The
business done at the fair, then, helped salvage and add life to the new nation's
publishing trade.[45]

Carey touched on class differences between small-town booksellers and major urban publishers. He suggested that interactions between these two groups created economic connections that led to "a more extensive and certain trade," resulting in a massive redistribution of capital. "Among the most important consequences of this institution," he wrote, was that "the humble printer or bookseller, with a small capital, is placed upon equal terms with his opulent neighbor." The humble shopkeeper was thus "saved from the expenses and fatigue" of scouring the countryside to sell his wares and secure new goods for his shelves. Instead, according to Carey, the literary fair encouraged a "fixed market" in which the struggling country seller could "participate in the profit, by exchange with the more opulent capitalist." Carey was suggesting that the nation's leading publishers, men like himself, acted out of benevolence in extending the reach of their businesses.

Carey may have flattered the large publishers, but he was clear about the necessity of cooperation, not competition, between the several branches of the publishing trade. Joining forces and working together would help solidify the new nation's book trade and shield it from the threat of foreign competition. "Every means by which we can improve these arts," he wrote, "tends to the public good, as well to the good of the individuals." London was the competition. "We should therefore enter into a generous emulation," Carey said, "not the rivalry of jealousy among ourselves, but competition with those countries, the excellence of whose productions already engross so immense a proportion of our market." Cooperation, then, would squeeze out European competition: "By employing our natural means, we shall possess a larger proportion than at present, of our natural commerce—we shall secure to our own country the circulation of vast sums which at present are carried into other countries, to invigorate their industry at the expense of our negligence, while we possess all the means required to secure the benefits to ourselves."

Carey expected these principles to circulate beyond the new Republic's port cities. "These views, pursued at Boston, New York, Philadelphia, Baltimore, and Charleston, S.C. would be soon followed by the lesser cities and towns," he wrote, a nod of encouragement that he hoped would inspire printers and booksellers to "communicate with each other." Carey's broadside concluded with the text of five resolutions passed by the attendees and designed to help the trade grow and remain competitive with Europe. Foremost was the insistence that printers and booksellers produce material texts on a par with European imports. Fair organizers maintained that printers must "use their utmost endeavors to improve the quality of the books they undertake to publish, in order to establish and support the reputation of the American manufacture of books, and render it deserving of the patronage of the friends of their country." The resolutions also encouraged printers and booksellers to remain in open dialogue with one another and build on the connections made at the fair. The "booksellers in the principle [*sic*] towns of the United States," Carey argued, should "form themselves into associations, for the purpose of corresponding with each other," a strategy that would "promote the general interest" of the trade. Most important, Carey suggested that American booksellers discontinue the importation of European texts if they could be printed domestically: "Resolved, that it be recommended to the importers of books, to discontinue as far as may be, the importation of all books, of which good and correct editions are printed in this country." While this was certainly a noble intention, it was not tenable in either the short or the long term, as booksellers continued to rely on London imports. Carey's message of cooperation between large producers and small peddlers, urban and rural markets, found a national audience in newspapers. The broadside was reprinted first in New York's *Commercial Advertiser* and the *Mercantile Advertiser* and then circulated in Newark and Elizabethtown, New Jersey, Alexandria, Virginia, Albany, New York, New Bedford, Massachusetts, and finally in Providence, Rhode Island.[46]

Collaboration between booksellers, printers, bookbinders, and other allied branches of the trade was made explicit by Gaine, Carey, and the toasts that came out of the first literary fair. That the booksellers and printers agreed on the need to protect the domestic production of books was a striking contrast to earlier, often tenuous alliances between merchants and mechanics. Like mechanics in the 1780s and early 1790s, Lawrence Peskin tells us, merchants pushed for "an active national government to direct the economy." But merchants and mechanics diverged greatly on what the government's role in the economy should look like. They happened to agree on "the need for state regulation to maintain a favorable balance of trade," but what set the two constituencies apart was manufacturing. "Unlike mechanics," Peskin writes, "the merchants continued to view foreign trade as the foundation of the national economy, and they rarely paid much attention to American manufacturing."[47] In general, most merchants remained committed to international trade and thus had little need for domestic manufacturing. And so, while most merchant organizations all but ignored the interests of mechanics in their public statements, booksellers stood in agreement with printers on the need for the American production of books. Failure to shield the domestic printing and bookbinding trades from the threat of European imports, they reasoned, would lead to certain ruin for the publishing trade as a whole, booksellers included.

As Gaine, Carey, and the fair organizers' toasts made clear, commitment to the cooperation between the several branches of the trade was the primary goal of the literary fair. The fair bolstered the trade by putting thousands of books produced in major markets like Boston, New York, and Philadelphia into circulation nationwide. The resolutions that circulated from town to town strongly encouraged booksellers, large and small, urban and rural, to keep alive the networks of exchange formed at the New York literary fair. In this way, Gaine and Carey suggested, the nation's booksellers could influence what was being published and distributed to readers throughout the countryside.

"When You Were Last in This City"

For large publishers, the first literary fair was a resounding success. While bringing together booksellers from disparate locations, forging usable trade networks, and creating a sense of urgency among members of the trade to publish *American* books, the fair increased the traffic in books moving beyond Philadelphia, New York, and Boston. It also allowed publishers with the largest stock to unload hundreds, if not thousands, of copies to smaller booksellers, exchanges that were as beneficial to wealthy publishers as they were to village shopkeepers.

The literary fair stimulated correspondence between booksellers and publishers that might otherwise never have occurred. Mathew Carey certainly benefited from his discussions with New York publishers. Two months after the fair, George F. Hopkins wrote to Carey to discuss an exchange of Bibles. "I have seen your favour," wrote Hopkins, assuring Carey that he would "take charge of the Bibles and make the best sales" in his power and pointing out that he had "sold only two dozen" of his supply. Hopkins reminded Carey that they had discussed an exchange of *The Federalist* but disappointed Carey with news that he would be unable to forward any. Hopkins noted that he had "already made arrangements with Mr. Humphreys and Mr. Bradford with respect to the Federalist, the latter of whom takes 50 sets for cash," adding that he was "not at liberty" to make any new deals with Philadelphia publishers.[48] John Harrisson, a New York printer who did presswork on a variety of projects, ranging from operas to almanacs, also wrote a follow-up letter to Carey. Harrisson, however, was terse, as Carey had yet to come through on an arrangement made at the fair. "In exchange with you last June there was due me 100 *Charlotte Temple* in sheets," he wrote, insisting that Carey ship them at the "first opportunity as the season is advancing to obstruct water communication between this City and yours."[49] The sense of urgency that emerged from the pages of promotional material created by the fair seems to have made a lasting impression. Writing to Carey less than a month after the fair, Thomas and James Swords shipped a "paper parcel . . . on board the Sloop Almena." In addition to the texts highlighted in their bill of lading, the brothers sent Carey a "small package containing 150 copies of the Booksellers Address," which was, in their estimation, "good enough to distribute."[50]

Much like Carey, Boston's John West used the fair to build a trade network. In the weeks after the fair, West corresponded with seven New York booksellers who had attended. On 10 June, for example, T. B. Jansen wrote to West to confirm that a shipment of books to West also included a "box & bundle for Mr. Isaiah Thomas Worcester which we have taken the liberty to trouble you with."[51] The following day, West received a letter from the New York printer John Tiebout, who pointed out that he had shipped an order of $93.50 intended for Worcester.[52] West and Samuel Campbell appear to have made an arrangement in New York, which Campbell alluded to in a letter to West in late June. "By the Ship *Adamant* which sails in 3 to 4 days you will receive a bundle containing the above," he wrote; "thank you to forward your articles at first opportunity & oblige."[53] West had a nearly identical arrangement with William Falconer. "By the sloop Liberty, Capt. Rawson," Falconer wrote in mid-July, "you will receive a bundle containing the above will thank you to forward the books I am to have from you as soon as you possibly can."[54]

The New York publisher Evert Duyckinck took advantage of the fair to forge trade networks while at the same time unloading large portions of his stock. Duyckinck arranged for a parcel to be shipped to Boston almost immediately after the close of the early June meeting. "I have ship'd . . . on board the schooner Betsy & Polly," he wrote on 16 June, "4 Campbell's Narrative, 6 Reeve's Letters, 3 Duncan's Cicero, 3 Denman's Medicine, 3 Cullen's Materia Medica, 6 Pleasures of Hope."[55] At the end of June, he wrote to Carey to follow up on two shipments bound for Philadelphia. "I have ship'd on board the schooner President . . . a paper package containing . . . 36 Duncan's logic, 24 Jachin & Boaz, 18 Caroline Licthfield, 8 Denman's Midwifery, 4 Evelina," totaling $88.[56] Duyckinck also sent his cheap books to a number of booksellers in twelve cities following the literary fair. Five of his correspondents between June and September 1802 appeared on the initial list of fair attendees. On 8 June, for example, Duyckinck shipped a package containing £16 16s worth of texts to Baltimore's Bonsall & Wiles; three days later, he exchanged £20 4s worth of inventory with Philadelphia's Thomas and William Bradford; a month later, he sent Philadelphia's Peter Bynberg a shipment worth £39 9s.[57] In November 1802, nearly six months after the fair, Duyckinck wrote to Carey regarding their ongoing exchange. "You may recollect when you were last in this City I mentioned to you I wanted a few of your Quarto Bibles which you then had in the Press," Duyckinck wrote. Reminding Carey of their agreement, Duyckinck proposed sending him "the N York Edition of the Quarto Bible in pay for them to which you assented." In addition to the Bible swap, Duyckinck noted that he had "in the Press an 12mo Edit. of Mackenzie's Voyage with the Map of his route" that he planned to sell for "125 cents," and told Carey that he could "have some when done if they are wanting."[58]

The enthusiasm generated by the fair did not last long, however. Thomas and James Swords, who had been involved in planning the New York event, told Carey that they had encountered some difficulty in planning the next fair, which was to be held in Philadelphia. The good will and rousing rhetoric so central to the literary fair's success seems to have died down, at least in New York. The brothers admitted to Carey that New York's printers and booksellers had difficulty justifying a trip to Philadelphia. Conceding that, aside from a citywide meeting in which they attempted to "get the Booksellers of this City to agree to certain propositions respecting a fair," or at least "a general Association of Booksellers" (though they considered this "impracticable"), the Swords brothers confessed that they had put little work into planning the Philadelphia fair. "It is true, we have thought but little on the business of the Fair," they disclosed, most likely owing to its relocation to Philadelphia. The organizational burden, it seemed, had shifted entirely to Carey. "As Father of the Project, we expect the labour will fall chiefly on your shoulders," the Swords brothers told Carey, admitting that this was "a poor excuse for ourselves." After seeming to shirk all of their former responsibilities, the brothers assured Carey that the next meeting of the fair would be a success. "You & Wm. Conrad will unquestionably have something prepared better doubtless, than any thing we could propose," they wrote, passing along all "assurances of acquiescence, at least as far as respect to ourselves."[59] Similarly, the New York printing firm of G. & R. Waite seemed disinclined to attend future fairs. Writing to Carey in November 1802, the Waite brothers confessed that they had "nothing worthwhile to attend the fair this season," while simultaneously continuing their exchange. "We would thank you, to let us have (if you can spare them) about 25 each of Charlotte Temple & Jackson's Bookkeeping & enclose them in some bookseller's parcel."[60] The momentum generated by the first literary fair seems to have dissipated almost as rapidly as it emerged.

Booksellers and printers, following in the tradition of fellow merchants and mechanics who had for years advocated greater protection of domestic manufacturing and the regulation of international trade, recognized that their economic interests were threatened by the continued importation of books from Europe. One result was the series of meetings that took place during the type controversy, followed several months later by the literary fair in New York. The rhetoric that dominated the meetings remained relevant for printers and booksellers promoting the American book trade. In an address to a July 1802 meeting of the Franklin Typographical Society, the journeyman printer Thomas Ringwood returned to theme of competitive balance with Europe.

Formerly the extent of the business carried on in our line went not beyond the daily news-papers, and a few of the lower order of books for use of schools. Now we not only supply the market with editions of the useful, but with almost all the elegant works; numbers of which are executed in a style equal to any from Europe, particularly those from the presses of Messrs. Swords, Hopkins, Oram, Collins, Heard, and others in this city. . . . It is also a subject of congratulation to us, that the efforts of the associated printers and booksellers have been so far successful as to produce American Editions of several classical works of considerable magnitude, which would not have been otherwise undertaken.[61]

At the 1804 literary fair, after handing out the commemorative medals, the attendees drafted a new constitution that provided for a board of directors with representatives from Boston, New York, Philadelphia, Baltimore, Albany, and Troy, New York. The board, which included New Yorkers James Swords and George Hopkins, could impose rules governing the American Company of Booksellers' transactions while also setting standard prices for interstate trade and regulating the quality of texts that would be distributed at future fairs.[62] Unfortunately, the fairs organized by the company did not extend beyond 1805, owing to the Yellow Fever epidemic that swept through New York. Despite the relatively short existence of the American Company of Booksellers, the two events discussed in this chapter promoted the labor of American publishers and printers by urging booksellers and their consumers to stock domestically produced texts and thus rely less on books imported from Europe.

5

EVERT DUYCKINCK AND
THE NATIONAL BOOK TRADE

In his 1852 speech on the early history of New York's publishing industry, John Francis suggested that few men had mattered more to how the trade developed than Evert Duyckinck. Francis described the bookseller and publisher as a well-respected yet quiet, stern man. Despite being "grave in his demeanor, and somewhat taciturn," Duyckinck was an "accommodating and courteous" businessman. He occupied "an ample and old-fashioned building, at the corner of Pearl-street and the Old Slip," which Francis had visited as a young man. "He must have been rich in literary recollections," Francis said, pointing out that Duyckinck had been for many years "quite extensively engaged as a publisher and seller." Francis commented on Duyckinck's reputation as a schoolbook publisher who had "largely dealt with that order of books, for elementary instruction, which were popular abroad, just about the close of our revolutionary war and at the adoption of our Constitution." Francis suggested that while the "city grew apace," Duyckinck was keenly attuned to the literary tastes and educational needs of residents, and that this made him a central figure in the rapid growth of the book trade in the early Republic.

> Mr. Duyckinck was gifted with great business talents, and esteemed as a man of punctuality and of rigid integrity in fiscal matters. He was the first who had the entire Bible, in duodecimo, preserved—set up in forms—the better to supply, at all times, his patrons. This was before stereotype plates were adopted. He gave to the Harpers the first job of printing they executed—whether Tom Thumb or Wesley's Primitive Physic, I do not know. The acorn has become the pride of the forest—the Cliff-street tree, whose roots and branches now ramify all the land. Duyckinck faithfully carried out the proverbs of Franklin, and the sayings of Noah Webster's *Prompter*. He was by birth and action a Genuine Knickerbocker.[1]

Despite Francis's best efforts to publicize Duyckinck's contributions to the American book trade, the life and career of the "Genuine Knickerbocker" has been overshadowed by his famous son, Evert Augustus Duyckinck, editor of a mid-nineteenth-century literary newspaper and the associate of Hawthorne, Poe, Melville, and John L. O'Sullivan. The elder Duyckinck was described by his *son's* biographer, Samuel Osgood, as "about forty years a bookseller," with a house on Old Slip and an adjoining shop in "Water Street in the rear, far down town in Old New York."[2] Apart from a few passing references, however, the elder Duyckinck's story has gone largely unnoticed. Yet Duyckinck was a key contributor to the expansion of the book trade in the early American Republic.[3]

Duyckinck's career in New York mirrored the dramatic structural changes that reshaped the American book trade and the larger market economy in the early nineteenth century. His long, steady career—which lasted from 1793 to 1830—spanned a number of seismic shifts in American political, economic, and social life. His was not an especially literary career, but rather one that served the disparate needs of the growing Republic. Duyckinck's surviving accounts and correspondence, spread across a number of archives, reveal that as a publisher he assumed what historian Robert A. Gross has called a "quintessentially capitalist role."[4] Duyckinck did not involve himself in the material production of his books; rather, he hired job printers to produce his books, a tactic that allowed him to create a large supply of reprints. He then moved his large, diverse catalogue of cheap, steady sellers, which included schoolbooks, devotionals, histories, travel narratives, popular European fiction, and inspirational biographies, across a vast distribution network that stretched from Nova Scotia to Florida. Duyckinck's ability to understand and take advantage of the young nation's reading habits was evident in his financial and social rise. He entered the New York publishing trade as a mechanic-turned-small-time shopkeeper, overseeing his brother-in-law's store, yet he retired a man of standing in the book trade—a self-styled Victorian gentleman of means surrounded by the trappings of New York's emerging bourgeoisie.[5]

Evert Duyckinck's accumulated financial records reveal his national ambitions as a publisher. Like other merchants in early America, Duyckinck tried to keep a careful record, so that all facets of his business remained transparent. Each of Duyckinck's fourteen daybooks—which Duyckinck kept mostly on his own, with only an occasional mark by his clerks Robert Lee and Anthony Tucker—contains approximately two years' worth of meticulously recorded transactions and consists of five to six hundred pages of daily business records. Early American merchants like Duyckinck typically used the Italian, or double-entry, system of bookkeeping, which, scholars have suggested, preserved the material record of an extensive kinship network. Duyckinck's painstakingly kept account books, which varied little in structure, content, or style for the entirety of his career, allowed him to keep track of each actor in his production and distribution networks. Indeed, a clear picture of the machinery of New York's publishing trade emerges from the pages of Duyckinck's accounts. Entries range from interactions with local booksellers who periodically bought texts for their shops to labor agreements with printers and bookbinders with whom he contracted to produce reprints of steady sellers. By curating the minutiae of daily life in their shops, merchants and artisans created in their account books a sense of clarity that provided stability in a constantly shifting and often unstable marketplace.[6]

Evert Duyckinck's business grew from a small Pearl Street bookshop into a national clearinghouse of best-selling educational and literary texts. Ever the astute businessman, Duyckinck took advantage of existing trade channels to forge his distribution network of bookshop owners and retail agents working on commission. While Duyckinck's wholesale business did little to create a uniquely American literary culture, his extensive trade networks helped bring cheap reprints of popular books to consumers in far-flung places.

"To Carry on the Business of Bookselling"

Evert Duyckinck's career did not follow the typical trajectory of printers who transformed themselves into publishers. Born in New York in 1764, Duyckinck worked for many years as a sailmaker just north of the waterfront. He was listed in the 1789 trade directory as a sailmaker on Front Street—a narrow alley running parallel to South Street—"near Lupton's wharf." Sailmakers like Duyckinck would have been part of a large, intricate shipbuilding enterprise comprising thirty separate skilled crafts, with each ship often taking a year to complete.[7]

Duyckinck may have had larger ambitions beyond stitching together sails. But it was not until the 1786 marriage of his sister to the bookseller Samuel Campbell that he contemplated leaving his profession behind. Seven years after the wedding, Duyckinck went into business with Campbell, creating "an equal and joint COPARTNERSHIP to carry on the Business of Bookselling and Stationery" for three years at 110 Pearl Street.[8] Duyckinck bought into the business with a down payment of £179 on a loan that carried a 7 percent interest rate. Campbell stocked the shop with nearly £800 worth of books and stationery. Even on such generous terms, and with what was probably a large stock of Campbell's books, Duyckinck entered a competitive, growing trade without any kind of formal training or apprenticeship.

Campbell had for many years been one of the city's leading printers and booksellers. Born in Edinburgh in July 1765, he arrived in New York by way of

Philadelphia in 1785, setting up his first bookshop on Hanover Square at the corner of the Old Slip. A year after going into business with Duyckinck, Campbell moved around the corner to 124 Pearl Street, an ideal spot for increased foot traffic given its proximity to the Bank of New York. It is likely that Campbell's former mentor, the Edinburgh publisher John Bell, helped support the business during his early years in New York, a common arrangement in colonial North America.[9]

Campbell set up Duyckinck's Pearl Street bookshop as a retail outlet for his extra stock. Beyond Campbell's original investment, Duyckinck was expected to pay Campbell "at or as near may be the original cost" for subsequent items that Campbell imported "or otherwise received"—in other words, books that Campbell either published himself or received through his exchange network. For his effort, Duyckinck was "entitled to the full half share of all the profits" of the store. While little additional evidence exists to document the partnership, Campbell's involvement seems to have been limited to supplying Duyckinck with books. Duyckinck was charged with carefully tending to the business and with keeping "a true and first account or accounts of every dealing or Transaction of said Company." The contract also required that Duyckinck compose a yearly inventory of stock, "with all debts due to, and from, the said Company."[10] Despite his being little more than a retail clerk, Duyckinck could at least count on a steady income working for one of the city's largest booksellers.

Printers, booksellers, and publishers went to great lengths to make the shipment of their books easier and less expensive. Indeed, many recognized that the expanse of the new Republic made shipment costly. To negotiate this challenge, many invested in various forms of transportation. Worcester's Isaiah Thomas, for example, bought shares in the hundreds of turnpikes that popped up throughout the mid-Atlantic region and New England at the turn of the nineteenth century.[11] Others invested in maritime transportation. In the span of three years, Duyckinck's new business partner purchased a controlling interest in three merchant ships. Buying shares in a ship was a common tactic that merchants used to strengthen their trading position. Shipping companies seldom owned maritime vessels, with the exception of whalers and steamers; rather, groups of merchants bought mercantile ships cooperatively.[12] In September 1792, for example, Campbell paid £700 to Oliver Bowen of Savannah, Georgia, for a stake in "the good ship or Vessell called the *Providence of Savannah*"—a three-masted schooner built in Providence, Rhode Island, sixty-seven feet long and with a "female image head."[13] Two years later, after he had gone into business with Duyckinck, Campbell bought shares in a two-hundred-ton ship called the *Vigilant,* and in July 1795 he paid £4,000 for access to the *Barrington.*[14] Typically, interest in ships ranged from $1,000 to $10,000, and owners were often a diverse group that included builders, masters, and merchants. It was not unusual, however, for a prosperous merchant to be the sole owner of a trading vessel.[15] By making this kind of investment, Campbell reduced the long-term cost of shipping books to distant ports.

Two years into his new career, Duyckinck began publishing books on his own, independent of Campbell. He mentioned the possibility of striking out on his own in a January 1795 letter to Philadelphia's Mathew Carey. Duyckinck apologized for a late shipment of books to Carey, "oweing to a disappointment in the printer," and said that he intended to "print several small things in the course of the next winter."[16] Duyckinck's accounts reveal his early arrangements with the city's printers. In November 1795, he hired William Hurtin and Andrew Commardinger to print thirty-nine hundred abridged copies of *Robinson Crusoe*. Shortly thereafter, in February 1796, Duyckinck commissioned the printer John Buel to print three thousand copies of John Macgowan's *Life of Joseph*. The next day, he met with John Tiebout and Edward O'Brien to discuss the printing of four thousand copies of George Keate's *Account of the Pelew Islands*.[17] All three texts eventually bore the imprint "printed for Evert Duyckinck & Company." By the end of 1796, Duyckinck had commissioned twenty-five printings, adding at least thirty-six thousand copies to his shop, a strong indication that he had ambitions to strike out on his own.

Rather than take on riskier projects, Duyckinck published large runs of inexpensive steady sellers. A fascinating example of his approach can be gleaned by studying his 1798 edition of Constantin-François Volney's *Travels Through Egypt and Syria,* a book that he published cooperatively and by subscription with the printer John Tiebout and fellow bookseller David Longworth. Ad hoc cooperative ventures prevented an oversaturation of the market should two publishers in a given location have an interest in publishing the same book.[18] As the printer responsible for producing the book, Tiebout took charge of the marketing campaign to secure subscribers. "This work will be printed on good paper, with a fair type," Tiebout boasted in an advertisement he placed in the Albany *Chronicle*, while also hinting that he and his partners would publish a "correct list of those patrons who may encourage the work" at the end of the text. Furthermore, their edition of Volney was to be issued in eight parts, "at the rate of two shillings per number."[19] Keeping their promise to publicize the success of their subscription campaign, Tiebout, Duyckinck, and Longworth published a list of 206 subscribers at the end of the first volume (table 5.1). Men dominated the subscription roles, though six women did lend their names to the text: Sarah Baker, Hannah Baldwin, a Miss Hubbard, Sarah Hurtin, Margaret Morgan, and Eleanor Paulding. Of the known subscribers, more than 60 percent worked with their hands. And while a number of physicians and teachers subscribed to the book, the paucity of professionals and merchants on the list is striking.

TABLE 5.1 Occupations of Subscribers to Evert Duyckinck's edition of Volney's *Travels Through Syria and Egypt* (1798)

Occupational Category	Subscribers (N)	Subscribers (%)
Artisan	69	61.0
Merchant	23	20.3
Professional	12	10.6
Unskilled	3	2.6
Politics	6	5.6
TOTAL	113	99.8
Occupation Unknown	93	

SOURCES: Volney, *Travels Through Syria and Egypt* (New York: Printed by J. Tiebout for E. Duyckinck & Co., 1798), list of subscribers, 2:299–300; Longworth, Shoemaker, Allen, and Tisdale, *Longworth's American Almanack* (1797); Longworth and Shoemaker, *Longworth's American Almanack* (1798).

A diverse cross-section of New York's mechanic community subscribed to Duyckinck's edition of Volney's *Travels*. Nearly one-quarter of the artisan subscribers, for example, were shoemakers. This can be explained partly by sheer numbers. At the time, shoemaking was one of the largest trades in the city. In 1805, for instance, Longworth's city directory listed nearly three hundred shoemakers who lived and worked in Manhattan; shoemakers were second only to carpenters in the total number that appeared in the trade directory.[20] While not exactly a desirable trade, as the historian Alfred F. Young has argued, young men with few prospects often turned to it. But shoemaking was not the only trade represented on Duyckinck's subscription list. Several different tradesmen subscribed, including bakers, carpenters, hairdressers, tailors, blacksmiths, butchers, printers, and sailmakers, along with a wire maker, a stoneware potter, a tin and copper worker, a venetian-blind manufacturer, and a cooper. The list also included a cart man named Josiah Corrington and two laborers, Abraham Day and Peter Winthrop. While Duyckinck's books probably had a broad literary and cultural appeal that would have been a draw to aspiring artisans, the cheapness of his reprints would have also been a selling point for working men and women who wanted to display books in their homes.[21]

Given his early successes, it did not take long for Duyckinck to establish his own business, independent of Campbell. In January 1799, six years after entering the publishing trade, Duyckinck dissolved the partnership with Campbell, purchasing the books still on hand at the Pearl Street shop—along with several reams of paper, sheepskins, receipt books, and twelve dozen sets of playing cards—for about £500. Schoolbooks and Bibles made up the majority of the stock, texts that would be staples in his business for many years. For example, the sale included eighteen copies of *A New Guide to the English Tongue* by Thomas Dilworth, seven pocket Bibles, five octavo Bibles, and fifty copies of Isaac Watts's *Psalms, Carefully Suited to the Christian Worship in the United States of America.* The buyout also included nearly three thousand copies of Noah Webster's *American Spelling-Book* in various stages of production.[22]

Duyckinck developed regional trade connections early in his career. His ambition to extend the reach of his bookshop may have led to the separation from Campbell, who probably expected little more than for Duyckinck to run his new store. Duyckinck's early trade networks emerge from statements of outstanding debts owed to him. And while this list is only a fraction of his early records, it suggests that Duyckinck's business was extensive, even early in his career as a bookseller. By March 1799, shortly after the dissolution of the partnership with Campbell, thirty-one booksellers throughout New England and the mid-Atlantic owed money to the now-defunct firm (table 5.2). Eight debtors lived in upstate New York, along with six in New Jersey and one in Philadelphia. One debtor, William Bartlett, resided in New Bern, North Carolina. In several cases, Duyckinck recorded the reason for the debt. For instance, Andrew G. Fraunces, indebted to Duyckinck for £5 2s, was listed in the assessment as "a Bankrupt"; Duyckinck also indicated that three New Yorkers, Wilbur Palmer of Stillwater, Benjamin Dodge of Dutchess County, and Thomas Wilber of Stephentown, had become insolvent. Duyckinck believed that Andrew Bostwick, who was late on a payment of less than one pound sterling, was dead.[23] Within a few short years, Evert Duyckinck had become a well-known publisher in the northeastern and mid-Atlantic states. After striking out on his own, Duyckinck's influence in New York and the nation's growing print market continued to grow.

"Education Has Acquired a New Complexion"

Evert Duyckinck soon became a leading figure in a campaign to educate the new nation's growing population. In the early years of the young Republic, publishers produced millions of books for schools, colleges, female seminaries, circulating libraries, and literary societies. The young nation's political elite, such as the renowned physician and educational reformer Benjamin Rush, knew all too well that upward mobility hinged on literacy cultivated by a text-based education. "The business of education has acquired a new complexion by the independence of our country," Rush wrote in 1798, adding that "the form of government we have assumed, has created a new class of duties to every American."[24] Duyckinck played a significant role in the national education crusade. During his thirty-five-year career, he published hundreds of thousands of inexpensive reprints of steadily selling schoolbooks for a national market.

TABLE 5.2 Debts Owed to the Co-Partnership of Evert Duyckinck and Samuel Campbell, March 1799

City, State	Accounts		Amount of Debt Owed	
	(*N*)	(%)	(£)	(%)
Fairfield, CT	2	6.4	13 15s	4.0
Berkshire, MA	2	6.4	17 2s	5.2
Stillwater, NY	1	3.2	35	10.7
Haverhill, NH	1	3.2	12 2s	3.7
Brattleboro, VT	2	6.4	30 8s	9.4
Pitts Town, NJ	1	3.2	9 11s	2.7
Cherry Valley, Otsego County, NY	1	3.2	11 7s	3.5
New Bern, NC	1	3.2	3 11s	0.9
Woodbridge, CT	1	3.2	9 13s	2.8
Newburgh, NY	3	9.6	15 5s	4.3
Dutchess County, NY	2	6.4	42 10s	12.9
Hanover, NY	1	3.2	6s	0.1
Stephentown, NY	2	6.4	38 10s	11.7
Redding, CT	1	3.2	3 15s	0.9
Sussex, NJ	1	3.2	10 9s	3.3
Albany, NY	1	3.2	13 1s	4.0
New Marlborough, MA	1	3.2	13 18s	4.0
Philadelphia, PA	1	3.2	7 8s	2.3
New Brunswick, NJ	2	6.4	4 8s	1.0
Hartford, CT	1	3.2	7 10s	2.1
Goshen, NY	1	3.2	4 13s	1.2
Middletown, NJ	1	3.2	4	1.2
Morristown, NJ	1	3.2	21 5s	6.6
TOTAL	31	99.2	329 7s	98.5

SOURCE: "Statement of Debts due to the Co-Partnership of Evert Duyckinck & Co., as taken from the Company's Ledger, New York," March 1799, Duyckinck Family Papers, box 60, folder 7, NYPL.

At the heart of the early Republic's new emphasis on education was the publishing trade. In the years after the Revolutionary War, American children, for the most part, had greater access to schools and books than they had had before the war. The first fifty years in the new nation's life witnessed a steady increase in the number of schools and academies that helped young Americans learn basic literacy. Education developed unevenly, however. New England far outpaced the mid-Atlantic region and the South in both the number of schools and the number of children attending those schools. Nevertheless, the simultaneous expansion of educational opportunity and the rise in literacy was a boon to the American publishing trade. Publishers like Evert Duyckinck recognized early on the economic possibilities of producing schoolbooks for a national market. By working diligently to supply the nation's schoolhouses, American publishers extended the reach of their businesses, as more and more readers demanded a wider variety of books. Publishers thus played an important role in helping teach the nation's growing population to read and write.[25]

Schoolbooks thus made up a significant portion of Duyckinck's known production. Of nearly 872,000 total copies, 255,000, or more than a quarter, were schoolbooks by Caleb Bingham, Noah Webster, Nathaniel Dwight, Lindley Murray, Thomas Dilworth, and others. Bingham and Dwight together accounted for nearly a hundred thousand Duyckinck imprints (table 5.3). Although it is significant that so much of Duyckinck's business involved publishing school-books written by a handful of writers, books intended for the schoolhouse made up a comparatively small percentage of his overall catalogue. Nineteen education titles account for more than 40 percent of the overall number of copies known to have been produced for him by the city's printers, but only about 10 percent of the total number of titles that appear in his daybooks. So, while there is no doubt that Duyckinck would have been known primarily as a supplier of school-books, he was involved in a far greater range of publishing pursuits, including, among many other genres, travel literature, fiction, and history. Indeed, it is likely that Duyckinck used the income generated by his involvement in the schoolbook trade to finance his other literary interests.

In search of educational texts for a national market, printers, booksellers, and publishers continued a long-standing colonial practice of reprinting books. Beginning in the 1730s, American booksellers began importing spelling books, and American printers reprinted them on their presses. Foremost among the many schoolbooks available in early America and the broader British Atlantic was Thomas Dilworth's *New Guide to the English Tongue*, first published in England in the early 1740s. Dilworth's guide proved immensely popular in North America, going through more than forty editions by 1785. Duyckinck published nearly ten thousand copies of Dilworth's schoolbooks. In addition to the copies of Dilworth's *New Guide to the English Tongue* that he inherited from Samuel Campbell in 1799, Duyckinck published several more editions of the classic English speller. In February 1803, for example, he requested that the printer Benjamin Gomez produce one thousand copies of the text. In 1823, long after the Dilworth speller had fallen out of fashion, Duyckinck had two thousand additional copies printed, probably the edition he published in 1820 with G. Long, Daniel D. Smith, and William B. Gilley.[26] Duyckinck also published suc-cessful runs and several thousand copies of Dilworth's popular mathematics text, *The Schoolmaster's Assistant*, in 1796, 1806, and 1810.[27]

TABLE 5.3 Most Popular Titles, 1795–1830

Copies (N)	Author and Title of Duyckinck Imprint
44,000	Caleb Bingham, *The American Preceptor: Being a New Selection of Lessons for Reading and Speaking; Designed for the Use of Schools*
41,500	Nathaniel Dwight, *A Short but Comprehensive System of the Geography of the World: by Way of Question and Answer, Principally Designed for Children and Common Schools*
37,900	*The Holy Bible*
30,000	Robert Gibson, *The Theory and Practice of Surveying: Containing All the Instructions Requisite for the Skilful Practice of This Art*
25,000	John Ely, *The Child's Instructor: Consisting of Easy Lessons for Children; On Subjects Which Are Familiar to Them, in Language Adapted to Their Capacities*
24,500	Noah Webster, *An American Selection of Lessons in Reading and Speaking: Calculated to Improve the Minds and Refine the Taste of Youth*
22,600	Lindley Murray, *The English Reader, or Pieces in Prose and Poetry, Selected from the Best Writers . . . with a Few Preliminary Observations on the Principles of Good Reading*
21,500	*The Book of Common Prayer*
20,500	Noah Webster, *A Grammatical Institute of the English Language: Comprising an Easy, Concise, and Systematic Method of Education*
15,500	John Perrin, *The Elements of French and English Conversation: With New, Familiar, and Easy Dialogues*
13,000	M. Berquin, *The Looking-Glass for the Mind, or Intellectual Mirror: Being an Elegant Collection of the Most Delightful Little Stories, and Interesting Tales in Prose and Verse*
12,800	Noah Webster, *The American Spelling-Book: Containing an Easy Standard of Pronunciation . . . In Three Parts*
11,650	François Pomey, *The Pantheon, Representing the Fabulous Histories of the Heathen God and Most Illustrious Heroes in a Plain and Familiar Method by Way of Dialogue*, trans. Andrew Tooke
10,000	John Perrin, *A Grammar of the French Tongue: Grounded Upon the Decisions of the French Academy.*
10,000	Caleb Bingham, *The Columbian Orator: Containing a Variety of Original and Selected Pieces, Together with Rules, Calculated to Improve Youth and Others in the Ornamental and Useful Art of Eloquence*
9,500	Lindley Murray, *English Grammar, Adapted to the Different Classes of Learners*
7,500	Benjamin Franklin, *The Life of Dr. Benjamin Franklin*
7,100	Daniel Defoe, *The Wonderful Life and Most Surprising Adventures of That Renowned Hero, Robinson Crusoe, Who Lived Twenty-Eight Years on an Uninhabited Island, Which He Afterwards Colonized.*
7,000	J. Hamilton Moore, *The Young Gentleman and Lady's Monitor, and English Teacher's Assistant*
6,500	Noah Webster, *Elements of Useful Knowledge, Containing a Historical and Geographical Account of the United States*
6,000	Thomas Dilworth, *The Schoolmaster's Assistant: Being a Compendium of Arithmetic, Both Practical and Theoretical*

SOURCE: Evert Duyckinck Daybooks, Duyckinck Family Papers, vols. 20–32, NYPL. For dates missing from the Duyckinck daybooks, see notes in table 5.5.

Hoping to build on the popularity of Dilworth's steadily selling texts, Noah Webster set out in 1783 to unify the new nation by standardizing the English language. While he had learned to read as a young boy using Dilworth's *New Guide*, Webster, in his experience as a teacher in Goshen, New York, considered the Dilworth text "the *oldest* and most imperfect guide we use in schools."[28] Even more significant than Dilworth's apparent shortcomings was the troublesome implication that Americans still looked to London for books that taught children how to read. Webster had "too much pride" to stand idly by while his country remained "indebted to Great Britain for books to learn our children the letters of the alphabet."[29] With this in mind, Webster pooled the necessary funds in 1783 to publish five thousand copies of a spelling book he designed himself. Shortly thereafter, Webster published a grammar book and a general reader intended to be used alongside his speller. It was not long before Webster's texts replaced Dilworth's as the books of choice in American schools. By 1830, Webster's *American Spelling-Book* was a publishing phenomenon, with more than three million copies in circulation.[30]

Webster revolutionized publishing in the new nation. As the sole author of his educational books, he took it upon himself to be involved in every facet of production and dissemination. Webster's most important concern was getting his books into the hands of readers. To accomplish this, he built a sophisticated network of printers charged with regional distribution. Samuel Campbell and, eventually, Evert Duyckinck became involved in Webster's ambitious plan to overhaul American education. Their role in Webster's crusade, however, was clouded by Campbell's seemingly dishonest business practices.

Webster was the first American author to take advantage of state and national copyright laws that granted sole intellectual ownership of written work to American authors. Oddly, however, the copyright laws did not clarify what role, if any, printers and publishers played in this newly codified legal framework. Authors like Webster thus "sold" their texts to printers and publishers, who took on the financial risk of production and distribution. As a result, books became valuable commodities to be bought, sold, and traded on the open market. Webster, as it turned out, was masterly in taking advantage of the state and federal copyright system. At the time, copyright laws allowed authors and publishers alike to create legal monopolies on certain books printed in the United States.[31]

Driven by his own national ambitions, Webster hoped to establish a magazine with broad literary appeal. In order to help raise the capital necessary to finance what he was calling the *American Magazine,* in October 1787 Webster hedged a desperate bet: he sold Samuel Campbell the sole rights to publish and disseminate his *American Spelling-Book* in New York, New Jersey, North Carolina, South Carolina, and Georgia for five years.[32] This was a tactic Webster often used as a way to give his schoolbooks the widest possible distribution, and it was a bargain for Campbell, who paid Webster only £80 for a profitable multi-state distribution network. Webster had begun selling copyrights to his texts in the 1780s in states with copyright regulations, and he continued this practice even after Congress passed a federal copyright law. As a result, Webster ended up with what James N. Green has called a "crazy quilt of licenses" spread out among several printers, each controlling a specific region of the country.[33] Taking advantage of his exclusive deal, Campbell churned out twenty thousand copies each year, beginning in 1787, until the expiration of the contract in 1792. Campbell went further, though, and extended his distribution network in 1789 above Long Island Sound into Connecticut, violating Webster's territorial agreement with another firm to distribute *The American Spelling-Book* in New England. Clearly annoyed by this violation of their arrangement, Webster fumed in a private letter that he had "long doubted" Campbell's honesty, revealing that Campbell had "cheated me before."[34] The relationship became so damaged that Webster sued, while Campbell continued to overstep his contract by printing large runs of the spelling book and shipping them to Hartford. Meanwhile, Webster's lawsuit against Campbell dragged on until 1797.[35]

The end of the partnership with Campbell proved even more acrimonious than Webster could have imagined. In 1792, Campbell published yet another cheap edition of Webster's book, his fourteenth in five years. Fed up with the constant wrangling with Campbell, Webster turned to the court of public opinion. He declared in the *Connecticut Courant* that Campbell's latest edition of the *American Spelling-Book* was "the most incorrect edition I have ever seen," that it contained "between two and three thousand errors in printing," and that he utterly disavowed the work.[36] In response, Campbell smugly insinuated that Webster was a "pedantic grammarian," "full of vanity and ostentation."[37] In order to protect his economic interests and his reputation as a publisher, and to discredit Webster's public charges, Campbell reached out to the printers of his fourteenth edition, New York's Thomas and James Swords. "We hereby certify that we printed for Samuel Campbell four half sheets of the American Spelling 14th ed.," wrote the Swords brothers, "and that we carefully read & corrected the proof sheets." Expressing confidence in their presswork, the Swords brothers said they had "every reason to believe" that the fourteenth edition was "fully accurate and as good in every respect as the copy it was printed from."[38] Campbell even went so far as to have an independent arbiter, the New York printer Charles Holt, compare the edition with one that Webster had personally vouched for. Holt "carefully examined and compared twelve pages" of the eleventh edition, printed in Hartford by Hudson & Goodwin, with Campbell's contested volume. While Holt found a number of errors in both, he considered the "fourteenth edition printed by S. Campbell in New York" to be "by far, more accurate

& correct."[39] This was not the end of the matter, however. One month before the expiration of the contract, Campbell printed a sizeable run—ninety thousand copies—of *The American Spelling-Book,* a dastardly move that gave him a massive surplus.[40] And then, in January 1793, Campbell unloaded £800 worth of inventory on his new business partner, Evert Duyckinck.

While it is not clear how many copies of the hotly contested fourteenth edition Duyckinck ended up with, his accounts reveal that he could move the book easily, given the high demand. Between May and December 1795, for example, Duyckinck completed thirty-nine transactions—totaling more than 830 copies—involving *The American Spelling-Book.* Between May and July, Duyckinck sold better than 250 copies of the book. In August, he moved ninety-four more copies, in addition to nearly five hundred between September and the end of the year.[41] While this total is but a fraction of the ninety thousand Campbell had printed prior to the conclusion of his contract with Webster, it does suggest that Duyckinck diligently traded, sold, and exchanged his many copies of Webster's popular speller.

Even though Duyckinck began his career by distributing disputed copies of Webster's spelling book, he continued publishing the "pedantic grammarian's" steadily selling schoolbooks for several years. Between 1797 and 1815, Duyckinck published ten editions of five Webster titles, including *The American Spelling-Book* in 1797, *A Grammatical Institute of the English Language* in 1798, 1801, and 1804, *An American Selection of Lessons in Reading and Speaking* in 1799, 1800, 1802, and 1804, *Elements of Useful Knowledge* in 1810, and, finally, *The Prompter* in 1815. These various editions amounted to *at least* sixty-four thousand copies (table 5.4). Given Webster's mastery of copyright law, Duyckinck paid Webster for the privilege of reprinting his popular texts. In early November 1803, for example, Duyckinck paid Webster $30 so that he could publish a sizeable run of *An American Selection of Lessons in Reading and Speaking,* a "reader" that Webster designed to work alongside the three volumes of his *Grammatical Institute of the English Language.* That very day, Duyckinck put in an order with the printer William W. Vermilye for fifteen thousand copies of the *American Selection* at six cents per copy, an order that eventually cost Duyckinck $900.[42] Thanks in no small way to Duyckinck's continued publication and distribution of Webster's inexpensive school texts, the new nation's growing population was afforded more opportunities to learn how to read, speak, and write.

Duyckinck did not publish Webster's schoolbooks exclusively, nor did Webster have a monopoly on the schoolbook market. In 1785, not long after Webster's *Grammatical Institute* first appeared, Caleb Bingham, a Boston school-teacher, published his first schoolbook, titled *The Young Lady's Accidence, or A Short and Easy Introduction to English Grammar.* Bingham went on to produce two influential patriotic readers. *The American Preceptor,* which first appeared

TABLE 5.4 Most Frequently Reprinted Authors, 1795–1830

Copies (N)	Author	Printings (N)	Titles (N)
64,300	Webster, Noah	18	4
54,000	Bingham, Caleb	15	2
41,500	Dwight, Nathaniel	10	1
41,100	Murray, Lindley	18	5
30,000	Gibson, Robert	41	1
28,100	Perrin, John	18	3
25,000	Ely, John	7	1
15,000	Berquin, M.	10	2
11,650	Tooke, Andrew	15	1
9,200	Dilworth, Thomas	7	2
6,576	Watts, Isaac	8	1
5,000	Goldsmith, Oliver	4	2
4,500	Clarke, John	4	2
4,174	Tisdale, Elkanah	7	1

SOURCE: Evert Duyckinck Daybooks, Duyckinck Family Papers, vols. 20–32, NYPL.

in 1794, sold 640,000 copies during its many print runs, while *The Columbian Orator*, a book Bingham first published in 1797, sold two hundred thousand copies nationwide.[43] Duyckinck supplied a number of Bingham's texts to the nation's print market, particularly *The American Preceptor*. Between 1800 and 1818, Duyckinck commissioned eleven printings of the book from six of the city's printers. In 1817, Duyckinck asked the printer John C. Totten to produce ten thousand copies of the *Preceptor*. The book did well enough that Duyckinck ordered an additional ten thousand copies the following year.[44] All told, Duyckinck distributed at least forty-four thousand copies of Bingham's *American Preceptor* and ten thousand copies of *The Columbian Orator* (table 5.3). Much like his distribution of Webster's popular spelling books, Duyckinck's publication of Bingham's *American Preceptor* and *Columbian Orator* on such a large scale reflects not only the growing demand for schoolbooks as "civic texts" but also Duyckinck's recognition of the public's need for particular titles.[45]

While Webster and Bingham remained steady sellers in the early years of the nineteenth century, books by the English author Lindley Murray greatly exceeded them in popularity. Born in 1745 to an old Quaker family of some means in Harper Tavern, Pennsylvania, Murray relocated to New York City in the early 1750s after living for a time in North Carolina. Murray and his family eventually fled New York at the end of the Revolutionary War, along with thousands of the city's Loyalists. After a long, strange journey, the Murrays settled on the outskirts of York, England. Once established there, the aging Murray embarked on an ambitious literary career. After self-publishing a book about mortality titled *The Power of Religion on the Mind in Retirement, Sickness, and Death*, he turned his attention to schoolbooks. In 1795, Murray finished his *English Grammar*, which quickly became an international best seller, soon to be followed by the equally popular *English Reader*, in 1799. After putting the hardships of the American Revolution behind him, Murray successfully rebounded in England and remade himself into arguably the Atlantic world's most celebrated schoolbook author.[46]

After arriving in the United States, Murray's schoolbooks became steady sellers almost overnight. American production of Murray's *English Grammar* and *English Reader*, in fact, outpaced Webster's schoolbooks. Beginning at the turn of the nineteenth century, Murray's schoolbooks went through a staggering 925 American editions, more than quadrupling Webster's still respectable 221 editions. Much of Murray's success in the United States can be traced to the New York printer Isaac Collins, who had the *English Reader* stereotyped in 1813. This shrewd maneuver allowed Collins to print Murray's schoolbooks in large numbers for a national market. By 1810, there were American editions of all of Murray's schoolbooks, and most American urban centers could claim their corner of the Murray market. Scholars have estimated that American publishers sold more than twelve million copies of Murray's schoolbooks in the first forty years of the nineteenth century. Murray was, by any estimation, the best-selling author in the world.[47]

Given the nationalist and often anti-British climate of the late 1790s, it is somewhat surprising that Murray's schoolbooks took off in the way that they did. The success of his books was especially unusual considering that Murray included nothing in his *English Reader* by an American author. This seeming contradiction did not go unnoticed by fellow American schoolbook author Lyman Cobb, who wrote several popular juvenile texts, including *The North American Reader* and the *Juvenile Reader*, and crowed, "The *English Reader* so largely used in our country does not contain a single piece or paragraph written by an American. Is this good policy? Is it patriotism? Shall the children of this great nation be compelled to read, year after year, none but the speeches and writings of men whose feelings and views are in direct opposition to our institutions and government?"[48]

Evert Duyckinck was one of many American publishers to take advantage of the ready availability of Murray's popular schoolbooks. The *English Reader* was especially profitable for a publisher looking to cash in on the high demand for schoolbooks. Duyckinck and the many other printers, booksellers, and publishers who produced the estimated twelve million copies of the texts did so without paying Murray a copyright fee. Because Murray wrote his schoolbooks after relocating to Great Britain following the British evacuation of New York, his work did not fall under the new state and federal copyright laws, though his brother John did file, unsuccessfully, for an American copyright in December 1798. Between 1804 and 1828, Duyckinck commissioned six printers to print more than forty-one thousand copies of Murray's books. Of particular note is a February 1819 order for seven thousand copies of *The English Reader,* printed by John C. Totten, who two years earlier had printed three thousand copies of the same text.[49] While his overall number of Murray schoolbooks is but a fraction of the more than twelve million produced in the early Republic from 1800 to 1840, Evert Duyckinck nonetheless took advantage of the opportunity to publish Murray's texts without incurring any copyright fees. Murray's books would have been a risk-free investment that Duyckinck could reproduce for a national market easily and cheaply.

Other than participating in the 1802 type controversy meeting and the literary fair that followed, Evert Duyckinck's involvement in the schoolbook trade was arguably the most political thing he did as a publisher. Publishers like Duyckinck took on the ambitious, and patriotic, projects of Webster and Bingham, distributing their books by the thousands throughout the countryside. Because the nation was expanding, the demand for schoolbooks was constant, something Duyckinck and many fellow publishers recognized. Because of this need, schoolbooks became the backbone of Duyckinck's business and probably helped finance his other literary interests as a publisher.

Evert Duyckinck's Extensive Print Network

Duyckinck's emergence as a formidable player in the book trade paralleled his city's rise as the commercial capital of the new nation. The growth of Manhattan's economy was largely the result of the "shipping boom" of the late 1790s and early 1800s. By the end of the eighteenth century, New York City had surged ahead of Philadelphia as the nation's most important port for domestic and international trade. By 1806, imports through New York's harbor were double the value of those arriving at Philadelphia. The city's exports increased as well. The reason for this boom in trade was quite simple: merchants and artisans alike had access to Manhattan Island's wide and deep harbor. The city's harbor allowed larger ships capable of transporting greater volumes of cargo to enter and leave much more easily than the shallow port of Philadelphia, which could be accessed only via the Delaware River. But the so-called shipping boom also had a downside. At the turn of the nineteenth century, Pearl and Water Street merchants began consolidating capital and joining forces with one another in large, powerful ventures, operations that forced smaller businesses and work-shops to move away from the waterfront. Scholars have observed that by the end of the eighteenth century, eight merchants controlled nearly 80 percent of the real estate near the harbor, while Pearl Street was lined with wholesale ware-houses. New York, even in the early days of the Republic, was fast becoming a heavily corporatized city in which a small coterie of men controlled most of the capital.[50]

The ease with which large merchant vessels could enter and leave New York's harbor—even in the coldest and iciest winter months—allowed the city to establish primacy in trade with Great Britain. Not long after the ratification of the Constitution, and cemented after Congress ratified the controversial Jay Treaty, more ships left Liverpool destined for Manhattan than for Philadelphia, Boston, Newport, Charleston, or Savannah. In addition to and because of its growing importance as a commercial seaport, New York quickly evolved into the nation's financial capital. By the early nineteenth century, the city was home to more banks and insurance firms than any other port city. And because of New York's increased prominence as a hub of international trade, the city drew young, aspiring merchants looking to make it big. In ten short years, between 1790 and 1800, the number of businessmen in New York quadrupled; in 1800, the city directories listed more than eleven hundred merchants.[51]

The rapid growth of Manhattan's economy led to a spatial transformation of the city. After prompting from both merchants and politicians alike, the city built South Street. As Edwin Burrows and Mike Wallace tell it, construction was accomplished by drop-hammering wooden poles "into the river bottom to form sea walls," after which "the water lot they enclosed was filled in with rubbish, earth, and cinder," a project that by 1801 had created "new wharves, slips, and piers" from "Whitehall to the Fly Market." [52] The West Side of the city, too, enjoyed a construction boom in order to accommodate more shipping traffic on the Hudson River. The city built West Street on top of a municipal landfill, and by 1810 the West Side docks boasted fifteen wharves. While this paled in com-parison to the more than thirty wharves across town, it signaled to observers like the intrepid British traveler John Lambert that New York was first in trade among American cities. "The wharfs were crowded with shipping, whose tall masts mingled with the buildings, and together with the spires and cupolas of the churches," Lambert wrote in November 1807 as his sloop sailed into the harbor. The New York of 1807, in his estimation, was "the first city in the United States for wealth, commerce, and population," and he noted the "lofty and well-built" English-style homes along Broadway and the "large commodious shops of every description," among them "book stores, print-shops, music-shops, jewelers, and silversmiths; hatters, linen-drapers, milliners, pastry-cooks, coach-makers, hotels, and coffee-houses."[53]

Lambert's enthusiasm for New York's splendor would not last long, how-ever. In April 1808, Lambert returned to Manhattan after touring South Carolina and Georgia, and his observations during his second tour of the city stood in striking contrast to his first impressions. Indeed, much had changed in a few short months. By April, the thriving commercial city was dominated by *"gloomy looks* and *long faces."* In late December 1807, Congress had laid an embargo "on all ships and vessels in the ports and harbors of the United States . . . bound to any foreign port or place."[54] Lambert vividly captured the "dismal aspect" of New York under the embargo:

> The embargo had now continued upwards of three months, and the salutary check which Congress imagined it would have upon the conduct of the belligerent powers was extremely doubtful, while the ruination of the com-merce of the United States appeared certain, if such a destructive measure was persisted in. Already had 120 failures taken place among the merchants and traders, to the amount of more than 5,000,000 dollars; and there were above 500 vessels in the harbor, which were lying up useless, and rotting for want of employment. Thousands of sailors were either destitute of bread, wandering about the country, or had entered into the British service. The merchants had shut up their counting-houses, and discharged their clerks, and the farmers refrained from cultivating their land; for if they brought their produce to market, they either could not sell at all, or were obliged to dispose of it for only a fourth of its value. In short, go where I would, the people were full of complaints.[55]

The city's jails, as a result of widespread insolvency, were overrun with debtors. Republican newspaper editor James Cheetham estimated that many of the city's nearly ten thousand laborers were without jobs. In response to the desperation he saw in the streets, alleys, and taverns of New York, Cheetham led a public campaign to pressure the city's Common Council to provide assistance to those in need. Heeding Cheetham's call, in January 1808 the council allocated emer-gency food rations, monetary relief, and public works employment for men unable to find work. Cheetham's heroic efforts on behalf of the city's working people led to the distribution of more than twenty-nine thousand food rations by April 1808.[56]

While ships rotted along the newly built and once-thriving South Street, and as merchants, artisans, and journeymen roamed the city seeking employ-ment, shelter, and food, Evert Duyckinck sat in the warmth of his Pearl Street office, poring over his account books by the glint of candlelight. Duyckinck was one of the few merchants in the city who weathered the storm caused by the Embargo Act. His business correspondence did not acknowledge the crisis then overtaking New York's economy. In early March, a month before Lambert returned to a ravaged city, Duyckinck sent a small parcel to Mathew Carey in Philadelphia that contained twenty-four copies of Samuel Pike's *Some Important Cases of Conscience Answered*. In an accompanying letter, Duyckinck also tipped his hand that he was trying to control the market for Lindley Murray's school-books, telling Carey that he was fixing the "Price of my Edit. of Murray's Exercises," instead of adhering to a quote stated in a prior letter. Two months after Lambert observed the ruins of Manhattan's thriving commercial district, Duyckinck apologized to Carey for the mistaken quote and promised to send the Murray books "in a few days," as soon as he received them from his binder.[57] As the edifices of New York's merchant and mechanic communities collapsed, Evert Duyckinck seemed indifferent to the chaos created by Jefferson's embargo. Rather, he continued on in his business, publishing inexpensive, steadily selling books for a national market.[58]

The American book trade was not immune to the wave of insolvencies that devastated the economy following the Embargo Act. Dozens of printers, book-sellers, and publishers, in port cities and small towns alike, faced bankruptcy. Of the sixty-four booksellers who attended the Philadelphia literary fair in 1803, only thirteen survived the embargo years. The War of 1812 brought a fresh wave of devastation. At the beginning of the war, New York's Isaac Riley—at the time, the city's largest publisher, with stock valued at more than $400,000—went bankrupt. Shortly thereafter, John Conrad shifted his troubled assets to a cred-itor, Samuel F. Bradford, who tanked two years later. Unlike many of his fellow publishers, Evert Duyckinck not only outlasted the recession but took advantage of the vacuum created by the collapse of so many large publishers. He was not alone in recognizing the opportunity for expansion. Mathew Carey also weath-ered the storm, mainly by publishing a variety of Bibles, both large and small, cheap and expensive. Similarly, Boston's Ebenezer Andrews invested heavily in copyrighted books and "valuable books" such as unique illustrated atlases that only his firm produced. Publishers like Carey and Andrews reacted to mass insolvency by cornering niche markets. Duyckinck approached the crisis quite differently. He continued to focus on financing the production of cheap, steady sellers, printed for him in large lots that he could move easily across a far-flung market.[59]

Duyckinck and his neighbors on Pearl and Water Streets survived the series of crises that ruined smaller printers and booksellers. Many, in fact, prospered in the years following the war. Duyckinck, for instance, claimed $9,000 of real property in 1815. Several men on Pearl and Water Streets claimed a larger stock when the city's tax assessors visited their shops. Isaac Collins & Company claimed $20,000, while Duyckinck's former partner, Samuel Campbell, claimed $14,000. The Swords brothers, just a few blocks away at 160 Pearl Street, claimed $10,000, as did the printers Amos Butler and Peter Mesier, while book-seller Thomas Ronalds, at 188 Pearl, claimed $13,000. These men claimed, on average, significantly more property than their fellow booksellers and printers around the city. The numbers suggest that Duyckinck and his neighbors weath-ered the embargo and the war years by consolidating and indeed expanding their businesses, while smaller printers and booksellers lived on the margins in the city's outer wards.[60]

Print remained a valued commodity even during recession and wartime. Despite the problems many printers, booksellers, and publishers faced during the Embargo of 1807 and the War of 1812, the city's trade continued to grow in the early nineteenth century. In fact, the number of men in the city's publishing trade gradually increased during the economic crises that plagued the city. By the time Andrew Jackson took possession of the presidential mansion and steam power enabled the rise of large, workshop-like factories that gradually replaced household modes of production, several hundred printers, bookbinders, book-sellers, and other allied tradesmen lived and worked in Manhattan.[61]

Duyckinck laid claim to the lower end of the American book trade and thus ignored shifting cultural trends and emerging literary tastes. In so doing, he confined his business to publishing large runs of cheap, popular sellers that would, unlike riskier projects, turn a steady profit. Between 1807, when the first embargo was enacted, and 1811, Duyckinck published nearly 180,000 copies of dozens of texts—and this is a conservative estimate in that we have only partial records for this period of his career (table 5.5). By the time rising tensions between the United States and Great Britain reached a boiling point, Duyckinck had accumulated the capital necessary to sustain his business without supple-menting his stock with imported books. During the war that followed, he pub-lished 89,000 copies of steadily selling books. While this may seem like a marked decline, only partial records exist for 1813 and 1815. Duyckinck's surviv-ing accounts, then, provide only a partial portrait of his overall publishing activity. Unfortunately, thirteen years of his accounts are either fragments or are missing from the archive entirely. If these years are averaged out on the basis of the twenty years of complete records, Duyckinck's total production of books during his career is probably closer to 1.2 million volumes.[62]

Duyckinck published his large stock of steadily selling educational and literary texts for a national market, working alongside and even competing with Philadelphia and New England publishers, who also imagined extending their networks of production and distribution across regional borders. Philadelphia publishers invested a great deal of time and capital in the Chesapeake region and points farther south. The Chesapeake Bay area, Baltimore especially, acted a gateway for mid-Atlantic merchants to reach southern port cities and towns. Sitting just beyond the reach of the Philadelphia's trading area, Baltimore's print

TABLE 5.5 Annual Production: Evert Duyckinck, 1795–1830

Year	Works (N)	Printings (N)	Printers (N)	Copies (N)	Year	Works (N)	Printings (N)	Printers (N)	Copies (N)
1795	5	10	8	11,700	1811[a]	3	6	2	4,400
1796	7	15	6	24,000	1813[b]	16	27	7	37,953
1799	7	13	8	18,650	1814	21	35	9	50,650
1800	14	28	6	71,200	1815[c]	2	2	2	400
1801	10	14	10	14,664	1816[d]	—	—	—	—
1802	14	25	11	27,626	1817	36	50	11	116,049
1803[e]	10	18	11	37,991	1818	25	35	8	52,450
1804	21	36	15	45,485	1819	13	16	4	30,250
1805	13	19	8	12,844	1820[f]	8	9	3	14,700
1806	12	23	10	29,874	1826[g]	3	4	3	4,196
1807	18	29	7	28,150	1827	17	28	4	32,450
1808	20	33	8	58,923	1828	15	18	3	34,470
1809	19	33	10	48,200	1829	8	17	3	18,250
1810	12	16	7	39,500	1830[h]	2	3	1	6,500
TOTAL COPIES					TOTAL COPIES				
1795–1800	125,550				1813–1816	89,003			
1801–1806	168,484				1817–1820	213,449			
1807–1811	179,173				1826–1830	95,866			

SOURCE: Evert Duyckinck Daybooks, Duyckinck Family Papers, vols. 20–32, NYPL.
[a] Vol. 27 (1811) only goes through 6 September.
[b] Vol. 28 (1813) only goes from May to December .
[c] Vol. 28 (1815) only goes to 18 January 1815.
[d] Vol. 29 begins on 26 December 1816.
[e] The records for 1803 are incomplete owing to an epidemic of Yellow Fever that forced New Yorkers to evacuate the city.
[f] Vol. 30 (1820) only goes through 1 April.
[g] Vol. 31 (1826) begins on 20 January.
[h] Vol. 32 (1830) only goes through 30 November.

market was up for grabs. Mathew Carey, working with his enigmatic itinerant salesman, the Reverend Mason Locke Weems, established a strong presence in the region. Over the course of their collaboration, Carey shipped nearly $20,000 worth of books to Weems, who then doled them out to subscribers and shop-keepers alike. By 1800, many of Carey's Philadelphia colleagues had followed his example and set up their own outposts in Chesapeake port towns. Through sheer force of will, Carey and Weems seemingly remade the southern book market and created reliance upon Philadelphia publishers for a steady supply of books.[63]

With Carey and his Philadelphia colleagues ostensibly in control of both the southern and western markets, Boston publishers held considerable sway over the Northeast. Worcester's Isaiah Thomas remained the region's most important publisher, largely because of his partnership with Boston's Ebenezer Andrews, his former apprentice. Just as Samuel Campbell had set up his protégé Evert Duyckinck in the early 1790s, Thomas supplied all of the tools Andrews could have possibly needed to get his Boston shop up and running. Aside from Thomas's substantial investment, Andrews could take on projects of his choice without any real oversight from his patron. Despite being something of a satellite branch in Thomas's publishing empire, Andrews sometimes published more books than Thomas did. As a result, Thomas and partners like Andrews controlled the New England print market, usually by creating commission partnerships with individual bookshops, unlike Carey's reliance on peripatetic salesmen like Mason Weems. Thomas thus created a sophisticated distribution network that stretched into a number of New England towns and port cities, from Worcester to Walpole, New Hampshire, Rutland, Vermont, and Portland, Maine. Andrews, likewise, worked with a number of commissioned booksellers in upstate New York and Baltimore. When taken together, James Green has argued, Thomas's network was "by far the largest book enterprise in the nation," and probably bigger than "most in Britain."[64]

After the dust had settled from the successive economic crises of the embargo and the War of 1812, Duyckinck expanded his distribution network into markets nominally controlled by Philadelphia and Boston publishers. Duyckinck's national book-distribution network rivaled in size, scope, and influence those of Carey, Thomas, and Andrews. Duyckinck made extensive use of retail agents to sell his cheap books on commission. Between 1813 and 1829, he worked with twenty-four booksellers in twenty cities across twelve states, ranging from Hanover, New Hampshire, and Baltimore, Maryland, to Georgetown, South Carolina, and Pensacola, Florida (table 5.6). Between the end of the War of 1812 and his retirement in 1830, Duyckinck shipped at least $65,000 worth of books and stationery to booksellers working with him on commission. Duyckinck offered generous commissions, with many retaining 25 to 33 percent of a book's retail price. The sheer reach of his business, and the liberal terms he offered, solidified Duyckinck's reputation as a reliable supplier of cheap books.[65]

Like many fellow booksellers and publishers in the early Republic, Duyckinck also participated in what scholars have called the "multiple imprint system" of book distribution. The multiple imprint system allowed publishers to extend their distribution networks at little or no risk to their overall business. Pioneered by Worcester's Isaiah Thomas and Philadelphia's Mathew Carey, printers and

TABLE 5.6 Booksellers on Commission with Evert Duyckinck, 1813–1829

Name	Years on Commission	City	State	Stock Received ($)	Discount (%)
John Beile	1826	Charleston	South Carolina	7.16	50
Franklin Betts	1817–1820	Baltimore	Maryland	25,018.44	33
William Burgess	1826–1827	Providence	Rhode Island	555.72	60
Nathan Camp	1817	Middletown	Connecticut	111.88	—
Clark & Lyman	1813–1819	Middletown	Connecticut	921.65	25
Cummings & Hilliard	1817–1818	Boston	Massachusetts	1,089.28	33
Peter Freeman	1828	Burlington	Connecticut	1,116.87	—
William Gibbes Hunt[a]	1820	Lexington	Kentucky	—	—
Christopher Hall	1818–1829	Norfolk	Virginia	3,167.37	33
John Hibbard	1818–1819	Hanover	New Hampshire	700.29	25
William S. Hunt[b]	1827	Pensacola	Florida	—	
Peter A. Johnson	1813–1817	Elizabethtown	New Jersey	10,054.22	25
George Long	1813–1814	New York	New York	2,397.66	25
George Lovejoy	1817	New York	New York	1,261.43	33
Robert Macgill	1813	Newburgh	New York	8.50	25
Joseph McIntyre	1819–1820	Salem	Massachusetts	1,558.75	33
Samuel Morgan	1826–1827	Albany	New York	4,777.00	—
Moses Scott	1814	Wilkes-Barre	Pennsylvania	192.86	—
Samuel Shaw	1818	Lansingburgh	New York	238.92	33
Skinner & Crosby	1817	Auburn	New York	601.59	33
Thomas M. Skinner	1818–1819	Albany	New York	1,811.80	33
Daniel Steele	1818–1819	Baltimore	Maryland	404.10	33
Eleazer Waterman	1818–1820	Georgetown	South Carolina	8,292.01	25
Erastus Worthington	1819	Brooklyn	New York	310.24	33
			TOTALS	64,597.74	

SOURCE: Evert Duyckinck Daybooks, Duyckinck Family Papers, vols. 20–32, NYPL. The value of stock received by each commission agent reflects Duyckinck's calculations, in that it reflects the individual discount he offered each correspondent. Duyckinck recorded the booksellers listed in this table as commissioned agents.

[a] William Gibbes Hunt was listed as a commission agent on 28 March 1820, which is the last page of vol. 30 of the Duyckinck Account Books; the amount listed is illegible.

[b] William S. Hunt was listed as a commission agent only once, in vol. 31, but the amount of stock he received, and the value of that stock, was not recorded.

booksellers formed large, mostly regional networks through which books in sheets were exchanged by the hundreds. Once the sheets were in hand, printers and booksellers simply added their own names to the imprint, a practice that allowed several men to share the financial risk of publishing a book. In this way, printers and booksellers saved money while also diversifying their stock. "Few firms had sufficient capital to take the whole risk on their titles," William Charvat tells us, and the result was the creation of a "loose intercity structure of tie-ups between particular booksellers," often identified as "correspondents" in account books and letters. Within the complexity of the multiple imprint system, Charvat points out, a correspondent served as a "co-publisher when he co-operated in the issue of a book" in which "a firm split the risk on a book which it had contracted to publish."[66]

Duyckinck did much of his business in the mid-Atlantic states and, to a lesser extent, New England (table 5.7). He retained two Manhattan booksellers—George Long and George Lovejoy, a former apprentice hailing from Stratford, Connecticut—to oversee his stake in the local market.[67] At the conclusion of Lovejoy's term as an apprentice, Duyckinck set him up two blocks away with $1,300 worth of books and stationery. Lovejoy, though, worked only one year for Duyckinck before disappearing from his patron's records.[68] In addition to the immediate New York market, Duyckinck dealt with several booksellers in upstate New York. Two of his retail agents—Samuel Morgan and Thomas M. Skinner—commanded Duyckinck's share of the Albany market, while Peter A. Johnson of Elizabethtown sold Duyckinck imprints in New Jersey. Duyckinck had a smaller presence in New England, corresponding with seven retail booksellers ranging from Middletown, Connecticut, to Hanover, New Hampshire, and several points in between, including Providence, Boston, and Salem. Duyckinck distributed his books evenly among his New England contacts, with booksellers on commission in Middletown and Burlington, Connecticut, receiving approximately the same amount of stock as those in Boston and Salem.[69]

For much of his career, Duyckinck did steady business with southern booksellers. Indeed, a majority of his commission accounts involved booksellers in Kentucky, Maryland, Virginia, South Carolina, and Florida. Prior to the American Revolution, southern booksellers had relied heavily on the English publishing trade to stock their shops. Once independence had been secured, however, many were forced to seek connections with northern publishers. What printing did occur in cities like Washington, D.C., Baltimore, Richmond, Charleston, and Savannah was very often either intensely local, such as the publication of sermons by area ministers, or related in some way to local or state government.[70] Printers and booksellers in the South, then, worked with publishers such as Duyckinck to line their shelves with the steady sellers that customers wanted. In the years during and after the War of 1812, Duyckinck shipped nearly $37,000

TABLE 5.7 Commission Accounts by Region, 1813–1829

Region, City, State	Accounts (N)	(%)	Stock Received[a] ($)	(%)
Mid-Atlantic				
Elizabethtown, NJ	1	4.1	10,054.22	15.5
Albany, NY	2	8.3	6,588.00	10.1
Auburn, NY	1	4.1	601.59	0.9
Brooklyn, NY	1	4.1	310.24	0.4
Lansingburgh, NY	1	4.1	238.92	0.3
New York, NY	2	8.3	3,659.09	5.6
Newburgh, NY	1	4.1	8.50	0
Wilkes-Barre, PA	1	4.1	192.86	0.2
TOTAL	10	41.2	21,653.42	33
New England				
Middletown, CT	2	8.3	1,033.53	1.6
Burlington, CT	1	4.1	1,116.87	1.7
Boston, MA	1	4.1	1,089.28	1.6
Salem, MA	1	4.1	1,558.75	2.4
Hanover, NH	1	4.1	700.29	1.0
Providence, RI	1	4.1	555.72	0.8
TOTAL	7	28.8	6,054.44	9.1
South				
Pensacola, FL	1	4.1	—	
Lexington, KY	1	4.1	—	
Baltimore, MD	2	8.3	25,416.07	39.3
Georgetown, SC	1	4.1	8,292.01	12.8
Charleston, SC	1	4.1	7.16	0
Norfolk, VA	1	4.1	3,167.37	4.9
TOTAL	7	28.8	36,882.61	57

SOURCE: Evert Duyckinck Daybooks, Duyckinck Family Papers, vols. 20–32, NYPL. The value of stock received by each commission agent reflects Duyckinck's calculations in that it reflects the individual discount he offered each correspondent.
[a] At discounted prices.

worth of stock to booksellers working on commission scattered throughout the South.[71]

Contrary to the suggestion that New York publishers largely bypassed the Chesapeake market, Duyckinck established connections with booksellers in Baltimore.[72] In May 1818, a Baltimore bookseller named Franklin Betts ran an advertisement in the Baltimore *Patriot & Mercantile Advertiser* claiming that his stock of New York–produced books was equal to what was being sold in Baltimore by "A PERSON who goes by the name of H. VICARY," an agent of the London publisher T. Kinnersley. Betts went on to assert that Vicary overcharged for subscriptions to Kinnersley's massive illustrated Bible, while books in Betts's shop could be obtained "one hundred percent cheaper"—a dubious claim, no doubt, but one sure to pique the interest of Baltimore *Patriot* readers.[73] Between 1817 and 1820, Betts received ninety-two shipments from Duyckinck worth more than $25,000 (table 5.8). The numbers in table 5.8, however, do not fully capture the extent of the partnership's activities. While Duyckinck's records do not survive for a five-year period between 1821 and 1826, it is likely that he continued shipments, as Betts advertised in the Baltimore *Patriot & Mercantile Advertiser* until May 1822.[74]

The pattern of shipments to Betts reflects Duyckinck's business model of publishing an assortment of titles that would appeal to broad cultural tastes and educational needs. A typical shipment from Duyckinck to Betts—in this case an April 1817 order, which Duyckinck shipped aboard the schooner *Resolve*—contained nearly two thousand individual items and forty-nine titles (table 5.9). The number of titles, however, is misleading. In this and similar shipments, Duyckinck listed only the number of chapbooks, not their titles; therefore, the number of titles Duyckinck sent to Betts greatly exceeded what was actually listed in the account book. The shipment was worth nearly $1,100, and after applying a generous discount, Duyckinck valued the order at $810.89. Aside from more than four hundred nonbook items, which included blank books, press papers, and ink powder, this order is representative of Duyckinck's business model, with its sharp focus on inexpensive educational texts and a lesser, but still notable, interest in literary and scholarly titles. For example, Betts ordered approximately the same number of belles lettres titles as educational works. The crucial difference was the number of copies and overall cost for each broad category. Duyckinck shipped 174 belles lettres items at a cost of $194,

TABLE 5.8 Franklin Betts (Baltimore, MD) Commission Account, 1817–1820

Year	Orders (N)	(%)	Stock Received ($)	(%)
1817	27	29.3	10,741.98	42.9
1818	31	33.6	9,636.52	38.5
1819	27	29.3	3,699.03	14.7
1820	7	7.6	940.91	3.7
TOTALS	92	99.8	25,018.44	99.8

SOURCE: Evert Duyckinck Daybooks, Duyckinck Family Papers, vols. 29 and 30, NYPL.

TABLE 5.9 Franklin Betts Commission Account Order, 9 April 1817

	Titles Ordered		Items Ordered		Cost of Order	
	(N)	**(%)**	**(N)**	**(%)**	**($)**	**(%)**
Belles Lettres						
Biography	2	3.5	8	0.4	9.00	0.8
Classics	6	10.7	50	2.5	70.00	6.4
Essays	1	1.7	2	0.1	2.50	0.2
Geography	3	5.3	62	3.2	54.00	4.9
History	1	1.7	2	0.1	3.00	0.2
Music	1	1.7	24	1.2	24.00	2.2
Novels	4	7.1	14	0.7	16.50	1.5
Travel	1	1.7	12	0.6	15.00	1.3
BELLES LETTRES TOTALS	19	33.4	174	8.8	194.00	17.5
Education						
Foreign Language	3	5.3	30	1.5	27.00	2.4
Juvenile	4	7.1	126	6.5	99.00	9.1
Misc. Chapbooks	Varied	—	528	27.3	49.50	4.5
Schoolbooks	15	26.7	444	22.9	251.75	23.2
EDUCATION TOTALS	22	39.1	1,128	58.2	427.25	39.2
Professional						
Medicine	2	3.5	4	0.2	15.00	1.3
PROFESSIONAL TOTALS	2	3.5	4	0.2	15.00	1.3
Reference						
Dictionaries	2	3.5	63	3.2	114.00	10.5
REFERENCE TOTALS	2	3.5	63	3.2	114.00	10.5
Religion						
Bibles	1	1.7	90	4.6	176.75	16.3
Misc. Religious texts	3	5.3	43	2.2	45.00	4.1
RELIGION TOTALS	4	7.0	133	6.8	221.75	20.4
Stationery						
Misc. Blank Books	5	8.9	156	8.0	91.63	8.4
Press Papers	1	1.7	144	7.4	12.00	1.1
Walker's Ink Powder	1	1.7	132	6.8	7.50	0.6
STATIONERY TOTALS	7	12.3	432	22.2	111.13	10.1
ORDER TOTAL	56	98.8	1,934	99.1	$1,083.13	99
					(272.24)	
					810.89	

SOURCE: Evert Duyckinck Daybooks, Duyckinck Family Papers, vol. 29, NYPL.

compared to the 1,128 educational texts Betts received in this shipment, valued at $427.25.[75]

For the duration of his brief career as a bookseller, Franklin Betts leaned heavily on Duyckinck to supply his shop. Indeed, the first advertisement Betts placed in the Baltimore *Patriot & Mercantile Advertiser,* touting books "just received and for sale," coincided with the start of his retail arrangement with Duyckinck.[76] And while Duyckinck's daybooks suggest that he set Betts up as clerk in a retail store, Betts looked to sell his large inventory to country sellers outside Baltimore.[77] By that time, he had received nineteen shipments from Duyckinck dating to January 1817, totaling $7,500.[78] The timing of his advertisements indicates that Betts sought to build his stock before going public. The advertisements he ran in the Baltimore *Patriot & Mercantile Advertiser* are little more than summaries of the shipments he received from Duyckinck. Between 1817 and 1820, Betts ran thirty-one advertisements in local newspapers highlighting his stock, though many were reprints. In April 1817, for example, Betts paid for an advertisement in the *Patriot* plugging the latest books from New York: "Just received and for sale by F. BETTS, 184 Market-Street, WRITINGS of Miss Hyde, with a sketch of her life, Tooke's Pantheon, Simson's Euclid, Clarke's Introduction, Adams' Latin Grammar, Perrin's Grammar and Exercises, Greek Testaments, Hardie's Corderii, together with many other articles."[79]

The books in this advertisement arrived intermittently in four shipments between mid-February and mid-April 1817, totaling more than $2,000. On 20 February, Betts received two copies of Robert Simson's corrected edition of *Elements of Geometry: Containing the First Six Books of Euclid,* along with twelve copies of Greek testaments. A few weeks later, in mid-March, six additional copies of Simson's *Elements of Geometry* and twelve copies of John Perrin and J. F. Tocquot's *Grammar of the French Tongue* arrived. Most of the texts highlighted in the advertisement, however, came to Betts in early April 1817. In the three-crate order, Duyckinck included four copies of *The Writings of Nancy Maria Hyde, of Norwich, Conn., Connected with a Sketch of Her Life,* twenty-four each of Andrew Tooke's *Pantheon* and John Clarke and James Hardie's *Introduction to the Making of Latin,* twelve copies of Alexander Adams's *Latin and English Grammar,* and six copies of Mathurin Cordier and James Hardie's *Corderii Colloquia, or Cordery's Colloquies.* Finally, forty-eight additional copies of Perrin and Tocquot's *Grammar of the French Tongue* arrived ten days before Betts placed the advertisement in the Baltimore *Patriot.*[80]

Over time, Duyckinck's collaboration with Franklin Betts began to pay off, as several additional Chesapeake booksellers followed his example and stocked their shops with Duyckinck imprints. Between 1813 and 1830, eight booksellers filled their Baltimore shops with nearly $2,000 worth of Duyckinck's books. But Duyckinck's influence in the Chesapeake was not limited to Baltimore. Near the end of his career, Duyckinck began working with several booksellers in Virginia, including three accounts in Richmond that totaled more than $7,500. Christopher Hall of Norfolk, for instance, received sixteen shipments from Duyckinck between 1818 and 1829, orders that totaled more than $3,000.[81] In January 1830, the Richmond bookseller Richard Sanxay wrote Duyckinck asking for several titles, including six common prayer books, six German language texts, sixteen dictionaries, two gardening texts, and one dozen atlases.[82] Likewise, the bookseller William H. Fitzwhylson received thirty-three shipments from Duyckinck between 1826 and 1829, totaling nearly $600. Both Fitzwhylson and Sanxay received a generous 60 percent discount. Such a steep discount suggests that Duyckinck, who by that time was in the twilight of his career, was trying to clear out his excess stock. These accounts paled in comparison, however, to Duyckinck's involvement with the Richmond bookseller John W. Nash. In a short four-year span, from 1826 to 1830, Nash received eighty-five shipments of books and stationery from New York, worth nearly $7,000, at a steep 60 percent discount.[83] Despite receiving such a large assortment of books on generous terms, Nash encountered financial difficulties. While we know little about him or his business, we do know that an apprentice in his shop named Joseph Williamson Randolph helped liquidate the shop's excess stock after Nash went out of business in 1830. While in the process of closing Nash's shop, Randolph purchased $200 worth of books for his new store, a transaction that probably included quite a few Duyckinck imprints.[84]

Duyckinck's influence in the South extended beyond the Chesapeake. Two South Carolina booksellers, John Beile of Charleston and Eleazer Waterman of Georgetown, sold Duyckinck imprints in their shops. While Beile worked for Duyckinck for only a brief period in 1826, Duyckinck's partnership with Waterman had a greater impact in South Carolina. In a short two-year period between July 1818 and March 1820, Duyckinck shipped twenty-five orders to Waterman that totaled nearly $8,300. Waterman was also active in Georgetown politics, serving the town as a district ordinary, a position to which he was appointed by the governor.[85] Two of Duyckinck's southern agents, William S. Hunt of Pensacola, Florida, and William Gibbes Hunt of Lexington, Kentucky, appear in Duyckinck's accounts, but neither the amount of stock they received nor the number of orders Duyckinck shipped them survive in the daybooks.[86]

Beyond the Chesapeake and points farther south, Duyckinck's growing distribution network also followed westward expansion. Duyckinck's dealings with three Ohio booksellers—Williamson & Strong, James Turnbull, and Gains Stebbens & Company—hint at one important development in the national book trade: the increased connectivity between interior towns and eastern port cities. Completion of the Erie Canal in the fall of 1825 opened new markets in the Ohio Valley by offering fast and relatively inexpensive transportation of goods. Given the sudden expansion of possible markets, Duyckinck took advantage of the new waterways. Turnbull, who operated a bookshop in Steubenville, a small river town in eastern Ohio, received four shipments from Duyckinck between May 1827 and May 1828 totaling $776.57. Several months later, in December 1828, Duyckinck shipped a parcel to Cincinnati's Williamson & Strong. And while these shipments pale in comparison to the connections he made in the Northeast, mid-Atlantic, and South, Duyckinck's growing westward network further suggests that he operated on a national scale.[87]

Evert Duyckinck was not the only New York publisher to recognize the possibilities of expanding west. After severing his partnership with Jonathan Seymour in 1808, George F. Hopkins embarked on a series of strange travels. He worked in the city, mostly on his own, until 1818, when he struck up a partnership with Benjamin F. Powers to open a printing office in Cincinnati. Hopkins's attempt to take his printing business to the Ohio Valley was short-lived, however. The printer David Bruce recalled in his memoir that Hopkins's decision to move west was sudden, irresponsible, and brought on by delusions of grandeur. "Mr. Hopkins was a worthy energetic printer," Bruce wrote, but he wasted his talents. Because of his ambition "to give elevation to the art of printing [he] conceived the idea of moving West—the better to carry out his extensive plans." Bruce mused that Hopkins "rashly withdrew from a profitable partnership with Mr. Jonathan Seymour and started for the western wilds declaring 'nothing short of a paper Mill would limit his ambitions, and that he would make books from the very rags!'" Hopkins's western businesses did not last long. He returned to New York in 1821, opening a printing shop on Pine Street. "After a year's absence Mr. Seymour was surprised to receive from him [Hopkins] a melancholy letter dated from a float boat down the Mississippi—passing the water front of the present city of Memphis," Bruce recalled. "The letter was an appeal for financial aid," Bruce sarcastically pointed out, because "the truth was Mr. George F. Hopkins had realised none of his utopian expectations if we omit the item of rags personified in his own garment."[88] Hopkins remained in New York, working alongside his son for many years, until he again felt the lure of adventure in 1838, relocating this time to Key West, Florida. He met a similar fate on his second adventure, slinking back to Gotham only a year after arriving in the Keys. He remained in New York as a printer until 1844, when he retired to New Jersey.[89]

As regional as much of Duyckinck's distribution was, we should not underestimate the difficulty in transporting such large numbers of books to places such as Hanover, New Hampshire. The journey to Hanover, roughly 270 miles from New York City, would have been difficult, no matter the course. Travel by stagecoach, while certainly arduous, would also have been prohibitively expensive for most booksellers and publishers in the early Republic. Indeed, as Cathy

Davidson has pointed out, the cost of a ten-mile journey could be as high as one dollar at the turn of the century. The cumbersome nature of book distribution, whether by land or by sea, places Duyckinck alongside other notable publishers in the early Republic, such as Carey and Thomas, for the simple reason that he sustained the kind of large-scale, wholesale business model of producing cheap books for a national market for much of his career, despite the logistical challenges.[90]

"The Books You Will Receive from Me Shall Be Well Bound"

Building networks of shopkeepers selling books on commission was not the only method publishers employed to expand their geographical reach. Duyckinck, like many of his peers, carried on the European tradition of exchanging books. Born out of the reprint trade, the exchange trade was a way for publishers to cross regional borders and enter into distant markets. Men like Duyckinck, Carey, Andrews, and Thomas also used the exchange trade to diversify their own inventories. The exchange trade was a simple operation: booksellers and publishers swapped books of equal value in various stages of production. Men of the trade often circulated their exchange catalogues—more or less one-page lists of available titles—between their friends and business partners in several cities. Typically, bound books would be exchanged for bound books while books in boards reciprocated a return of titles in a similar material state. Little if any money ever changed hands, since publishers exchanged items of equal value. Implicit in the practices of the exchange trade was a type of economic nationalism. Rather than turn to London for a large supply of steadily selling titles, publishers with enough capital would have thousands of copies of a particular text printed, and would then almost immediately place them in a box destined for another market. Much of the exchange trade in the early nineteenth century was built on the agreements made at the early literary fairs. In this way, a publisher like Duyckinck could tap into a national print market without risking much in the process. By circulating his books on exchange, he could increase the possibility of doing interstate business.[91]

Evert Duyckinck participated extensively in the exchange trade, so much so that in 1820 he started maintaining a separate account book in order to keep track of what had become a large, complex network of fellow booksellers. Working within the constraints of the exchange trade, Duyckinck cultivated relationships with more than 140 booksellers in more than three dozen cities spread across thirteen states and the District of Columbia. Many of his exchange partners resided in the mid-Atlantic and New England (table 5.10). Duyckinck kept seventy exchange accounts with mid-Atlantic shopkeepers, including book-

TABLE 5.10 Booksellers on Exchange with Evert Duyckinck by Region, 1820–1830

Region, City, State	Accounts (N)	(%)	Stock Received ($)
Mid-Atlantic			
Albany, NY	8	5.5	4,739.87
Canandaigua, NY	1	0.6	614.25
Catskill, NY	1	0.6	30.00
Cooperstown, NY	2	1.3	260.00
Ithaca, NY	1	0.6	163.80
Lansingburgh, NY	3	2.0	486.00
Rochester, NY	1	0.6	1,128.10
Troy, NY	1	0.6	178.00
Utica, NY	3	2.0	3,041.50
Elizabethtown, NJ	1	0.6	648.75
Morristown, NJ	1	0.6	257.59
New Brunswick, NJ	1	0.6	76.50
Newark, NJ	1	0.6	62.50
Trenton, NJ	1	0.6	36.00
Philadelphia, PA	41	28.4	34,854.70
Pittsburgh, PA	3	2.0	832.25
TOTAL	70	47.2	47,409.81
New England			
Bridgeport, CT	3	2.0	2,237.00
Bristol, CT	1	0.6	65.42
Hartford, CT	9	6.2	9,763.07
Middletown, CT	3	2.0	895.75
New Haven, CT	6	4.1	2,203.20
Newport, RI	1	0.6	170.50
Norwich, CT	1	0.6	244.00
Rutland, VT	1	0.6	372.25
Hallowell, ME	2	1.3	1,908.00
Boston, MA	19	13.1	27,462.30
Greenfield, MA	1	0.6	237.00
Northampton, MA	1	0.6	736.00
Salem, MA	1	0.6	823.25
Concord, NH	3	2.0	1,622.85
Exeter, NH	1	0.6	883.50
Keene, NH	1	0.6	162.50

(Continued)

TABLE 5.10 (Continued)

Region, City, State	Accounts (N)	(%)	Stock Received ($)
Providence, RI	2	1.3	483.00
Brattleboro, VT	1	0.6	295.00
Bellows Falls, VT	2	1.3	468.00
TOTAL	59	39.3	51,032.59
South			
Baltimore, MD	8	5.5	6,936.45
Charleston, SC	1	0.6	52.00
Richmond, VA	4	2.7	756.00
Savannah, GA	1	0.6	240.00
Washington, D.C.	1	0.6	100.00
TOTAL	15	10.0	8,084.45

SOURCE: Evert Duyckinck Exchange Book, Duyckinck Family Papers, vol. 35, NYPL.

sellers in new and growing markets such as Rochester, Cooperstown, and Ithaca and locations farther west like Pittsburgh. Duyckinck exchanged with booksellers in the northern reaches of New England, including Hallowell, Maine, Brattleboro, Rutland, and Bellows Falls, Vermont, and Concord, Exeter, and Keene, New Hampshire. And while he did not exchange as many texts with southern booksellers, he still kept track of fifteen accounts that sent more than $8,000 worth of his stock to Baltimore, Maryland, Richmond, Virginia, Savannah, Georgia, and Charleston, South Carolina.[92]

Given the nature of the exchange trade, it is not surprising that Duyckinck was especially active in swapping books with Philadelphia and Boston booksellers. He traded nearly $35,000 worth of stock with more than forty Philadelphia booksellers. Duyckinck also worked with nineteen men of the trade in Boston, swapping books valued at more than $27,000. He exchanged books with John West, one of Boston's leading publishers. The correspondence between Duyckinck and West, along with Duyckinck's detailed accounts, represents the kind of rigidly formulaic transactions that occurred within the exchange trade. In December 1799, for example, Duyckinck informed West that he had begun work on "an edition of Perrin's [French] Grammar" and that he would gladly exchange it for a few of "such works as I may want . . . either of your own print or books printed by others in Boston." Duyckinck insisted that the exchange involve bound books. "The books you will receive from me shall be well bound," he wrote, "therefore shall expect the same from you."[93]

Unlike the many printers, booksellers, bookbinders, and publishers who floundered in the difficult economic climate brought on by the embargo and the War of 1812, Evert Duyckinck prospered. And while many of his fellow publishers narrowed their specializations, Duyckinck published a broad array of inexpensive steady sellers for a national market. Duyckinck competed with Boston and Philadelphia publishers for influence in the Northeast, mid-Atlantic region, and South, and he positioned himself well for this kind of expansion by making key connections in Maryland, Virginia, and South Carolina. In the course of doing so, Duyckinck contracted with dozens of booksellers to sell his books on commission and kept track of a complex exchange network. In this way, Duyckinck mirrored the practices of influential publishers like Worcester's Isaiah Thomas and Philadelphia's Mathew Carey. Further west, Duyckinck formed relationships with booksellers along the Ohio River in the Northwest Territory, a sign of the Erie Canal's transformative role in reshaping the American economy. By the time he retired in 1830, Duyckinck had made himself into one of the leading publishers in the new nation.

A House on Bleecker Street

Over the course of his long career, Duyckinck expanded his business from a small Pearl Street retail shop into a large interstate wholesaling firm. By the time he retired in 1830, his private life bore little resemblance to his early days as a New York artisan. In November 1829—following the example of affluent urban refugees who sought a more refined, sociable community away from lower Manhattan's noisy financial and manufacturing sector—Duyckinck moved his family to a new, fashionable neighborhood in the Eighth Ward.[94] This rapidly developing area near John Jacob Astor's Vauxhall Gardens was designed to create a sense of separation in both geography and class. Men in charge of development along Bleecker Street sought and received permission from the city government to rename a block "LeRoy Place," a shrewd rhetorical move that aimed to distinguish it from surrounding neighborhoods.[95] Duyckinck's new neighborhood thus teemed with row houses situated on tree-lined streets that were, according to Edwin Williams's 1833 New York guidebook, comparable in "beauty and taste" to the most resplendent of European palaces.[96]

By 1830, an increasing number of well-to-do members of the trade maintained a residence separate from their shops. As historians have noted, the integrated household economy in which journeyman and apprentice resided under the same roof with their master gradually disappeared. The household, then, was used less and less as a space of economic production and more as a quiet escape from the tumult of the downtown marketplace. As a result, a newer, more fluid spatial arrangement between employer and worker emerged in which wealthier booksellers and printers moved to residential neighborhoods while keeping their places of business in the densely packed quarters of the older lower wards. Booksellers and printers began taking advantage of the newly devoted commercial space. Many displayed their wares in the front of the building and used the upstairs for excess stock; the rear of the building was typically used for keeping up the accounts. This interior spatial shift also affected shop employees. No longer under the auspices of their masters, journeymen often relocated to the ramshackle tenant neighborhoods that began sprouting up in the early nineteenth century, still hoping someday to become heads of their own households. The average percentage of men of the trade who maintained two addresses, as listed in the annual trade directories, increased in the 1820s. In 1821, for instance, fifty-two men of the trade maintained separate residences. Five years later, this number had risen to seventy-five, and by 1830, 162 printers, booksellers, and bookbinders had both a business and a separate home address.[97]

Duyckinck distanced himself from his artisanal past by filling his new Bleecker Street home with the trappings of gentility. In particular, the house featured two important markers of refinement: the formal parlor and the dedicated library. In addition to the large mahogany table that was the focal point of their dining room, the family furnished their parlor with window chairs, a rocking chair and cushions, plated candlesticks, a mantle clock, and carpeting. Scholars have suggested that carpeting created an invisible barrier between the tumultuous world of the marketplace and the carefully constructed parlor of polish and repose. The new house also had a considerable library of 250 finely bound English books and a large assortment of "valuable" American editions lining several mahogany bookcases. Libraries and dining rooms became prominent architectural additions to the homes of well-to-do nineteenth-century families. The library, while conveying to visitors a sense intellectual and material refinement, was meant to be a comfortable and relaxed retreat. A library like the one in Duyckinck's home stood in contrast to the formal parlor. Families could gather in the library to read books, write letters, and engage in learned conversation. Mahogany and rosewood desks, along with a mahogany bureau, dotted Duyckinck's library, indicating that he probably attended to personal and business correspondence there in the evenings, away from his lower Manhattan office.[98]

The abundance of mahogany furniture in Evert Duyckinck's home is telling. The visibly striking wood had been prized among European and American elites since the early eighteenth century and was recognized as an important marker of refinement and gentility. By the time the Duyckinck family filled their new

Bleecker Street home with the beautiful, highly varnished wood, however, it had become much easier to acquire. Inexpensive and more easily harvestable wood often served as the basis for furniture pieces, as craftsmen increasingly used only the beautiful veneers, giving the illusion of a solid piece of mahogany furniture. At the same time, mahogany fell out of style, so that by the time the Duyckinck family moved to Bleecker Street, the furniture was beginning to be viewed as stodgy and old-fashioned.[99]

Given the length of his career and the reach of his book distribution, it is not surprising that Evert Duyckinck set his family up in such a refined way. What his Bleecker Street home reveals to us was Duyckinck's conscious attempt not only to distance himself from his former life as a South Street sailmaker but also to place himself among the city's elite merchants and professionals. This required a commitment to a more refined lifestyle, separate from the tight confines of the lower Manhattan shop. Unlike many men who came and went in the trade over the course of his long career, Duyckinck found more lasting expression in his home, just down the street from LeRoy Place.

In April 1830, Evert Duyckinck was one of the eighteen booksellers who gathered in New York for a trade sale. Duyckinck's appearance at the Panorama Room that Tuesday morning marked his final public contribution to the American book trade. Taking advantage of this regional gathering, Duyckinck used the sale to unload his large inventory, which far exceeded that of the other participants. He brought nearly two hundred titles, while the next-largest contributor offered only fifty-nine. He also sought to rid his store of thirty-two copperplate engravings, including a set of eight for *Don Quixote*, an image of George Washington's tomb, a set of nine plates for *Domestic Cookery*, and plates for insertion in Benjamin Franklin's *Autobiography* that would add a visual dimension to the book.[100] Duyckinck's attempt to liquidate his stock at the 1830 trade sale, then, suggests that he was contemplating retiring from the business.

Not long after the trade sale, letters began arriving at Duyckinck's shop congratulating him on his retirement.[101] In May, Richmond's Richard Sanxay wrote that "on your retiring from business, permit me to express my regret that the trade should have lost so valuable a member." A month later, Thomas Skinner of Auburn, New York, commended Duyckinck for the "successful prosecution" of his publishing business.[102] Duyckinck retired at a transitional moment for the American book trade, as large firms such as Harper & Brothers and Carey & Lea wrestled for control of the print marketplace, competing for the right to publish the latest, greatest popular authors while also taking advantage of improved technologies—stereotype plates and cylinder papermaking, among others—that gradually reshaped shop labor and, by extension, the American publishing trade.[103]

While the promotion of nationalism, literary or otherwise, was never Evert Duyckinck's intent, his surviving financial records reveal that he participated in and helped shape a national print market in the early American Republic. Duyckinck exploited the lower end of the book trade, producing steadily selling reprints for national distribution. Readers in distant parts of the nation, then, became unified by his imprints, which they carried in jacket pockets, read quietly by candlelight, or used in the local schoolhouse. When taken together, Duyckinck's accumulated distribution systems made up a national network of 168 booksellers who sold his titles in fifty-three towns and municipalities in sixteen states. The story of the elder Evert Duyckinck shows that not only did a national print market exist in the early Republic—it flourished.

Print and Memory in an Age of Change

On the day before his seventeenth birthday, in November 1833, the aspiring littérateur Evert Augustus Duyckinck buried his father. Services took place in Saint Thomas Church, at the corner of Broadway and Houston Street. A local newspaper, which had been in print nearly as long as Evert Duyckinck had been in business, remembered the sixty-nine-year-old bookseller as "an old and respectable inhabitant of this city, and for many years one of its most extensive booksellers and publishers."[1] According to Evert Augustus, the funeral was a large, friendly affair despite the melancholy circumstances. "It was nearly dark when the funeral took place," he remarked in his diary, "and the dimly lighted church with the notes of the organ made the scene yet more solemn." Several of Duyckinck's colleagues, including John Lang, Thomas A. Ronalds, and James Swords, came together one last time to carry their friend from Saint Thomas to his final resting place. The ceremony, then, was a celebration of the austere Duyckinck's career. "Every mark of respect has been paid to the memory of my honored parent," wrote the younger Duyckinck. The service included an Anglican bishop and two other members of the church. In his diary, Evert Augustus tersely described fulfilling the last wishes of his father. "My respected parent had at times requested me if any thing happened to him to take his place and conduct family worship at evening by reading a portion of scripture and prayer," he said. "This I did last evening."[2]

Evert Duyckinck's death, and the funeral that followed, was as much a celebration of his life as it was an important symbolic transition for the publishing trade. The New York trade had become increasingly mechanized and controlled by a few large firms and shops that hired, and paid a pittance to, poorly trained former apprentices and vagabond journeymen who wended their way from the countryside in search of sustenance. Historians have pointed out that technological change created a crisis within the printing trade in the late 1820s and early 1830s. Before 1820, typesetters and pressmen had been highly skilled artisans. The introduction of the steam-powered cylindrical press, which had become all too common in the larger Manhattan shops in the 1830s, allowed an untrained boy to operate the machine. The highly skilled pressman, so the story goes, suddenly became irrelevant. Around the time of Duyckinck's funeral, there was what one historian calls a "glut of skilled labor" in New York, where printing had become big business as skilled labor became obsolete.[3] While hand-press printing shops still dotted the countryside, power-press firms took over the port cities. Thus, as publishers became less reliant on the household model of production, shops that had experienced tremendous growth in the 1820s monopolized much of the printed output and subsequent distribution by combining all facets of production under one roof and employing hundreds of hapless journeymen printers-turned-workers. Indeed, as the January 1834 issue of the *Booksellers' Advertiser* pointed out, the Harper & Brothers firm was thriving. "Ten Years ago these brothers worked the press with their own hands, and it is within that time that they have commenced publishing; now they give constant employment to nearly 200 persons—and, indirectly, to many more—they are diffusing knowledge to millions—and their names are familiar wherever the English language is spoken."[4] Printers and bookbinders, once proud, highly skilled artisans, quickly became wage earners in large shops that had started to resemble factories. Meanwhile, aging printers—proud men reared in the old system of apprenticeship, itinerancy, economic independence, and trade interdependence—began anxiously contemplating their place in an industry that was undergoing dramatic technological and structural change. Their apprehension was palpable.[5]

Evert Duyckinck's funeral marked the end of an era while also representing a structural shift in the larger publishing industry. Duyckinck was one of the last of a dying breed of preindustrial publishers. Unlike most of the men who would become "publishers" in the early Republic, Duyckinck was not trained as a printer. He used household modes of production, outsourcing the labor for imprints that bore his name like so many fellow early Republic publishers. Duyckinck was laid to rest by a number of aging artisans, who for many years donned their leather aprons to produce the cheap reprints that bore his name. Duyckinck dove head first into the trade without any type of formal training and did so with making money in mind. Indeed, New Yorkers who knew Duyckinck considered him something of a transformative figure. "Duyckinck faithfully carried out the proverbs of Franklin," concluded John Francis, using his "great business talents" to transform the early American book trade. Duyckinck's popular reprints "must have been issued by his enterprise in innumerable thousands throughout the old thirteen states," to the point where Francis considered his business to have been "among the beginnings of that American reprint practice, still prevailing among us, of having in reprints of even the most important works from abroad, for better circulation."[6] Evert Duyckinck's funeral, then, occurred at a time when his trade—in New York and elsewhere in Jacksonian America—was at a crossroads.

James Swords understood well what was happening in the book trade. In May 1830, roughly six months before Duyckinck passed away, Swords began taking stock of his career. Then sixty-six years old and nearing the end of his life, Swords sat down to write his friend Isaiah Thomas, himself an aging printer and resident of Worcester, Massachusetts, noted as much for his famous flight from Boston to western Massachusetts in 1775, his printing press in tow, as he was for founding the American Antiquarian Society in 1812. The subject of this particular note was an answer to Thomas's request that Swords donate his life's work to the society's library. "I was in due course favoured with your very kind letter of the eighteenth last," Swords wrote, noting the pride he took in delivering work that he and his brother had published. "My trifling donation recently merited all this notice—and yet the notice was gratifying to me, inasmuch as, besides the assurance of an agreeable acceptance on your part, it officially certified my being placed on the list of donors to an institution of great merit, whose claims rest on all who feel an interest in the general welfare of this country."[7] Time, it seems, was catching up with James Swords and his aging colleagues.

For years, Thomas and James Swords operated one of the city's most productive printing shops. The brothers were born in the 1760s to Mary and Lieutenant Thomas Swords, a Saratoga County farmer, as discontent with British imperial policies began to simmer. While the Swords family held Loyalist sympathies, they, like many Americans at the time, feigned neutrality until Thomas Sr.'s arrest in May 1776 for refusing to lead a colonial military unit. At the outbreak of hostilities, the family sought refuge in New York City, where the brothers apprenticed under the Tory printer James Robertson. While in New York during the British occupation, they did presswork for the *Royal Gazette* and the *Royal American Gazette* in addition to producing a one-page genealogical broadside. In 1783, the Swords family became part of the massive relocation of Loyalists, moving, along with approximately thirty thousand fellow souls, to the Canadian Maritime provinces. After the family settled in Shelburne, Nova Scotia, the brothers took up printing. While there, they published the *Port Roseway Gazetteer* with Robertson in a small shop that became an important social and cultural center. Their stay in Nova Scotia, however, was short-lived. In 1786, the brothers returned to New York City, opening a shop on Pearl Street. In their first publication, a reprint of *A Narrative of the Expedition to Botany Bay,* they included an advertisement announcing the establishment of their firm. "T. and J. Swords, Printers, Respectfully inform their Friends and the Public, that, having established a PRINTING-OFFICE in this City, they intend prosecuting their Business in all its Branches, with Elegance and Propriety."[8]

Once established in the city, the brothers remained active printers until 1832. In 1833, James Swords retired from the firm, assuming the presidency of the Washington Fire Insurance Company, a position he held until his death in September 1846. Thomas continued in the trade until 1843, bringing his son Edward and Thomas Naylor Stanford aboard. While together, the Swords brothers published a number of noteworthy literary, scientific, and religious periodicals, including the *Medical Repository* from July 1797 to July 1807, the short-lived *Monthly Magazine, and American Review,* the *United States Christian Magazine,* the *Christian Journal and Literary Register,* which they published for thirteen years between January 1817 and December 1830, and their yearly pocket almanac, which they printed from 1816 to 1832. The brothers also published many Columbia College dissertations while also developing close ties with the city's Episcopal church. In addition to scientific and religious publications, the Swords brothers had connections to elite literary circles in New York. For seven years they published the *New-York Magazine, or Literary Repository,* an eclectic monthly they founded in 1790 that touched on a variety of topics dear to New York's emerging literary scene, including politics, religion, science, morality, public virtue, domesticity, humor, literature, and poetry.[9]

James Swords's letters to the Antiquarian Society reveal the anxieties of a man, once a leading figure in the city's publishing trade, now enfeebled and openly questioning the lasting importance of his work and the work of his friends. Yet despite the apprehensions he felt about how history would remember him, Swords tried to actively solidify his reputation during a time of what one scholar has called "intense historical consciousness," as the men so intimately involved in the early years of the Republic "wrestled with their accomplishments and legacy."[10] Swords prepared packages for shipment to Worcester with a sense of urgency, while simultaneously reflecting on the importance of his work. "I have on this day put on board the Providence packet sloop *Victory,*" he wrote to Thomas, "a small package to your address, with orders to forward it by the canal line of transportation, which I presume is the safest and most speedy mode of conveyance." Swords noted that the package included copies of the *Christian Journal* and three volumes of the *Monthly Magazine, and American Review,* which lasted from April 1799 to December 1800. Swords concluded his letter to Thomas by commenting on the importance of preserving their not-too-distant artisanal past. "There are also some other trifles, which can scarcely excite an interest in any but those who, like yourself, have a desire to hand down to posterity the labour of their predecessors as of those of their own time," he wrote.[11]

Not all printers and booksellers in the twilight of their careers contemplated their place in American history. For many, just making ends meet was a deciding factor in what to do with the books in their stores. Indeed, many wills drawn up by aging printers and booksellers read like desperate pleas for help. Several booksellers requested that the executors of their estates liquidate their shops' stock as a way to help their families through financial difficulties. In December 1830, William Banks Gilley, a Broadway bookseller, passed away in debt. While he left all of his furniture, bedding, and "Kitchen Stuff" to his wife, Harriet, he asked his executors that his "Stock in trade be disposed of" and that the "proceeds of such sale" be used to pay off his business debts. Should any cash be left over, Gilley specified, it was to be used "towards the payment of the mortgage on the property in Broadway where I now reside."[12] Gilley's burdens may have been too much for his family to take on, however. In February 1831, just a few weeks after his death, Harriet put "the Store and dwelling part of the House" at 94 Broadway—"not surpassed by any in the city for the Bookselling and Stationery business"—up for sale. In addition to the house, she aimed to sell her husband's "whole stock in trade," which included a large selection of history books.[13] Harriet made the difficult decision after trying, unsuccessfully, to keep the shop afloat following Gilley's death. William Burgess, who died two years after Gilley, found himself in a similar predicament toward the end of his life. Much like Gilley, Burgess directed his executors to sell his "real and personal property" at 97 Fulton Street as a way to meet his creditor's demands.[14]

James Swords's collaboration with the Antiquarian Society lasted fourteen years and coincided with a national campaign by the AAS to collect and preserve the new nation's printed history. Christopher Columbus Baldwin, a Harvard-trained lawyer and former publisher of the *Worcester Magazine and Historical Journal* and the *National Aegis,* became the Antiquarian Society's second librarian after Thomas. Baldwin collected as much of the nation's history in print as he could. It was, for him at least, a project that involved preserving the output of the nation's presses, whether newspapers, books, pamphlets, or magazines. Baldwin assiduously wrote to publishers, printers, and newspapermen, asking for all items created using their individual presses. Newspapers became Baldwin's particular obsession. "I have taken the liberty of troubling you with this communication to request of you to present to the American Antiquarian Society a copy of the *National Intelligencer* from its first establishment to the present time," he wrote in April 1832 to the longtime editors of the venerable paper, which had been published since 1800 in Washington, D.C.[15] Baldwin made similar requests of Hezekiah Niles of Baltimore, Jacob B. Moore, editor of the *New Hampshire Patriot,* Asa M'Farland of the *Concord Register & New Hampshire Statesman,* William Duane, long the publisher of the Philadelphia *Aurora,* and Samuel Woodward of Weathersfield, Connecticut, whom Baldwin asked for copies of the *Courant,* the *Mercury,* and the *Connecticut Gazette.*[16]

Baldwin relied on James Swords to collect items produced in New York. In April 1832, he requested that Swords gather as many of the city's publications as possible. "And these facts are communicated with the request that you would lend us your influence in procuring for us a series of some of the leading city newspapers for the last 20 or 30 years," Baldwin wrote, adding that he would also be grateful for any and all "city or state registers, or city directory ancient or modern." In a follow-up letter, Baldwin acknowledged the absurdity of this request, while continuing to insist upon its importance.

> In my communication to you under date of 19th of April, I expressed the wish that we could procure a file of some one of your leading City papers for the last 20 or 30 years. I am not ignorant how much I ask for. My experience has excused me of the difficulty of obtaining files for much shorter period. But old news papers are a kind of property that, generally, are little thought of & so much so that even ancient volumes are not infrequently taken for wrapping or sold to the paper maker. . . . I should be wanting in courage to ask for these favours if they were for me individually or for a mere local institution. But the objects of the Antiquarian Society are external to the whole American Continent. There is nothing local or limited about it. Every thing which relates to American History in any shape whatever is desirable.[17]

Why did these men suffer such anxiety over the preservation of print, by definition an ephemeral source? Perhaps the answer lies in how the industry changed in the 1830s, and the type of consumer that emerged as a result. American consumers in the 1830s had greater access to a wider variety of cheap print—ranging from the penny press to sensationalistic novels and urban sketches—than they had ever had before, and as the nineteenth century progressed, print became even more disposable. Indeed, print became the "debris left behind by everyday people" thanks to the "promiscuous circulation" of texts and people in the rapidly changing social and economic landscape of Jacksonian America, as historian David Henkin tells us.[18] What once had been cherished family heirlooms, to be read time and again, printed texts were fast becoming something to consume and then dispose of, whether by passing them along or, more often, discarding them altogether. Efforts by men like Baldwin and Swords, then, were as much an exercise in the construction of individual and institutional memory as they were a desperate attempt to preserve an increasingly disposable past.[19]

Yet the increasing disposability of print in the nineteenth century only partly explains this anxiety. The efforts to preserve the printed history of the United States amounted to an unspoken commentary on the ways in which the publishing trade, and the nation more broadly, was changing in the 1830s and 1840s. Much had happened in American social, economic, and political life by 1833, and this was certainly true of the publishing trade. Three years after the aged leaders of the New York publishing trade gathered to bury Evert Duyckinck, the young New York publisher George Palmer Putnam used the city's trade magazine to offer effusive, yet short-sighted, praise of the book trade's economic and geographic expansion. "Our publishing trade appears to be flourishing," he wrote, imploring booksellers and printers to take stock of the number of books published and shipped to locations near and far. Putnam did not simply point out the greater volume of texts being moved at higher rates of return. He seemed particularly focused on technological improvements and how these changes amped up productivity, forever altering labor relations between masters and journeymen: "In this age of ballooning and railroading—printing by steam—where the machinery of book-making is such, that it is only necessary to put your rags in the mill and they come out Bibles—all ready printed—there is no telling what human invention will accomplish next. We like this go-ahead of spirit."[20]

The dramatic explosion of print and the expansion of its geographic reach in the 1830s—the "go-ahead of spirit" Putnam endorsed so enthusiastically—are often associated with increased mechanization in printing and papermaking. As scholars have argued, printing had not changed all that much since the late fifteenth century until the invention of the cylindrical steam press, which made its first domestic appearance in 1825 at the office of the New York *Daily Advertiser*. Increased mechanization in paper production, which simplified how paper was made from rags, greatly increased the number of books, newspapers, pamphlets, and magazines printed each year. Stereotype plates further enabled publishers to print more books at greater speeds because typesetters no longer had to reset the text one page at a time. These structural changes in the trade, coinciding with dramatic improvements in transportation that occurred in the 1820s and beyond, created a ready national print market in the 1830s.[21]

The decline of household modes of production, the gradual disappearance of the printer-publisher archetype, and the introduction of new printing and papermaking technologies must have deepened the understandable anxieties of the men still around to witness how the world they had made was fading away. The entrepreneurial impulse overtaking the antebellum publishing trade—represented by the likes of Putnam—was hardly a swan song for a preindustrial printer like James Swords. Men like Swords had been key players in the machinery of New York's rapidly growing book trade, yet they became, as the 1830s progressed, increasingly irrelevant. Indeed, the eighteenth-century artisanal world of household production either faded away entirely or was reoriented by a few wealthy master printers who opened large-scale shops that began resembling factories, employing hundreds of workers on technologically advanced machinery.[22]

But were the structural and technological changes that revolutionized the trade in the 1830s and 1840s, and the anxieties they spawned, really all that dramatic? To be sure, technology was a driving force in the explosion of print that enveloped the countryside in what historian Daniel Walker Howe has identified as the earliest manifestation of a "national market for published material" after 1830.[23] Yet, as I have tried to show in this book, New York City's printers, booksellers, and publishers built sophisticated distribution networks that extended far beyond Manhattan well before 1830. Men in New York's publishing trade helped to shape a national print market in the early Republic. The national distribution of books was big business for men like Evert Duyckinck. New York's publishers connected disparate American readers together, whether through a cheap reprint of a popular education text or an audacious conservative commentary.[24]

It turns out, then, that Dr. John Francis was wrong at the 1852 Typographical Society banquet. Francis wrapped up his "Reminiscences" by commenting on the superiority of the press in the 1850s as compared with the early nineteenth century. "I have already remarked on the superior ability of the press of our present days in comparison with that of the period through which some of us have lived," he said. Francis insisted that the technologically advanced press in use in 1852 New York had "swelled its dimensions" and "increased the excellence of its material."[25] It is likely that Samuel Loudon, Samuel Campbell, John Ward Fenno, Mathew Carey, and Evert Duyckinck would have disagreed with Francis's dismissal of the early book trade's productivity and reach. In fact, Duyckinck and his colleagues blurred the boundaries between regional and national markets and helped build up the nation in print.

NOTES

·····················

Introduction

1. Francis, "Reminiscences of Printers," 253–54. For an overview of Francis's life and career, see "The Late Dr. Francis: Sketch of His Life and Personal Character," *New York Times*, 11 February 1861.

2. Francis, "Reminiscences of Printers," 254, 255.

3. Ibid., 260, 261, 262.

4. Ibid., 264, 265.

5. For an overview of this process, see Warner, *Letters of the Republic*, 1–33. On the "public sphere," see Habermas, *Structural Transformation*. For work that uses the "public sphere" as a category of analysis, see Calhoun, *Habermas and the Public Sphere*; Grasso, *Speaking Aristocracy*; Brooke, "Ancient Lodges"; Brooke, "'Read by the Whole People'"; and Brooke, "Consent, Civil Society."

6. Clemens, "Consumer Culture," 589; Gross, "Introduction: An Extensive Republic." For consumer culture in early America, see Breen, *Marketplace of Revolution*; Bushman, *Refinement of America*; Jaffee, *New Nation of Goods*. For an overview of print culture and the place of the book trade in early America, see Davidson, *Revolution and the Word*; Green, "Rise of Book Publishing"; Amory and Hall, *Colonial Book in the Atlantic World*. For the distinction between "printers," "booksellers," and "publishers," see Remer, *Printers and Men of Capital*.

7. Waldstreicher, *Perpetual Fetes*; Pasley, *"Tyranny of Printers"*; Furstenberg, *Name of the Father*; Hoeflich, *Legal Publishing*; Eastman, *Nation of Speechifiers*; Brown, *Knowledge Is Power*; John, *Spreading the News*. For recent work that places communication at the heart of the American Revolution, see Warner, *Protocols of Liberty*; Breen, *American Insurgents, American Patriots*. For the perils involved in the development of "American" cultural identity independent of Great Britain, see Yokota, *Unbecoming British*. For recent criticism of much of this scholarship, see Loughran, *Republic in Print*; Gross, "Introduction: An Extensive Republic," 8.

8. See especially Remer, *Printers and Men of Capital*. For more on Philadelphia and Boston, see Green, "Rise of Book Publishing." For recent work on the Baltimore and South Carolina book trades, see Arndt, "Bringing Books into Baltimore"; Raven, *London Booksellers*. For mid-nineteenth-century New York publishers, see Greenspan, *George Palmer Putnam*; Exman, *House of Harper*. For the rise of New York's publishing trade in the mid-nineteenth century, see Wallace, *Media Capital*; Henkin, *City Reading*. For the intersection of print and religion in the early Republic, see Nord, *Faith in Reading*; Wosh, *Spreading the Word*. For the rise of the "penny press," see Cohen, *Murder of Helen Jewett*; Nerone, "Mythology of the Penny Press." For New York and, broadly, the market economy, see Murphy, *Building the Empire State*; Greenberg, *Advocating the Man*.

9. For the "imagined community" created by print, see Anderson, *Imagined Communities*, 38, 42–43, 46. For criticism of Anderson's theory in early American studies, see Loughran, *Republic in Print*, 5–6, 9, 12. For an economic approach to book history, see Hruschka, *How Books Came to America*; Remer, *Printers and Men of Capital*; Green, "Rise of Book Publishing"; Charvat, *Literary Publishing in America*. For a mid-nineteenth-century perspective on Boston that relies heavily on financial accounts, see Winship, *American Literary Publishing*. For an English perspective, see Raven, *Business of Books*; St. Clair, *Reading Nation*.

Chapter 1

1. Silver, *American Printer*, 67–68.

2. Ibid.; Thomas, *Printing in America*, 1:303–4.

3. Silver, "Aprons Instead of Uniforms," 132; Lorenz, *Hugh Gaine*, 125. Work on Samuel Loudon's life and career is somewhat limited. See especially Vail, "Patriotic Pair"; Wall, "Samuel Loudon (1727–1813)"; Brennan, "Shaped by Revolution"; Connor, "Robert Bell and Samuel Loudon."

4. "The Memorial of Samuel Loudon of the City of New York, Printer," 27 January 1784, Typographical Library Records, box 11, Rare Book and Manuscript Library, Columbia University; *Constitution of the State of New-York.*

5. Thorburn, *Fifty Years' Reminiscences,* 75; Vail, "Patriotic Pair," 391–92.

6. Botein, "'Meer Mechanics.'" For a recent challenge to Botein's argument, see Adelman, "'Constitutional Conveyance.'" For the role of print in state building, see Frankel, *States of Inquiry.*

7 .For what little biographical information is available for Loudon's life before New York, see "Samuel Loudon," Printers' File, AAS. Brennan relies on Wall's date of 1727 as Loudon's year of birth. See Brennan, "Shaped by Revolution," 24; Wall, "Samuel Loudon (1727–1813)," 75.

8. *New-York Mercury,* 15 October 1753.

9. For a discussion of consumer culture in the Atlantic world in the eighteenth century, see Breen, *Marketplace of Revolution;* McConville, *King's Three Faces;* Hartigan-O'Connor, *Ties That Buy.*

10. *New-York Mercury,* 19 September 1757.

11. "Release Granted to Philip John Schuyler," 16 January 1768, Miscellaneous Manuscript Collection, New York State Library.

12. Loudon to Schuyler, 26 May 1769, Philip Schuyler Papers, box 1, no. 1365, NYPL.

13. Loudon to Schuyler, 6 April 1773, ibid., box 2, no. 1367.

14. Loudon to Schuyler, 29 May 1773, ibid., no. 1368.

15. *New-York Gazette: and the Weekly Mercury,* 17 May 1773.

16. Loudon to Schuyler, 19 June and 20 August 1773, Philip Schuyler Papers, box 2, nos. 1369 and 1370, NYPL.

17. Burrows and Wallace, *Gotham,* 194. For demographic changes in the mid-eighteenth century, see Bailyn, *Peopling of British North America.*

18. Loudon to Schuyler, 22 July 1774, Philip Schuyler Papers, box 2, no. 1373, NYPL. For immigration, see Miller, *Emigrants and Exiles;* Miller et al., *Irish Immigrants.*

19. *New-York Mercury,* 23 December 1771.

20. Loudon to Elijah Backus, 2 September 1773, quoted in Brennan, "Shaped by Revolution," 27.

21. Glynn, "New York Society Library," 501, 504.

22. Beales and Green, "Libraries and Their Users," 399–400. For more on circulating libraries in colonial and early national New York, see Keep, *New York Society Library,* 108–11; Raddin, *Hocquet Caritat,* esp. chap. 2; Zboray, *Fictive People,* esp. chap. 11. For studies of circulating libraries in other parts of early America, see Roeber, "German and Dutch Books," 309, 312; Winton, "Southern Book Trade," 238–40.

23. Schlesinger, *Prelude to Independence,* 222.

24. *Rivington's New-York Gazetteer, or The Connecticut, Hudson's River, New-Jersey, and Quebec Weekly Advertiser,* 30 December 1773.

25. *New-York Gazette: and the Weekly Mercury,* 31 January 1774.

26. Ibid., 7 November 1774.

27. Ibid., 21 November 1774. For women and reading in the Atlantic world, see Hackel and Kelly, *Reading Women;* Kerber, *Women of the Republic;* Branson, *Fiery Frenchified Dames,* esp. chap. 1; Zboray and Zboray, "Political News and Female Readership."

28. Beales and Green, "Libraries and Their Users," 403.

29. Hendrickson, *Rise and Fall of Alexander Hamilton,* 303–4; Allgor, *Perfect Union,* 28–29.

30. First Charging Ledger, NYSL, 6, 8, 28, 29, 30, 31, 33, 34, 81. See also King, *Books and People,* 278.

31. *New-York Gazette,* 29 April 1776; *New-York Journal,* 23 May 1776.

32. Wilson, *Memorial History,* 534.

33. *Independent New-York Gazette,* 22 November 1783; *New-York Morning Post,* 2 December 1783; *New-York Packet,* 10 November 1786; *New-York Journal, or The Weekly Register,* 16 November 1786.

34. New York *Daily Advertiser,* 10 November 1786; *New-York Morning Post,* 10 November 1786. Catharine is mentioned as the proprietor of the coffeehouse in an advertisement in the 20 November 1787 issue of the *New-York Journal* pertaining to the subscription of the paper itself. "Subscriptions for this paper (printed every day at *six dollars,* and once a week at *Two Dollars* per annum) are received, in this city by the Printer hereof, by Mrs. Bradford at the merchants Coffee House, and by Messrs Hodge, Allen, berry & Rogers, and Campbell, booksellers." *New-York Journal,* 20 November 1787. See also King, *Books and People,* 278.

35. First Charging Ledger, NYSL, 298.

36. Thomas, *Printing in America*, 1:310–12.

37. *Life of Dr. Benjamin Franklin*, 23. For a discussion of the physical demands of the printing trades, see Pasley, *Tyranny of Printers*, 25; Rorabaugh, *Craft Apprentice*; Silver, *American Printer*; Wroth, *Colonial Printer*.

38. *New-York Journal, or The General Advertiser*, 21 December 1775. The original title of the *Packet*, according to the prospectus in the *Journal*, was the *New-York Packet, or The North-American General Advertiser*.

39. Schlesinger, *Prelude to Independence*, 51–53.

40. *New-York Packet, and the American Advertiser*, 4 January 1776. Loudon changed the name of his newspaper back and forth between the *New-York Packet* and the *New-York Packet, and the American Advertiser*. See also Brennan, "Shaped by Revolution," 36–37.

41. Breen, *American Insurgents, American Patriots*, 99–101. See also Carp, *Rebels Rising*, chap. 2; Brown, *Knowledge Is Power*; Warner, *Protocols of Liberty*. For the theory that informs much of the scholarly discussion of the role of print in shaping politics in early America, see Anderson, *Imagined Communities*.

42. For work on the challenges printers faced, especially the threat of violence, see Nerone, *Violence Against the Press*, chap. 1. For an overview of colonial newspapers, see Copeland, *Colonial American Newspapers*; Clark, *Public Prints*. For newspapers and the American Revolution, see Schlesinger, *Prelude to Independence*; Humphrey, *American Revolution and the Press*.

43. Schlesinger, *Prelude to Independence*, 72, 83, 185.

44. Waldstreicher, *Runaway America*, 12–13. See also Dyer, *Biography of James Parker*, 80–81, 95; Paltsits, "John Holt—Printer and Postmaster"; McAnear, "James Parker Versus John Holt," 77–78.

45. Waldstreicher, *Runaway America*, 13–14.

46. Ibid., 15–17.

47. Schlesinger, *Prelude to Independence*, 222.

48. Thomas, *Printing in America*, 1:307.

49. Ibid., 2:123.

50. Chopra, *Unnatural Rebellion*, 41; Thomas, *Printing in America*, 1:307–10, 2:120–24; Chopra, "Printer Hugh Gaine," 274–75.

51. *Rivington's New-York Gazetteer, or The Connecticut, Hudson's River, New-Jersey, and Quebec Weekly Advertiser*, 11 August 1774; Botein, "Printers and the American Revolution," 36–39.

52. *Rivington's New-York Gazetteer, or The Connecticut, Hudson's River, New-Jersey, and Quebec Weekly Advertiser*, 22 April 1773.

53. Thomas, *Printing in America*, 2:120–21. For more on Rivington's neutrality, see Botein, "Printers and the American Revolution," 36–39, 43–47; Buel, "Freedom of the Press," 60–61. For more on press neutrality in colonial North America, see Martin, *Free and Open Press*; Botein, "'Meer Mechanics.'"

54. Burrows and Wallace, *Gotham*, 220.

55. Thomas, *Printing in America*, 2:121.

56. Walett, *Patriots, Loyalists, and Printers*, 36; Chopra, "Printer Hugh Gaine," 274–75.

57. Galloway, *Candid Examination*, 31, 49, 33–34. For a brief analysis of Rivington's publication of Galloway's pamphlet, see Chopra, "Printer Hugh Gaine," 275.

58. *Thomas's Massachusetts Spy, or The Worcester Gazette*, 8 December 1775.

59. Thomas, *Printing in America*, 2:121; Breen, *American Insurgents, American Patriots*, 235–37; Chopra, "Printer Hugh Gaine," 274–75; Burrows and Wallace, *Gotham*, 220, 224, 226–27; Botein, "Printers and the American Revolution," 39. For more on Isaac "King" Sears, see Maier, *Old Revolutionaries*, chap. 2; Countryman, *People in Revolution*, 39, 59, 63, 124–25, 144.

60. Loudon to Dudley Woodbridge, 29 March 1776, quoted in Wall, "Samuel Loudon (1727–1813)," 78.

61. Burrows and Wallace, *Gotham*, 223–26.

62. Loudon to Woodbridge, 29 March 1776, quoted in Wall, "Samuel Loudon (1727–1813)," 78. For New York's preparations, see Burrows and Wallace, *Gotham*, 227–28.

63. [Inglis], *Deceiver Unmasked*, iii.

64. "Petition of Samuel Loudon, Printer," 28 March 1776, in *Calendar of Historical Manuscripts*, 1:273. The information and quotations in the following three paragraphs are from this source.

65. Jones, *History of New York*, 64–65; Connor, "Robert Bell and Samuel Loudon," 56; Levy, *Emergence of a Free Press*, 175. See also Countryman, *People in Revolution*, 125; Nerone, *Violence Against the Press*, 36; Tiedemann, *Reluctant Revolutionaries*, 246.

66. *New-York Gazette: and the Weekly Mercury,* 2 September 1776.

67. Gilje and Pencak, *Age of the Constitution,* 13–14.

68. Norwich *Packet and the Connecticut, Massachusetts, New-Hampshire, and Rhode-Island Weekly Advertiser,* 9 December 1776. See also Caulkins, *History of Norwich,* 332.

69. Humphrey, *American Revolution and the Press,* 187–89.

70. Fishkill *New-York Packet,* 16 January 1777.

71. "Appointment of Hugh Gaine as Printer to the Province of New York," Typographical Library Records, 1576–[ca. 1950], box 7, Rare Book and Manuscript Library, Columbia University.

72. Chopra, "Printer Hugh Gaine," 271–73; *Journals of Hugh Gaine,* 1:4, 51–54.

73. Chopra, "Printer Hugh Gaine," 271–73; Chopra, *Unnatural Rebellion,* 80–83, 86, 88, 90, 242; *Journals of Hugh Gaine,* 1:4, 51–54. For a biography of Gaine, see Lorenz, *Hugh Gaine.*

74. Loudon to Isaac Beers, 3 November 1777, quoted in Brennan, "Shaped by Revolution," 69–70.

75. Quoted in Humphrey, *American Revolution and the Press,* 181.

76. Quoted in ibid., 183.

77. Fishkill *New-York Packet,* 1 August 1776.

78. Ibid., 11 March and 29 April 1778, quoted in Brennan, "Shaped by Revolution," 70–71, 73 (see also 74).

79. Cambridge *New England Chronicle,* 20 June 1776; Humphrey, *American Revolution and the Press,* 180–81.

80. Fishkill *New-York Packet,* 29 August 1776.

81. Brennan, "Shaped by Revolution," 50, 58.

82. Ibid., 58–59.

83. Fishkill *New-York Packet,* 27 March 1783.

84. Ibid., 10 April 1783.

85. Ibid.

86. Ibid., 28 August 1783. For more on negligent newspaper subscribers, see Steffen, "Newspapers for Free." For Loudon's return to New York, see Brennan, "Shaped by Revolution," 81–92.

87. Loudon to Woodbridge, 27 August 1783, quoted in Brennan, "Shaped by Revolution," 86–87.

88. Duer, *New-York as It Was,* 8.

89. James Duane to Polly Duane, 22 December 1783, Duane Family Papers, MS 179, NYHS. See also Burrows and Wallace, *Gotham,* 265.

90. Burrows and Wallace, *Gotham,* 265–66.

91. Loudon to Alexander McDougall, 26 September 1783, quoted in Brennan, "Shaped by Revolution," 87–89.

92. Ibid.

93. For more on the fires that threatened New York during the revolutionary era, see Carp, "Night the Yankees Burned Broadway."

94. Burrows and Wallace, *Gotham,* 256, 259–60. For more on fears of British evacuation among New York Loyalists, see Chopra, *Unnatural Rebellion,* esp. 197–201. For the reestablishment of New York after the war, see Countryman, *People in Revolution,* 191–296.

95. Wood, *Cries of New-York,* 12, 14, 25, 27, 36. Wood, a printer and children's bookseller, was contributing to a literary genre dating to the sixteenth century and documenting the sights, sounds, and, most important, the "cries" of working people in cities like Paris, London, Nuremberg, and Vienna, and later Boston, New York, Baltimore, and Philadelphia. For more on the urban "cries" genre, see Shesgreen, *Images of the Outcast,* 2.

96. For more on the geography of the New York publishing trade in the early days of the Republic, see Smith, "World the Printers Made," 28–129. For a discussion of the economic landscape of New York in this era, see Blackmar, *Manhattan for Rent.* For more on the Tontine Coffee House, see "The Constitution and Nominations of the Subscribers to the Tontine Coffee-House," Tontine Coffee House Records, NYHS; Burrows and Wallace, *Gotham,* 312, 318, 320, 326, 339, 410, 445, 597, 756.

97. New York *Independent Journal, or The General Advertiser,* 17 November 1783; *New-York Evening Post,* 4 September 1782 and 25 July 1783.

98. *Independent Gazette, or The New-York Journal Revived,* 5 February 1784; *New-York Journal and State Gazette,* 18 March 1784. Greenleaf's first issue of the *New-York Journal* appeared on 18 January 1787.

99. New York *Daily Advertiser,* 16 March 1785.

100. For advertising in early American newspapers, see Mott, *American Journalism*, 56; Pasley, *"Tyranny of Printers,"* 31; Keyes, "Early American Advertising," 18, 73–130.

101. Samuel Loudon Account Book, 1785–1789, Samuel Loudon Papers, AAS; *Loudon's New-York Packet*, 7 March 1785; Franks, *New-York Directory*. Loudon changed the name of the paper several times in a short time span. On 11 November 1784, for instance, he changed the title to *Loudon's New-York Packet*. Only a few months later, on 16 May 1785, he changed the name again, this time back to the *New-York Packet*. Loudon made no additional changes to the masthead prior to the paper's folding in January 1792.

102. *Loudon's New-York Packet*, 24 February 1785.

103. Ibid.

104. Ibid., 28 February and 3 March 1785.

105. Ibid., 28 February 1785.

106. Ibid., 31 January 1785.

107. Ibid., 28 February 1785; Samuel Loudon Account Book, 1785–1789, Samuel Loudon Papers, AAS. For studies that focus on advertisements promising rewards for runaways in colonial, revolutionary, and early national America, see Franklin and Schweninger, *Runaway Slaves;* Gellman, *Emancipating New York;* Hodges and Brown, *"Pretends to Be Free";* Meaders, *Dead or Alive;* Smith and Wojtowicz, *Blacks Who Stole Themselves;* Waldstreicher, *Runaway America.*

108. Samuel Loudon Account Book, 1785–1789, Samuel Loudon Papers, AAS. For the textual arrangements of newspapers, see Barnhurst and Nerone, *Form of News.*

109. For a discussion of newspaper subscribers in the early Republic, see Steffen, "Newspapers for Free."

110. The tenth session of the state legislature met in New York City between 12 January and 21 April 1787. The eleventh met in Poughkeepsie from 9 January to 22 March 1788, and the twelfth relocated to Albany from 11 December 1788 to 3 March 1789. *Journal of the Assembly of the State of New-York at Their Eleventh Session; Journal of the Assembly of the State of New-York at Their Tenth Session; Journal of the Assembly of the State of New-York at Their Twelfth Session.*

111. Quoted in Wall, "Samuel Loudon (1727–1813)," 88.

112. Samuel Loudon Account Book, 1785–1789, Samuel Loudon Papers, AAS. As I indicated, most of the shipments in 1787 took place in June and July. Loudon filled two orders in April, seven in May, 119 in June, twenty-eight in July, three in August, three in September, one in October, and two in December. The pattern was similar in 1788. Between April and November 1788, Loudon filled ninety-six orders: four in April, one in May, thirty-five in June, thirty-one in July, five in August, nine in September, nine in October, and two in November.

113. On Andrew Onderonk and early paper making in New York, see Bidwell, *American Paper Mills*, 198–99.

114. "Memorial of Samuel Loudon, Printer," 13 January 1790, Samuel Loudon Papers, folder 1, AAS. For a rich discussion of the relationship between citizens and the state regarding entitlement politics, see Jensen, *Patriots, Settlers.*

115. "Ledger of Monies Paid & Owed to Samuel Loudon, Printer to the State of New York," 19 March 1790, Samuel Loudon Papers, folder 1, AAS.

116. "Memorial of Samuel Loudon, Printer," 19 March 1790, ibid.

117. "Memorial of Samuel Loudon, Printer," 20 March 1790, ibid.

118. Unsigned, undated note from the New York State Legislature, delivered to Samuel Loudon, ibid. For the various items in a printer's shop, see Wroth, *Colonial Printer*, 63, 65. For a discussion of the debt crisis facing the states after the American Revolution, see Holton, *Unruly Americans.*

119. *New-York Packet*, 5 May 1789, 3 February 1791, 26 January 1792; New York *Diary, or Loudon's Register*, 15 February 1792.

120. Ronalds and Loudon to Carey, 13 September 1805, Lea & Febiger Records, box 54, HSP.

121. Ronalds and Loudon to Carey, 21 December 1805, ibid.

122. "Thomas & James Ronalds," Printers' File, AAS.

123. Robert Thompson, James Eastburn, and Edward Mitchell to Mathew Carey, 24 December 1806, Lea & Febiger Records, box 57, HSP; *Archaeologica Americana*, 5:312; Thorburn, *Fifty Years' Reminiscences*, 75.

Chapter 2

1. Winthrop Sargent Diary, 13 October 1793, Winthrop Sargent Papers, MS 11, Ohio Historical Society; Cadou, Crump, and McLeod, *Dining with the Washingtons*, 37, 38.

2. Gordon to Gates, 31 August 1784, Thomas Addis Emmet Collection, NYPL, reproduced in "Letters of the Reverend William Gordon," 506; Gordon to Washington, 19 December 1776, ibid., 329.

3. Gordon to Washington, 8 March 1784, ibid., 506.

4. Harris, *Discourse, Delivered at Dorchester,* 9–10, quoted in Furstenberg, *Name of the Father,* 65.

5. Ford, "Introductory Note," in "Letters of the Reverend William Gordon," 302.

6. For Gordon's encounter with Ezra Stiles, see ibid., 303–4; *Literary Diary of Ezra Stiles,* 1:107.

7. For Gordon's already hardened opinions toward his home country prior to his arrival in America, see Gordon to James Bowdoin, 18 May 1770, Winthrop Papers, MHS. For a discussion of his criticism of the Declaration of Independence, see Pilcher, "William Gordon and the History," 449–50.

8. For a discussion of subscription and its local and elite context, see Farren, "Subscription"; Nord, "Republican Literature."

9. For "story papers" in the nineteenth century, see Davidson, *Revolution and the Word,* 75–77.

10. For work on the "revolutionary historians," see Messer, *Stories of Independence;* Cheng, *Plain and Noble Garb;* Cohen, *Revolutionary Histories;* Shaffer, *Politics of History;* Callcott, *History in the United States;* Gay, *Loss of Mastery;* Davies, "Muse of the Revolution"; Friedman and Shaffer, "Mercy Otis Warren"; Kalinowska, "Three Early Historians"; King, "'Pen of the Historian'"; McDonnell, "National Identity."

11. For a discussion of "founders chic," see the introduction to Pasley, Robertson, and Waldstreicher, *Beyond the Founders,* 1.

12. For work on David Ramsay, see Shaffer, *To Be an American;* Friedman and Shaffer, "David Ramsay and the Quest"; Kornfeld, "From Republicanism to Liberalism"; Messer, "From a Revolutionary History."

13. Quoted in Green, "Rise of Book Publishing," 78; Brunhouse, "Ramsay's Publication Problems."

14. Aitken and Ramsay quoted in Sher, *Enlightenment and the Book,* 539.

15. Robert Aitken, Waste Book, 1771–1802, Robert Aitken Papers, LCP.

16. Ibid.

17. Green tells us that after peace was brokered in 1783, Aitken slashed the price of his domestically produced Bible in order to compete with cheap, imported British Bibles, a move, Green writes, that took him "to the brink of ruin." See Green, "Rise of Book Publishing," 77; Sher, *Enlightenment and the Book,* 539. For Aitken's daughter, see Hudak, *Early American Women Printers,* 547–75.

18. Pilcher, "William Gordon and the History," 451, 455–56.

19. Gordon to Washington, 17 December 1776, in Force, *American Archives,* 3:1265–66.

20. Gordon to Adams, 27 March 1777, in *Papers of John Adams,* 5:132–34.

21. Gordon to Washington, 23 July 1778, in Hoth, *Papers of George Washington,* 16:140–41.

22. Gordon to Washington, 13 August 1783, in "Letters of the Reverend William Gordon," 498–500.

23. Gordon to Adams, 27 March 1777, in *Papers of John Adams,* 5:132–34.

24. Gordon to Gates, 7 June 1777, in "Letters of the Reverend William Gordon," 342–43.

25. Resolution of the Legislature, 5 July 1777, in *Acts and Resolves . . . Massachusetts Bay,* 20:71.

26. "Letters of the Reverend William Gordon," 498–500, 312–13n.

27. Gordon to Adams, 5 June 1777, in *Papers of John Adams,* 5:216–18.

28. Gordon to Gates, 2 September 1777, in "Letters of the Reverend William Gordon," 357.

29. Gordon to Gates, 16 March 1778, ibid., 391–92.

30. Gordon to Washington, 30 August 1781, and Gordon to Gates, 16 October 1782, both in ibid., 457–58 and 473–75, respectively.

31. *Diary and Autobiography of John Adams,* 2:174; Pilcher, "William Gordon and the History," 452n11. Pilcher also describes Gordon's well-publicized spat with John Hancock, whom he accused of misusing funds. Gordon also angered Alexander Hamilton by accusing him of plotting to overthrow the Continental Congress. Pilcher, "William Gordon and the History," 452; "Letters of the Reverend William Gordon," 338. For Hancock's problems as treasurer of Harvard College, see Allan, *John Hancock,* 266–70.

32. Gordon to Adams, 7 September 1782, in "Letters of the Reverend William Gordon," 471.

33. Gordon to Washington, 18 June 1783, ibid., 491–92.

34. Gordon to Gates, 24 January 1783, ibid., 479–80.
35. Gordon to Washington, 26 February 1783, ibid., 484.
36. *Salem Gazette*, 24 August 1784.
37. Gordon's successful petition was reported in the Boston *Independent Chronicle and Universal Advertiser* on 26 August 1784; the Boston *Continental Journal and Weekly Advertiser* on 26 August 1784; *Thomas's Massachusetts Spy, or The Worcester Gazette* on 26 August 1784; the Newburyport *Essex Journal and the Massachusetts and New-Hampshire General Advertiser* on 27 August 1784; the *Boston Gazette* on 30 August 1784; the Hartford *American Mercury* on 30 August 1784; the New London *Connecticut Gazette* on 10 September 1784; the Philadelphia *Pennsylvania Packet, and General Advertiser* on 9 September 1784; and the Trenton *New-Jersey Gazette* on 27 September 1784.
38. *New-York Packet*, 2 September 1784.
39. *Providence Gazette*, 25 September 1784.
40. Gordon to Greene, 12 and 26 September 1785, in "Letters of the Reverend William Gordon," 517–18, 520–21.
41. For the emergence of the subscription trade in early America, see Farren, "Subscription." For work on local manufacturing and the emergence of a national marketplace in the early Republic, see Jaffee, *New Nation of Goods*. For the role of peddlers in American economic life in the early Republic, see Rainer, "'Sharper' Image." For work on the subscription trade in England, see Robinson and Wallis, *Book Subscription Lists*.
42. Farren, "Subscription," 10.
43. Ibid., 13, 156. Farren found 180 lists of subscribers' names in eighteenth-century America (156n1).
44. Ibid., 157–59. For the reluctance of consumers to subscribe to books, see Davidson, *Revolution and the Word*, 86.
45. *New-York Packet*, 16 January 1786; Farren, "Subscription," 13–14; for a broadside version of the proposal, see Gordon, *Proposals for printing by subscription . . .* (Roxbury, Mass., 1785), Broadsides Collection, no. B4398 MA, John Hay Library, Brown University.
46. *New-York Packet*, 16, 23, 30 January and 2, 9 February 1786; Philadelphia *Pennsylvania Journal*, 23 January 1786; *Providence Gazette*, 4 February 1786; Trenton *New-Jersey Gazette*, 6 February 1786; Portsmouth *New-Hampshire Gazette*, 18 February 1786; Charleston *Columbian Herald*, 20 February 1786; Hartford *Connecticut Courant and Weekly Intelligencer*, 20 February 1786; *Carlisle Gazette, and the Western Repository of Knowledge*, 1 March 1786. The longtime publisher of the *Carlisle Gazette*, George Kline, changed the title of his newspaper several times between 1785 and 1817. Between 1785 and 1793, the paper was known as the *Carlisle Gazette, and the Western Repository of Knowledge*. In 1793, the title was shortened to the *Carlisle Gazette*. On 8 January 1794, the title changed yet again, to *Kline's Carlisle Weekly Gazette*. Between 22 January and 19 March 1794, however, the title was again shortened to the *Carlisle Gazette*, reverting back to *Kline's Carlisle Weekly Gazette* on 26 March 1794. Years later, on 3 August 1810, Kline changed the title to *Kline's Weekly Carlisle Gazette*. Seven years after that, on 10 November 1817, Kline merged with the *Spirit of the Times*, creating the *Spirit of the Times & Carlisle Gazette*.
47. Gordon to Greene, 24 November 1785, and Gordon to Washington, 28 November 1785, both in "Letters of the Reverend William Gordon," 524 and 525, respectively.
48. *Diaries of George Washington*, 3:15.
49. *New-York Packet*, 16 January 1786; Philadelphia *Pennsylvania Journal*, 28 January 1786; *Providence Gazette*, 4 February 1786; Trenton *New-Jersey Gazette*, 6 February 1786; Portsmouth *New-Hampshire Gazette, or Fowle's New-Hampshire Gazette and the General Advertiser*, 18 February 1786; Charleston *Columbian Herald, or The Patriotic Courier of North America*, 20 February 1786; Hartford *Connecticut Courant and Weekly Intelligencer*, 20 February 1786; *Carlisle Gazette, and the Western Repository of Knowledge*, 1 March 1786.
50. John Eliot to Jeremy Belknap, 8 February 1786, in "Letters of the Reverend William Gordon," 533n2.
51. *New-York Packet*, 16, 23, 30 January, 2, 9 February 1786; Trenton *New-Jersey Gazette*, 6, 13 February 1786; *Carlisle Gazette, and the Western Repository of Knowledge*, 1, 8 March 1786; Charleston *Columbian Herald*, 20 February, 9, 16, 27 March, 6, 10 April 1786; Philadelphia *Pennsylvania Journal*, 28 January, 1, 4, 15 February, 1, 8, 11, 15, 22, 29 March, 4, 8, 15, 19, 26 April, 6, 10, 20 , 24 May, 3, 14, 17, 21, 24 June, 22, 26 July, 16, 19, 23, 26 August, and 9 September 1786. For a recent study of advertising practices in early America, see Keyes, "Early American Advertising."
52. Gordon to Osgood, 10 January 1786, and Gordon to Greene, 24 November 1785, both in "Letters of the Reverend William Gordon," 529 and 524, respectively.

53. New London *Connecticut Gazette,* 21 April 1786; *New-York Packet,* 29 April 1786.

54. Gordon to Gates, 16 October 1782, and Gordon to Temple, 1 February 1786, both in "Letters of the Reverend William Gordon," 473–75 and 609, respectively; Gordon to Temple, 15 March 1786, Winthrop Papers, MHS.

55. Norwich, Conn., *Packet, or The Country Journal,* 23 February 1786; Boston *Independent Ledger and the American Advertiser,* 13 March 1786.

56. Eliot to Belknap, 15 March 1786, in "Letters of the Reverend William Gordon," 535n5.

57. Philadelphia *Pennsylvania Packet, and Daily Advertiser,* 17 August 1786. On 21 September 1784, the printers of the *Pennsylvania Packet, and General Advertiser* changed the title of the paper slightly, to the *Pennsylvania Packet, and Daily Advertiser.*

58. Pilcher, "William Gordon and the History," 453; Ford, "Introductory Note," in "Letters of the Reverend William Gordon," 306.

59. Gordon to Washington, 16 February 1789, George Washington Papers, Series 4, Library of Congress, Washington, D.C.

60. Gordon to Bowdoin, 28 September 1786, Winthrop Papers, MHS.

61. Barker, *Newspapers, Politics, and English Society,* 15; Harris, *Rise of the Press,* 33; Harris, *Patriot Press,* 28–31.

62. Harris, *Rise of the Press,* 33.

63. Barker, *Newspapers, Politics, and English Society,* 67–68.

64. Harris, *Rise of the Press,* 36.

65. Maier, *From Resistance to Revolution,* 162–69.

66. Barker, "Stockdale, John."

67. Pilcher, "William Gordon and the History," 453; Adams's marginalia quoted in Haraszti, "More Books from the Adams Library," 119–22.

68. Pilcher, "William Gordon and the History," 453; Adams to Elbridge Gerry, 1813, quoted in Austin, *Life of Elbridge Gerry,* 1:520.

69. Pilcher, "William Gordon and the History," 454; Anonymous, "Recollections of a Bostonian," in Niles, *Principles and Acts of the Revolution,* 482.

70. Boston *Massachusetts Centinel,* 18 October 1786.

71. For Philadelphia, see the *Independent Gazetteer,* 30 October 1786, and the *Freeman's Journal, or The North-American Intelligencer,* 1 November 1786; for South Carolina, see the Charleston *Columbian Herald, or The Patriotic Courier of North America,* 9 November 1786, and the Charleston *Morning Post and Daily Advertiser,* 9 November 1786.

72. Boston *Massachusetts Centinel,* 21 October 1786.

73. *Thomas's Massachusetts Spy, or The Worcester Gazette,* 16 March 1786, reprinted in the New York *Daily Advertiser,* 25 March 1786.

74. See *Charter, Bye-Laws, and Names.*

75. Members checked out Ramsay's *History of the Revolution in South Carolina* fifty-eight times and his general *History of the American Revolution* thirty-seven times. See First Charging Ledger, NYSL.

76. Ibid. For Robinson, see Smith, *City of New York,* 47.

77. First Charging Ledger, NYSL, 6, 8, 28, 29, 30, 31, 33, 34, and 81. See also King, *Books and People,* 278.

78. First Charging Ledger, NYSL, 298.

79. *Federal Gazette and Philadelphia Evening Post,* 23 February 1789.

80. Ibid.

81. The proposal appeared in the Elizabethtown *New-Jersey Journal, and Political Intelligencer,* 25 February, 4 March, 1, 15, 29 April, 6 May 1789; Boston *Independent Chronicle and Universal Advertiser,* 19 March and 4 June 1789; Hartford *Connecticut Courant and Weekly Intelligencer,* 30 March 1789; Savannah *Georgia Gazette,* 9 April 1789; and the Poughkeepsie *Country Journal,* 16 June 1789.

82. "Sir, The Subscribers, having taken into their serious consideration, the general utility attending a friendly correspondence among the booksellers and printers of the United States of America." Circular letter dated New York, 10 January 1789, signed by Hugh Gaine, Robert Hodge, Samuel Campbell, Thomas Allen, and William Ross, and addressed to William Young, Philadelphia, Michael Zinman Collection of Early American Imprints, no. 10470.F, LCP. See also Green, "Rise of Book Publishing," 82.

83. For the subscription list, see Hawkesworth, *New Voyage, Round the World*, 1–17.

84. Gross, "Introduction: An Extensive Republic," 28–29; see also Remer, *Printers and Men of Capital*, 90–91.

85. New York *Daily Advertiser*, 14 May 1789.

86. Ibid., 31 August 1789.

87. Ibid.

88. Ibid. The notice was reprinted twice in the New York *Daily Advertiser*, on 5 and 9 September 1789. The notice was also published in the *New-York Daily Gazette*, 15, 16, and 19 October 1789.

89. On Rousseau, Montesquieu, and early novels published by subscription, see Davidson, *Revolution and the Word*, 86–87. Davidson counts subscribers to the Bryan text from Connecticut, Kentucky, Louisiana, Maryland, New York, North Carolina, Ohio, Pennsylvania, South Carolina, and Virginia. Farren points to books published after the Revolution and finds that the "numbers of subscribers listed ranges between 92 and 873," with the median "being 483 and the average about 370." Farren, "Subscription," 169.

90. Gordon, *History of the Rise, Progress, and Establishment* (New York, 1789), 3:3–28, Michael Zinman Collection of Early American Imprints, no. 109860, and the McNeil Americana Collection, no. 112560, LCP. What follows are some bibliographical notes taken directly from the LCP online catalogue entry: 3v.: maps; 21cm (8vo). Maps engraved by Cornelius Tiebout. Pagination: v. 1: [13], 26–443, [1] folded leaf of plates; v. 2: [11], 26–474, [2], p. [1] folded leaf of plates; v. 3: [37], 18–446 [i.e., 448] p. Errors in paging: v. 1, pages 341, 429, and 433 misnumbered 413, 492, and 343; v. 3, numbers 183–184 repeated in pagination. Signatures: v. 1, [A]² B₄ D-3I₄ 3K² (3K2 verso blank); v. 2, [A]1 B₄ D-3M₄ 3O² (3O2 blank); v. 3, pi1 C-E₄ [F]1 ²E₄ ³A-3H₄. Subscribers' names, v. 3, initial p. [3]-28]. Includes Index. For more detailed bibliographical information, see the Library Company's online catalogue entry, accessed 1 July 2016, http://dc02kg0559na.hosted.exlibrisgroup.com:48992/F?func=direct&doc_number=000291595.

91. Gordon, *History of the Rise, Progress, and Establishment* (New York, 1789), 3:3–28.

92. Ibid.

93. I am indebted to Jim Green of the Library Company of Philadelphia for his assistance in comparing the New York and London editions of Gordon's *History*.

94. For subscribing practices in early America, including women subscribers, see Nord, "Republican Literature," 47–48.

95. *New-York Gazette*, 26 November 1764.

96. *New-York Journal, or The General Advertiser*, 15 January 1767.

97. Ibid., 12 November 1767. John continued to advertise his available stock during the revolutionary crisis. See ibid., 20 May 1773; *Rivington's New-York Gazetteer, or The Connecticut, Hudson's River, New-Jersey, and Quebec Weekly Advertiser*, 5 May 1774.

98. Unrecorded will of John Laboyteaux, 21 May 1780, in *Collections of the New-York Historical Society*, 199–200.

99. *Independent Gazette, or The New-York Journal Revived*, 24 January 1784.

100. *New-York Morning Post, and Daily Advertiser*, 3 March 1789. For the entire run, see March through December 1789. On 23 February 1785, the *New-York Morning Post* altered its title slightly, to the *New-York Morning Post, and Daily Advertiser*.

101. Ibid., 9, 10, 11, 14, 16, 18, 23, 24, 25 March 1789.

102. New York *Daily Advertiser*, 6 March 1789.

103. Ibid., 7 March 1789. For Childs's serialization, see ibid., 9, 10, 11, 12, 13, 14, 16, 17, 19, 24, 25, 26 March 1789.

104. Ibid., 4 March 1789.

105. Crane, "Publius in the Provinces," 589–90; Loughran, *Republic in Print*, 119–20, 467n20. For recent work on the publication history of "The Federalist," see Bucci, "John Jay and 'The Fœderalist.'"

106. Davidson, *Revolution and the Word*, 163.

107. Libby, "Critical Examination."

108. Boston *Herald of Freedom*, 3 July 1789.

109. New York *Daily Advertiser*, 9 July 1789.

110. Ibid., 11 July 1789; Gordon to Gates, 25 February 1786, and Gordon to Washington, 9 April 1786, both in "Letters of the Reverend William Gordon," 535 and 536, respectively.

111. New York *Daily Advertiser*, 11 July 1789.

Chapter 3

1. Philadelphia *Gazette of the United States*, 21 December 1798.
2. For a discussion of the development of the Republican newspaper network and its contribution to the development of party politics in the new nation, see Pasley, *"Tyranny of Printers,"* 48–78.
3. Philadelphia *Aurora, and General Advertiser*, 7 August 1798. For a narrative of this strange affair, see Tagg, *Benjamin Franklin Bache*, 349–51.
4. Philadelphia *Aurora, and General Advertiser*, 8 August 1798.
5. Philadelphia *Gazette of the United States*, 8 August 1798. For a discussion of the overtly masculine politics of honor, see Ellis, *Founding Brothers*, chap. 1; Freeman, *Affairs of Honor*.
6. Philadelphia *Aurora, and General Advertiser*, 9 August 1798; Philadelphia *Gazette of the United States*, 9 August 1798.
7. Philadelphia *Gazette of the United States*, 9 August 1798.
8. For the best biographical treatment of John Ward Fenno, see Hench, "Letters of John Fenno."
9. Remer, *Printers and Men of Capital*, 36; District of Columbia *Cabinet*, 6 October 1800.
10. For literary politics in the early Republic, see Dowling, *Literary Federalism*; Kaplan, *Men of Letters*; Waterman, *Republic of Intellect*; Barnard, Kamrath, and Shapiro, *Revising Charles Brockden Brown*; Watts, *Romance of Real Life*; Kerber, *Federalists in Dissent*. For Hocquet Caritat, see Raddin, *Hocquet Caritat*; Shapiro, *Culture and Commerce*.
11. See Giles, *Transatlantic Insurrections*, 2; Tennenhouse, *Importance of Feeling English*; Yokota, *Unbecoming British*; Tamarkin, *Anglophilia*; Giles, *Atlantic Republic*; Giles, *Remapping of American Literature*; Shapiro, *Culture and Commerce*.
12. Fenno to Dickins, 25 July and 7 August 1800, Loudoun Mansion Papers, box 27, HSP.
13. For printers and libel cases, see Pasley, *"Tyranny of Printers,"* 124, 141, 171, 189, 265, 266, 270–71, 277.
14. Hench, "Letters of John Fenno . . . Part 1," 303. For circulation of the judgment, see New York *Commercial Advertiser*, 1 December 1800; District of Columbia *Washington Federalist*, 2 December 1800; New York *Daily Advertiser*, 2 December 1800; Alexandria *Times, and the District of Columbia Daily Advertiser*, 3 December 1800; Wilmington, Del., *Mirror of the Times General Advertiser*, 3 December 1800; Hagerstown *Maryland Herald and Elizabeth-town Advertiser*, 4 December 1800; Harrisburg *Oracle of Dauphin and Harrisburgh Advertiser*, 8 December 1800; Newport, R.I., *Newport Mercury*, 9 December 1800; Boston *Massachusetts Mercury*, 9 December 1800; *Salem Gazette*, 9 December 1800; *Thomas's Massachusetts Spy, or The Worcester Gazette*, 10 December 1800; *Providence Journal, and Town and Country Advertiser*, 10 December 1800; New Bedford *Columbian Courier*, 12 December 1800; Newburyport *Herald and Country Gazette*, 12 December 1800; Portland, Maine, *Jenks' Portland Gazette*, 15 December 1800; Bennington *Vermont Gazette*, 15 December 1800; District of Columbia *Cabinet*, 16 December 1800; Charleston *South-Carolina State Gazette, and Timothy's Daily Advertiser*, 17 December 1800; Charleston *Carolina Gazette*, 18 December 1800; Augusta, Ga., *Chronicle*, 20 December 1800.
15. Pasley, *"Tyranny of Printers,"* 3, 46–47. For more on the political divide that emerged in the 1790s, see Elkins and McKitrick, *Age of Federalism*; Sharp, *American Politics in the Early Republic*; Cunningham, *Jeffersonian Republicans*.
16. Pasley, *"Tyranny of Printers,"* 46–47. For colonial printers as "meer mechanics," see Botein, "'Meer Mechanics.'"
17. Pasley, *"Tyranny of Printers,"* 20, 25–26, 57–60, 130, 192, 298, 299; Gross, "Introduction: An Extensive Republic," 20–21. For more on the economics of newspaper editing in the early Republic, see Steffen, "Newspapers for Free"; Silver, *American Printer*.
18. Hench, "Letters of John Fenno . . . Part 1," 299–302; Pasley, "Two National Gazettes," 55; Pasley, *"Tyranny of Printers,"* 48–78; Humphrey, *Press of the Young Republic*, xiv, 42, 44, 45.
19. Pasley, "Two National Gazettes," 56–57; John Fenno, "An Address, Boston, January 1, 1789," in Hench, "Letters of John Fenno . . . Part 1," 312, 299.
20. Philadelphia *Gazette of the United States*, 15 April 1789; Pasley, "Two National Gazettes," 58.
21. Humphrey, *Press of the Young Republic*, 45; Pasley, "Two National Gazettes," 61–62.
22. Fenno to Ward, 30 March 1800, in Hench, "Letters of John Fenno . . . Part 2," 233.
23. Lewis Morris to Joseph Dennie, 14 February 1799, in Lanzendörfer, "From the Periodical Archives," 98–99.
24. Ibid.; Fenno to Dennie, 12 February 1799, ibid., 99.

25. Ellis, "Joseph Dennie and His Circle"; Richards, "Dennie, Joseph"; Lanzendörfer, "From the Periodical Archives," 99.

26. Philadelphia *Gazette of the United States*, 30 April 1800.

27. Ellis, "Joseph Dennie and His Circle," 130; Philadelphia *Gazette of the United States*, 28 May 1800.

28. Burrows and Wallace, *Gotham*, 315–28. For political developments in New York, see Young, *Democratic Republicans of New York*, 33–58, 83–108, 231–56, 392–412, 445–67; for the Clintons, see Cornog, *Birth of Empire;* for Tammany Hall, see Mushkat, *Tammany.*

29. Burrows and Wallace, *Gotham*, 324–31. For the Alien and Sedition Acts, see Pasley, *"Tyranny of Printers,"* 105–31. For the "Revolution of 1800," see the essays in Horn, Lewis, and Onuf, *Revolution of 1800.* For the lingering influence of Federalists after the so-called Revolution of 1800, see Lampi, "Federalist Party Resurgence."

30. New York *American Citizen and General Advertiser*, 31 May 1800.

31. On Cobbett and Fenno's collaboration, see Daniel, *Scandal and Civility;* Pasley, *"Tyranny of Printers,"* 100–103; List, "Role of William Cobbett."

32. For recent work on Rush's libel case against Cobbett, see Myrsiades, *Law and Medicine.* The standard biographies on Cobbett are Spater, *William Cobbett*, and Green, *Great Cobbett.*

33. New York *Daily Advertiser*, 4 June 1800; *New-York Gazette and General Advertiser*, 4 June 1800.

34. Cobbett's farewell was reprinted in the Philadelphia *Gazette of the United States*, 6 June 1804; the Alexandria *Times, and the District of Columbia Daily Advertiser*, 9 June 1800; Boston *J. Russell's Gazette, Commercial and Political*, 9 June 1800; the Newburyport *Herald and Country Gazette*, 20 June 1800; the Litchfield, Conn., *Farmer's Monitor*, 24 June 1800; the Brookfield, Mass., *Political Repository*, 24 June 1800; the Charleston *City Gazette and Daily Advertiser*, 25 June 1800; *Thomas's Massachusetts Spy, or The Worcester Gazette*, 25 June 1800; the Georgetown, S.C., *Gazette*, 28 June 1800; the Leominster *Telescope, or American Herald*, 3 July 1800; the Providence *United States Chronicle*, 3 July 1800; and the Windsor *Spooner's Vermont Journal*, 15 July 1800.

35. Fenno to Dickins, 19 October 1801, Loudoun Mansion Papers, box 27, HSP. For Burr and the Manhattan Company, see Murphy, "'Very Convenient Instrument.'"

36. Longworth and Shoemaker, *Longworth's American Almanack* (1800).

37. New York *Daily Advertiser*, 4 June 1800; *New-York Gazette and General Advertiser*, 4 June 1800.

38. William Cobbett Account Book, AAS; Gaines, "William Cobbett's Account Book," 304.

39. Estate Inventory of John Ward Fenno, John Ward Fenno Papers, NYHS.

40. For the advertisement for the novels, see *New-York Gazette and General Advertiser*, 23 August 1800. For the carpentry texts, see New York *Daily Advertiser*, 7 October 1800. For history book advertisements, see *New-York Gazette and General Advertiser*, 6, 22, 25, 27 September and 16 October 1800; New York *Daily Advertiser*, 15 November 1800. For what Fenno classified as the "best London editions" of "Law Books," see New York *Daily Advertiser*, 13, 18 September 1800. For travel literature, see *New-York Gazette and General Advertiser*, 18, 19, 24 October 1800. For poetry, see New York *Daily Advertiser*, 26, 27 November 1800; *New-York Gazette and General Advertiser*, 26, 28 November 1800; New York *Commercial Advertiser*, 27 October 1801. For gardening books, see New York *Daily Advertiser*, 7 October 1800, 20 February 1801.

41. Fenno to Dickins, 15 June 1801, Loudoun Mansion Papers, box 27, HSP.

42. Johnson to Mr. Fellows, 18 June 1795, Joseph Johnson Letterbook, Pforzheimer Collection of Shelley and His Circle, A-RD 09, NYPL. For Fellows, see Duncan and Tiebout, *New-York Directory.*

43. Johnson to Thomas and James Swords, 4 October 1800 and 10 March 1801, Joseph Johnson Letterbook, NYPL. Johnson wrote to the brothers several more times—in May 1802, February, June, and July 1803, May, September, and November 1805, August 1807, and June and October 1808.

44. Books Imported by T. & J. Swords, 9 November 1801, Book Trades Collection, MSS boxes B, box 2, folder 1, AAS.

45. Johnson to Thomas and James Swords, 26 June and 4 October 1808, Joseph Johnson Letterbook, NYPL; Braithwaite, *Romanticism, Publishing, and Dissent*, 179; Chard, "Joseph Johnson," 73.

46. *New-York Gazette and General Advertiser*, 4 October 1800.

47. New York *Daily Advertiser*, 1 January 1801.

48. Ibid., 29 October 1800. On d'Ivernois, see d'Ivernois, *Historical and Political Survey.* See also Whatmore, "D'Ivernois, Sir Francis."

49. New York *Daily Advertiser*, 29 October 1800. For Gifford's life and career, see Stephen and Smith, "Gifford, John."

50. Fenno to Dickins, 21 February 1801, Loudoun Mansion Papers, box 27, HSP.

51. For work on Madame de Genlis, see Shapiro, *French Women Poets*, 476–77. See also Schaneman, "Rewriting 'Adèle et Théodore'"; Schroder, "Going Public"; Trouille, "Toward a New Appreciation"; Wahba, "Madame de Genlis in England"; Walker, "Producing Feminine Virtue."

52. Keyes, "Early American Advertising," 102–10. For more on book catalogues in in early America, see Winans, *Descriptive Checklist.*

53. Fenno, *Supplementary Catalogue*, 11–12, 23–24, 20; Liebersohn, *Aristocratic Encounters*, 35–36.

54. For work on Boucher, see Zimmer, *Jonathan Boucher;* Clark, "Jonathan Boucher and the Toleration"; Zimmer and Kelly, "Jonathan Boucher"; Middleton, "Colonial Virginia Parson"; Clark, "Jonathan Boucher"; Fall, "Rev. Jonathan Boucher"; Evanson, "Jonathan Boucher"; Calhoon, "Boucher, Jonathan."

55. Fenno, *Supplementary Catalogue*, 13.

56. "Appendix to the Two Sermons on Absalom and Ahitophel," in Boucher, *View of the Causes and Consequences*, 438.

57. New York *American Citizen*, 8 December 1800, reprinted in the District of Columbia *Cabinet*, 16 December 1800, and the Norwich, Conn., *Courier*, 4 February 1801.

58. Quoted in Pasley, *"Tyranny of Printers,"* 100.

59. Estate Inventory of John Ward Fenno, John Ward Fenno Papers, NYHS.

60. Fenno had on hand 107 copies of thirty-four belles lettres titles in boards, three copies of education texts, twenty copies of professional titles, nineteen copies of seven reference titles, and twenty-four Bibles. Most of the books he stored in sheets were belles lettres texts, including 2,740 copies of six titles and 350 copies of two religious texts. For more on the storage of books in boards and sheets, see Winship, *American Literary Publishing*, 131.

61. New York *Daily Advertiser*, 4 June 1800; *New-York Gazette and General Advertiser*, 4 June 1800; Fenno, *Supplementary Catalogue*, 7.

62. Gilmartin, *Writing Against Revolution*, 119–21. See also Gilmartin, *Print Politics;* Barker, *Newspapers, Politics, and English Society;* Harris, *Rise of the Press;* Thompson, *Making of the English Working Class;* Thompson, *Customs in Common.* For recent work on periodicals and political culture in the early American Republic, see Haberman, "Magazines, Presentation Networks"; Haberman, "Provincial Nationalism."

63. *Anti-Jacobin Review* 1 (1798): 2, quoted in Gilmartin, *Writing Against Revolution*, 110.

64. See Gilmartin, *Writing Against Revolution*, 98, 99, 105, 110, 137, 141, 151, 155, 171, 221.

65. The periodicals noted above are listed in the Estate Inventory of John Ward Fenno, John Ward Fenno Papers, NYHS.

66. Fenno to Dickins, 13 October 1800, Loudoun Mansion Papers, box 27, HSP.

67. Philadelphia *Gazette of the United States*, 25 October 1800.

68. New York *Daily Advertiser*, 16 May 1801.

69. Armstrong, "Commotions of a New-York May-Day." See also Burrows and Wallace, *Gotham*, 392–93; New York *Daily Advertiser*, 11 and 26 May 1801. City directories beginning in 1801 listed Fenno's address as 141 Broadway. See Longworth, *Longworth's American Almanac* (1801); Longworth and Shoemaker, *Longworth's American Almanac* (1802).

70. For work on Caritat, see especially Raddin, *Hocquet Caritat;* Shapiro, *Culture and Commerce*, 143, 159, 160, 265. For a discussion of Caritat's "Literary Assembly," see Burrows and Wallace, *Gotham*, 378; Verhoeven, "'This Blissful Period,'" 20–23, 38n58. For Caritat's circulating library, see Davidson, *Revolution and the Word*, 88–90.

71. Burrows and Wallace, *Gotham*, 340; Sandoval-Strausz, *Hotel*, 24.

72. Estate Inventory of John Ward Fenno, John Ward Fenno Papers, NYHS.

73. Ibid.; William Cobbett Account Book, AAS; Gaines, "William Cobbett's Account Book," 310–12. Cobbett's account book lists six New England booksellers (three in Boston and one each in New Haven, Connecticut, Newburyport, Massachusetts, and Pittsfield, Massachusetts); thirty-six in the mid-Atlantic (thirteen in New York City, fifteen in Philadelphia, and one each in Albany, New York, Carlisle, Lancaster, Pittsburgh, and Reading, Pennsylvania, and one each in Trenton, New Jersey, and Wilmington, Delaware); and nineteen in the South (ten in Maryland—three in Baltimore, two in Easton, three in Fredericktown, and one each in Georgetown Crossroads and Williamsport; eight in Virginia—three in Norfolk, two in Richmond, and one each in Alexandria, Chambersburg, Petersburg; and one in Savannah, Georgia). For a discussion of commission networks, see Remer, *Printers and Men of Capital*, 82.

74. William Cobbett Account Book, AAS; Gaines, "William Cobbett's Account Book," 310–12.

75. See Remer, *Printers and Men of Capital*, 70–71. For a sampling of the texts published and distributed by the Conrad family, see *Constitutions of the United States*. The bookseller's catalogue of John Conrad & Co., Philadelphia, M. & J. Conrad & Co., Baltimore, and Rapin, Conrad & Co., Washington, D.C., is included at the end.

76. Davis, *Travels of Four Years*, 222–23, 225. See also Pilkington and Vernon, *Methodist Publishing House*, 129.

77. Fenno to Dennie, 17 January 1800, Meredith Papers, *Port Folio* section, HSP. For Francis Asbury, see Wigger, *American Saint*.

78. Parker, "Asbury Dickins, Bookseller," 465.

79. Kaplan, *Men of Letters*, 141. See also Dowling, *Literary Federalism*; Richards, "Dennie, Joseph"; Ellis, "Joseph Dennie and His Circle."

80. Fenno to Dickins, 13 August 1800, Loudoun Mansion Papers, box 27, HSP.

81. Fenno to Dickins, 21 February 1801, ibid.

82. Fenno to Dickins, 25 July 1800, ibid. For Hill's career as a bookseller, see a variety of advertisements in Baltimore newspapers. For example, the *Federal Gazette & Baltimore Daily Advertiser*, 19 November 1801, noted that the "Clerical Candidates, a Poem" was available for sale at the "Bookstores of George Hill, Andrews & Butler, and Warner & Hanna."

83. Hill to Dickins, 18 June 1801, Loudoun Mansion Papers, box 27, HSP.

84. Hill to Dickins, 1 July 1801, ibid.

85. Fenno to Dickins, 23 January, 10 February, 19 February, 20 July, and 21 August 1801, ibid.

86. Kaplan, *Men of Letters*, 140–41.

87. Fenno to Dickins, 15 July 1801, Loudoun Mansion Papers, box 27, HSP.

88. C. W. Hare to Dickins, 26 October 1801, Notice of Summons, quoted in Parker, "Asbury Dickins, Bookseller," 480–81. For work on debt in early America, see Mann, *Republic of Debtors*.

89. Copy, dated 3 December 1803, of "General Power of Attorney Executed by Asbury Dickins in Favor of Thomas W. Armat," 27 October 1801, Loudoun Mansion Papers, box 27, HSP.

90. Parker, "Asbury Dickins, Bookseller," 481.

91. List of debts and assets, n.d., endorsed "Dickins Estate," Loudoun Mansion Papers, box 27, HSP.

92. Fenno to Rodman, 8 January 1802, ibid.

93. "Mr. Asbury Dickins in Account with the Estate of John Ward Fenno," as drawn up by John Rodman, 24 May 1802, ibid.

94. Fenno to Dickins, 16 March 1801, ibid.

95. Dickins to Armat, 22 February 1802, quoted in Parker, "Asbury Dickins, Bookseller," 482.

96. Armat to Dickins, n.d., Loudoun Mansion Papers, box 27, HSP.

97. Agreement for purchase between David Hogan and Thomas W. Armat, 25 July 1805, ibid.

98. See Parker, "Asbury Dickins, Bookseller," 482–83.

99. See Pasley, *"Tyranny of Printers,"* 105–75; Pasley, "1800 as a Revolution."

100. Ezra Sargeant, "E. Sargeant, & Co.," New York *Daily Advertiser*, 29 April 1802.

Chapter 4

1. *New-York Evening Post*, 20 June 1804; Hackenberg, "Getting the Books Out"; Green, "Rise of Book Publishing," 94, 111–12; Kaser, "Origin of the Book Trade."

2. American Association of Booksellers, Silver Medal, 1804, Arts and Artifacts Collection, LCP. For stories that mention the booksellers' medal ceremony, see *New-York Evening Post*, 20 June 1804; Litchfield, Conn., *Monitor*, 20 June 1804; Kingston, N.Y., *Plebeian*, 20 June 1804; New York *Herald*, 23 June 1804; Peacham, Vt., *Green Mountain Patriot*, 26 June 1804; New York *Morning Chronicle*, 29 June 1804; Boston *New-England Palladium*, 3 July 1804; Alexandria *Expositor, for the Country*, 7 June 1804; Fredericktown *Republican Gazette*, 13 July 1804; Fredericktown *Hornet*, 17 July 1804. For work on the symbolism of medals, see Albertson, "Society of the Cincinnati"; Hofer, "Case of the Mystery Medal"; Olson, "Franklin's Commemorative Medal"; Olson, *Emblems of American Community*; Prins, "Two George Washington Medals"; Richardson, "Cassin Medal"; Schleiner, "Infant Hercules."

3. "Agreement Between Noah Webster and George F. Hopkins," 13 May 1797, Noah Webster Papers, series 4, MssCol 3258, box 8, NYPL.

4. "Agreement Between Noah Webster & George Foliet Hopkins," 17 October 1797, ibid. Hopkins also worked with Webster on the *Minerva*; see New York *Minerva*, 2 May 1796, 15 May and 30 September 1797; New York *Spectator*, 4 October 1797. Hopkins dissolved his *Spectator* part-

nership with Webster in 1799; see New York *Spectator*, 3 July 1799. For more on the dissolution of this partnership, see New York *Commercial Advertiser*, 1 July 1799.

5. Steffen, "Newspapers for Free"; Pasley, *"Tyranny of Printers,"* 77; Clark, *Public Prints*, 7, 168.

6. Agreement between Webster and Hopkins, 17 October 1797, Noah Webster Papers, NYPL.

7. "Dissolution of partnership Between Noah Webster and George F. Hopkins," 6 April 1799, ibid., series 4, box 8.

8. *Life of Thurlow Weed*, 1:57. For more on Weed, see Van Deusen, *Thurlow Weed*.

9. For work on the long tradition in the early Republic of manufacturing protectionism, see Peskin, *Manufacturing Revolution*, 65–92. Peskin's discussion of popular neomercantilists stands in contrast to the "republican" and "capitalist" interpretations of political economy in the early Republic. See McCoy, *Elusive Republic*; Appleby, *Capitalism and a New Social Order*. See also Rockman, *Scraping By*, 42.

10. Peskin, *Manufacturing Revolution*, 61, 64.

11. Burrows and Wallace, *Gotham*, 306–7.

12. Kielbowicz, *News in the Mail*, 34. For work on newspaper reprinting and the circulation of information, see especially Steffen, "Newspapers for Free." For the significance of newspapers to social, cultural, and political life in the early Republic, see Pasley, *"Tyranny of Printers."* For the influence of the post office on newspaper circulation, which, by extension, enabled the free circulation of papers from city to city, editor to editor, see John, *Spreading the News*, 32–33. See also, all by Kielbowicz, "Speeding the News"; "Modernization, Communication Policy"; and "News Gathering by Mail." For the general speed with which information traveled in early America, see Pred, *Urban Growth*.

13. *New-York Evening Post*, 25 February 1802.

14. "Protection to Manufactures, communicated to the House of Representatives," in Lowrie and Clarke, *American State Papers*, 7th Cong., 1st sess., 10 February 1802, 730. Coleman reprinted the announcement of the congressional duty in the *Evening Post* one day after it appeared in the Philadelphia *Aurora*. William Duane, the *Aurora*'s printer, had learned of the announcement on 10 February 1802 while in Washington, D.C., and he immediately sent word to Philadelphia, where it appeared in the *Aurora* on 15 February 1802. The announcement then appeared in the *Daily Advertiser*, followed a day later by the *American Citizen and General Advertiser*. See Philadelphia *Aurora*, 15 February 1802; *New-York Evening Post*, 16 February 1802; New York *Daily Advertiser*, 17 February 1802; New York *American Citizen and General Advertiser*, 17 February 1802.

15. "Petition to the U.S. Congress by Archibald Binny & James Ronaldson Favoring the Remitting of Duties on Regulus of Antimony," 8 January 1802, Book Trades Collection, MSS boxes "B," box 2, AAS. The AAS copy is a photostat of the original manuscript, which is held by the National Archives in Washington, D.C. For work on Binny and Ronaldson, see Lee, "Infant Manufactures"; Silver, *Typefounding in America*. For a focused study of this petition, see Silver, "Printers' Lobby."

16. *New-York Evening Post*, 1 March 1802; "Petition of Sundry Printers and Booksellers of the City of New York," 8 March 1802, Book Trades Collection, MSS boxes "B," box 2, AAS.

17. "Petition of Sundry Printers and Booksellers," 8 March 1802, AAS.

18. "Petition to the U.S. Congress by the Franklin Typographical Society of the City of New York," 15 March 1802, AAS, folder 2. For early trade union activism, including typographical societies, see Lause, *Some Degree of Power*; Rock, *Artisans of the New Republic*; Wilentz, *Chants Democratic*; Rock, Gilje, and Asher, *American Artisans*; Stevens, *New York Typographical Union*.

19. "Petition to the U.S. Congress by the Franklin Typographical Society," 15 March 1802, AAS.

20. Baltimore *Federal Gazette*, 24 February 1802.

21. "Petition of the Subscribers, Printers and Others, of the City of Baltimore," reprinted in Silver, "Printers' Lobby," 225.

22. Charleston *Times*, 15 March 1802; "Memorial to the U.S. Congress by Subscribers, Printers, Booksellers, & Stationers in Charleston, S.C., Expressing Their Opposition to the Proposed Duty Increase on Printing Type," 30 March 1802, Book Trades Collection, box 2, folder 2, AAS.

23. Peskin, *Manufacturing Revolution*, 72, 73.

24. For the 1804 tariff, see Silver, "Printers' Lobby," 228.

25. Morgan, *Evolution of a Trade Association*, 30–31. See also Growoll, *Book Trade Bibliography*.

26. New York *Commercial Advertiser*, 21 December 1801.

27. Peskin, *Manufacturing Revolution*, 69; see 65–71 for a discussion of Carey's ideology. See also Remer, *Printers and Men of Capital*, 55–65; Rowe, *Mathew Carey*.

28. Peskin, *Manufacturing Revolution*, 69.

29. *Salem Gazette*, 29 December 1801.

30. See Boston *Commercial Gazette*, 28 December 1801; *Providence Journal, and Town and Country Advertiser*, 30 December 1801; Salem, Mass., *Impartial Register;* 31 December 1801; New Bedford *Columbian Courier*, 1 January 1802; Rutland, Vt., *Herald*, 11 January 1802; Norwich, Conn., *Courier*, 13 January 1802; New London *Bee*, 13 January 1802; Portsmouth *New-Hampshire Gazette*, 5 January 1802; *Thomas's Massachusetts Spy, or The Worcester Gazette*, 6 January 1802; *United States Oracle, and Portsmouth Advertiser*, 16 January 1802; Leominster *Telescope, or American Herald*, 11 March 1802; Dedham, Mass., *Columbian Minerva*, 23 March 1802; New York *Mercantile Advertiser*, 8 April 1802; New Bedford *Columbian Orator*, 23 April 1802.

31. New York *Commercial Advertiser*, New York *Daily Advertiser*, and *New-York Evening Post*, 14 April 1802; New York *American Citizen and General Advertiser* and New York *Mercantile Advertiser*, 15 April 1802; *New-York Gazette and General Advertiser*, 16 April 1802; New York *Herald* and New York *Spectator*, 17 April 1802.

32. Philadelphia *Gazette of the United States*, 15 April 1802; *Philadelphia Gazette and Daily Advertiser* and Philadelphia *Poulson's American Daily Advertiser*, 17 April 1802; Boston *Independent Chronicle and Universal Advertiser*, 22 April 1802; *Salem Gazette*, 23 April 1802; *Providence Gazette*, 24 April 1802; Salem, Mass., *Impartial Register*, 26 April 1802; Dedham, Mass., *Columbian Minerva*, and Norwich *Connecticut Centinel*, 27 April 1802; New London *Bee* and New London *Connecticut Gazette*, 28 April 1802; Brattleboro *Federal Galaxy*, 10 May 1802.

33. New York *Commercial Advertiser*, 1 June 1802.

34. Philadelphia *Gazette of the United States*, 2 June 1802.

35. New York *Commercial Advertiser*, 2 June 1802; see also New York *Spectator*, 2 June 1802.

36. Philadelphia *Gazette and Daily Advertiser* and Philadelphia *Poulson's American Daily Advertiser*, 5 June 1802; Baltimore *Republican, or Anti-Democrat*, 7 June 1802; New London *Connecticut Gazette* and Norwich, Conn., *Courier*, 9 June 1802; Windham, Conn., *Herald*, 10 June 1802; *Providence Gazette*, 12 June 1802; Newport *Rhode-Island Republican*, 19 June 1802; Cooperstown *Otsego Herald, or Western Advertiser*, 17 June 1802; *Kline's Carlisle Weekly Gazette*, 23 June 1802; Burlington *Vermont Centinel*, 24 June 1802; Walpole, N.H., *Farmer's Weekly Museum, or Literary Gazette*, 29 June 1802.

37. New York *Daily Advertiser*, 2 June 1802. See also Philadelphia *Poulson's American Daily Advertiser*, 4 June 1802; Albany *Gazette*, 7 June 1802; Concord *Courier of New Hampshire*, 1 July 1802. While each of the notices ran the statement that more booksellers were expected, a full tally was never published.

38. Hodges, *New York City Cartmen*.

39. Waldstreicher, *Perpetual Fetes*, 26. For more on public celebrations as expressions of solidarity, national, political, or otherwise, see Newman, *Politics of the Street*. For tavern culture in early America, see Conroy, *In Public Houses;* Salinger, *Taverns and Drinking;* Thompson, *Rum Punch and Revolution*.

40. New York *Mercantile Advertiser*, 7 June 1802. For a discussion of how the typographical societies evoked the memory of Franklin in their toasts, see especially Eastman, *Nation of Speechifiers*, 161–64, 166–67. For more on the unusual connection between Faustus and Gutenberg at the New York literary fair, see Wall-Randell, "'Doctor Faustus,'" 260; Johns, "Faust and the Pirates."

41. New York *Mercantile Advertiser*, 7 June 1802.

42. The toasts were reprinted in Philadelphia *Poulson's American Daily Advertiser*, 9 June 1802; Alexandria *Times, and the District of Columbia Daily Advertiser*, 11 June 1802; Baltimore *Republican, or Anti-Democrat*, 11 June 1802; Portsmouth *New Hampshire Gazette*, 22 June 1802; Keene *New-Hampshire Sentinel*, 26 June 1802; and the Brattleboro *Federal Galaxy*, 28 June 1802.

43. [Gaine], *Oration Delivered Before the Booksellers*. For a discussion of Gaine's speech, see Remer, *Printers and Men of Capital*, 62–63.

44. [Gaine], *Oration Delivered Before the Booksellers*.

45. [Carey], *To the Booksellers* (the quotations in the next three paragraphs are from this source). Remer identifies Carey as the likely author of the broadside; see *Printers and Men of Capital*, 62–63, 174n67. The broadside was reprinted a week later, on 14 June 1802, in two New York newspapers, the *Commercial Advertiser* and the *Mercantile Advertiser*.

46. It appeared in the Newark, N.J., *Centinel of Freedom* and Elizabethtown *New-Jersey Journal, and Political Intelligencer*, 15 June 1802; Alexandria *Times, and the District of Columbia Daily Advertiser*, 18 June 1802; Albany *Centinel*, 22 June 1802; New Bedford *Columbian Courier*, 25 June 1802; and *Providence Gazette*, 26 June 1802.

47. Peskin, *Manufacturing Revolution*, 80.

48. Hopkins to Carey, 3 August 1802, Lea & Febiger Records, box 38, HSP. For work on the circulation of *The Federalist*, see Loughran, *Republic in Print*, 105–58. See also Alexander, *Selling of the Constitutional Convention*.

49. Harrisson to Carey, 23 November 1802, Lea & Febiger Records, box 38, HSP.

50. T. & J. Swords to Carey, 26 June 1802, ibid., box 39.

51. Jansen to West, 10 June 1802, West, Richardson & Lord Business Records, MSS boxes W, box 3, AAS.

52. Tiebout to West, 11 June 1802, ibid., box 5.

53. Campbell to West, 24 June 1802, ibid., box 1.

54. Falconer to West, 17 July 1802, ibid., box 2. For a discussion of John West, see Warren, "John West—Bookseller." On the Boston book trade in the early Republic, see Silver, *Boston Book Trade*.

55. Duyckinck to West, 16 June 1802, West, Richardson & Lord Business Records, box 2, AAS. For the record of shipment, see Evert Duyckinck Daybook, 15 June 1802, Duyckinck Family Papers, vol. 22, MssCol 873, NYPL.

56. Duyckinck to Carey, 28 June 1802, Lea & Febiger Records, box 37, HSP. For Duyckinck's notes on the shipment, see Evert Duyckinck Daybook, 19 and 23 June 1802, Duyckinck Family Papers, vol. 22, NYPL.

57. Evert Duyckinck Daybook, 8 and 11 June and 19 July 1802, Duyckinck Family Papers, vol. 22, NYPL.

58. Duyckinck to Carey, 22 November 1802, Lea & Febiger Records, box 37, HSP.

59. T. & J. Swords to Carey, 27 September 1802, ibid., box 39.

60. G. & R. Waite to Carey, 30 November 1802, ibid., box 40.

61. Ringwood, *Address, Delivered Before the Franklin Typographical Association*, 18.

62. Morgan, *Evolution of a Trade Association*, 31.

Chapter 5

1. Francis, "Reminiscences of Printers," 260–61.

2. Osgood, *Evert Augustus Duyckinck*, 2.

3. For work on Evert Augustus Duyckinck, see Widmer, *Young America;* Miller, *Raven and the Whale;* Mize, "Contributions of Evert A. Duyckinck"; Roche, "Literary Gentleman"; Wells, "Evert Duyckinck's Literary World."

4. Gross, "Introduction: An Extensive Republic," 7.

5. For work on the reprint trade in early America, see McGill, *Culture of Reprinting;* Green, "Rise of Book Publishing," 76–91; Remer, *Printers and Men of Capital*, 12, 51, 53, 54, 64, 88, 160.

6. For a useful summary of accounting methods, see Davies, *New and Concise System*, 3–4. On business accounting in early America, see especially Remer, *Printers and Men of Capital*, 101–6; Winship, *American Literary Publishing*, 24–27, 36–37. For a discussion of double-entry accounting, see Chatfield, *History of Accounting Thought*, 44–51. For a useful discussion of the language of accounting and the creation of kinship networks, see Ditz, "Secret Selves, Credible Personas"; Siskind, *Rum and Axes*, 52; Block, *Postindustrial Possibilities*, 19. For further discussion of double-entry accounting and its usefulness for historical analysis, see Densmore, "Nineteenth-Century Account Books," 6; Edwards, "Early Bookkeeping"; Yamey, "Scientific Bookkeeping."

7. For a discussion of this transformation of printers into publishers, see Remer, *Printers and Men of Capital*, 3. For a general overview of New York's waterfront, see McKay, *South Street*. For a discussion of sail making and shipbuilding in early America, see Smith, *"Lower Sort,"* 78; Bridenbaugh, *Colonial Craftsman*, 92–94.

8. "Contract between Samuel Campbell and Evert Duyckinck," 1 January 1793, Duyckinck Family Papers, MssCol 873, box 62, NYPL.

9. Green, "Rise of Book Publishing," 81; McDougall, "Charles Elliot's Book Adventure," 202; "Samuel Campbell," Printers' File, AAS; Campbell, *Samuel Campbell's Sale Catalogue*.

10. Contract between Campbell and Duyckinck, 1 January 1793, Duyckinck Family Papers, NYPL.

11. Davidson, *Revolution and the Word*, 80.

12. See Albion, *Rise of New York Port*, 266–70.

13. "Bill of Sale for the Ship Providence," Samuel Campbell Collection (Phi 114), box 1, folder 1, HSP.

14. "Bill of Sale for the Ship Barrington," ibid.

15. See Albion, *Rise of New York Port*, 266–70.

16. Duyckinck to Carey, 7 January 1795, Lea & Febiger Records, box 6, HSP.

17. Evert Duyckinck Daybook, 13 November 1795, 25 and 26 February 1796, Duyckinck Family Papers, vol. 20, NYPL.

18. Green, "Rise of Book Publishing," 91.

19. Albany *Chronicle*, 9 April 1798. I compared the names on the subscription lists in the two 1798 printings of Volney's *Travels Through Egypt and Syria* (one printed for Evert Duyckinck, the other for David Longworth, both held in the Michael Zinman Collection of Early American Imprints at the LCP) to names in the 1797 and 1798 city trade directories, which provided occupational data. See Longworth and Shoemaker, *Longworth's American Almanack* (1798).

20. Rock, *Artisans of the New Republic*,13; Nord, "Republican Literature," 50; Longworth, *Longworth's American Almanack* (1805).

21. Young, "George Robert Twelves Hews," 570–71; For more detailed data on the Volney subscription list, see Smith, "'Elements of Useful Knowledge,'" 512–14.

22. "Purchase Sheet, Evert Duyckinck bought of Samuel Campbell," 1 January 1799, Duyckinck Family Papers, box 60, NYPL.

23. "Statement of Debt due to & from the Copartnership of Evert Duyckinck & Company, from their Ledger, 1799," ibid. Three such assessments exist in the Duyckinck Family Papers at the NYPL. See "Statements of the Debts due to & from the Copartnership of Evert Duyckinck & Company from their Ledger, 1799, 1801, 1804," ibid. Little actual variance exists in the three assessments, as many debtors in 1799 were still unable to fulfill their financial obligations to Duyckinck by 1804.

24. Rush, "Modes of Education," 686; Kelley, "Introduction: Educating the Citizenry," 269.

25. Moran and Vinovskis, "Schools," 286–87; see also Brown, *Strength of a People*.

26. Monaghan and Monaghan, "Schoolbooks," 304–5; Monaghan, *Learning to Read and Write*, 81–88, 91–104, 213–33, 390–91; Crain, *Story of A*. For numbers on Duyckinck's publication of Dilworth's spelling book, see Evert Duyckinck Daybook, Duyckinck Family Papers, vols. 23 and 30, NYPL.

27. For numbers on Duyckinck's publication of Dilworth's *Schoolmaster's Assistant*, see Evert Duyckinck Daybook, Duyckinck Family Papers, vols. 21 and 26, NYPL.

28. Quoted in Kramer, *Imagining Language in America*, 44.

29. Quoted in Monaghan and Monaghan, "Schoolbooks," 304; see also Monaghan, *Common Heritage*, 51. For Webster's national ambitions, see Lepore, *A Is for American*, 5–6, 15–37.

30. Monaghan and Monaghan, "Schoolbooks," 305–8; Monaghan, *Common Heritage*, 227.

31. McGill, "Copyright," 198; Green, "Rise of Book Publishing," 100.

32. Noah Webster Journal, 31 October 1787, Noah Webster Papers, NYPL. The best account of the Campbell affair can be found in Monaghan, *Common Heritage*, 78–81. See also Unger, *Noah Webster*, 139, 151; Kendall, *Forgotten Founding Father*, 92; Ellis, *After the Revolution*, 161–212; Warfel, *Noah Webster*; Skeel, *Writings of Noah Webster*.

33. Green, "Rise of Book Publishing," 100.

34. Webster to Hudson & Goodwin, 20 February 1789, Noah Webster Papers, box 1, NYPL; Monaghan, *Common Heritage*, 77–79.

35. "Statement Detailing Accusations Against Samuel Campbell," 28 February 1789, Noah Webster Papers, box 10, NYPL.

36. Hartford *Connecticut Courant*, 17 September 1792; Skeel, *Writings of Noah Webster*, 19–20; Warfel, *Noah Webster*, 73.

37. Quoted in Warfel, *Noah Webster*, 73.

38. Thomas and James Swords to Campbell, 22 September 1792, Samuel Campbell Collection (Phi 114), box 1, HSP.

39. Holt to Campbell, 24 September 1792, ibid.

40. Webster to Hudson & Goodwin, 23 January 1795, Noah Webster Papers, box 1, NYPL. Scholars disagree on the precise number of copies Campbell printed. Warfel puts it at a hundred thousand, a number that Moss and Kendall have repeated. Monaghan, however, uses ninety thousand. See Monaghan, *Common Heritage*, 79; Warfel, *Noah Webster*, 73; Kendall, *Forgotten Founding Father*, 92; Moss, *Noah Webster*, 25.

41. Evert Duyckinck Daybook, 29 May, 1, 6, 9, 18, 30 June, 2, 7, 9, 15, 20, 24 July, 20, 30 August, 11, 25 September, 11, 12, 13, 30 November, 3, 5, 8, 9, 10, 11, 12, 16, 18, 24, 26, 28, 29 December 1795, Duyckinck Family Papers, vol. 20, NYPL.

42. Evert Duyckinck Daybook, 5 November 1803, ibid., vol. 23; Monaghan and Monaghan, "Schoolbooks," 308.

43. For the number of copies sold, see Blight, *Columbian Orator,* xiii–xvii.

44. Evert Duyckinck Daybook, 11 March 1817, 28 October 1818, Duyckinck Family Papers, vol. 29, NYPL.

45. For a discussion of Bingham's publications, see Monaghan and Monaghan, "Schoolbooks," 308–9. For a discussion of Bingham's works as civic texts, see Furstenberg, *Name of the Father,* 147–66, 241–45.

46. For work on Murray's schoolbooks, see Monaghan, *Murrays of Murray Hill,* 92–103; Tieken-Boon van Ostade, *Two Hundred Years.*

47. Monaghan and Monaghan, "Schoolbooks," 309; Monaghan, *Murrays of Murray Hill,* 92–103.

48. Cobb, *New North American Reader,* v–vi; Monaghan, *Murrays of Murray Hill,* 95.

49. Evert Duyckinck Daybook, Duyckinck Family Papers, vols. 23, 24, 25, 28, 29, 30, 33, NYPL. For Duyckinck's Murray imprints, see the bibliography.

50. Burrows and Wallace, *Gotham,* 333–38. For more on Pearl Street in the early Republic, see Blackmar, *Manhattan for Rent,* 23, 82–84; Albion, *Rise of New York Port,* 43, 63, 280; Blumin, *Emergence of the Middle Class,* 78–83, 86; Johnson and Wilentz, *Kingdom of Matthias,* 18–19; Kouwenhoven, *Historical Portrait of New York,* 132; Wyatt-Brown, *Lewis Tappan,* 41–77.

51. Burrows and Wallace, *Gotham,* 334, 336, 337.

52. Ibid., 338.

53. Lambert, *Travels Through Canada,* 2:49, 55–56. Biographical information on Lambert, apart from his travel narratives, is limited. For a brief summary of his life, see Roy, "Lambert, John"; Rock, *Artisans of the New Republic,* 79; Burrows and Wallace, *Gotham,* 338, 339, 373, 374, 411–12; Wilentz, *Chants Democratic,* 27.

54. Lambert, *Travels Through Canada,* 2:295. See also the New York *American Citizen,* New York *Public Advertiser,* and New York *Spectator,* all 26 December 1807. For discussion of the embargo as foreign policy, see Kaplan, *Entangling Alliances with None;* Perkins, *Prologue to War;* Sears, *Jefferson and the Embargo;* Spivak, *Jefferson's English Crisis.* For an overview of the economic impact of the embargo and the War of 1812 on early American commerce, see Lipsey, "U.S. Foreign Trade." See also Gilchrist, *Growth of the Seaport Cities.* On 30 September 1802, the *American Citizen and General Advertiser* became simply the *American Citizen.*

55. Lambert, *Travels Through Canada,* 2:294–95.

56. New York *American Citizen,* 1 January 1808; *Minutes of the Common Council,* 4:703, 5:79. For a discussion of poor and debtor relief in New York during the embargo, see Cray, *Paupers and Poor Relief;* Daitsman, "Labor and the Welfare State"; Folsom, *Impatient Armies of the Poor;* Mohl, "Poverty in Early America."

57. Duyckinck to Carey, 1 March and 30 May 1808, Lea & Febiger Records (Collection 227B), box 62, HSP.

58. Carey sent Duyckinck several letters in response to Duyckinck's shipments in March and May 1808. The surviving copies of the letters, hastily recorded by a clerk in a letter book, are mostly illegible. See Carey to Duyckinck, 3, 21 March, 9 May 1808, Mathew Carey Letterbook, vol. 25, ibid.

59. Green, "Rise of Book Publishing," 96–98.

60. New York City record of assessment, Manhattan, First Ward, 1815, Municipal Archives of the City of New York. For the comparative tax data on printers, booksellers, bookbinders, and publishers in New York, see Smith, "World the Printers Made," 116–19.

61. For data on the growth of the publishing trade in late eighteenth- and early nineteenth-century New York, see Smith, "World the Printers Made," 43; Burrows and Wallace, *Gotham,* 338; Morgan, *Evolution of a Trade Association,* 32.

62. Evert Duyckinck Daybook, Duyckinck Family Papers, vols. 20–32, NYPL. Duyckinck's records for 1803 are incomplete owing to an epidemic of Yellow Fever that forced New Yorkers to evacuate the city. Vols. 27–32 are fragments of the overall business records.

63. Green, "Rise of Book Publishing," 87–88; Ford and Skeel, *Mason Locke Weems,* 2:15, 64–65, 113.

64. Green, "Rise of Book Publishing," 89–90; Shipton, *Isaiah Thomas,* 50; Davidson, *Revolution and the Word,* 81.

65. Remer, *Printers and Men of Capital,* 82–83.

66. Charvat, *Profession of Authorship,* 40–41.

67. "Labor Indenture of George Lovejoy to Evert Duyckinck," 22 January 1813, Duyckinck Family Papers, box 62, NYPL. Duyckinck entered into the contract with Ezekiel Lovejoy of Stratford, Connecticut, binding George to Duyckinck's shop for four years, one month, and fourteen days.

68. Evert Duyckinck Daybook, 10 April 1817, ibid., vol. 29. For Lovejoy's location, see *Longworth's Pocket Almanack*.

69. Evert Duyckinck Daybook, Duyckinck Family Papers, vols. 20–32, NYPL.

70. Green, "Rise of Book Publishing," 121.

71. Evert Duyckinck Daybook, Duyckinck Family Papers, vols. 20–32, NYPL.

72. Green, "Rise of Book Publishing," 88.

73. Baltimore *Patriot & Mercantile Advertiser*, 21 May 1818. For work on Kinnersley's large, annotated, and illustrated subscription Bible (and others like it), see Bentley, "Holy Pirates," 381–82; Tebbel, *History of Book Publishing*, 183.

74. See Baltimore *Patriot & Mercantile Advertiser*, 11, 19 December 1821, and 6 March and 22 May 1822.

75. Evert Duyckinck Daybook, 9 April 1817, Duyckinck Family Papers, vol. 29, NYPL.

76. Baltimore *Patriot & Mercantile Advertiser*, 8 April 1817. According to the account books, Duyckinck's first shipment to Betts, totaling $292.93, was delivered to Baltimore on 8 January aboard the sloop *Hiram*. See Evert Duyckinck Daybook, 8 January 1817, Duyckinck Family Papers, vol. 29, NYPL.

77. Baltimore *Patriot & Mercantile Advertiser*, 16 October 1817.

78. See Evert Duyckinck Daybook, 8 January, 20 February, 14 March, 9, 19 April, 2, 14, 26 May, 1, 14, 29 July, 16 August, 3, 5, 10, 23, 30 September, and 7 October 1817, Duyckinck Family Papers, vol. 29, NYPL.

79. Baltimore *Patriot & Mercantile Advertiser*, 29 April 1817. Between March 1817 and March 1820, Betts ran thirteen original ads in this newspaper; there were thirty-one total ads during this period, but many were repeats. Each ad covered the intermediate shipments. See ibid., 25 March, 8, 23, 29 April, 18 July, 16 October, 12 November 1817; 10 January, 6 March, 20, 22 April, 21 May, 11 July 1818; 15, 18 March, 17 June 1820; 11, 19 December 1821; 6 March and 22 May 1822. For Duyckinck's shipments to Betts, see Evert Duyckinck Daybook, Duyckinck Family Papers, vols. 29 and 30, NYPL.

80. See Evert Duyckinck Daybook, 20 February, 14 March, 9, 19 April 1817, Duyckinck Family Papers, vol. 29, NYPL. The 20 February shipment was $664.00, 14 March was $323.33, 9 April was $810.39, and 19 April was $252. Duyckinck did not publish his own edition of Euclid until 1824. The edition he shipped to Betts was one that he received in an exchange with another publisher.

81. Evert Duyckinck Daybook, ibid., vols. 29–32.

82. Sanxay to Duyckinck, 19 January 1830, ibid., box 60.

83. Evert Duyckinck Daybook, ibid., vols. 31, 32; Evert Duyckinck Ledger, ibid., vol. 38.

84. Strohm, "J. W. Randolph," 547. For more detailed statistics on Duyckinck's involvement with southern booksellers, see Smith, "'Elements of Useful Knowledge,'" 532–34.

85. Charleston *City Gazette and Daily Advertiser*, 1 August 1817.

86. Smith, "'Elements of Useful Knowledge,'" 532–34. The Hunt and Gibbes Hunt incomplete records are due to the fragmented nature of the Duyckinck daybooks. In the case of William Gibbes Hunt, his entry as a commission agent was recorded on 28 March 1820, at the very end of vol. 30, which concluded with 1 April 1820. Frustratingly, the final amount listed is illegible. In the case of William S. Hunt, only one entry exists in vol. 31, and it lists him as a commission agent without a summary of his stock or the amount received. See Evert Duyckinck Daybook, Duyckinck Family Papers, vols. 30 and 31, NYPL.

87. Evert Duyckinck Daybook, 17, 18 May 1827, 10 May and 29 December 1828, Duyckinck Family Papers, vol. 31, NYPL. For work on the Erie Canal, see Howe, *What Hath God Wrought*, 117–20, 138, 216–18, 221, 237–38, 241, 246, 252; Sellers, *Market Revolution*, 41–43, 79, 103, 110, 112, 130, 132, 158, 185, 195, 216–20, 227–28, 230–31, 237, 285, 293, 391–92. See also Cornog, *Birth of Empire*; Sheriff, *Artificial River*; Shaw, *Erie Water West*; Larson, *Internal Improvement*.

88. "Autobiography of David Bruce, or Then and Now," n.d., miscellaneous manuscripts filed under David Bruce, NYHS. For David Bruce and his life as a printer and type founder in New York, see Stevens, *New York Typographical Union*, 37–39; Lause, *Some Degree of Power*, 25, 51–52, 116–17; Pretzer, "'Paper Cap and Inky Apron.'"

89. "George F. Hopkins," Printers' File, AAS.

90. Davidson, *Revolution and the Word*, 80.

91. Remer, *Printers and Men of Capital*, 79–82; Green, "Rise of Book Publishing," 83–84; Keyes, "Early American Advertising," 81–82.

92. Evert Duyckinck Exchange Book, Duyckinck Family Papers, vol. 35, NYPL.

93. Duyckinck to West, 16 December 1799, West, Richardson & Lord Business Records, box 2, AAS.

94. Deed for no. 56 Bleecker Street, 2 November 1829, Duyckinck Family Papers, box 62, NYPL. According to city tax records, Duyckinck's personal wealth had steadily increased during the economic crises, rising from $2,500 total claimed property in 1808 to $10,000 in 1816. Unfortunately, the ambiguity of the tax assessments does not allow any further inquiry, as many men—Duyckinck included—did not differentiate between personal property and inventory. Record of tax assessment for the City of New York, First Ward, 1808, 1809, 1813, 1815, 1816, Municipal Archives. First Ward records do not exist for 1810, 1811, and 1814.

95. Blackmar, *Manhattan for Rent*, 164; Bushman, *Refinement of America*, 355–56.

96. Burrows and Wallace, *Gotham*, 458–59; Williams and Disturnell, *New York as It Is*, 12.

97. Blackmar, *Manhattan for Rent*, 99–103, 131, 133, 171–73; Rosebrock, *Counting-House Days*, 31; Wall, "Separation of the Home," 186–87. For data on men in the trade with separate residences, see Smith, "World the Printers Made," 127–28.

98. "List of silverware & furniture in the Estate of Evert Duyckinck," June 1837, Duyckinck Family Papers, box 62, NYPL. This document lists only the type of book rather than the actual title. For material culture in the early Republic, see Jaffee, *New Nation of Goods*, x; Bushman, *Refinement of America*, 256–57, 265. See also Cole and Williamson, *American Carpet Manufacture*.

99. See Anderson, *Mahogany*, esp. 184–209, 250–92.

100. Of the eighteen firms at the sale, ten were from Philadelphia, two were from Boston, two were from Hartford, and two were from New York. See Peaslee and Cowperthwait, *First Day's Catalogue*, BDSDS.1830F, Broadsides Collection, AAS.

101. While he remained active in the firm until the spring of 1830, Duyckinck turned over the day-to-day activities of his business to Orville A. Roorbach, a former apprentice, in 1825. For Roorbach's apprenticeship term with Duyckinck, see *Library Journal*, August 1897, 385.

102. Sanxay to Duyckinck, 21 May 1830, Skinner to Duyckinck, 21 June 1830, Duyckinck Family Papers, box 60, NYPL.

103. In August 1817, Duyckinck asked John and James Harper to print two thousand copies of Seneca's *Morals*. For Duyckinck's record of this transaction, see Evert Duyckinck Daybook, 5 August 1817, ibid., vol. 29; prospectus of *Seneca's Morals*, James Harper Papers, series 3, box 5, Rare Book and Manuscript Library, Columbia University. Harper scholars frequently mention this as a momentous occasion for the young brothers. See Casper, "Case Study: Harper & Brothers," 128.For the standard biography of the Harpers, see Exman, *House of Harper*. For a discussion of the reorganization of labor in the nineteenth century, see Green, "Rise of Book Publishing," 113–27; Sokoloff, "Transition from the Artisanal Shop." For a discussion of the shift to plate usage, see Winship, "Printing with Plates."

Afterword

1. New York *Commercial Advertiser*, 21 November 1833.

2. Diary of Evert Augustus Duyckinck, 23 November 1833, Duyckinck Family Papers, vol. 5, NYPL.

3. Rorabaugh, *Craft Apprentice*, 76–77.

4. [John] West and [John] Trow, "Statistics," in *Booksellers' Advertiser, and Monthly Register of New Publications, American and Foreign*, January 1834, 41.

5. See Lause, *Some Degree of Power*. For a discussion of these broad market and labor shifts, see Rockman, *Scraping By*; Johnson, *Shopkeeper's Millennium*; Laurie, *Artisans into Workers*. For the New York context, see Wilentz, *Chants Democratic*; Gilje, *Road to Mobocracy*; Rock, *Artisans of the New Republic*; Greenberg, *Advocating the Man*.

6. Francis, "Reminiscences of Printers," 260.

7. Swords to Thomas, 25 May 1830, box 6 (1812–1959), AAS Archives, AAS.

8. Bookseller advertisement, *A Narrative of the Expedition to Botany Bay* (New York: Reprinted by T. and J. Swords, 1789), AC901.M33 vol. 40, no. 4, Special Collections, University of

Virginia; "Thomas and James Swords," Printers' File, AAS; *In Memory of James R. Swords*; Cold-well, "T. & J. Swords, Printers," 211–12; Johnston, "T. & J. Swords," 16; Nord, "Republican Litera-ture"; AhKao and Wolfe, "American Bibliographical Notes." For more on the Swords brothers' partner, James Robertson, and on their career in Canada, see Robertson, "Loyalist Printers"; Tremaine and Fleming, *Bibliography of Canadian Imprints*, 615; Thomas, *Printing in America*, 1:192–93, 313, 2:91–92, 210, 126–27. The American Antiquarian Society possesses a photostat of the Swords brothers' first publication, a one-page broadside commemorating their father's life. See "Thomas Swords, born at Marybarrow (Queen's County), Ireland, on Sunday, June 19, 1738:—Died at New-York, on Sunday, January 16, 1780," Broadsides Collection, AAS. For the estimate of the Loyalist diaspora, see Jasanoff, "Other Side of Revolution," 208.

9. "Thomas Swords," Printers' File, AAS; Coldwell, "T. & J. Swords, Printers," 211–12; Johnston, "T. & J. Swords," 17. For a list of books published by the Swords brothers, see Swords and Swords, *Books Printed and Sold*, Dated Pamphlets Collection, AAS. For work on the emer-gence of literary societies in early New York, see Bender, *New York Intellect*, 32–33; Shields, *Civil Tongues and Polite Letters*, 322–23; Waterman, *Republic of Intellect*. For the Swords brothers and the *New York Magazine*, see Nord, *Communities of Journalism*, 175–98.

10. Freeman, *Affairs of Honor*, 264.

11. Swords to Thomas, 25 May 1830, box 6, AAS Archives, AAS.

12. William B. Gilley, probated will, Probated Wills, J1043–92, Liber 67, NYSA.

13. New York *Commercial Advertiser*, 10 February 1831.

14. William Burgess, probated will, Probated Wills, 25 April 1832, J1043–92, Liber 68, NYSA.

15. Baldwin to Messrs. Gale and Seaton of Washington, D.C., 13 April 1832, Christopher Colum-bus Baldwin Letterbook, octavo vol. 5, Baldwin Papers, AAS. For background on Baldwin, see Larkin and Sloat, *Place in My Chronicle*. For more on the drive by historical societies to collect docu-ments, see Henle, "Preserving the Past"; Freeman, *Affairs of Honor*, 262–88.

16. Baldwin to Niles, Esq., of Baltimore, 18 April 1832; Baldwin to Moore, 23 May 1832; Baldwin to M'Farland, 24 May 1832; Baldwin to Duane, 17 September 1832; and Baldwin to Wood-ward, 31 October 1832, all in Baldwin Letterbook no. 5, Baldwin Papers, AAS. For work on Gales & Seaton and the *National Intelligencer*, see Ames, *History of the National Intelligencer*. For a recent biography of William Duane, see Little, *Transoceanic Radical*.

17. Baldwin to Swords, 19 April and 3 May 1832, Baldwin Letterbook no. 5, Baldwin Papers, AAS.

18. Henkin, *City Reading*, ix, x. For the variety of print in mid-nineteenth-century New York and elsewhere, see Cohen, Gilfoyle, and Lefkowitz Horowitz, *Flash Press*; Cohen, *Murder of Helen Jewett*; Erickson, "Welcome to Sodom."

19. For the evolution of early American reading habits, see Hall, *Cultures of Print*, 36–78.

20. Putnam's essay appeared in the *Booksellers' Advertiser, and Monthly Register of New Publi-cations, American and Foreign*, March 1836, 1, quoted in Remer, *Printers and Men of Capital*, 149–52.

21. For a broad overview of these changes in the 1820s and 1830s, see Howe, *What Hath God Wrought*, 203–42. For an intensive study of the publishing trade in antebellum America, see Zboray, *Fictive People*. For papermaking in nineteenth-century America, see McGaw, *Most Wonder-ful Machine*. For the trade in the 1840s and beyond, see Casper et al., *Industrial Book*.

22. Remer, *Printers and Men of Capital*, 151.

23. Howe, *What Hath God Wrought*, 227.

24. Gross, "Introduction: An Extensive Republic," 6; Loughran, *Republic in Print*, xviii–xix.

25. Francis, "Reminiscences of Printers," 265.

BIBLIOGRAPHY

....

Primary Sources

MANUSCRIPT COLLECTIONS

American Antiquarian Society (Worcester, Mass.) (AAS)
  AAS Archives, 1812–Present
  Book Trades Collection, 1726–1939
  Broadsides Collection
  Christopher Columbus Baldwin Papers, 1816–1835
  Dated Books Collection
  Dated Pamphlets Collection
  Printers' File
  Samuel Loudon Papers, 1785–1790
  West, Richardson & Lord Business Records, 1792–1855
  William Cobbett Account Book, 1796–1800

Columbia University, Rare Book and Manuscript Library (New York, N.Y.)
  Harper & Brothers Records, 1817–1829
  James Harper Papers, 1800–1925
  Typographical Library Records

Historical Society of Pennsylvania (Philadelphia, Pa.) (HSP)
  Booksellers' Company of Philadelphia, Minutes, 1802–1803
  Edward Carey Gardiner Collection
  Lea & Febiger Records, 1785–1982 (bulk 1796–1882)
  Loudoun Mansion (Germantown) Papers, 1696–1939
  Meredith Papers
  Samuel Campbell Collection
  Simon Gratz Collection
  Stauffer Collection

John Hay Library, Brown University (Providence, R.I.)
  Broadsides Collection

Library Company of Philadelphia (Philadelphia, Pa.) (LCP)
  Arts and Artifacts Collection
  Binny and Ronaldson Papers (McAllister Collection)
  Mathew Carey Collection, 1802–1826
  McNeil Americana Collection
  Michael Zinman Collection of Early American Imprints
  Rare Books Collection
  Robert Aitken Papers
  Young and Woodward Business Papers (McAllister Collection)

Library of Congress (Washington, D.C.)
  George F. Hopkins Correspondence
  George Washington Papers, Series 4
  Robert Moore Papers, 1813–1817

Massachusetts Historical Society (Boston, Mass.) (MHS)
  Winthrop Papers (Bowdoin-Temple Papers)

Municipal Archives of the City of New York, Surrogate Court of New York, 31 Chamber Street
(New York, N.Y.)
  Jury Lists, New York City, 1816, 1819, 1821
  Record of Assessment, Manhattan, 1808–1830

New-York Historical Society (New York, N.Y.) (NYHS)
  Duane Family Papers, 1700–1945
  John Ward Fenno Papers
  Miscellaneous Account Books and Book Inventories
  Miscellaneous Manuscripts Filed Under David Bruce
  Record of Assessment, Manhattan
  Tontine Coffee House Records

New York Public Library: Astor, Lenox and Tilden Foundations (New York, N.Y.) (NYPL)
  Carl H. Pforzheimer Collection of Shelley and His Circle
  Joseph Johnson Letterbook, 1795–1810
  Manuscripts and Archives Division
  Duyckinck Family Papers, 1793–1889
  Noah Webster Papers, 1764–1833
  Philip Schuyler Papers
  Thomas Addis Emmet Collection

New York Society Library (New York, N.Y.) (NYSL)
  First Charging Ledger, 1789–1792

New York State Archives (Albany, N.Y.) (NYSA)
  Probated Wills, 1787–1829
  Records of Wills and Probates,
      1787–1822
  Surrogate's Court Record of Wills and Probates, 1787–1879

New York State Library (Albany, N.Y.)
  Miscellaneous Manuscript Collection

Ohio Historical Society (Columbus, Ohio)
  Winthrop Sargent Papers, 1776–1865

NEWSPAPERS AND PERIODICALS
  Connecticut
  Hartford: *American Mercury; Connecticut Courant and Weekly Intelligencer*
  Litchfield: *Farmer's Monitor; Monitor*
  Middletown: *Middlesex Gazette*
  New Haven: *Connecticut Journal*
  New London: *Bee; Connecticut Gazette*
  Norwich: *Courier; Connecticut Centinel; Packet and the Connecticut, Massachusetts, New-
      Hampshire, and Rhode-Island Weekly Advertiser; Packet, or The Country Journal*
  Windham: *Herald*

  Delaware
  Wilmington: *Mirror of the Times General Advertiser*

District of Columbia
Cabinet; Washington Federalist; National Intelligencer

Georgia
Augusta: *Chronicle*
Savannah: *Georgia Gazette*

Maine
Portland: *Jenks' Portland Gazette; Gazette*

Maryland
Baltimore: *Federal Gazette; Federal Gazette & Baltimore Daily Advertiser; Patriot & Mercantile Advertiser; Republican, or Anti-Democrat;
Telegraph*
Fredericktown: *Hornet; Republican Gazette*
Hagerstown: *Maryland Herald and Elizabeth-town Advertiser*

Massachusetts
Boston: *Boston Gazette; Columbian Sentinel; Commercial Gazette; Continental Journal
and Weekly Advertiser; Daily Advertiser; Herald of Freedom; Independent Chronicle
and Universal Advertiser; Independent Ledger and the American Advertiser; J. Russell's Gazette, Commercial and Political; Massachusetts Centinel; Massachusetts
Magazine, or Monthly Museum; Massachusetts Mercury; New-England Palladium;
Patriot*
Brookfield: *Political Repository*
Cambridge: *New England Chronicle, or Essex Gazette*
Dedham: *Columbian Minerva*
Leominster: *Telescope, or American Herald*
New Bedford: *Columbian Courier; Columbian Orator*
Newburyport: *Essex Journal and the Massachusetts and New-Hampshire General Advertiser; Herald and Country Gazette*
Pittsfield: *Sun*
Salem: *Impartial Register; Salem Gazette*
Worcester: *Thomas's Massachusetts Spy, or The Worcester Gazette*

New Hampshire
Concord: *Courier of New Hampshire*
Keene: *New-Hampshire Sentinel*
Portsmouth: *New-Hampshire Gazette; New-Hampshire Gazette, or Fowle's New-
Hampshire Gazette and the General Advertiser; United States Oracle, and Portsmouth Advertiser*
Walpole: *Farmer's Weekly Museum, or Literary Gazette; New Hampshire Journal, or
Farmer's Weekly Museum*

New Jersey
Elizabethtown: *New-Jersey Journal, and Political Intelligencer*
Newark: *Centinel of Freedom*
Trenton: *New-Jersey Gazette*

New York
Albany: *Argus; Centinel; Chronicle; Daily Advertiser; Gazette; Plough Boy and Journal of
the Board of Agriculture; Register*
Ballston Spa: *Gazette; Independent American*

Cooperstown: *Otsego Herald, or Western Advertiser*
Fishkill: *New-York Packet; New-York Packet, and the American Advertiser*
Goshen: *Orange County Patriot*
Hudson: *Northern Whig; Bee*
Kingston: *Plebeian*
New York: *American Citizen; American Citizen and General Advertiser; American Magazine; Booksellers' Advertiser; Bowery Republican; Le Bulletin; Chronicle Express; Commercial Advertiser; Corrector; Daily Advertiser; Daily Items, for Mechanics; Diary, or Loudon's Register; Herald; Independent Gazette, or The New-York Journal; Independent Gazette, or The New-York Journal Revived; Independent Journal, or The General Advertiser; Independent New-York Gazette; Independent Republican; Journal, and State Gazette; Library Journal; Loudon's New-York Packet; Mercantile Advertiser; Minerva; Monthly Magazine, and American Review; Morning Chronicle; New-York Daily Gazette; New-York Evening Post; New-York Gazette; New-York Gazette and General Advertiser; New-York Gazette: and the Weekly Mercury; New-York Gazette, or The Weekly Post-Boy; New-York Journal; New-York Journal and Daily Patriotic Register; New-York Journal and State Gazette; New-York Journal, or The General Advertiser; New-York Journal, or The Weekly Register; New-York Mercury; New-York Morning Post; New-York Morning Post, and Daily Advertiser; New-York Packet; Public Advertiser; Publisher's Weekly; Rivington's New-York Gazetteer, or The Connecticut, Hudson's River, New-Jersey, and Quebec Weekly Advertiser; Shamrock; Spectator; Times; Weekly Inspector; Weekly Visitor*
Norwich: *Republican Agriculturalist*
Poughkeepsie: *Northern Post; Country Journal*

Pennsylvania
Carlisle: *Carlisle Gazette; Carlisle Gazette, and the Western Repository of Knowledge; Kline's Carlisle Weekly Gazette; Spirit of the Times & Carlisle Gazette*
Harrisburg: *Oracle of Dauphin and Harrisburgh Advertiser*
Philadelphia: *American Museum; Aurora, and General Advertiser; Federal Gazette and Philadelphia Evening Post; Freeman's Journal, or The North-American Intelligencer; Gazette of the United States; Grojan's Philadelphia Public-Sale Report; Independent Gazetteer; Pennsylvania Herald; Pennsylvania Journal; Pennsylvania Packet, and Daily Advertiser; Pennsylvania Packet, and General Advertiser; Philadelphia Gazette and Daily Advertiser; Poulson's American Daily Advertiser*
Wilkes-Barre: *Gleaner*

Rhode Island
Newport: *Newport Mercury; Rhode-Island Republican*
Providence: *Patriot; Providence Gazette; Providence Journal, and Town and Country Advertiser; Rhode-Island American; United States Chronicle*

South Carolina
Charleston: *Carolina Gazette; City Gazette and Daily Advertiser; Columbian Herald; Columbian Herald, or The Patriotic Courier of North America; Morning Post and Daily Advertiser; South-Carolina State Gazette, and Timothy's Daily Advertiser; Times*
Georgetown: *Gazette*

Vermont
Bennington: *News-Letter; Vermont Gazette*
Brattleboro: *Federal Galaxy; Reporter*

Burlington: *Vermont Centinel*
Peacham: *Green Mountain Patriot*
Rutland: *Herald*
Windsor: *Spooner's Vermont Journal*

Virginia
Alexandria: *Expositor, for the Country; Times, and the District of Columbia Daily Advertiser*

Other Printed Primary Sources

The Acts and Resolves, Public and Private, of the Province of the Massachusetts Bay, to Which Are Prefixed the Charters of the Province, with Historical and Explanatory Notes, and an Appendix, Resolves, Etc., 1777–1778. Vol. 20. Boston: Wright & Potter, 1918.

Adams, John. *Diary and Autobiography of John Adams.* Edited by Lyman H. Butterfield. Vol. 2. Cambridge: Belknap Press of Harvard University Press, 1961.

———. *Papers of John Adams.* Vol. 5, *August 1776–March 1778.* Edited by Robert J. Taylor. Cambridge: Harvard University Press, 2006.

Archaeologica Americana: Transactions and Collections of the American Antiquarian Society. Vol. 5. Worcester: Printed for the Society by William Manning, 1820.

Armstrong, Amy. "On the Commotions of a New-York May-Day." *Monthly Magazine, and American Review for the Year 1799* (New York: T. and J. Swords, 1800), vol. 1, 84.

Austin, James T., ed. *The Life of Elbridge Gerry, with Contemporary Letters.* Vol. 1. Boston: Wells and Lilly, 1828.

Bingham, Caleb. *The American Preceptor: Being a New Selection of Lessons for Reading and Speaking.* Boston: Manning and Loring, 1794.

———. *The American Preceptor: Being a New Selection of Lessons, for Reading and Speaking.* New York: Published by Evert Duyckinck, John C. Totten, Printer, 1817.

———. *The Columbian Orator: Containing a Variety of Original and Selected Pieces; Together with Rules; Calculated to Improve Youth and Others in the Ornamental and Useful Art of Eloquence.* Boston: Printed by John West for the author, 1797.

———. *The Young Lady's Accidence, or A Short and Easy Introduction to English Grammar.* Boston: Printed by Greenleaf and Freeman, 1785.

Boucher, Jonathan. *A View of the Causes and Consequences of the American Revolution: in Thirteen Discourses, Preached in North America between the Years 1763 and 1775: With an Historical Preface.* London: Printed for G. G. and J. Robinson, 1797.

Calendar of Historical Manuscripts Relating to the War of the Revolution: In the Office of the Secretary of State, Albany, N.Y. Vol. 1. Albany: Weed, Parsons and Co., 1868.

Campbell, Samuel. *Samuel Campbell's Sale Catalogue of Books, for 1794. Comprehending above Fifty Thousand Volumes, in Arts, Sciences, and Miscellaneous Literature; Forming a General Assortment of the Principal Authors, Ancient and Modern.* New York: Published by Samuel Campbell, 1794.

[Carey, Mathew]. *To the Booksellers of the United States.* New York, 1802.

Caritat, Hocquet. *The Feast of Reason and the Flow of the Soul. A New *explanatory Catalogue of H. Caritat's General & Increasing Circulating Library. Intended Also to Answer the Purpose of a Sale Catalogue, Respecting Those Marked with a Star (*), Which H. Caritat Has an Assortment Of, for Sale, in His Book-Store, No. 153, Broad-Way.* New York: Printed by M. L. & W. A. Davis, 1799.

The Charter, Bye-Laws, and Names of the Members of the New-York Society Library. With a Catalogue of the Books Belonging to the Said Library. New York: Printed by Hugh Gaine, 1789.

Clarke, John, and James Hardie. *An Introduction to the Making of Latin, Comprising, After an Easy, Compendious Method, the Substance of the Latin Syntax, with Proper English Examples, to Which Is Subjoined a Succinct Account of the Affairs of Ancient Greece and Rome, with Rules for the Gender of Nouns.* New York: Printed by John C. Totten for Evert Duyckinck, 1811.

Cobb, Lyman. *Cobb's New North American Reader, or Fifth Reading Book.* New York: Caleb Bartlett, 1845.

Collections of the New-York Historical Society for the Year 1902. New York: Printed for the Society, 1902.

The Constitution of the State of New-York. Fishkill: Printed by Samuel Loudon, 1777.

The Constitutions of the United States, According to the Latest Amendments, to Which Are Prefixed, the Declaration of Independence, and the Federal Constitution, with the Amendments. Philadelphia: Printed for Robert Campbell, 1800.

Cordier, Mathurin, and James Hardie. *Corderii Colloquia, or Cordery's Colloquies, with a Translation of the First Forty, to Which Is Added, a Vocabulary.* New York: E. Duyckinck, 1816.

Davies, Benjamin. *A New and Concise System of Book-Keeping, According to the Italian Method of Double Entry, Adapted to the Commerce of the United States.* Philadelphia: Benjamin Johnson, 1819.

Davis, John. *Travels of Four Years and a Half in the United States of America: During 1798, 1799, 1800, 1801, and 1802.* Edited by Alfred J. Morrison. New York: H. Holt, 1909.

Defoe, Daniel. *The Wonderful Life and Most Surprising Adventures of That Renowned Hero, Robinson Crusoe, Who Lived Twenty-Eight Years on an Uninhabited Island. Which He Afterwards Colonized.* New York: Printed by Hurtin & Commardinger, for E. Duyckinck & Co., 1795.

Dilworth, Thomas. *A New Guide to the English Tongue.* Brooklyn: Printed by T. Kirk for E. Duyckinck, 1802.

———. *A New Guide to the English Tongue in Five Parts.* New York: Published for E. Duyckinck, D. D. Smith, W. B. Gilley, and G. Long, 1820.

———. *The Schoolmaster's Assistant: Being a Compendium of Arithmetic, Both Practical and Theoretical.* New York: Printed by M'Farlane & Long for Evert Duyckinck, 1806.

———. *The Schoolmaster's Assistant, Being a Compendium of Arithmetic, Both Practical and Theoretical.* New York: E. Duyckinck, 1810.

———. *The Schoolmaster's Assistant: Being a Compendium of Arithmetic, Both Practical and Theoretical.* New York: E. Duyckinck and R. M'Dermut, 1810.

———. *The Schoolmaster's Assistant: Being a Compendium of Arithmetic, Both Practical and Theoretical in Five Parts.* New York: Printed by Mott & Lyon for S. Campbell, E. Duyckinck, and Co., 1796.

d'Ivernois, Francis. *Historical and Political Survey of the Losses Sustained by the French Nation, in Population, Agriculture, Colonies, Manufactures, and Commerce, in Consequence of the Revolution and the Present War. From the French of Sir Francis d'Ivernois. To Which Is Added, a Supplement.* London: printed for J. Wright, 1799.

Duer, William Alexander. *New-York as It Was During the Latter Part of the Last Century: An Anniversary Address Delivered Before the St. Nicholas Society of the City of New York, December 1st, 1848.* New York: Stanford and Swords, 1849.

Duncan, William. *The New-York Directory, and Register, for the Year 1791: Illustrated with a New and Accurate Plan of the City, and Part of Long-Island, Exactly Laid Down, Agreeable to the Latest Survey.* New York: T. and J. Swords, 1791.

———. *The New-York Directory, and Register, for the Year 1792: Illustrated with a New and Accurate Plan of the City, and Part of Long-Island, Exactly Laid Down, Agreeably to the Latest Survey*. New York: T. and J. Swords, 1792.

Duncan, William, and Cornelius Tiebout. *The New-York Directory, and Register, for the Year 1795. Illustrated with a New and Accurate Plan*. New York: Printed for the editor, by T. and J. Swords, 1795.

Fenno, John Ward. *Supplementary Catalogue, Consisting of Books, Imported from London, per the Latest Arrivals, by J. W. Fenno, No. 141, Hanover-Square, October, 1800*. New York: Printed by John Furman, 1800.

Force, Peter, ed. *American Archives: A Documentary History of the United States of America, from the Declaration of Independence, July 4, 1776, to the Definitive Treaty of Peace with Great Britain, September 3, 1783*. Vol. 3. Fifth series. Washington, D.C.: Prepared and Published Under Authority of Acts of Congress, 1853.

Ford, Paul Leicester, and Emily Ellsworth Ford Skeel, eds. *Mason Locke Weems, His Works and Ways, in Three Volumes*. Vol. 2. New York, 1929.

Francis, John W. "Reminiscences of Printers, Authors, and Booksellers in New-York." *International Magazine of Literature, Art, and Science* 5 (February 1852): 253–66.

Franklin, Benjamin. *The Life of Dr. Benjamin Franklin*. New York: Printed and sold by T. and J. Swords, 1794.

Franks, David C. *The New-York Directory, Containing a Valuable and Well Calculated Almanack*. New York: Printed by Shepard Kollock, 1786.

Gaine, Hugh. *The Journals of Hugh Gaine, Printer*. Edited by Paul Leicester Ford. 2 vols. New York: Dodd, Mead, 1902.

[———]. *An Oration Delivered Before the Booksellers Convened in New-York, at Their First Literary Fair, June 4th, 1802*. New York, 1802.

Galloway, Joseph. *A Candid Examination of the Mutual Claims of Great-Britain, and the Colonies: With a Plan of Accommodation on Constitutional Principles*. New York: Printed by James Rivington, 1775.

Gifford, John. *A Letter to the Earl of Lauderdale, Containing Strictures on His Lordship's Letters, to the Peers of Scotland*. London: printed at the Anti-Jacobin Press, by T. Crowder for T. N. Longman and O. Rees, 1800.

Gordon, William. *The History of the Rise, Progress, and Establishment, of the Independence of the United States of America: Including an Account of the Late War; and of the Thirteen Colonies, from Their Origin to That Period*. London: Printed for the Author, 1788.

———. *The History of the Rise, Progress, and Establishment, of the Independence of the United States of America: Including an Account of the Late War; and of the Thirteen Colonies, from Their Origin to That Period. By William Gordon, D.D. In Three Volumes*. New York: Printed by Hodge, Allen, and Campbell, 1789.

———. "Letters of the Reverend William Gordon, Historian of the American Revolution, 1770–1799." Edited by Worthington C. Ford. *Proceedings of the Massachusetts Historical Society* 63 (October 1929–June 1930): 303–613.

Harris, Thaddeus Mason. *A Discourse, Delivered at Dorchester, Dec. 29, 1799: Being the Lord's Day After Hearing the Distressing Intelligence of the Death of General George Washington, Late President of the United States, and Commander in Chief of the American Armies*. Charlestown, Mass.: Printed by Samuel Etheridge, 1800.

Hawkesworth, John. *A New Voyage, Round the World, in the Years 1768, 1769, 1770, and 1771*. New York: Printed by James Rivington for William Aikman, 1774.

Hench, John B., ed. "Letters of John Fenno and John Ward Fenno, 1779–1800; Part 1: 1779–1790." *Proceedings of the American Antiquarian Society* 89, no. 2 (1979): 299–368.

———. "Letters of John Fenno and John Ward Fenno, 1779–1800; Part 2: 1792–1800." *Proceedings of the American Antiquarian Society* 90, no. 1 (1980): 163–234.

Hodge, Robert, Thomas Allen, and Samuel Campbell. *The New-York Directory, and Register, for the Year 1790: Illustrated with an Accurate and Elegant Plan of the City of New-York, and Part of Long-Island, Including the Suburbs, with All the Streets, Lanes, Public Buildings, Wharves.* New York: Hodge, Allen, and Campbell, 1790.

[Inglis, Charles]. *The Deceiver Unmasked, or Loyalty and Interest United: In Answer to a Pamphlet Entitled Common Sense.* New York: Printed by Samuel Loudon, 1776.

In Memory of James R. Swords: Notes of a Meeting of the New York Publishers' Association, and Others Connected with the Trade, at Appletons' Building, Broadway, June 20. New York: New York Publishers' Association, 1855.

Journal of the Assembly of the State of New-York at Their Eleventh Session, Begun and Holden at Poughkeepsie in Dutchess County, the Ninth Day of January, 1788. Poughkeepsie: Printed for Samuel and John Loudon, printers to the State, 1788.

Journal of the Assembly of the State of New-York at Their Tenth Session, Begun and Holden in the City of New-York, the Twelfth Day of January, 1787. New York: Printed by Samuel and John Loudon, printers to the state, 1787.

Journal of the Assembly of the State of New-York at Their Twelfth Session, Begun and Holden at the City of Albany, the Eleventh Day of December, 1788. Albany: Printed by Samuel and John Loudon, printers to the state, 1789.

Keate, George. *An Account of the Pelew Islands, Situated in the Great South Sea. Composed from the Journals of Capt. Henry Wilson, and His Officers; Who, in August, 1783, Were There ship-Wrecked in the Antelope Packet.* New York: Printed by Tiebout & O'Brien, for Evert Duyckinck and Co., 1796.

Kurland, Philip B., and Ralph Lerner, eds. *The Founders' Constitution.* Vol. 1. Chicago: University of Chicago Press, 1987.

Lambert, John. *Travels Through Canada, and the United States of North America, in the Years 1806, 1807, and 1808, to Which Are Added Biographical Notices and Anecdotes of Some of the Leading Characters in the United States.* Vol. 2. London: Printed for C. Cradock and W. Joy, 1814.

Larkin, Jack, and Caroline Sloat, eds. *A Place in My Chronicle: A New Edition of the Diary of Christopher Columbus Baldwin, 1829–1835.* Worcester: American Antiquarian Society, 2010.

Longworth, David, ed. *Longworth's American Almanac, New York Register, and City Directory, for the Twenty-Sixth Year of American Independence.* New York: David Longworth, 1801.

———, ed. *Longworth's American Almanack, New York Register, and City Directory, for the Thirtieth Year of American Independence.* New York: David Longworth, 1805.

———, ed. *Longworth's Pocket Almanack, and New-York and United States Kalendar, for 1817.* New York: Published by David Longworth, 1817.

Longworth, David, and Abraham Shoemaker, eds. *Longworth's American Almanac, New-York Register, and City Directory, for the Twenty Seventh Year of American Independence.* New York: David Longworth, 1802.

———, eds. *Longworth's American Almanack, New-York Register, and City Directory, for the Twenty-Fifth Year of American Independence.* New York: Printed and published by D. Longworth, 1800.

———, eds. *Longworth's American Almanack, New-York Register, and City Directory, for the Twenty-Third Year of American Independence: Containing Most Things Useful in a Work of This Kind.* New York: Printed for the publisher, by T. & J. Swords, 1798.

Longworth, David, Abraham Shoemaker, J. Allen, and Elkanah Tisdale, eds. *Longworth's American Almanack, New-York Register, and City Directory, for the Twenty-Second*

Year of American Independence: Containing Most Things Useful in a Work of This Kind: Embellished with a View of the New Theatre. New York: Printed for the editor, by T. & J. Swords, 1797.

Lowrie, Walter, and Matthew St. Claire Clarke, eds. *American State Papers: Documents, Legislative and Executive, of the Congress of the United States, from the First Session of the First to the Third Session of the Thirteenth Congress. Finance.* Vol. 1, 1789–1802. Washington, D.C.: Gales and Seaton, 1832.

Macgowan, John. *The Life of Joseph, the Son of Israel. In Eight Books. Chiefly Designed to Allure Young Minds to a Love of the Sacred Scriptures.* New York: Printed by John Buel, for E. Duyckinck & Co., 1796.

M'Comb, John, and Cornelius Tiebout, eds. *The New York Directory, and Register, for the Year 1789: Illustrated with an Accurate and Elegant Plan of the City of New-York, and Part of Long-Island, Including the Suburbs, with All the Streets, Lanes, Public Buildings, Wharves, &c. Exactly Laid Down, from the Latest Survey.* New York: Printed for Hodge, Allen, and Campbell, 1789.

Minutes of the Common Council of the City of New York, 1784–1831. Vols. 4 and 5. New York: M. B. Brown, 1917.

Murray, Lindley. *An Abridgment of L. Murray's English Grammar with an Appendix.* New York: Printed for E. Duyckinck, by L. Nichols, 1804.

———. *English Exercises, Adapted to Murray's English Grammar: Designed for the Benefit of Private Learners, as Well as for the Use of Schools.* New York: Published by Evert Duyckinck, 1808.

———. *The English Reader, or Pieces in Prose and Poetry: Selected from the Best Writers.* New York: Evert Duyckinck, 1815.

———. *The English Reader, or Pieces in Prose and Poetry Selected from the Best Writers, Designed to Assist Young Persons to Read.* New York: Evert Duyckinck, 1819.

———. *The English Reader, or Pieces in Prose and Poetry: Selected from the Best Writers: With a Few Preliminary Observations on the Principles of Good Reading.* New York: Evert Duyckinck, 1807.

———. *Introduction to the English Reader.* New York: Evert Duyckinck, 1822.

———. *Introduction to the English Reader: With Rules and Observations for Assisting Children to Read with Propriety.* New York: E. Duyckinck, 1811.

———. *Key to the Exercises Adapted to Murray's English Grammar.* New York: Published by E. Duyckinck, 1809.

Niles, Hezekiah. *Principles and Acts of the Revolution in America, or an Attempt to Collect and Preserve Some of the Speeches, Orations, and Proceedings, with Sketches and Remarks on Men and Things, and Other Fugitive or Neglected Pieces, Belonging to the Men of the Revolutionary Period in the United States.* Baltimore: W. O. Niles, 1822.

Peaslee, John P., and Hulings Cowperthwait. *First Day's Catalogue, Second New-York Trade Sale—April, 1830: Catalogue of Books to Be Sold Without Reserve, in Lots to Suit the Trade, on Tuesday Morning at the Panorama Sales Room, 157, Broadway.* New York, 1830.

Perrin, John, and J. F. Tocquot. *A Grammar of the French Tongue, Grounded upon the Decisions of the French Academy Wherein All the Necessary Rules, Observations, and Examples Are Exhibited in a Manner Entirely New.* New York: Evert Duyckinck, 1816.

Pomey, François. *The Pantheon, Representing the Fabulous Histories of the Heathen Gods and Most Illustrious Heroes in a Plain and Familiar Method by Way of Dialogue.* Translated by Andrew Tooke. New York: Evert Duyckinck, 1816.

Price, Richard. *Observations on the Nature of Civil Liberty, the Principles of Government, and the Justice and Policy of the War with America: To Which Is Added, an Appendix,*

Containing, a State of the National Debt, an Estimate of the Money Drawn from the Public by the Taxes; and an Account of the National Income and Expenditure since the Last War. New York: S. Loudon, 1776.

Ringwood, Thomas. *An Address Delivered Before the Franklin Typographical Association of New-York, and a Select Company, on the Fifth of July, 1802: In Commemoration of the Twenty-Seventh Anniversary of American Independence, and of the Third of the Association.* New York: Printed by Southwick and Crooker, 1802.

Rush, Benjamin. "Of the Modes of Education Proper in a Republic." In *The Founders' Constitution*, edited by Philip B. Kurland and Ralph Lerner, 1:686–87. Chicago: University of Chicago Press, 1987.

Sherwood, Samuel. *The Church's Flight into the Wilderness: An Address on the Times.* New York: Printed by S. Loudon, 1776.

Smith, Thomas E. V. *The City of New York in the Year of Washington's Inauguration, 1789.* New York: A. D. F. Randolph, 1889.

Stiles, Ezra. *The Literary Diary of Ezra Stiles.* Edited by Franklin Bowditch Dexter. New York: C. Scribner, 1901.

Swords, Thomas, and James Swords. *Books Printed and Sold by T. & J. Swords, No. 160 Pearl-Street, New-York.* New York: T. & J. Swords, 1807.

Thomas, Isaiah. *The History of Printing in America: With a Biography of Printers, in Two Volumes.* New York: Burt Franklin, 1874.

Thorburn, Grant. *Fifty Years' Reminiscences of New-York, or Flowers from the Garden of Laurie Todd: Being a Collection of Fugitive Pieces Which Appeared in the Newspapers and Periodicals of the Day, for the Last Thirty Years.* New York: D. Fanshaw, 1845.

Volney, Constantin-François. *Travels Through Egypt and Syria, in the Years 1783, 1784 & 1785. Containing the Present Natural and Political State of Those Countries; Their Productions, Arts, Manufactures & Commerce; with Observations on the Manners, Customs and Government of the Turks & Arabs. By M. C-F. Volney. Translated from the French. In Two Volumes.* New York: Printed by John Tiebout, for David Longworth, 1798.

———. *Travels through Egypt and Syria, in the Years 1783, 1784 & 1785. Containing the Present Natural and Political State of Those Countries; Their Productions, Arts, Manufactures & Commerce; with Observations on the Manners, Customs and Government of the Turks & Arabs. By M. C-F. Volney. Translated from the French. In Two Volumes.* New York: Printed by J. Tiebout, for E. Duyckinck & Co., 1798.

Washington, George. *The Diaries of George Washington, 1748–1799.* Edited by John Clement Fitzpatrick. Vol. 3. Boston: Houghton Mifflin, 1925.

———. *The Papers of George Washington, Revolutionary War Series.* Vol. 16, July–September 1778. Edited by David R. Hoth. Charlottesville: University of Virginia Press, 2006.

Webster, Noah. *An American Selection of Lessons in Reading and Speaking: Being the Third Part of a Grammatical Institute of the English Language.* New York: Evert Duyckinck, 1802.

———. *An American Selection of Lessons in Reading and Speaking: Being the Third Part of a Grammatical Institute of the English Language.* New York: W. W. Vermilye for Evert Duyckinck, 1804.

———. *An American Selection of Lessons in Reading and Speaking: Calculated to Improve the Minds and Refine the Taste of Youth.* New York: Printed for E. Duyckinck, R. Magill, N. Judah, P. A. Mesier, C. Davis, J. Harrisson, and B. Gomez, 1799.

———. *An American Selection of Lessons in Reading and Speaking: Calculated to Improve the Minds and Refine the Taste of Youth.* New York: Printed by G. and R. Waite, for Evert Duyckinck, 1800.

———. *The American Spelling-Book Containing an Easy Standard of Pronunciation*. New York: Printed for, and sold by, Samuel Campbell, 1792.

———. *The American Spelling-Book: Containing an Easy Standard of Pronunciation. Being the First Part of a Grammatical Institute of the English Language. In Three Parts.* New York: Printed by W. A. Davis for T. Allen, E. Duyckinck & Co., N. Judah, P. A. Mesier, and D. Dunham, 1797.

———. *Elements of Useful Knowledge, Containing a Historical and Geographical Account of the United States.* New York: Published by Evert Duyckinck, 1810.

———. *A Grammatical Institute of the English Language.* New York: Printed by L. Nichols & Co. for E. Duyckinck, 1801.

———. *A Grammatical Institute of the English Language: Comprising an Easy, Concise, and Systematic Method of Education. Designed for the Use of English Schools in America.* New York: Printed by Robert Wilson, for Evert Duyckinck & Co., 1798.

———. *A Grammatical Institute of the English Language: Part Second.* New York: Printed for E. Duyckinck by L. Nichols, 1804.

———. *The Prompter, or A Commentary on Common Sayings and Subjects Which Are Full of Common Sense, the Best Sense in the World.* New York: Published by E. Duyckinck, 1815.

Weed, Thurlow. *Life of Thurlow Weed, Including His Autobiography and a Memoir.* 2 vols. New York: Da Capo Press, 1970.

Williams, Edwin, and J. Disturnell. *New York as It Is.* New York: T. R. Tanner, 1833.

Wood, Samuel. *The Cries of New-York.* New York: Printed and sold by Samuel Wood, 1814.

Secondary Sources

Adelman, Joseph M. "'A Constitutional Conveyance of Intelligence, Public and Private': The Post Office, the Business of Printing, and the American Revolution." *Enterprise and Society* 11, no. 4 (2010): 709–52.

AhKao, Roxane, and Susan J. Wolfe. "American Bibliographical Notes: A Query by Isaiah Thomas on the New York Press." *Proceedings of the American Antiquarian Society* 94, no. 1 (1984): 149–57.

Albertson, Karla Klein. "The Society of the Cincinnati." *Early American Life* 20, no. 3 (1989): 32–42.

Albion, Robert Greenhalgh. *The Rise of New York Port, 1815–1960.* New York: C. Scribner's Sons, 1939.

Alexander, John K. *The Selling of the Constitutional Convention: A History of News Coverage.* Madison, Wisc.: Madison House, 1990.

Allan, Herbert S. *John Hancock: Patriot in Purple.* New York: Macmillan, 1948.

Allgor, Catherine. *A Perfect Union: Dolley Madison and the Creation of the American Nation.* New York: Henry Holt, 2006.

Ames, William E. *A History of the National Intelligencer.* Chapel Hill: University of North Carolina Press, 1972.

Amory, Hugh, and David D. Hall, eds. *The Colonial Book in the Atlantic World.* Vol. 1 of *A History of the Book in America.* Chapel Hill: University of North Carolina Press, 2007.

Anderson, Benedict. *Imagined Communities: Reflections on the Origin and Spread of Nationalism.* New York: Verso, 1991.

Anderson, Jennifer L. *Mahogany: The Costs of Luxury in Early America.* Cambridge: Harvard University Press, 2012.

Appleby, Joyce Oldham. *Capitalism and a New Social Order: The Republican Vision of the 1790s.* New York: New York University Press, 1984.

Arndt, S. C. "Bringing Books into Baltimore: Tracing Networks of Importation, 1760–1825." *Book History* 16 (2013): 62–88.

Bailyn, Bernard. *The Peopling of British North America: An Introduction.* New York: Knopf, 1986.

Barker, Hannah. *Newspapers, Politics, and English Society, 1695–1855.* New York: Longman, 2000.

———. "Stockdale, John (c. 1749–1814)." In *Oxford Dictionary of National Biography*, online ed., edited by David Cannadine. Oxford: Oxford University Press, 2004. Accessed 3 January 2017. http://www.oxforddnb.com/view/article/26541.

Barnard, Philip, Mark Kamrath, and Stephen Shapiro, eds. *Revising Charles Brockden Brown: Culture, Politics, and Sexuality in the Early Republic.* Knoxville: University of Tennessee Press, 2004.

Barnhurst, Kevin G., and John C. Nerone. *The Form of News: A History.* New York: Guilford Press, 2001.

Beales, Ross W., and James N. Green. "Libraries and Their Users." In *A History of the Book in America*, vol. 1, *The Colonial Book in the Atlantic World*, edited by Hugh Amory and David D. Hall, 399–404. Chapel Hill: University of North Carolina Press, 2007.

Bender, Thomas. *New York Intellect: A History of Intellectual Life in New York City, from 1750 to the Beginnings of Our Own Time.* New York: Knopf, 1987.

Bentley, G. E., Jr. "The Holy Pirates: Legal Enforcement in England of the Patent in the Authorized Version of the Bible, ca. 1800." *Studies in Bibliography* 50 (1997): 372–89.

Bidwell, John. *American Paper Mills, 1690–1832: A Directory of the Paper Trade, with Notes on Products, Watermarks, Distribution Methods, and Manufacturing Techniques.* Hanover: Dartmouth College Press, 2012.

Blackmar, Elizabeth. *Manhattan for Rent, 1785–1850.* Ithaca: Cornell University Press, 1989.

Blight, David W., ed. *The Columbian Orator.* New York: New York University Press, 1998.

Block, Fred L. *Postindustrial Possibilities: A Critique of Economic Discourse.* Berkeley: University of California Press, 1990.

Blumin, Stuart M. *The Emergence of the Middle Class: Social Experience in the American City, 1760–1900.* New York: Cambridge University Press, 1989.

Botein, Stephen. "'Meer Mechanics' and an Open Press: The Business and Political Strategies of Colonial American Printers." *Perspectives in American History* 9 (1975): 127–225.

———. "Printers and the American Revolution." In *The Press and the American Revolution*, edited by Bernard Bailyn and John B. Hench, 11–58. Boston: Northeastern University Press, 1980.

Braithwaite, Helen. *Romanticism, Publishing, and Dissent: Joseph Johnson and the Cause of Liberty.* New York: Palgrave, 2003.

Branson, Susan. *These Fiery Frenchified Dames: Women and Political Culture in Early National Philadelphia.* Philadelphia: University of Pennsylvania Press, 2001.

Breen, T. H. *American Insurgents, American Patriots: The Revolution of the People.* New York: Hill and Wang, 2010.

———. *The Marketplace of Revolution: How Consumer Politics Shaped American Independence.* New York: Oxford University Press, 2004.

Brennan, Denis P. "Shaped by Revolution: Samuel Loudon and the *New-York Packet*, 1776–1783." Master's thesis, State University of New York at Albany, 1992.

Bridenbaugh, Carl. *The Colonial Craftsman.* Chicago: University of Chicago Press, 1961.

Brooke, John L. "Ancient Lodges and Self-Created Societies: Voluntary Association and the Public Sphere in the Early Republic." In *Launching the "Extended Republic":*

The Federalist Era, edited by Ronald Hoffman and Peter J. Albert, 273–359. Charlottesville: University Press of Virginia, 1996.

———. "Consent, Civil Society, and the Public Sphere in the Age of Revolution and the Early American Republic." In *Beyond the Founders: New Approaches to the Political History of the Early American Republic*, edited by Jeffrey L. Pasley, Andrew W. Robertson, and David Waldstreicher, 207–50. Chapel Hill: University of North Carolina Press, 2004.

———. "Reason and Passion in the Public Sphere: Habermas and the Cultural Historians." *Journal of Interdisciplinary History* 29, no. 1 (1998): 43–67.

———. "To Be 'Read by the Whole People': Press, Party, and Public Sphere in the United States, 1789–1840." *Proceedings of the American Antiquarian Society* 110, no. 1 (2000): 41–118.

Brown, Richard D. *Knowledge Is Power: The Diffusion of Information in Early America, 1700–1865*. New York: Oxford University Press, 1991.

———. *The Strength of a People: The Idea of an Informed Citizenry in America, 1650–1870*. Chapel Hill: University of North Carolina Press, 1997.

Brunhouse, Robert. "David Ramsay's Publication Problems." *Papers of the Bibliographical Society of America* 39, no. 1 (1945): 51–67.

Bucci, Richard. "John Jay and 'The Fœderalist, No. V': A Bibliographical Discussion." *Papers of the Bibliographical Society of America* 105, no. 3 (2011): 377–406.

Buel, Richard. "Freedom of the Press in Revolutionary America: The Evolution of Libertarianism, 1760–1820." In *The Press and the American Revolution*, edited by Bernard Bailyn and John B. Hench, 59–98. Boston: Northeastern University Press, 1980.

Burrows, Edwin G., and Mike Wallace. *Gotham: A History of New York City to 1898*. New York: Oxford University Press, 1999.

Bushman, Richard L. *The Refinement of America: Persons, Houses, Cities*. New York: Knopf, 1992.

Cadou, Carol Borchert, Nancy Carter Crump, and Stephen A. McLeod, eds. *Dining with the Washingtons: Historic Recipes, Entertainment, and Hospitality from Mount Vernon*. Chapel Hill: University of North Carolina Press, 2011.

Calhoon, Robert M. "Boucher, Jonathan (1738–1804)." In *Oxford Dictionary of National Biography*, online ed., edited by David Cannadine. Oxford: Oxford University Press, 2004. Accessed 3 January 2017. http://www.oxforddnb.com/view/article/2972.

Calhoun, Craig J., ed. *Habermas and the Public Sphere*. Cambridge: MIT Press, 1992.

Callcott, George H. *History in the United States, 1800–1860: Its Practice and Purpose*. Baltimore: Johns Hopkins University Press, 1970.

Carp, Benjamin L. "The Night the Yankees Burned Broadway." *Early American Studies* 4, no. 2 (2006): 471–511.

———. *Rebels Rising: Cities and the American Revolution*. New York: Oxford University Press, 2007.

Casper, Scott E. "Case Study: Harper & Brothers." In *A History of the Book in America*, vol. 2, *An Extensive Republic: Print, Culture, and Society in the New Nation, 1790–1840*, edited by Robert A. Gross and Mary Kelley, 128–36. Chapel Hill: University of North Carolina Press, 2010.

Casper, Scott E., Jeffrey D. Groves, Stephen W. Nissenbaum, and Michael Winship, eds. *The Industrial Book, 1840–1880*. Vol. 3 of *A History of the Book in America*. Chapel Hill: University of North Carolina Press, 2007.

Caulkins, Frances Manwaring. *History of Norwich, Connecticut: From Its Possession by the Indians, to the Year 1866*. Hartford, Conn.: H. P. Haven, 1866.

Chard, Leslie F. "Joseph Johnson: Father of the Book Trade." *Bulletin of the New York Public Library* 79 (1975): 51–82.

Charvat, William. *Literary Publishing in America, 1790–1850.* Amherst: University of Massachusetts Press, 1993.

———. *The Profession of Authorship in America, 1800–1870.* New York: Columbia University Press, 1992.

Chatfield, Michael. *A History of Accounting Thought.* Hinsdale, Ill.: Dryden Press, 1974.

Cheng, Eileen K. *The Plain and Noble Garb of Truth: Nationalism and Impartiality in American Historical Writing, 1784–1860.* Athens: University of Georgia Press, 2008.

Chopra, Ruma. "Printer Hugh Gaine Crosses and Re-Crosses the Hudson." *New York History* 90, no. 4 (2009): 271–85.

———. *Unnatural Rebellion: Loyalists in New York City During the Revolution.* Charlottesville: University of Virginia Press, 2011.

Clark, Charles E. *The Public Prints: The Newspaper in Anglo-American Culture, 1665–1740.* New York: Oxford University Press, 1994.

Clark, Michael D. "Jonathan Boucher and the Toleration of Roman Catholics in Maryland." *Maryland Historical Magazine* 71, no. 2 (1976): 194–204.

———. "Jonathan Boucher: The Mirror of Reaction." *Huntington Library Quarterly* 33, no. 1 (1969): 19–32.

Clemens, Paul G. E. "The Consumer Culture of the Middle Atlantic, 1760–1820." *William and Mary Quarterly* 62, no. 4 (2005): 577–620.

Cohen, Lester H. *The Revolutionary Histories: Contemporary Narratives of the American Revolution.* Ithaca: Cornell University Press, 1980.

Cohen, Patricia Cline. *The Murder of Helen Jewett: The Life and Death of a Prostitute in Nineteenth-Century New York.* New York: Knopf, 1998.

Cohen, Patricia Cline, Timothy J. Gilfoyle, and Helen Lefkowitz Horowitz. *The Flash Press: Sporting Male Weeklies in 1840s New York.* Chicago: University of Chicago Press, 2008.

Coldwell, Chris. "T. & J. Swords, Printers During the Federal Period to Doctors, Scientists, Friendly and Calliopean Clubbers, and Other New York Literati, as Well as High Churchists, and the Occasional Presbyterian." *Confessional Presbyterian* 2, no. 1 (2006): 211–36.

Cole, Arthur Harrison, and Harold F. Williamson. *The American Carpet Manufacture: A History and an Analysis.* Cambridge: Harvard University Press, 1941.

Connor, Christina. "Robert Bell and Samuel Loudon: The Dissemination of Information, the Freedom of the Press, and Book Publishing During the Age of Revolution in America." Master's thesis, State University of New York at Albany, 2006.

Conroy, David W. *In Public Houses: Drink and the Revolution of Authority in Colonial Massachusetts.* Chapel Hill: Published for the Institute of Early American History and Culture by the University of North Carolina Press, 1995.

Copeland, David A. *Colonial American Newspapers: Character and Content.* Newark: University of Delaware Press, 1997.

Cornog, Evan. *The Birth of Empire: DeWitt Clinton and the American Experience, 1769–1828.* New York: Oxford University Press, 1998.

Countryman, Edward. *A People in Revolution: The American Revolution and Political Society in New York, 1760–1790.* Baltimore: Johns Hopkins University Press, 1981.

Crain, Patricia. *The Story of A: The Alphabetization of America from the New England Primer to the Scarlet Letter.* Stanford: Stanford University Press, 2000.

Crane, Elaine F. "Publius in the Provinces: Where Was 'The Federalist' Reprinted Outside New York City?" *William and Mary Quarterly* 21, no. 4 (1964): 589–92.

Cray, Robert E. *Paupers and Poor Relief in New York City and Its Rural Environs, 1700–1830.* Philadelphia: Temple University Press, 1988.

Cunningham, Noble E. *The Jeffersonian Republicans: The Formation of Party Organiza-tion, 1789–1801*. Chapel Hill: Published for the Institute of Early American His-tory and Culture by the University of North Carolina Press, 1957.

Daitsman, George. "Labor and the Welfare State in Early New York." *Labor History* 4, no. 3 (1963): 248–56.

Daniel, Marcus Leonard. *Scandal and Civility: Journalism and the Birth of American Democracy*. New York: Oxford University Press, 2009.

Davidson, Cathy N. *Revolution and the Word: The Rise of the Novel in America*. Exp. ed. New York: Oxford University Press, 2004.

Densmore, Christopher. "Understanding and Using Early Nineteenth-Century Account Books." *Midwestern Archivist* 5, no. 1 (1980): 5–19.

Ditz, Toby. "Secret Selves, Credible Personas: The Problematics of Trust and Public Display in the Writing of Eighteenth-Century Philadelphia Merchants." In *Pos-sible Pasts: Becoming Colonial in Early America*, edited by Robert Blair St. George, 219–42. Ithaca: Cornell University Press, 2000.

Dowling, William C. *Literary Federalism in the Age of Jefferson: Joseph Dennie and the Port Folio, 1801–1812*. Columbia: University of South Carolina Press, 1999.

Dyer, Alan. *A Biography of James Parker, Colonial Printer*. Troy: Whitston, 1982.

Eastman, Carolyn. *A Nation of Speechifiers: Making an American Public After the Revolu-tion*. Chicago: University of Chicago Press, 2010.

Edwards, James Don. "Early Bookkeeping and Its Development into Accounting." *Busi-ness History Review* 34, no. 4 (1960): 446–58.

Elkins, Stanley M., and Eric L. McKitrick. *The Age of Federalism: The Early American Republic, 1788–1800*. New York: Oxford University Press, 1993.

Ellis, Harold Milton. "Joseph Dennie and His Circle: A Study in American Literature from 1792 to 1812." *Studies in English*, no. 3 (15 July 1915): 9–285.

Ellis, Joseph J. *After the Revolution: Profiles of Early American Culture*. New York: W. W. Norton, 1979.

———. *Founding Brothers: The Revolutionary Generation*. New York: Knopf, 2000.

Erickson, Paul Joseph. "Welcome to Sodom: The Cultural Work of City-Mysteries Fic-tion in Antebellum America." PhD diss., University of Texas at Austin, 2005.

Evanson, Philip. "Jonathan Boucher: The Mind of an American Loyalist." *Maryland Historical Magazine* 58, no. 2 (1963): 123–36.

Exman, Eugene. *The House of Harper: The Making of a Modern Publisher*. New York: Harper Perennial, 2010.

Fall, Ralph Emmett. "The Rev. Jonathan Boucher, Turbulent Tory (1738–1804)." *Histori-cal Magazine of the Protestant Episcopal Church* 36, no. 4 (1967): 323–56.

Farren, Donald. "Subscription: A Study of the Eighteenth-Century American Book Trade." PhD diss., Columbia University, 1982.

Folsom, Franklin. *Impatient Armies of the Poor: The Story of Collective Action of the Unemployed, 1808–1942*. Boulder: University Press of Colorado, 1991.

Frankel, Oz. *States of Inquiry: Social Investigations and Print Culture in Nineteenth-Century Britain and the United States*. Baltimore: Johns Hopkins University Press, 2006.

Franklin, John Hope, and Loren Schweninger. *Runaway Slaves: Rebels on the Plantation*. New York: Oxford University Press, 1999.

Freeman, Joanne B. *Affairs of Honor: National Politics in the New Republic*. New Haven: Yale University Press, 2001.

Friedman, Lawrence J., and Arthur H. Shaffer. "David Ramsay and the Quest for an American Historical Identity." *Southern Quarterly* 14, no. 4 (1976): 351–71.

———. "Mercy Otis Warren and the Politics of Historical Nationalism." *New England Quarterly* 48, no. 2 (1975): 194–215.

Furstenberg, François. *In the Name of the Father: Washington's Legacy, Slavery, and the Making of a Nation.* New York: Penguin Books, 2006.

Gaines, Pierce W. "William Cobbett's Account Book." *Proceedings of the American Antiquarian Society* 78, no. 2 (1968): 299–312.

Gay, Peter. *A Loss of Mastery: Puritan Historians in Colonial America.* New York: Vintage Books, 1968.

Gellman, David Nathaniel. *Emancipating New York? The Politics of Slavery and Freedom, 1777–1827.* Baton Rouge: Louisiana State University Press, 2006.

Gilchrist, David T., ed. *The Growth of the Seaport Cities, 1790–1825.* Charlottesville: University Press of Virginia, 1967.

Giles, Paul. *Atlantic Republic: The American Tradition in English Literature.* Oxford: Oxford University Press, 2006.

———. *The Global Remapping of American Literature.* Princeton: Princeton University Press, 2011.

———. *Transatlantic Insurrections: British Culture and the Formation of American Literature, 1730–1860.* Philadelphia: University of Pennsylvania Press, 2001.

Gilje, Paul A. *The Road to Mobocracy: Popular Disorder in New York City, 1763–1834.* Chapel Hill: Published for the Institute of Early American History and Culture by the University of North Carolina Press, 1987.

Gilje, Paul A., and William Pencak, eds. *New York in the Age of the Constitution, 1775–1800.* Rutherford, N.J.: Associated University Presses, 1992.

Gilmartin, Kevin. *Print Politics: The Press and Radical Opposition in Early Nineteenth-Century England.* New York: Cambridge University Press, 1996.

———. *Writing Against Revolution: Literary Conservatism in Britain, 1790–1832.* New York: Cambridge University Press, 2007.

Glynn, Tom. "The New York Society Library: Books, Authority, and Publics in Colonial and Early Republican New York." *Libraries and Culture* 40, no. 4 (2005): 493–529.

Grasso, Christopher. *A Speaking Aristocracy: Transforming Public Discourse in Eighteenth-Century Connecticut.* Chapel Hill: Published for the Omohundro Institute of Early American History and Culture by the University of North Carolina Press, 1999.

Green, Daniel. *Great Cobbett: The Noblest Agitator.* London: Hodder and Stoughton, 1983.

Green, James N. "The Rise of Book Publishing." In *A History of the Book in America,* vol. 2, *An Extensive Republic: Print, Culture, and Society in the New Nation, 1790–1840,* edited by Robert A. Gross and Mary Kelley, 75–127. Chapel Hill: University of North Carolina Press, 2010.

Greenberg, Joshua R. *Advocating the Man: Masculinity, Organized Labor, and the Household in New York, 1800–1840.* New York: Columbia University Press, 2007.

Greenspan, Ezra. *George Palmer Putnam: Representative American Publisher.* University Park: Pennsylvania State University Press, 2000.

Gross, Robert A. "Introduction: An Extensive Republic." In *A History of the Book in America,* vol. 2, *An Extensive Republic: Print, Culture, and Society in the New Nation, 1790–1840,* 1–52. Chapel Hill: University of North Carolina Press, 2010.

Gross, Robert A., and Mary Kelley, eds. *An Extensive Republic: Print, Culture, and Society in the New Nation, 1790–1840.* Vol. 2 of *A History of the Book in America.* Chapel Hill: University of North Carolina Press, 2010.

Growoll, Adolf. *Book Trade Bibliography in the United States in the Nineteenth Century.* New York: E. B. Hackett, Brick Row Book Shop, 1939.

Haberman, Robb K. "Magazines, Presentation Networks, and the Cultivation of Authorship in Post-Revolutionary America." *American Periodicals* 18, no. 2 (2008): 141–62.

———. "Provincial Nationalism: Civic Rivalry in Postrevolutionary American Magazines." *Early American Studies* 10, no. 1 (2012): 162–93.

Habermas, Jürgen. *The Structural Transformation of the Public Sphere: An Inquiry into a Category of Bourgeois Society*. Translated by Thomas Burger and Frederick Lawrence. Cambridge: MIT Press, 1989.

Hackel, Heidi Brayman, and Catherine E. Kelly, eds. *Reading Women: Literacy, Authorship, and Culture in the Atlantic World, 1500–1800*. Philadelphia: University of Pennsylvania Press, 2008.

Hackenberg, Michael. "Getting the Books Out: Trade Sales, Parcel Sales, and Book Fairs in the Nineteenth-Century United States." In *Getting the Books Out: Papers of the Chicago Conference on the Book in Nineteenth-Century America*, edited by Michael Hackenberg, 4–25. Washington, D.C.: Center for the Book at the Library of Congress, 1985.

Hall, David D. *Cultures of Print: Essays in the History of the Book*. Amherst: University of Massachusetts Press, 1996.

Haraszti, Zoltan. "More Books from the Adams Library." *Boston Public Library Quarterly* 3 (1951): 109–26.

Harris, Robert. *A Patriot Press: National Politics and the London Press in the 1740s*. Oxford: Clarendon Press, 1993.

———. *Politics and the Rise of the Press: Britain and France, 1620–1800*. New York: Routledge, 1996.

Hartigan-O'Connor, Ellen. *The Ties That Buy: Women and Commerce in Revolutionary America*. Philadelphia: University of Pennsylvania Press, 2009.

Hendrickson, Robert A. *The Rise and Fall of Alexander Hamilton*. New York: Van Nostrand Reinhold, 1981.

Henkin, David M. *City Reading: Written Words and Public Spaces in Antebellum New York*. New York: Columbia University Press, 1998.

Henle, Alea. "Preserving the Past, Making History: Historical Societies in the Early Republic." PhD diss., University of Connecticut, 2012.

Hodges, Graham Russell. *New York City Cartmen, 1667–1850*. New York: New York University Press, 1986.

Hodges, Graham Russell, and Alan Edward Brown. *"Pretends to Be Free": Runaway Slave Advertisements from Colonial and Revolutionary New York and New Jersey*. New York: Garland, 1994.

Hoeflich, M. H. *Legal Publishing in Antebellum America*. New York: Cambridge University Press, 2010.

Hofer, Margaret K. "The Case of the Mystery Medal." *New York Journal of American History* 65, no. 4 (2004): 18–23.

Holton, Woody. *Unruly Americans and the Origins of the Constitution*. New York: Hill and Wang, 2007.

Horn, James, Jan Ellen Lewis, and Peter S. Onuf, eds. *The Revolution of 1800: Democracy, Race, and the New Republic*. Charlottesville: University of Virginia Press, 2002.

Howe, Daniel Walker. *What Hath God Wrought: The Transformation of America, 1815–1848*. New York: Oxford University Press, 2007.

Hruschka, John. *How Books Came to America: The Rise of the American Book Trade*. University Park: Pennsylvania State University Press, 2012.

Hudak, Leona M. *Early American Women Printers and Publishers, 1639–1820*. Metuchen, N.J.: Scarecrow Press, 1978.

Humphrey, Carol Sue. *The American Revolution and the Press: The Promise of Independence*. Evanston: Northwestern University Press, 2013.

———. *The Press of the Young Republic: 1783–1883*. Westport, Conn.: Greenwood Press, 1996.

Jaffee, David. *A New Nation of Goods: The Material Culture of Early America*. Philadelphia: University of Pennsylvania Press, 2010.

Jasanoff, Maya. "The Other Side of Revolution: Loyalists in the British Empire." *William and Mary Quarterly* 65, no. 2 (2008): 205–32.

Jensen, Laura. *Patriots, Settlers, and the Origins of American Social Policy.* New York: Cambridge University Press, 2003.

John, Richard R. *Spreading the News: The American Postal System from Franklin to Morse.* Cambridge: Harvard University Press, 1998.

Johns, Adrian. "Faust and the Pirates: The Cultural Construction of the Printing Revolution." In *The Nature of the Book: Print and Knowledge in the Making,* 324–79. Chicago: University of Chicago Press, 1998.

Johnson, Paul E. *A Shopkeeper's Millennium: Society and Revivals in Rochester, New York, 1815–1837.* New York: Hill and Wang, 2004.

Johnson, Paul E., and Sean Wilentz. *The Kingdom of Matthias: A Story of Sex and Salvation in Nineteenth-Century America.* New York: Oxford University Press, 1994.

Johnston, Paul. "T. & J. Swords, Early New York Printers." *Book Collector's Packet* 1, no. 3 (1932): 16–17.

Jones, Thomas. *History of New York During the Revolutionary War and of the Leading Events in the Other Colonies at That Period.* Edited by Edward Floyd de Lancey. 2 vols. New York: New-York Historical Society, 1879.

Kalinowska, Fryderyka. "Three Early Historians of the American Revolution." *American Studies in Scandinavia* 3, no. 2 (1970): 25–46.

Kaplan, Catherine O'Donnell. *Men of Letters in the Early Republic: Cultivating Forums of Citizenship.* Chapel Hill: Published for the Omohundro Institute of Early American History and Culture by the University of North Carolina Press, 2008.

Kaplan, Lawrence S. *Entangling Alliances with None: American Foreign Policy in the Age of Jefferson.* Kent: Kent State University Press, 1987.

Kaser, David. "The Origin of the Book Trade Sales." *Papers of the Bibliographical Society of America* 50, no. 3 (1956): 296–302.

Keep, Austin Baxter. *History of the New York Society Library: With an Introductory Chapter on Libraries in Colonial New York, 1698–1776.* New York: Printed for the Trustees by De Vinne Press, 1908.

Kelley, Mary. "Introduction: Educating the Citizenry." In *A History of the Book in America,* vol. 2, *An Extensive Republic: Print, Culture, and Society in the New Nation, 1790–1840,* edited by Robert A. Gross and Mary Kelley, 269–72. Chapel Hill: University of North Carolina Press, 2010.

Kendall, Joshua C. *The Forgotten Founding Father: Noah Webster's Obsession and the Creation of an American Culture.* New York: G. P. Putnam's Sons, 2010.

Kerber, Linda K. *Federalists in Dissent: Imagery and Ideology in Jeffersonian America.* Ithaca: Cornell University Press, 1970.

———. *Women of the Republic: Intellect and Ideology in Revolutionary America.* Chapel Hill: Published for the Institute of Early American History and Culture by the University of North Carolina Press, 1980.

Keyes, Carl Robert. "Early American Advertising: Marketing and Consumer Culture in Eighteenth-Century Philadelphia." PhD diss., Johns Hopkins University, 2007.

Kielbowicz, Richard B. "Modernization, Communication Policy, and the Geopolitics of News, 1820–1860." *Critical Studies in Mass Communication* 3, no. 1 (1986): 21–35.

———. "News Gathering by Mail in the Age of the Telegraph: Adapting to a New Technology." *Technology and Culture* 28, no. 1 (1987): 26–41.

———. *News in the Mail: The Press, Post Office, and Public Information, 1700–1860s.* New York: Greenwood Press, 1989.

———. "Speeding the News by Postal Express, 1825–1861: The Public Policy Privileges for the Press." *Social Science Journal* 22, no. 1 (1985): 49–63.

King, Marion. *Books and People: Five Decades of New York's Oldest Library*. New York: Macmillan, 1954.

King, Martha J. "The 'Pen of the Historian': Mercy Otis Warren's History of the American Revolution." *Princeton University Library Chronicle* 72, no. 2 (2011): 513–31.

Kornfeld, Eve. "From Republicanism to Liberalism: The Intellectual Journey of David Ramsay." *Journal of the Early Republic* 9, no. 3 (1989): 289–313.

Kouwenhoven, John Atlee. *The Columbia Historical Portrait of New York: An Essay in Graphic History in Honor of the Tricentennial of New York City and the Bicentennial of Columbia University*. Garden City, N.Y.: Doubleday, 1953.

Kramer, Michael P. *Imagining Language in America: From the Revolution to the Civil War*. Princeton: Princeton University Press, 1992.

Lampi, Philip J. "The Federalist Party Resurgence, 1808–1816." *Journal of the Early Republic* 33, no. 2 (2013): 255–81.

Lanzendörfer, Tim. "From the Periodical Archives: Joseph Dennie, the Value of the Editor, and the Creation of the *Port Folio*." *American Periodicals* 22, no. 1 (2012): 94–106.

Larson, John Lauritz. *Internal Improvement: National Public Works and the Promise of Popular Government in the Early United States*. Chapel Hill: University of North Carolina Press, 2001.

Laurie, Bruce. *Artisans into Workers: Labor in Nineteenth-Century America*. New York: Hill and Wang, 1989.

Lause, Mark A. *Some Degree of Power: From Hired Hand to Union Craftsman in the Preindustrial American Printing Trades, 1778–1815*. Fayetteville: University of Arkansas Press, 1991.

Lee, Jennifer B. "Infant Manufactures: Early Typefounding in Philadelphia." *Printing History* 11, no. 2 (1989): 28–40.

Lepore, Jill. *A Is for American: Letters and Other Characters in the Newly United States*. New York: Knopf, 2002.

Levy, Leonard W. *Emergence of a Free Press*. New York: Oxford University Press, 1985.

Libby, Orin Grant. "A Critical Examination of Gordon's History of the American Revolution." *Annual Report of the American Historical Association for the Year 1899* (1900): 365–88.

Liebersohn, Harry. *Aristocratic Encounters: European Travelers and North American Indians*. New York: Cambridge University Press, 1998.

Lipsey, Robert E. "U.S. Foreign Trade and the Balance of Payments, 1800–1913." In *The Cambridge Economic History of the United States*, edited by Stanley L. Engerman and Robert E. Gallman, 722–27. New York: Cambridge University Press, 2000.

List, Karen K. "The Role of William Cobbett in Philadelphia's Party Press, 1794–1799." *Journalism Monographs* 82 (1983): 1–41.

Little, Nigel. *Transoceanic Radical, William Duane: National Identity and Empire, 1760–1835*. London: Pickering and Chatto, 2008.

Lorenz, Alfred Lawrence. *Hugh Gaine: A Colonial Printer-Editor's Odyssey to Loyalism*. Carbondale: Southern Illinois University Press, 1972.

Loughran, Trish. *The Republic in Print: Print Culture in the Age of U.S. Nation Building, 1770–1870*. New York: Columbia University Press, 2007.

Maier, Pauline. *From Resistance to Revolution: Colonial Radicals and the Development of American Opposition to Britain, 1765–1776*. New York: Knopf, 1972.

———. *The Old Revolutionaries: Political Lives in the Age of Samuel Adams*. New York: Knopf, 1980.

Mann, Bruce H. *Republic of Debtors: Bankruptcy in the Age of American Independence*. Cambridge: Harvard University Press, 2002.

Martin, Robert W. T. *The Free and Open Press: The Founding of American Democratic Press Liberty, 1640–1800*. New York: New York University Press, 2001.

McAnear, Beverly. "James Parker Versus John Holt." *Proceedings of the New Jersey Historical Society* 59, nos. 2–3 (1941): 77–95, 198–212.

McConville, Brendan. *The King's Three Faces: The Rise and Fall of Royal America, 1688–1776*. Chapel Hill: Published for the Omohundro Institute of Early American History and Culture by the University of North Carolina Press, 2006.

McCoy, Drew R. *The Elusive Republic? Political Economy in Jeffersonian America*. Chapel Hill: Published for the Institute of Early American History and Culture by the University of North Carolina Press, 1980.

McDonnell, Michael. "National Identity and the American War for Independence Reconsidered." *Australasian Journal of American Studies* 20, no. 1 (2001): 3–17.

McDougall, Warren. "Charles Elliot's Book Adventure in Philadelphia, and the Trouble with Thomas Dobson." In *Light on the Book Trade: Essays in Honour of Peter Isaac*, edited by Barry McKay John Hinks, and Maureen Bell, 197–212. London: Oak Knoll Press and the British Library, 2004.

McGaw, Judith A. *Most Wonderful Machine: Mechanization and Social Change in Berkshire Paper Making, 1801–1885*. Princeton: Princeton University Press, 1987.

McGill, Meredith L. *American Literature and the Culture of Reprinting, 1834–1853*. Philadelphia: University of Pennsylvania Press, 2003.

———. "Copyright." In *A History of the Book in America*, vol. 2, *An Extensive Republic: Print, Culture, and Society in the New Nation, 1790–1840*, edited by Robert A. Gross and Mary Kelley, 198–210. Chapel Hill: University of North Carolina Press, 2010.

McKay, Richard C. *South Street: A Maritime History of New York*. New York: G. P. Putnam's Sons, 1934.

Meaders, Daniel. *Dead or Alive: Fugitive Slaves and White Indentured Servants Before 1830*. New York: Garland, 1993.

Messer, Peter C. "From a Revolutionary History to a History of Revolution: David Ramsay and the American Revolution." *Journal of the Early Republic* 22, no. 2 (2002): 205–33.

———. *Stories of Independence: Identity, Ideology, and History in Eighteenth-Century America*. DeKalb: Northern Illinois University Press, 2005.

Middleton, Arthur P. "The Colonial Virginia Parson." *William and Mary Quarterly* 26, no. 3 (1969): 425–40.

Miller, Kerby A. *Emigrants and Exiles: Ireland and the Irish Exodus to North America*. New York: Oxford University Press, 1985.

Miller, Kerby A., Arnold Schrier, Bruce D. Boling, and David N. Doyle, eds. *Irish Immigrants in the Land of Canaan: Letters and Memoirs from Colonial and Revolutionary America, 1675–1815*. New York: Oxford University Press, 2003.

Miller, Perry. *The Raven and the Whale: The War of Words and Wits in the Era of Poe and Melville*. New York: Harcourt, Brace, 1956.

Mize, George Edwin. "The Contributions of Evert A. Duyckinck to the Cultural Development of Nineteenth Century America." PhD diss., New York University, 1954.

Mohl, Raymond A. "Poverty in Early America, a Reappraisal: The Case of Eighteenth-Century New York City." *New York History* 50, no. 1 (1969): 5–27.

Monaghan, Charles. *The Murrays of Murray Hill*. Brooklyn: Urban History Press, 1998.

Monaghan, Charles, and E. Jennifer Monaghan. "Schoolbooks." In *A History of the Book in America*, vol. 2, *An Extensive Republic: Print, Culture, and Society in the New Nation, 1790–1840*, edited by Robert A. Gross and Mary Kelley, 304–17. Chapel Hill: University of North Carolina Press, 2010.

Monaghan, E. Jennifer. *A Common Heritage: Noah Webster's Blue-Back Speller*. Hamden, Conn.: Archon Books, 1983.

————. *Learning to Read and Write in Colonial America*. Amherst: University of Massachusetts Press, 2005.

Moran, Gerald F., and Maris A. Vinovskis. "Schools." In *A History of the Book in America*, vol. 2, *An Extensive Republic: Print, Culture, and Society in the New Nation, 1790–1840*, edited by Robert A. Gross and Mary Kelley, 286–303. Chapel Hill: University of North Carolina Press, 2010.

Morgan, Charlotte E. *The Origin and History of the New York Employing Printers' Association: The Evolution of a Trade Association*. New York: Columbia University Press, 1930.

Moss, Richard J. *Noah Webster*. Boston: Twayne, 1984.

Mott, Frank Luther. *American Journalism: A History, 1690–1960*. New York: Macmillan, 1962.

Murphy, Brian Phillips. *Building the Empire State: Political Economy in the Early Republic*. Philadelphia: University of Pennsylvania Press, 2015.

————. "'A Very Convenient Instrument': The Manhattan Company, Aaron Burr, and the Election of 1800." *William and Mary Quarterly*, 3rd ser., 65, no. 2 (2008): 233–66.

Mushkat, Jerome. *Tammany: The Evolution of a Political Machine, 1789–1865*. Syracuse: Syracuse University Press, 1971.

Myrsiades, Linda S. *Law and Medicine in Revolutionary America: Dissecting the Rush v. Cobbett Trial, 1799*. Bethlehem: Lehigh University Press, 2012.

Nerone, John C. "The Mythology of the Penny Press." *Critical Studies in Mass Communication* 4, no. 4 (1987): 376–404.

————. *Violence Against the Press: Policing the Public Sphere in U.S. History*. New York: Oxford University Press, 1994.

Newman, Simon P. *Parades and the Politics of the Street: Festive Culture in the Early American Republic*. Philadelphia: University of Pennsylvania Press, 1997.

Nord, David Paul. *Communities of Journalism: A History of American Newspapers and Their Readers*. Urbana: University of Illinois Press, 2001.

————. *Faith in Reading: Religious Publishing and the Birth of Mass Media in America*. New York: Oxford University Press, 2004.

————. "A Republican Literature: A Study of Magazine Reading and Readers in Late Eighteenth-Century New York." *American Quarterly* 40, no. 1 (1988): 42–64.

Olson, Lester C. "Benjamin Franklin's Commemorative Medal Libertas Americana: A Study in Rhetorical Iconology." *Quarterly Journal of Speech* 76, no. 1 (1990): 23–45.

————. *Emblems of American Community in the Revolutionary Era: A Study in Rhetorical Iconology*. Washington, D.C.: Smithsonian Institution Press, 1991.

Osgood, Samuel. *Evert Augustus Duyckinck, His Life, Writings and Influence*. Boston: D. Clapp and Son, 1879.

Paltsits, Victor Hugo. "John Holt—Printer and Postmaster." *Bulletin of the New York Public Library* 24 (1920): 483–99.

Parker, Peter J. "Asbury Dickins, Bookseller, 1798–1801, or The Brief Career of a Careless Youth." *Pennsylvania Magazine of History and Biography* 94, no. 4 (1970): 464–83.

Pasley, Jeffrey L. "1800 as a Revolution in Political Culture: Newspapers, Celebrations, Voting, and Democratization in the Early Republic." In *The Revolution of 1800: Democracy, Race, and the New Republic*, edited by James Horn, Jan Ellen Lewis, and Peter S. Onuf, 121–52. Charlottesville: University of Virginia Press, 2002.

————. "The Two National Gazettes: Newspapers and the Embodiment of American Political Parties." *Early American Literature* 35, no. 1 (2000): 51–86.

————. *"The Tyranny of Printers": Newspaper Politics in the Early American Republic*. Charlottesville: University Press of Virginia, 2001.

Pasley, Jeffrey L., Andrew W. Robertson, and David Waldstreicher, eds. *Beyond the Founders: New Approaches to the Political History of the Early American Republic.* Chapel Hill: University of North Carolina Press, 2004.

Perkins, Bradford. *Prologue to War: England and the United States, 1805–1812.* Berkeley: University of California Press, 1961.

Peskin, Lawrence A. *Manufacturing Revolution: The Intellectual Origins of Early American Industry.* Baltimore: Johns Hopkins University Press, 2003.

Pilcher, George W. "William Gordon and the History of the American Revolution." *Historian* 34, no. 3 (1972): 447–64.

Pilkington, James Penn, and Walter N. Vernon. *The Methodist Publishing House: A History.* Nashville: Abingdon Press, 1968.

Pred, Allan Richard. *Urban Growth and the Circulation of Information: The United States System of Cities, 1790–1840.* Cambridge: Harvard University Press, 1973.

Pretzer, William S. "'Of the Paper Cap and Inky Apron': Journeymen Printers." In *A History of the Book in America,* vol. 2, *An Extensive Republic: Print, Culture, and Society in the New Nation, 1790–1840,* edited by Robert A. Gross and Mary Kelley, 160–71. Chapel Hill: University of North Carolina Press, 2010.

Prins, Harald E. L. "Two George Washington Medals: Missing Links in the Chain of Friendship Between the United States and the Wabanaki Confederacy." *Maine Historical Society Quarterly* 28, no. 4 (1989): 226–34.

Raddin, George Gates. *Hocquet Caritat and the Early New York Literary Scene.* Dover, N. J.: Dover Advance Press, 1953.

Rainer, Joseph T. "The 'Sharper' Image: Yankee Peddlers, Southern Consumers, and the Market Revolution." *Business and Economic History* 26, no. 1 (1997): 27–46.

Raven, James. *The Business of Books: Booksellers and the English Book Trade, 1450–1850.* New Haven: Yale University Press, 2007.

———. *London Booksellers and American Customers: Transatlantic Literary Community and the Charleston Library Society, 1748–1811.* Columbia: University of South Carolina Press, 2002.

Remer, Rosalind. *Printers and Men of Capital: Philadelphia Book Publishers in the New Republic.* Philadelphia: University of Pennsylvania Press, 1996.

Richards, Jeffrey H. "Dennie, Joseph." In *American National Biography Online.* New York: Oxford University Press, 2000. Accessed 3 January 2017. http://www.anb.org/articles/16/16-00448.html.

Richardson, Edgar P. "The Cassin Medal." *Winterthur Portfolio* 4 (1968): 75–82.

Robertson, Marion. "The Loyalist Printers: James and Alexander Robertson." *Nova Scotia Historical Review* 3, no. 1 (1983): 83–93.

Robinson, F. J. G., and Peter John Wallis. *Book Subscription Lists: A Revised Guide.* Newcastle upon Tyne: H. Hill, 1975.

Roche, Arthur John. "A Literary Gentleman in New York: Evert A. Duyckinck's Relationship with Nathaniel Hawthorne, Herman Melville, Edgar Allan Poe, and William Gilmore Simms." PhD diss., Duke University, 1973.

Rock, Howard B. *Artisans of the New Republic: The Tradesmen of New York City in the Age of Jefferson.* New York: New York University Press, 1979.

Rock, Howard B., Paul A. Gilje, and Robert Asher, eds. *American Artisans: Crafting Social Identity, 1750–1850.* Baltimore: Johns Hopkins University Press, 1995.

Rockman, Seth. *Scraping By: Wage Labor, Slavery, and Survival in Early Baltimore.* Baltimore: Johns Hopkins University Press, 2009.

Roeber, A. Gregg. "German and Dutch Books and Printing." In *A History of the Book in America,* vol. 1, *The Colonial Book in the Atlantic World,* edited by Hugh Amory and David D. Hall, 298–313. Chapel Hill: University of North Carolina Press, 2007.

Rorabaugh, W. J. *The Craft Apprentice: From Franklin to the Machine Age in America.* New York: Oxford University Press, 1986.

Rosebrock, Ellen Fletcher. *Counting-House Days in South Street: New York's Early Brick Seaport Buildings.* New York: South Street Seaport Museum, 1975.

Rowe, Kenneth Wyer. *Mathew Carey: A Study in American Economic Development.* Baltimore: Johns Hopkins University Press, 1933.

Roy, Jacqueline. "Lambert, John." In *Dictionary of Canadian Biography*, vol. 5. Toronto: University of Toronto, 1983. Accessed 29 June 2015. http://www.biographi.ca/en/bio/lambert_john_5E.html.

Salinger, Sharon V. *Taverns and Drinking in Early America.* Baltimore: Johns Hopkins University Press, 2002.

Sandoval-Strausz, A. K. *Hotel: An American History.* New Haven: Yale University Press, 2007.

Schaneman, Judith Clark. "Rewriting 'Adèle et Théodore': Intertextual Connections Between Madame de Genlis and Ann Radcliffe." *Comparative Literature Studies* 38, no. 1 (2001): 31–45.

Schleiner, Winfried. "The Infant Hercules: Franklin's Design for a Medal Commemorating American Liberty." *Eighteenth-Century Studies* 10, no. 2 (1976): 235–44.

Schlesinger, Arthur M. *Prelude to Independence: The Newspaper War on Britain, 1764–1776.* New York: Knopf, 1958.

Schroder, Anne L. "Going Public Against the Academy in 1784: Mme de Genlis Speaks Out on Gender Bias." *Eighteenth-Century Studies* 32, no. 3 (1999): 376–82.

Sears, Louis Martin. *Jefferson and the Embargo.* Durham: Duke University Press, 1927.

Sellers, Charles. *The Market Revolution: Jacksonian America, 1815–1846.* New York: Oxford University Press, 1991.

Shaffer, Arthur H. *The Politics of History: Writing the History of the American Revolution, 1783–1815.* Chicago: Precedent, 1975.

———. *To Be an American: David Ramsay and the Making of the American Consciousness.* Columbia: University of South Carolina Press, 1991.

Shapiro, Norman R. *French Women Poets of Nine Centuries: The Distaff and the Pen.* Baltimore: Johns Hopkins University Press, 2008.

Shapiro, Stephen. *The Culture and Commerce of the Early American Novel: Reading the Atlantic World-System.* University Park: Pennsylvania State University Press, 2008.

Sharp, James Roger. *American Politics in the Early Republic: The New Nation in Crisis.* New Haven: Yale University Press, 1993.

Shaw, Ronald. *Erie Water West: A History of the Erie Canal, 1792–1854.* Lexington: University Press of Kentucky, 1990.

Sher, Richard B. *The Enlightenment and the Book: Scottish Authors and Their Publishers in Eighteenth-Century Britain, Ireland, and America.* Chicago: University of Chicago Press, 2006.

Sheriff, Carol. *The Artificial River: The Erie Canal and the Paradox of Progress, 1817–1862.* New York: Hill and Wang, 1996.

Shesgreen, Sean. *Images of the Outcast: The Urban Poor in the Cries of London.* Manchester: Manchester University Press, 2002.

Shields, David S. *Civil Tongues and Polite Letters in British America.* Chapel Hill: Published for the Institute of Early American History and Culture by the University of North Carolina Press, 1997.

Shipton, Clifford Kenyon. *Isaiah Thomas: Printer, Patriot, and Philanthropist, 1749–1831.* Rochester: Leo Hart, 1948.

Silver, Rollo G. *The American Printer, 1787–1825.* Charlottesville: Published for the Bibliographical Society of the University of Virginia by the University Press of Virginia, 1967.

———. "Aprons Instead of Uniforms: The Practice of Printing, 1776–1787." *Proceedings of the American Antiquarian Society* 87, no. 1 (1977): 111–94.

———. *The Boston Book Trade, 1800–1825.* New York: New York Public Library, 1949.

———. "Printers' Lobby: Model 1802." *Studies in Bibliography* 3 (1950): 207–28.

———. *Typefounding in America, 1787–1825.* Charlottesville: Published for the Bibliographical Society of the University of Virginia by the University Press of Virginia, 1965.

Siskind, Janet. *Rum and Axes: The Rise of a Connecticut Merchant Family, 1795–1850.* Ithaca: Cornell University Press, 2002.

Skeel, Emily Ellsworth Ford. *A Bibliography of the Writings of Noah Webster.* New York: New York Public Library, 1958.

Smith, Billy G. *The "Lower Sort": Philadelphia's Laboring People, 1750–1800.* Ithaca: Cornell University Press, 1990.

Smith, Billy G., and Richard Wojtowicz. *Blacks Who Stole Themselves: Advertisements for Runaways in the Pennsylvania Gazette, 1728–1790.* Philadelphia: University of Pennsylvania Press, 1989.

Smith, Steven Carl. "'Elements of Useful Knowledge': New York and the National Book Trade in the Early Republic." *Papers of the Bibliographical Society of America* 106, no. 4 (2012): 487–538.

———. "A World the Printers Made: Print Culture in New York, 1783–1830." PhD diss., University of Missouri, 2013.

Sokoloff, Kenneth L. "Was the Transition from the Artisanal Shop to the Nonmechanized Factory Associated with Gains in Efficiency? Evidence from the U.S. Manufacturing Censuses of 1820 and 1850." *Explorations in Economic History* 21, no. 4 (1984): 351–82.

Spater, George. *William Cobbett: The Poor Man's Friend.* 2 vols. New York: Cambridge University Press, 1982.

Spivak, Burton. *Jefferson's English Crisis: Commerce, Embargo, and the Republican Revolution.* Charlottesville: University Press of Virginia, 1979.

St. Clair, William. *The Reading Nation in the Romantic Period.* New York: Cambridge University Press, 2004.

Steffen, Charles G. "Newspapers for Free: The Economies of Newspaper Circulation in the Early Republic." *Journal of the Early Republic* 23, no. 3 (2003): 381–419.

Stephen, Leslie, and Adam I. P. Smith. "Gifford, John (1758–1818)." In *Oxford Dictionary of National Biography*, online ed., edited by David Cannadine. Oxford: Oxford University Press, 2004. Accessed 3 January 2017. http://www.oxforddnb.com/view/article/10665.

Stevens, George A. *New York Typographical Union No. 6: A Study of a Modern Trade Union and Its Predecessors.* Albany: J. B. Lyon Co., 1913.

Strohm, Robert F. "J. W. Randolph." In *Virginia Law Books: Essays and Bibliographies*, edited by William Hamilton Bryson, 547–57. Philadelphia: American Philosophical Society, 2000.

Tagg, James. *Benjamin Franklin Bache and the Philadelphia Aurora.* Philadelphia: University of Pennsylvania Press, 1991.

Tamarkin, Elisa. *Anglophilia: Deference, Devotion, and Antebellum America.* Chicago: University of Chicago Press, 2008.

Tebbel, John William. *A History of Book Publishing in the United States*. New York: R. R. Bowker, 1972.

Tennenhouse, Leonard. *The Importance of Feeling English: American Literature and the British Diaspora, 1750–1850*. Princeton: Princeton University Press, 2007.

Thompson, E. P. *Customs in Common: Studies in Traditional Popular Culture*. New York: New Press, 1991.

———. *The Making of the English Working Class*. New York: Pantheon Books, 1964.

Thompson, Peter. *Rum Punch and Revolution: Taverngoing and Public Life in Eighteenth-Century Philadelphia*. Philadelphia: University of Pennsylvania Press, 1999.

Tiedemann, Joseph S. *Reluctant Revolutionaries: New York City and the Road to Independence, 1763–1776*. Ithaca: Cornell University Press, 1997.

Tieken-Boon van Ostade, Ingrid. *Two Hundred Years of Lindley Murray*. Münster: Nodus Publikationen, 1996.

Tremaine, Marie, and Patricia Fleming. *A Bibliography of Canadian Imprints, 1751–1800*. Toronto: University of Toronto Press, 1999.

Trouille, Mary. "Toward a New Appreciation of Mme de Genlis: The Influence of Les Battuécas on George Sand's Political and Social Thought." *French Review* 71, no. 4 (1998): 565–76.

Unger, Harlow G. *Noah Webster: The Life and Times of an American Patriot*. New York: John Wiley and Sons, 1998.

Vail, R. W. G. "A Patriotic Pair of Peripatetic Printers: The Up-State Imprints of John Holt and Samuel Loudon, 1776–1783." In *Essays Honoring Lawrence C. Wroth*, edited by Frederick R. Goff, 391–422. Portland, Maine: Athoensen Press, 1951.

Van Deusen, Glyndon G. *Thurlow Weed, Wizard of the Lobby*. Boston: Little, Brown, 1947.

Verhoeven, W. M. "'This Blissful Period of Intellectual Liberty': Transatlantic Radicalism and Enlightened Conservatism in Brown's Early Writings." In *Revising Charles Brockden Brown: Culture, Politics, and Sexuality in the Early Republic*, edited by Philip Barnard, Mark Kamrath, and Stephen Shapiro, 7–40. Knoxville: University of Tennessee Press, 2004.

Wahba, Magdi. "Madame de Genlis in England." *Comparative Literature* 13, no. 3 (1961): 221–38.

Waldstreicher, David. *In the Midst of Perpetual Fetes: The Making of American Nationalism, 1776–1820*. Chapel Hill: Published for the Omohundro Institute of Early American History and Culture by the University of North Carolina Press, 1997.

———. *Runaway America: Benjamin Franklin, Slavery, and the American Revolution*. New York: Hill and Wang, 2004.

Walett, Francis G. *Patriots, Loyalists, and Printers: Bicentennial Articles on the American Revolution*. Worcester: American Antiquarian Society, 1976.

Walker, Lesley H. "Producing Feminine Virtue: Strategies of Terror in Writings by Madame de Genlis." *Tulsa Studies in Women's Literature* 23, no. 2 (2004): 213–36.

Wall, Alexander J. "Samuel Loudon (1727–1813), Merchant, Printer and Patriot: With Some of His Letters." *New-York Historical Society Quarterly* 6 (1922): 75–92.

Wall, Diana DiZerega. "The Separation of the Home and Workplace in Early Nineteenth-Century New York City." *American Archaeology* 5, no. 3 (1985): 185–89.

Wallace, Aurora. *Media Capital: Architecture and Communications in New York City*. Urbana: University of Illinois Press, 2012.

Wall-Randell, Sarah. "'Doctor Faustus' and the Printer's Devil." *Studies in English Literature, 1500–1900* 48, no. 2 (2008): 259–81.

Warfel, Harry R. *Noah Webster: Schoolmaster to America*. New York: Macmillan, 1936.

Warner, Michael. *The Letters of the Republic: Publication and the Public Sphere in Eighteenth-Century America*. Cambridge: Harvard University Press, 1990.

Warner, William Beatty. *Protocols of Liberty: Communication Innovation and the American Revolution*. Chicago: University of Chicago Press, 2013.

Warren, Dale. "John West—Bookseller." *New England Quarterly* 6, no. 3 (1933): 613–19.

Waterman, Bryan. *Republic of Intellect: The Friendly Club of New York City and the Making of American Literature*. Baltimore: Johns Hopkins University Press, 2007.

Watts, Steven. *The Romance of Real Life: Charles Brockden Brown and the Origins of American Culture*. Baltimore: Johns Hopkins University Press, 1994.

Wells, Daniel Arthur. "Evert Duyckinck's Literary World, 1847–1853: Its Views and Reviews of American Literature." PhD diss., Duke University, 1972.

Whatmore, Richard. "D'Ivernois, Sir Francis (1757–1842)." In *Oxford Dictionary of National Biography*, online ed., edited by David Cannadine. Oxford: Oxford University Press, 2009. Accessed 3 January 2017. http://www.oxforddnb.com/view/article/98254.

Widmer, Edward L. *Young America: The Flowering of Democracy in New York City*. New York: Oxford University Press, 1999.

Wigger, John H. *American Saint: Francis Asbury and the Methodists*. New York: Oxford University Press, 2009.

Wilentz, Sean. *Chants Democratic: New York City and the Rise of the American Working Class, 1788–1850*. New York: Oxford University Press, 2004.

Wilson, James Grant. *The Memorial History of the City of New-York: From Its First Settlement to the Year 1892*. Vol. 4. New York: New York History Company, 1893.

Winans, Robert B. *A Descriptive Checklist of Book Catalogues Separately Printed in America, 1693–1800*. Worcester: American Antiquarian Society, 1981.

Winship, Michael. *American Literary Publishing in the Mid-Nineteenth Century: The Business of Ticknor and Fields*. New York: Cambridge University Press, 1995.

———. "Printing with Plates in the Nineteenth-Century United States." *Printing History* 5, no. 2 (1983): 15–26.

Winton, Calhoun. "The Southern Book Trade in the Eighteenth Century." In *A History of the Book in America*, vol. 1, *The Colonial Book in the Atlantic World*, edited by Hugh Amory and David D. Hall, 224–46. Chapel Hill: University of North Carolina Press, 2007.

Wosh, Peter J. *Spreading the Word: The Bible Business in Nineteenth-Century America*. Ithaca: Cornell University Press, 1994.

Wroth, Lawrence C. *The Colonial Printer*. Charlottesville: Dominion Books, 1964.

Wyatt-Brown, Bertram. *Lewis Tappan and the Evangelical War Against Slavery*. Cleveland: Press of Case Western Reserve University, 1969.

Yamey, B. S. "Scientific Bookkeeping and the Rise of Capitalism." *Economic History Review* 1, nos. 2–3 (1949): 99–113.

Yokota, Kariann Akemi. *Unbecoming British: How Revolutionary America Became a Postcolonial Nation*. New York: Oxford University Press, 2011.

Young, Alfred F. *The Democratic Republicans of New York: The Origins, 1763–1797*. Chapel Hill: Published for the Institute of Early American History and Culture by the University of North Carolina Press, 1967.

———. "George Robert Twelves Hewes (1742–1840): A Boston Shoemaker and the Memory of the American Revolution." *William and Mary Quarterly* 38, no. 4 (1981): 561–623.

Zboray, Ronald J. *A Fictive People: Antebellum Economic Development and the American Reading Public*. New York: Oxford University Press, 1993.

Zboray, Ronald J., and Mary Saracino Zboray. "Political News and Female Readership in Antebellum Boston and Its Region." *Journalism History* 22, no. 1 (1996): 2–14.

Zimmer, Anne Y. *Jonathan Boucher, Loyalist in Exile.* Detroit: Wayne State University Press, 1978.

Zimmer, Anne Young, and Alfred H. Kelly. "Jonathan Boucher: Constitutional Conservative." *Journal of American History* 58, no. 4 (1972): 897–922.

INDEX

· · · · · · · · · · · · · · · · · · · ·

Page numbers followed by *t* refer to tables. Those followed by n refer to notes, with note number.